A Herefordshire Miscellany

A HEREFORDSHIRE MISCELLANY

Commemorating 150 Years of the Woolhope Club

Edited by
David Whitehead and John Eisel

LAPRIDGE PUBLICATIONS
2000

First published in 2000 by
Lapridge Publications
22 Broomy Hill, Hereford HR4 0LH

© 2000

ISBN 1 899290 08 7

British Library Cataloguing in Publication Data
A catalogue record for this book is available
from the British Library

Designed by Paul Latcham and David Postle
and set in Garamond 11/12

Printed and bound in Great Britain by
Biddles Limited, Guildford and King's Lynn

A HEREFORDSHIRE MISCELLANY is published in the year 2000 for the Subscribers whose names are listed at the end of the book.

This book is number: **315**

THE CONTRIBUTORS

ANTHEA BRIAN

JOHN EISEL

DEREK FOXTON

ROGER FRENCH

JOAN GRUNDY

BERYL HARDING

HEATHER HURLEY

PAUL LATCHAM

ALAN MORRIS

JEAN O'DONNELL

DERRYAN PAUL

RUTH E. RICHARDSON

GRAHAM ROBERTS

JOHN ROSS

RON SHOESMITH

ROSAMUND SKELTON

BRIAN SMITH

PETER THOMSON

JIM TONKIN

MURIEL TONKIN

DAVID WHITEHEAD

NB. The first 500 copies of *A Herefordshire Miscellany* have been signed by the contributors – a far greater number than was intended. Paul and Valerie Latcham would like to express their appreciation for the cheerful and willing way that this was carried out.

Standard Abbreviations

BL British Library
HCA Hereford Cathedral Archive
HCL Hereford Cathedral Library
HL Hereford Library
HRO Herefordshire Record Office
PRO Public Record Office
RCHM Royal Commission on Historical Monuments
TWNFC Transactions of the Woolhope Naturalists' Field Club

Decorations

The decorative printers' head-pieces used above the title of each article have been borrowed from a number of seventeenth- to early twentieth-century books, mostly of Herefordshire interest. The sources are as follows:

LOCATION	SOURCE
Pages 17, 65	*Account of the Family of Landon of Monnington and Credenhill, co. Hereford* (Privately printed, 1912).
Pages 95, 139, 163, 178	*A Copy of the Poll...for the County of Hereford...1754...* (Gloucester, 1754).
Page 153	[John Beale], *Herefordshire Orchards, a Pattern for all England* (London, 1657).
Page 193	Thomas Bisse, *A Sermon preached at...Hereford, August 14, 1716* (London, 1716).
Page 15	Thomas Bisse, *A Sermon preach'd at St Peter's in Hereford, October 4, 1725...* (London, 1726).
Pages 82, 125, 247	F. T. Havergal, *Monumental Inscriptions in the Cathedral Church of Hereford* (London, Walsall and Hereford, 1881).
Page 109	F. T. Havergal, *Memorials of Fredrick Arthur Gore Ouseley...* (London, Walsall and Hereford, 1889).
Page 37	J. E. Harting, *The Birds of Shakespeare...* (London, 1871).
Pages 47, 205	J. H. James, *Herefordia, A Poem* (London, 1861).
Pages 57, 256, 287	[Richard Rawlinson], *The History and Antiquities of the City and Cathedral-Church of Hereford...* (London, 1717).
Page 272	*Lascelles & Co's Directory and Gazetteer of Herefordshire...* (Birmingham, 1851).
Contents page, 219	C. J. Robinson, *A History of the Castles of Herefordshire and their Lords* (London & Hereford, 1869).
Pages 27, 235	C. J. Robinson, *A History of the Mansions and Manors of Herefordshire* (London & Hereford, 1873).

The Index

The index for this sesquicentenary volume has been compiled by Woolhope Club member Dr John Bowman of London to whom the publishers extend their thanks.

CONTENTS.

List of Pictorial Illustrations

Maps, Plans, etc.

Foreword by Basil Butcher

The only possible explanation for my being asked to write this foreword is that I am one of the longest-standing members of our famous field club.

There must be many members far more worthy of this honour, though no one could be more interested in the work of the club. I have been unable for some years, through knee trouble, to attend the outings. But fortunately, thanks to the great work by Muriel and Jim Tonkin, all is recorded in our excellent *Transactions*.

There can be few similar clubs with such a splendid collection of experts, each in their own field, writing for their transactions.

Herefordshire should be proud to have a club which can produce such a fine commemorative book as this.

In the words of our motto I *Hope on* and *Hope Ever* that the club will go from strength to strength.

Hereford, October 2000

Vivian of Hereford.

Woolhope Naturalist's Field Club Centenary Photograph
Near Dormington Wood   On the Woolhope Dome.
23rd June 1951.

The 1951 club photograph with Basil Butcher at the centre of the front row (sitting).

Photo: Vivian of Hereford

Biographical Notices of the Contributors

Dr Anthea Brian, a biologist, came to Herefordshire in 1974, joining the Woolhope Club in the same year; she was president in 1982. Much involved in the Herefordshire Nature Trust, she is researching the history of Lower House Farm and its lands in the former open-field township of Tupsley.

Dr John C. Eisel, a retired lecturer in mathematics, was at school in Hereford, since when he has had a deep interest in the history of the city. He now enjoys spending time on his main research interests in church bells and bell ringing. He is a past president of the Woolhope Club and served as field secretary for five years.

Derek Foxton is a retired dental surgeon who has been interested in photography since he was a boy. His interest in old photographs of Hereford has led to his building up a considerable collection of images, culled from many sources, to add to his own photographs. He has published several books based on his collection and work.

Dr Roger French, now partly retired, lectures at the University of Cambridge and is a Fellow of Clare Hall. In 1967 he and his wife Anne bought a cottage, with a cider mill, in Checkley, on the edge of the estates once owned by Roger of Hereford. His interest in cider led to the publication of *The History and Virtues of Cyder*, London, 1982.

Joan Grundy formerly worked for the Ministry of Agriculture, Fisheries and Food. She is a founder-member of the Rare Breeds Survival Trust, and has a particular interest in farm live-stock. Her current work as an adult education tutor draws on her other special interests which are vernacular architecture and landscape archaeology.

Beryl Harding moved to Hereford after nearly twenty years teaching biology and geography. She joined the Woolhope Club in 1980, since serving on various committees, and was president during 1997-8. She is much involved with Herefordshire Nature Trust and has been one of the mayor's city guides for the last eight years.

Heather Hurley has lived in Herefordshire for over twenty-five years and, as chairman of the Ross Civic Society's Rights of Way Committee and volunteer for the county's Countryside Service, has been actively involved in preserving and improving rights of way. She has published various books and contributed to the Woolhope *Transactions*.

Paul Latcham came to Hereford in 1974 to set up with Valerie Latcham the Hereford Bookshop, which they jointly ran until 1998. He is a collector and student of bookplates and has contributed to journals at home and abroad on bookplate subjects. Lapridge Publications was formed in 1991.

Alan Morris has lived in Herefordshire since 1965, taught chemistry at the Cathedral School for thirty-three years, and has been a member of the Woolhope Club since 1966. He has had a life-long interest in ancient coins and antiquities, particularly those of the Roman and Stuart periods, and has contributed to numismatic journals.

Richard K. Morriss was assistant director of the City of Hereford Archaeology Unit. He worked on the recording and analysis of Caradoc Court in 1989 and produced the interim report. He is now an independent archaeological consultant and consultant archaeologist to the dean and chapter of Birmingham cathedral.

Jean O'Donnell has been a member of the Woolhope Club since 1964 and was president in 1970 and 1996. She was formerly tutor-organiser for the Workers' Educational Association in

Herefordshire and Shropshire. She lectures in local history, the Victorian period and literature and is a founder member of the Hereford Guild of Guides.

Derryan Paul took a degree in classics before training as an archivist. She was assistant archivist in Hereford Record Office from 1963 to 1965 and has since worked as archivist, librarian and college and university lecturer and is currently studying the care of churches in Herefordshire 1662-1762.

Ruth E. Richardson was born in Hereford, taught history for several years, and is currently teaching archaeology. She was chairman of the city of Hereford archaeological committee, is a past president of the Woolhope Club, general editor of the Herefordshire Field-Name Survey and co-organiser of the Hereford Millennium Air Survey.

Graham Roberts was city surveyor of Hereford 1965-91 with wide technical and management duties, and was made an honorary freeman of the city on his retirement. He has been a member of the Woolhope Club since 1968 and compiled Hereford's official guides 1969-80 and the Three Choirs Festival programme books in the 1970s.

Dr John Ross was a consultant physician at Hereford, 1961-85. He has published articles on renal disease, the effects of severe exertion, medical history and on resistance activities in Italy during World War II. Since retirement he has been active with Herefordshire Nature Trust and continues to help run the Hereford Post-Graduate Medical Centre.

Ron Shoesmith was director of the City of Hereford Archaeology Unit from 1974 until 1998. He now works as a archaeological consultant and is preparing research reports on Goodrich and Clun castles for English Heritage. He is consultant archaeologist to the dean and chapter of Hereford cathedral.

Rosamund E. Skelton has been a member of the Woolhope Club since 1965 and Recorder for Deserted Medieval Villages since 1968. She is currently chairman of the Archaeological Research Section. Her interest in medieval settlement was inspired through participating in the archaeological excavations at Wharram Percy in Yorkshire.

Brian S. Smith was county archivist of Gloucestershire 1968-80. He was assistant secretary 1980-81 and secretary 1982-92 of the Royal Commission on Historical Manuscripts, after which he retired to Herefordshire. He is the author of books and articles on historical subjects and is vice-president of the British Records Association.

Peter Thomson is a former teacher of geography who spent his youth in the Pennines looking at birds and flowers when he should have been doing other things. His interest in geology arose from contact with an inspiring teacher and a love of the countryside. He has been a member of the Woolhope Club since the 1960s and is a past president.

J. W. Tonkin came to Herefordshire as first headmaster of Wigmore High School. He has been an extra-mural lecturer 1954 onwards; buildings recorder for the Woolhope Club since 1964, editor of the *Transactions* since 1967, secretary since 1985 and president in 1967, 1973 and 1984. President of Vernacular Architecture Group 1980-83.

Muriel Tonkin came to Hereford in 1963 from Cornwall and has been assistant secretary of the Woolhope Club since 1966 and assistant treasurer since 1968. She was president in 1974, 1983 and 1994. Her special interests are in genealogy, local history and historical research.

David Whitehead has lived and worked in Herefordshire, his adopted county, since 1970. He is a past president of the Woolhope Club and has written and lectured extensively on many aspects of the county's history, specialising latterly in its architectural and landscape history.

The Woolhope Club

J. W. TONKIN

The club was founded in 1851 as a result of the geological discoveries in Hereford-shire at that time and to follow up lectures with field visits. The name is taken from the Woolhope Dome, a Silurian geological feature, its full name being The Woolhope Naturalists' Field Club.

Membership was at first limited to forty; this was raised to fifty in 1860 and after 1866 there was no limit. Ladies were not admitted until 1954 and junior members, over 14, in 1968.

The object was to observe and report, hold field meetings and meetings for lectures and discussion.

The *Transactions* were first published in 1866, since when they have been published annually. The early proceedings were collected from newspaper reports and the club's minutes and were published in 1907. Indexes to the *Transactions* were published in 1911, 1939, 1957 and 1989, and a catalogue of the library in 1941.

In 1870 Mr (later Sir) James Rankin built a museum in Hereford, to which the club gave its collections, and added a public library on the understanding that the club should have a permanent home in the building, which was completed in 1874. A room on the first floor named the Woolhope Room became the club's meeting place and houses its library. The city librarian became the club's honorary librarian.

There have been a number of publications, from *The Herefordshire Pomona* in 1874, to *A Concise List of Seals belonging to the Dean and Chapter of Hereford Cathedral* in 1966. In 1954 a volume entitled *Herefordshire: its natural history, archaeology, and history...*, a collection of essays on its history and work, was published to celebrate the centenary of the club's foundation.

From its earliest days the club had visited archaeological and architectural sites as well as studying the natural history and geology; this fact was recognised in 1893 when Rule 1 was amended to read 'for the practical study, in all its branches of the Natural History and Archaeology of Herefordshire and the districts immediately adjacent'.

The club has benefited from five bequests to its library. The first was in 1918 when Miss Madeline Hopton left her manuscript of Herefordshire crosses to the club and her collection of fifty-eight volumes on wayside crosses. The second was by C. A. Benn, OBE, president in 1939 and 1940, of his collection of books on the Norman period. The biggest bequest was by George Marshall, FSA in 1952; he had been president in 1922 and secretary 1917-46. The fourth and fifth were given by non-members: In 1971 Mr V. E. Murray left the club his library of botanical books and in 1998 Mr G. W. Smith bequeathed his collection of photographs.

In 1962 it was agreed that the long services of Mr F. C. Morgan should be marked by an annual lecture by a visiting speaker of national repute in his/her chosen subject.

The President's Badge was given to the club in 1951 to commemorate its centenary and in memory of George Marshall, FSA.

At a special general meeting held on 20 May 1965, it was agreed that members could form sections to pursue research into particular interests. The Archaeological Research Section was formed soon after, holding its first meeting on 8 July, and the Natural History Section much later with its first meeting on 20 November, 1976.

Like any voluntary body the club is dependent on the services of its officers. Secretaries have served for as long as thirty years and assistant secretaries/treasurers even longer, the current holder of the office having now completed thirty-three years.

Among the presidents the club has included a bishop of Hereford, two deans, and an archdeacon, a cathedral canon and prebendaries of the diocese. A number of ex-officers of the services have also held the office, some retired regular servicemen, others war-time officers.

After the admission of ladies to membership, Mrs Leeds became the first lady president in 1959 and has been followed by seven others serving eleven years between them.

This mixture of professional men and women – accountants, doctors, agricultural, electrical and mechanical engineers, journalists, lawyers, lecturers, librarians and teachers – is representative of the club membership, and their varied experience has contributed so much over the past 150 years.

Editors of the *Transactions* have also given long service. Mr F. C. Morgan has already been mentioned and the current editor has been in office since 1967.

The annual programme of the club consists of eight winter meetings and six field visits in the summer, four whole days and two half-day. For a number of years there was a week's visit to another part of the country.

In 1991 the club held its winter annual meeting on 7 December in the Woolhope Room as it had done since 1874, but the next meeting had to be held in a committee room at Shirehall because new fire regulations limited the attendance to forty. The Woolhope Room still houses the club's library which has been carefully catalogued, checked and cleaned by two senior members of the committee, one of them an ex-president, and is used for committee meetings and some specialist meetings.

Thus the club's 750 or so members still carry on the traditions set by its founders in 1851. Little did they dream of an annual *Transactions* of some 150 pages going out not only to ordinary members but to fifty institutional members all over the world.

Founders of the Woolhope Club

J. H. ROSS

It is not easy nowadays to make original contributions to knowledge about our surroundings without specialised training and technical backing, but 200 years ago educated men, trained in the classics, medicine and theology, living away from academic centres, increasingly realised that they could make observations and draw conclusions from them which could be of interest locally or even nationally. They often had the time to do this, away from their professional commitments and, what was more, it was enjoyable to go into the countryside and make the observations; it could be a pleasant outdoor alternative to field sports (Sir Roderick Murchison, the great geologist and an honorary member of the Woolhope Club 'urged on by his wife, gave up the joys of foxhunting for the more sublime pleasures of scientific research').[1]

An interest in natural history and their surroundings was being encouraged in all strata of society by publications and lectures. Gilbert White, for example, had urged such interests when he wrote, in 1788, that he was 'also of the opinion that if stationary men would pay some attention to the districts on which they reside, and would publish their thoughts respecting the objects that surround them, from such materials might be drawn the most complete county-histories, which are still wanting in several parts of this kingdom'.[2] Hugh Miller of *The Old Red Sandstone* fame had written in 1841: 'My advice to young working-men desirous of bettering their circumstances and adding to the amount of their enjoyment, is a very simple one...Learn to make a right use of your eyes; the commonest things are worth looking at – even stones and weeds, and the most familiar animals'.[3]

Ten years later in Herefordshire there were still many unaware of such advice and one of our early members, remembering the days leading to the formation of the club, later wrote: 'To some of us it was a revelation to hear that the familiar fields and woods, the quarries and sea-side cliffs might reasonably be consulted direct if we would expand, or check, or even comprehend the teaching of books and lectures'.[4] There were however others in Hereford, already keen naturalists, anxious to share, increase and organise their activities and dissatisfied with the existing facilities – these were our founders.

It is not easy to give a date for our foundation. The first recorded meeting of the Woolhope Naturalists' Field Club was on Tuesday, 13 April 1852 when minutes were written and the rules of the club were listed for the first time. This might therefore be considered the foundation day but as H. Cecil Moore wrote in 1907, when he gathered together the publications of the club from 1852 to 1865, it has always been considered that the club was formed towards the end of 1851.[5] Moore thought that the list of thirty members and seven honorary members in the first minutes indicated 'that the formation of the Club had received mature consideration preliminary to the first record of its proceedings'.

There had certainly been discussions during 1851 by some members of the Hereford Literary, Philosophical and Antiquarian Society about the formation of a field club. Such discussions are occasionally hinted at in reports of this society's meetings and memories of them were recorded in later years, somewhat infrequently. From such sources the prime founders can be identified.

The Reverend W. S. Symonds is said to have drawn the attention of the society to the formation of field clubs elsewhere; the Berwickshire Naturalists' Field Club founded in 1831, the Tyneside later and then the Cotteswold in the neighbouring county of Gloucestershire in 1846. He is supposed to have done this, according to the *Hereford Times* of 22 May 1852, when he gave a lecture to the Society in 1851 or 1852 and this report is repeated by H. Cecil Moore and quoted by F. C. Morgan in 1951[6] but, in the *Transactions of the Herefordshire Natural History, Literary, Philosophic and Antiquarian Society,*[7] there is no recorded lecture by him until 30 November 1852, some months after the Woolhope Club's first activities; possibly he made his comments at a meeting when there was another lecturer but they are not recorded. But was it Symonds who was advocating such a club three years before this in an anonymous letter to the *Hereford Journal* of 25 April 1849? It stressed the need for a 'Naturalists' Field Club' in Herefordshire, mentioning the wealth of material which could be studied in the county and listing eight rules of the Tyneside Club which bear close resemblance to some of the Woolhope Club's rules; the letter was signed with the pseudonym 'Physiologos'. It has been suggested that this was Symonds, which seems very likely.[8]

M. J. Scobie, a keen geologist, apparently stimulated by Sir Roderick Murchison's *Silurian System*, spoke during 1851 to other members of the society about the formation of a club to explore the geology of the district.

At the same time, the Reverend W. H. Purchas was very keen to promote the study of botany in Herefordshire, 'almost an untrodden field'.[9] He discussed forming a local club for this purpose with Dr H. G. Bull who suggested that he should give a lecture on British ferns to the Literary, Philosophical and Antiquarian Society and then 'ventilate the idea of a Field Club'. This he did on 26 March 1852 (the *Hereford Times* of 3 April 1852, which has been quoted several times later, gave 2 April as the date of the lecture – this cannot be correct for, three days before, the *Hereford Journal* of 31 March had already reported the meeting as being on 26 March). Dr Bull gave the vote of thanks on that occasion and noted that the society was beginning to take a greater interest in their surroundings 'after hearing almost unceasingly lectures upon things of antiquity'; he suggested summer excursions devoted to botanical research with subsequent publication by the society which 'would tell the people in ages to come that it had existed usefully'.[10] Purchas recounted, about fifty years later, that at the end of the evening Bull told him that he had been talking to Scobie, who was upset by Purchas's plan to form a botanical club as it might interfere with his intention to form a geological club. Purchas, however, replied that he was delighted to hear about Scobie's plan and suggested joining forces to have a club for the field study of all branches of natural history. Scobie and Purchas were introduced, others joined in the discussion and further meetings were held at Bull's or Scobie's houses. It is likely also that Andrew Rowan who addressed the club frequently in early years and who lived just round the corner from Bull was involved. A remarkable man, he was a medical doctor, qualified analytical chemist, insurance agent, and ran both a hatter's shop in Broad Street, Hereford, and a noisome business emptying the cess pools of Hereford and producing manure for farmers.

Dr Bull's comments are the only contemporary recorded hints of dissatisfaction with the Literary, Philosophical and Antiquarian Society ('Natural History' some-times appeared in its title); later, Symonds spoke of 'the great general apathy that formerly existed in the public mind respecting natural history'[11] and there were comments about the need for 'personal investigation of natural science'. However, it is not clear why this society (founded in 1836) was not adapted to become or include a field club. The society did have some lectures on natural history, specimens were collected and exhibited by members, and there were expeditions to places of interest in the county. In 1852, after the formation of the Woolhope Club, there was no summer excursion and the society's president blamed this on the weather, but was it related to the Woolhope's blossoming activities? The president, during the next winter, referring to the interval since their previous meeting, said to the members, without elaboration 'during the time that had elapsed since they had parted, there had been some circumstances calling for notice by the members as a body' – was this a reference to the formation of their rival?[12] Members and attendances fell off, there were financial problems and the Literary, Philosophical and Antiquarian Society was wound up in 1869.

The 26 March 1852, when Bull, Purchas and Scobie initiated discussions, would therefore seem to be the most important date in the story of the founding of the club. It is however remarkable that only eighteen days after these apparently tentative plans for formation, on 13 April 1852, the club was in existence with rules, thirty members and seven honorary members.

Thomas Blashill joined the club in its first year and when president in the Jubilee Year 1901 recorded some of the details of its foundation which I have related. He spoke of 'the three originators of the Club' and I think that he meant Bull, Scobie and Purchas. Symonds, T. T. Lewis and R. M. Lingwood certainly took part in the preliminary discussions also. These six can therefore be considered our founders. The lives and contributions of these men whom we should remember with gratitude will be considered.

DR HENRY GRAVES BULL (1818-1885) [13,14]

Dr Bull (Pl. 1) was probably the most influen-tial founder of the club and its most active member for thirty-four years. We are fortu-nate that he came to Hereford, for after an outstanding record as a student he could surely have made his career in a central teaching hos-pital. The son of a doctor (a keen botanist) in Pitsford, Northamptonshire, he was appren-ticed aged 16 to a physician in Northampton and later studied medicine in Edinburgh and Paris.[15,16] He graduated MD in Edinburgh win-ning a gold medal and two other prizes. In 1841 he applied and was interviewed for the post of house physician at the Herefordshire General Infirmary but was not appointed; the interviewers must have been impressed by his qualifications but the job had been promised to another before Bull's arrival. Fortunately he decided to set up a practice for himself in Hereford and after a while rented Number

Plate 1. Henry Graves Bull, MD.

One St John Street where he lived for the rest of his life and where his nine children were born.

His activities in Hereford were all-embracing. First and foremost he must have been an excellent doctor with a large practice. He became a physician to the Hereford Infirmary, worked at the Hereford Dispensary, was a founder member of the Herefordshire Medical Association, doctor to the gaol and gave valuable evidence from his own records at enquiries into Hereford's health and sanitation. He was innovative and was giving ether anaesthetics with a machine of his own design only a month after ether had first been used in England.[17] His philanthropic activities were many; he was a JP and was actively connected with libraries and schools. His was a large, happy and sociable family.

His observations on Herefordshire and his communications about them to the Woolhope Club must have taken up much of his time away from patients and hospital management but there is no evidence that he ever neglected his medical work in pursuit of his other activities. His articles in the *Transactions* for the first ten years were mostly botanical, later he wrote on historical, archaeological, zoological and other subjects. His observations were always recorded in great detail and his articles were full of literary references, evidence of his omnivorous reading. His first article 'The Mistletoe in Herefordshire' in 1864 takes up thirty-five pages and introduces much history and even theology, and his books are full of quotations from the poets (twenty-eight quotations accompany notes on the nightingale in his *Notes on the Birds of Herefordshire*, and there are nine in the introduction to the volume).

The Woolhope Club remembers Henry Bull particularly for his contributions to mycology and pomology and through these he gained national fame. In 1867 the Reverend Mr Keys read a paper to the club, written by his wife, on field mushrooms. Bull gave a speech of thanks, twice as long as the lecture and packed just as full of facts about these mushrooms.[18] This was the first public display of his great interest in fungi, exemplified in later years by articles and paintings relating to them and by his involvement with the famous Hereford Fungus Forays which started in 1868. It has generally been considered that the forays were his creation, but Mark Lawley recently found letters from Bull to Thomas Blashill which indicated that Edwin Lees, a Worcestershire botanist, first suggested them and that Bull was reluctant for some reason to arrange them until Lees was able to be present and lend his authority to establish them.[19] However, Bull became the prime organiser of these events, a most important feature of the Woolhopian programme for twenty-four years. Mycologists from all over England and Europe were attracted to Hereford for four days of searching for fungi. Bull was 'the life and soul of these outings into the autumn woods, at the annual fungus banquet and at the receptions in his drawing-room where all were invited to drink coffee and listen to papers and discussions on mycological subjects'. At the 1878 dinner, Bull helped to prepare the meal and 'dispensed these savoury and steaming viands with his own hands to the fifty-two diners'.[20] These meetings led to the foundation in 1896 of the British Mycological Society which looks on Bull as a founder.

His greatest achievement was probably in pomology – apple lore. He became interested in the local varieties of apple, especially of the cider apple, and proposed the production of an authoritative publication, which the club decided to sponsor. Dr Robert Hogg, an expert with a European reputation, wrote the descriptions, while Bull's daughter Edith and a Miss Ellis painted seventy-six plates representing 432 apples and pears, working in the Bulls' drawing room ('in this their labour of love they have spent all the sunshiny hours of eight autumnal seasons in succession' wrote

Edith's father.)[21] The work was begun in 1876 and completed in 1884. Two magnificent volumes, *The Herefordshire Pomona*, resulted and they achieved international repute: most of the first 100 pages consist of introductory essays by Bull, packed with quotations and historical references.

In 1884 the Seine-Inférieure Pomological Exhibition took place in Rouen, and the club sent Drs. Bull and Hogg and another member as exhibitors. They left Hereford with four large crates containing 248 varieties of fruit and samples of six kinds of the best cider and two of perry. They were awarded six medals and a *diplome d'honneur*. Dr Bull, never at a loss, made a long speech – in French – to the pomological delegates after a banquet. This was no simple speech of thanks but a historical lecture partly aimed at proving that the cider growers of Normandy had come there from Wales in the sixth century AD.[22] One week after his return from Rouen he was in action at the annual fungus forays and at the associated banquet he outlined his ambitious plans for further Woolhope publications – a book on the flora of the county in the following year, on the birds the year after, and then on the fungi. Sadly not all of these plans were to be realised. He became less active in 1885, although he continued to read long papers to his beloved club. He took part in the eighteenth annual fungus foray, reading a paper and leading a discussion on two of the evenings but became ill soon afterwards and died, aged 67, on 31 October. It is said that, on his deathbed, he corrected the manuscript of *Notes on the Birds of Herefordshire*.

THOMAS TAYLOR LEWIS (1801-1858) [23]

Thomas Lewis was a modest man whose careful observations of his surroundings in Herefordshire became recognised nationally. There is no written record of his taking part in the discussions leading to the foundation of the club but he must have done so in 1851 and 1852 for he already had a considerable reputation as a geologist and regular contact with Bull and Scobie; Thomas Blashill, in remembering the early days, includes him amongst the founders.

He was born in Ludlow to a family which owned coal and ironworks at Titterstone Clee and when a boy collected rocks and fossils in that area. He went to school far away in Cheam, Surrey and there met Elizabeth Penfold whom he was to marry in 1827 after eight years courtship. At Cambridge he studied for the church but also attended the lectures of Professor Adam Sedgwick a geologist who emphasised the need for fieldwork.

His future father-in-law obtained for him the curacy at Aymestrey in 1826 and he became devoted to that neighbourhood. Sadly, Elizabeth died there in 1829 following childbirth. Lewis worked hard in his parish and from the time of his arrival there, began, as he later wrote 'zealously to collect the fossils which were everywhere in abundance, strewed over the roads and fields'.[24] His careful work enabled him to distinguish five rock formations below the Old Red Sandstone and led, on 17 July 1831, to his meeting the great geologist Roderick Murchison who was studying the 'Transition Series' of rocks in the Welsh borders.[25] Lewis demonstrated to Murchison some of his findings in the Aymestrey area during the next few days and later said about their first meeting 'One of the most interesting events in my life…there dawned upon me the vision of the deep interest of the then comparatively unknown county in which it was my very good fortune and happiness to be dwelling , and to the true development of which I had unknowingly discovered the key and made some progress'.[26] Friendship developed between these two men through such an absorbing common interest which was breaking new ground. Lewis sent crates of fossils to Murchison in London and correspondence was frequent. Lewis's letters were sometimes long and detailed, recording his careful observations and yet, on one occasion the modest vicar wrote: '...The whole of my labour must be regarded by you only in the light of a humble collection of fossils in my parochial rambles'.[27]

Lewis was offered the rectorship of Hopton, not far from Aymestrey, a better appointment than his curacy, but refused, wishing to remain 'in a very beautiful and interesting parish'. There may have been another factor in his decision: Elizabeth Ferguson, owner of Yatton Court in Aymestrey. They were married in 1838, in spite of the opposition of Elizabeth's father, 'an irascible admiral', who never spoke to them subsequently. Elizabeth encouraged Lewis's scientific interests and he became a corresponding friend of T. H. Huxley and Charles Darwin and frequently attended meetings of the Royal Society in London. He was promoted to vicar of Bridstow near Ross-on-Wye in 1842 but he and his family returned regularly to his beloved Aymestrey.

He died in October 1858, aged 57, about nine months after a disabling stroke. His praises were sung locally by the Woolhope Club – 'One of Herefordshire's best and most accomplished men' and nationally in the *Gentleman's Magazine* – 'Mr Lewis was indeed, one of those unostentatious labourers to whom science often owes much more than it acknowledges'. His collection of fossils went to the British Museum, and the fossils named after him, especially some Silurian brachiopods, assure he is remembered by palaeontologists.

The above quotation from the *Gentleman's Magazine*, other published comments and a letter of Lewis's indicate that his scientific work was not fully recognised and that Murchison was here at fault. Early in their acquaintance he did however make known his obligation to Lewis 'whose unceasing researches have contributed very essentially towards the zoological illustration of this memoir'. This was in a paper in which Murchison made a considerable error. It is said that Lewis pointed out the mistake and in a later paper on the transition rocks of the Welsh borderlands Murchison corrected the error but made no mention of Lewis or others who had helped with this work.[28]

Murchison published his magnificent volume *The Silurian System* in 1839; the preface expressed thanks to seventeen friends who had helped him, but there was no mention of Lewis. However, Lewis was included in a list of fossil collectors and in a passage about a Ludlow stratum; Murchison wrote 'I have preferred naming it after the beautiful village of Aymestry [sic] where the rock is fully and clearly laid open and where its fossil contents have been elaborately worked out by my friend the Reverend T. T. Lewis'. Comments about inadequate acknowledgements must have been made; Dr W. H. Fitton (later President of the Geological Society), who had visited Aymestrey, made a point of giving credit to Lewis when he reviewed Murchison's book in the *Edinburgh Review* in 1841. He mentioned the work that Lewis had done before Murchison and wrote 'the researches of this gentleman deserve a permanent place in the history of the subject' and said that Murchison fully agreed with this. He also said that Lewis 'rejoiced' that his work had fallen into the hands of a greater geologist.[29]

In 1854 Murchison published *Siluria, the History of the Oldest Known Rocks Containing Organic Remains* and sent a copy to Lewis who wrote a letter of thanks but added his great disappointment that 'his early researches' were so little acknowledged and 'flattered myself, as others thought that...you would record these a little more in detail'. He wrote of a 'mortified pride, divested, I think, of any unfriendly feeling towards yourself'.[30] He concluded this letter, a masterly combination of congratulations on the publication and of tactfully expressed disappointment, by saying that his wife and other ladies had urged him to throw his letter into the fire but 'in justice to myself I cannot'. It is not known if Murchison replied to this letter but he did write to the Woolhope Club in the same year excusing attendance because of illness and included 'In reference to the classification of the upper Silurian rocks, my most efficient assistant was my valued friend, the Rev T. T. Lewis of Aymestry [sic]. That gifted but modest individual first obtained the true key to the subdivision of those rocks…' In a preface to a later edition of *Siluria* in 1859, he paid a tribute to Lewis somewhat deflated by saying that Lewis's original work had been 'most serviceable in enabling me to establish the correct order of the Upper Silurian rocks…' Murchison sent a copy of the book to Mrs Lewis four months after Lewis's death with a letter in which 'I have endeavoured to do justice to the scientific merits of your excellent and lamented husband'.[31] He wrote that he had felt 'real sorrow' when the death had been announced but had not written in order to save her writing back – strange; if he had felt 'real sorrow' surely he would have written four months earlier.

The Woolhope Club has never been in doubt about the fine work done by Lewis whom they once called 'the grandfather of the Silurian System', Sir Roderick Murchison being 'the father'.[32]

WILLIAM HENRY PURCHAS (1823-1903)[33]

Purchas (Pl. 2) was another modest vicar whose painstaking botanical work was nationally recognised. At his lecture on British ferns to the Hereford Literary and Philosophical Society on 26 March 1852 the formation of a Hereford field club was seriously discussed.

He was born in Ross-on-Wye where his father was a wine merchant and, as the oldest son, went into this business for several years, but when his younger brothers were old enough to take over he became free to pursue the religious career which he had always hoped for. He went to Durham University aged thirty-two, was ordained in December 1857 and then worked in Derbyshire for eight years, Gloucestershire for five years and in North Staffordshire until his death aged 80. He became interested in botany as a young man, entomology having been his main hobby as a boy. Many years later he wrote that he had '…more and more seen as I continued to give attention to British Botany that Herefordshire was almost an untrodden field, and my constant correspondence with the late Mr Hewet C. Watson, the father of British Geographical Botany, made me see this the more strongly'.[34] The geographical distribution of plants in

Plate 2. The Reverend William Henry Purchas, founder and botanist.

Herefordshire became his particular interest. His botanical work in Herefordshire cannot have been easy considering that his years at university and his subsequent career took him so far away. He must have started his mapping of the county into fourteen districts during holidays from Durham, recruiting others to help him, but the work became more difficult with ordination in 1857 and, although part one of his 'Flora of Herefordshire' appeared in the *Transactions* in 1866, it is not surprising that the full results were not published until 1889, in conjunction with the Reverend Augustin Ley.

It would appear that he enjoyed studying plant genera the identification of whose species was particularly difficult and, at that time, still confused – brambles, roses and hawkweeds for example. As Augustin Ley later wrote '...the study of British brambles was a hopelessly puzzling affair; it involved trying to fit some 150 forms into thirty to forty descriptions, and resembled the attempt to force 150 apples into a basket designed to contain 40...', and as has been written recently '...to prove parentage of individual bramble-bushes would require the considerable resources of a well-equipped laboratory for sequencing genes...'[35]

Purchas was a member of the Botanical Society of London and in regular touch with the leading botanists in the country. He published at least twenty papers in national botanical journals but Ley maintained that due to his modesty, Purchas's observations of real scientific value were never recorded – such as observations on the ripening of orchid seeds and on 'the uniform perishing of the terminal bud in certain species of *Salix*, so that the next year's growth starts from the first lateral bud'.

WILLIAM S. SYMONDS (1818-1887) [36]

William Symonds was born in 1818 at Elsden near Kington and educated at Cheltenham and Christ's College Cambridge. He was appointed curate at Offenham near Evesham in 1843 and it was there he became interested in geology after being shown a collection of fossils by a parishioner. In 1845 he became vicar of Pendock, between Ledbury and Tewkesbury. He made contact with, and learned much from, the leading geologists Hugh Strickland, Charles Lyell and Roderick Murchison.

The Malvern Hills became a special interest of his and he published a paper in the *Quarterly Journal of the Geological Society* on observations made during the construction of the Ledbury tunnel. An excellent lecturer, he was in great demand to speak at meetings (Bull commented on '...his great learning in geology and happy knack he has of conveying information in clear and forcible language...').[37]

He was active with the Cotteswold Field Club and Worcester Natural History Society during 1851 when he joined the discussions leading to the formation of the Woolhope Club. In 1853 he founded the Malvern Naturalists Field Club and was its president for eighteen years, but he continued to attend Woolhope meetings and was that club's president in 1854. He wrote forty-three papers, several historical novels and edited the papers of the geologist Hugh Miller. When coal was found at Newent in the 1860s there were great expectations as to its extent and value. Symonds warned the promoters that they would be disappointed but his warnings were disregarded; he was proved correct and 'the undertaking was abandoned after great loss'. Murchison acknowledged his work on the 'transition' strata in his *Siluria* (1859). It was not just in the west of England that his interests lay, he apparently visited Scotland, Ireland and Belgium with geological intent.

He was a great supporter of Darwin and spoke about his doubts as to the truth of some bible stories (he could not believe that Noah's ark could possibly have held representatives of all the world's species), but his faith in a 'God of Nature' was not impaired. When his health failed he went to live with his daughter and her husband, Sir Joseph Hooker, the botanist.

MACKAY JOHN SCOBIE (1819-1853)

Scobie (Pl. 3) was the first secretary of the club and it was probably he who most stimulated action towards its founding. Lewis, soon after Scobie's premature death, spoke of his 'talent, business habits, perseverance and integrity' and considered the club 'indebted to him for its formation'.[38]

Plate 3. Mackay John Scobie, the first secretary.

Sadly, there is little known about this young energetic man outside his Woolhope activities. He grew up in Ross-shire and came to work in Hereford in the National Provincial Bank and as an insurance agent. His interest in geology had been stimulated by reading Hugh Miller's *The Old Red Sandstone*. It was probably from this book that he learned that the Old Red in Herefordshire 'enjoyed the reputation of being particularly destitute of organic remains'.[39] This he viewed 'with no small regret' and therefore became interested in the Silurian strata and the Woolhope area but 'found the distance from Hereford too great for an ordinary walk, which only my leisure could afford me'. However, studying nearer Hereford, he discovered the 'Hagley Dome' a protrusion of Downton Sandstones and Upper Ludlow Shale near Bartestree. This 'had escaped for 20 years all other explorers, including the staff of the Ordnance Survey'.[40] Hugh E Strickland FRS, an honorary member of the club, published an account of the Dome in the *Quarterly Journal of the Geological Society of London*, November 1852.

Scobie found a previously undescribed Silurian fossil, a *Pterygotus*, and figured actively in all the early Woolhope outings. He was elected Fellow of the Geological Society of London on 16 June 1852, proposed by Strickland and Murchison and described as 'a gentleman much attached to geology'.

There is little doubt that he would have contributed much more to the club and to geological studies if he had not died, aged 34, in 1853. A few days before he died someone commented to him that he had a good many irons in the fire and he replied that 'he desired to know something of everything, but everything of something, and that thing is geology'.[41]

ROBERT MAULKIN LINGWOOD

There is little information available about the first president of the club. He is mentioned as a founder but the few brief accounts of the discussions preceding foundation do not include his name. Blashill, writing about the early days and founders has little to say about him. He lived at Lyston, Llanwarne, and was high sheriff of Herefordshire in 1848. He presided at club events in 1852 but no presidential address by him is recorded. Later he attended meetings and was honorary secretary in 1864 and 1865, but did not contribute to discussions or papers except in 1853 with a list of birds, and in 1860 with a list of Herefordshire fauna and of the average dates of appearance near his home of birds, butterflies and flowers, 1850-57. In February 1866, the retiring president mentioned that Lingwood had retired to the Continent.

REFERENCES

[1] S. J. Gould, *Ever Since Darwin* (1980), 126.

[2] G. White, *The Natural History of Selborne*(1789), 'Advertisement' to original edition.

[3] H. Miller, *The Old Red Sandstone* (1852), 5th edition, 33-34.

[4] T. Blashill, *TWNFC* (1902), 288-299.

[5] H. C. Moore, *TWNFC* (1852-1865), Introduction (1907).

[6] F. C. Morgan, *Herefordshire* (1951), 2.

[7] *Transactions of the Herefordshire Natural History, Literary, Philosophic and Antiquarian Society*, Hereford City Library FLC 506. This volume consists of reports from the *Hereford Times*.

[8] I. Cohen, *TWNFC*, XXV (1957), 348.

[9] W. H. Purchas, quoted by T.Blashill, *TWNFC* (1902), 289.

[10] H. G. Bull, *Hereford Journal*, 31 March 1852.

[11] W. S. Symonds, *TWNFC* (1853), 55.   [12] op cit. in note 7, 30 Nov. 1852.

[13] C. W. Walker, *TWNFC*, XXXVI (1958), 66-75. This article supplied much information about the life of Dr Bull.

[14] J. H. Ross, *Journal of Medical Biography* 4 (1996), 94-99.

[15] H. G. Bull, Obituary, *British Medical Journal* (1885), II, 999.

[16] Death of Dr Bull of Hereford, *Hereford Times*, 7 November 1885.

[17] *Hereford Journal*, 3 February 1847.   [18] H. G. Bull, *TWNFC* (1867), 75-79.

[19] M. Lawley, *The Bygone Botanists of Herefordshire* (1995), 12-13.

[20] *TWNFC* (1878), 119.

[21] H. G. Bull & R. Hogg (eds.), *The Herefordshire Pomona* II (1876-85).

[22] *TWNFC* (1884), 227-240.

[23] B. Colloms, *Victorian Country Parsons* (1977). This book supplied much information about the life of Lewis.

[24] *TWNFC* (1858), 226.

[25] J. C. Thackray, 'T. T. Lewis and Murchison's Silurian System', *TWNFC* (1977), 187.

[26] T. T. Lewis, *TWNFC* (1854), 100.   [27] Thackray op cit. in note 25, 188.   [28] Ibid, 190.

[29] W. Fitton, 'The Silurian System', *The Edinburgh Review*, LXII (1841), 10-13.

[30] T. T. Lewis, 15 July 1854. In 'Sir Archibald Geikie papers', Edinburgh University Library, EUL, MSGen, 523/58.

[31] R. Murchison's letter to Mrs Lewis, 2 Feb 1859. This is in the possession of Mrs G. Hodges of Aymestrey, great, great granddaughter of Lewis, who kindly showed it to me.

[32] *TWNFC* (1853), 54.

[33] *TWNFC* (1903), 341-343. This obituary by the Reverend Augustin Ley has supplied much of the information about the life of Purchas.

[34] Blashill op cit. in note 4, 289. Blashill quoting Purchas.

[35] Lawley op cit. in note 19, 9.

[36] The Reverend J. D. La Touche, President of the Caradoc Field Club wrote a monograph about Symonds which provided this account of his life and work.

[37] H. G. Bull, *TWNFC* (1866), 240.   [38] T. T. Lewis, *TWNFC* (1853), 47.

[39] M. J. Scobie, *TWNFC* (1853), 5.   [40] T. T. Lewis, *TWNFC* (1854), 103.

[41] Blashill op cit. in note 4, 291.

Photographs from the Geoffrey Smith Collection

JEAN O'DONNELL AND DEREK FOXTON

GEOFFREY WALTER SMITH 1929-1998

Although he was not a member, Geoffrey Smith left a substantial legacy to the Woolhope Club when he died. He also left to the club library his collection of photographs mounted in albums. He lived in a modest house at 2 Crescent Cottages in Clarkson Lane, off Ledbury Road. It seems to have been his family home, for there are many photographs of the *Rose and Crown* opposite and its gardens with relatives included. He was apparently the sole survivor of a large local family and was of a solitary nature. Geoffrey Smith was a Herefordian who continued his father's interest in photographs of the local scene, copying many from books, Woolhope *Transactions*, postcards and the local papers. He was a true collector. Most of the photographs have been published previously but this is a selection from the most interesting of those remaining. The source is unknown but is probably a family album.

Plate 1. *Men in Bowler Hats in Broad Street.* They seem to be leaving the cathedral after some important event. Due to the exposure there appears to be a light dusting of snow but the child is lightly clad and the men are not wearing overcoats. A woman in a hat stands outside the women's reading room of the Free Library while a policeman strides by. The gates are shut indicating a Sunday after 1898 when the women's reading room was established. The photograph may have been taken by Walter Pritchard who lived in the house from where this was taken.

Plate 2. *Suffragette meeting in St Peter's Square 1908 addressed by Miss Gladys Keevil.* The campaign to secure votes for women started in 1903 led by Mrs Emmeline Pankhurst. Speakers were met with hostility from men and some women. This gallant woman has a stain from a thrown missile down her dress. All the spectators are wearing hats. The campaign for women's suffrage was halted in 1914 when war broke out. After its conclusion , women over 30 were given the vote and this was extended to all women over 21 in 1929.

Plate 3. Opposite top: *The Cenotaph in High Town.* After the Great War of 1914-18 war memorials were erected across the country. In Hereford a temporary one was built of wood in High Town. On the front are the words *Live thou for England as I for England died.* The march-by is led by uniformed men followed by those in civilian dress and is possibly the ceremony to dedicate the memorial. The fine stone Eleanor Cross in St Peter's Square by L. W. Barnard of Cheltenham was dedicated in 1922. A lamp standard and trough were removed to make room. The balcony next to the Butter Market is crowded with spectators; others are at the windows and on the roof. In addition to the many Union Jacks hung from the windows is a solitary French flag. The shops to the west of the Butter Market were replaced by Lloyds Bank in 1928. Clarkson and Stewart was founded in 1790 and sold provisions and wine.

Plate 4. Opposite bottom: *Greenland's Fire, 1930.* This photograph was taken by Percy Pritchard from the first floor of his tailor's shop at 1 Commercial Street. The fire is in Greenland's department store on the site of the present Marks and Spencers. Boots is on the other side where films are being advertised. Greenland's had expanded from two small premises in High Street 1890 to the large and elegant store in the photograph; they closed when Marks and Spencers rebuilt their store here in 1965.

Plate 5. *Marchant's, 3 High Street.* Many older Herefordians will remember the fragrant smell of roasted coffee which emanated from these half-timbered premises. It had been a grocer's for over 150 years. There were three Marchant brothers who had shops within a hundred yards of each other. This photograph shows the part of the building which was retained by Littlewood's when they rebuilt their store in 1965. The façade dates from 1600 and was a town house and shop with a medieval stone cellar. There is a fine gas lamp which is no longer there. This part, with its balcony, can be seen inserted into Littlewood's shop where its seems incongruous to the visitor. It was moved from its position in Marchant's by Messrs Pynfolds of London using long jacks and a wooden frame to move it on rollers and a plate railway at a cost of £100 a yard. It stood by the Old House in High Town for six months until it was replaced in Littlewood's new store.

Plate 7. *The May Fair in Broad Street, c1905.* The annual May Fair (St Ethelbert's Fair) was held by the bishop until 1838 when the city council took it over and reduced it from nine days to three. In medieval times the whole town was taken over by the bishop's men and the tolls taken at the six city gates went to the bishop and the dean and chapter. Fairs were for trading as well as amusements but by the time this photograph was taken the fun fair was well established with its coconut shies, fat ladies and boxing booths. In this photograph only women and children can be seen with a gypsy stall-holder in the foreground.

Plate 6. Opposite: *The Judge's Lodgings, 5 Commercial Street, 1936.* This photograph was taken just before the house was demolished, to be replaced by the new Odeon cinema in 1937. It was built at the same time as the Shire Hall to accommodate the judge during the assizes. The horses for the judge's coach were hired from Bastion mews stables. The coach is now at Churchill House Museum. The judge was rehoused at The Crescent, Bodenham Road during the assizes and then at Carfax on Aylestone Hill, the former home of Mr Carless, the town clerk. Next to the house was a fine ironmongers called Workman's. The new Odeon cinema, built by a Hereford firm, Peake & Sons, cost £28,000 and seated 1133. The site is now occupied by shops built in 1987.

Plate 8. *The entrance to Jordan's Boat Yard, c1885.* This is a rare view of buildings on the S.W. of the bridge in Hereford. Over the open entrance can be seen the name *...and Cock's Bark Yard*(?). Bark ricks were a common sight by the river as oak bark was imported for tanning on the many trows which moved produce. Near here was the terminus of the tramway which went to Abergavenny and South Wales but which became redundant with the advent of the railway in 1853. Jordan's boat yard by the bridge was famous and Richard Jordan, boat builder, lived at 55 St Martin's Street. Later, his son W. H. Jordan moved to Wyebridge House where his father had been apprenticed to a boat-builder, a Mr Jeffries. In 1884 it cost two ladies 1s 0d to hire a boat. The shop next to the bridge was a tobacconist's, Mr J. Ward. At one time it was Chesterfield's the water diviner and well digger. The wattle-and-daub panels can be seen to the side of the building.

Plate 9. Opposite top: *Salvation Army on Hereford Bridge.* The march is led by the Salvation Army band sometime in the 1960s. The Hereford Citadel Corps celebrated their centenary in 1982. Today the new Left Bank riverside restaurant has replaced the old showrooms of Mead and Tomkinson. Built by Richard Sully for his motor business, its arcaded windows and balcony look like a boat house. It was a coach building business as early as 1876 when it was owned by John Watkins.

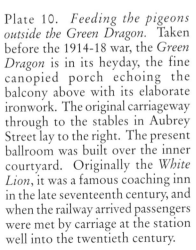

Plate 10. *Feeding the pigeons outside the Green Dragon.* Taken before the 1914-18 war, the *Green Dragon* is in its heyday, the fine canopied porch echoing the balcony above with its elaborate ironwork. The original carriageway through to the stables in Aubrey Street lay to the right. The present ballroom was built over the inner courtyard. Originally the *White Lion*, it was a famous coaching inn in the late seventeenth century, and when the railway arrived passengers were met by carriage at the station well into the twentieth century.

Plate 13. *Whitney-on-Wye Toll Bridge.* The overturned barrels are from a brewer's dray with a roof. The photograph is looking down river while the crowd looking at the accident are fascinated by the camera. This bridge is famous for its mixture of timber and masonry spans dating from *c*1802. There is no sign of the stone arches on either side and the men are standing on the dried-up river bed. The river has changed course here several times; dramatically so in 1730 when the church found itself on the opposite bank. There are scaffold poles as if it was being repaired.

Plate 11. Opposite top: *Delivery man in Venn's Road.* The baker is bringing orders from Roberts and Sons, proprietors of the Cafe Royal, to residents of the narrow Venn's Road, previously Parry's Lane. Cox's cottage, with its thatched roof, is in the background. The original Venn Road was Kyrle Street but it was renamed when Reverend John Venn died in 1890 because he had lived at Beechwood in Parry's Lane. The delivery van has wonderful oil lamps each side. Roberts was a firm of bakers and pastry cooks situated at 16 St Peter's Street where they were established before 1858. In 1913 they had a stall in the Butter Market.

Plate 12. Opposite bottom: *The Carrots, Hampton Bishop, c1908.* This country pub is still popular but has been modernised. In 1914 the proprietor was Charles Wheatstone, farmer. There was Richard Wheatstone as landlord in 1858 and, except for James Watkins in 1876, the same family was there for over sixty years. There is a family group in the foreground with a pony trap and a cyclist is resting against the wall with a drink. Close to the river Wye it was popular with fishermen. One of the pools, famous for its big salmon, was known as 'The Carrots Pool'.

Plate 14. *Weobley, next to the Unicorn Inn.* A wealden-style house with wooden shutters outside the windows is unusual in Herefordshire but there is another at Weobley, around the corner in Broad Street. Cart horses and the sheepdog emphasize the quiet rural street. In 1858 there was a landlady, Mary Ann Lloyd. Around the time of the photograph, in 1905, the landlord, William Jones, was also a nail maker.

Plate 15. *Floods in Greyfriars Avenue.* Boats were evidently in demand during the bad floods of February 1950. There was a whirlwind in the area between the Black Mountains and Hay-on-Wye, bringing down trees and damaging farm buildings. Heavy downpours caused the rivers Wye and Severn to rise rapidly and large tracts of meadowland were awash. Perhaps these wooden rowing boats came to the rescue from the rowing club just upstream.

Birds of Herefordshire and their Habitats

BERYL HARDING

Herefordshire is transitional between the lowland areas of England and the Welsh uplands. It is fringed to the west by the Black Mountains and their foothills, to the east and south by the Malverns and the Forest of Dean and to the north and east by the Clifton-on-Teme uplands, the Bromyard Downs and the hills from Ludlow to Presteigne. The lowland areas form 65% of the county and are broken by higher land in the Woolhope, Garway, Aconbury, Dinmore and Wormsley hills. Amid the agriculture of the lowlands these hills are often wooded, providing habitats for wildlife.

MOORLAND

There is a marked lack of lowland heath in Herefordshire but upland heath or moorland occurs in the Black Mountains where the soils are mostly acidic and dominated by ling with crowberry and bilberry, purple moor grass and mat grass. On these moorlands Ravens, Buzzard, Red Grouse, Wheatear, Meadow Pipit and Ring Ouzel are to be found. The latter two are summer migrants but the Ring Ouzel is not common as the county lacks sufficient high ground. Diminishing numbers nest on the slopes of the Cat's Back and Olchon valley and can be seen on lower ground, during spring and autumn passage, feeding in small groups on berries in the autumn. The Wheatear is maintaining its numbers. These plus Whinchat and Stonechat can be seen and heard on Hergest Ridge.

Buzzards have gradually spread eastward through the county during the century since gamekeeper persecution has been reduced. Ravens also have been spreading eastward during the last fifty to sixty years, being frequently seen anywhere in the county but more abundant in the west. They are on a population high now having been once rendered extinct in the county from shooting. It had become a rare breeding resident by the turn of the century – probably the last nest was shot out in 1880 at Kentchurch. Increasingly recognised now to be harmless to pheasants it even has protection on some sporting estates.

The Peregrine falcon is a powerful bird requiring precipitous clifftop ledges for nesting. Since the reduction of persecution the Welsh population has gradually risen to 300 pairs and has been moving eastward to Cheshire, Shropshire and Herefordshire – some have even reached the cliffs of Dover as the next precipitous land to the east. Their spread is severely limited by the lack of suitable nesting sites and they are in competition for similar ledges with Ravens. However, Ravens make several nests each year so some can be taken up by Peregrines. The two species can co-exist in harmony, apart from occasional sparring.

The nesting success of the Peregrines at the guarded site of Symonds Yat has sadly not been mirrored in Herefordshire. Peregrines use the same site year after year and those in the Darren area of the Black Mountains were successful in 1995. The species as a whole reached their lowest ebb in 1962 then the ban on organochloride pesticides allowed some recovery. During the seventies and eighties a gradual resumption of nest sites and breeding occurred in Wales but not in the Darren until 1979. According to records kept by Dr Charles Walker, they bred successfully until 1985 but since then breeding has been sporadic with eggs often failing to hatch. About four pairs now nest in the county with varying success.

The Red Kite can occasionally be seen in the county. It is still a very rare vagrant and although breeding in the past it has yet to do so again – a pair has been seen in the Eastnor deer-park but are not yet nesting. The Red Grouse is a rare resident breeder in the Black Mountains. The Black Grouse bred in limited numbers during the last century but have not done so since 1939. In the sheltered tree-lined hedges of the Olchon valley Redstarts and Pied Flycatchers nest.

WOODLAND

Herefordshire is fortunate in still retaining much native woodland, although replanting is not always of indigenous species; for example, in wetter areas alder and willow have been replanted with poplar. The invertebrate populations of native trees far exceeds that of non-native so providing more food for birds. The oak alone has 240 species of Lepidoptera as well as many other insect species, so the breeding of the Nuthatch, various tits and other woodland birds has evolved to coincide with the peak of the Oak Moth caterpillar. When the spring is cold and wet the oaks are later coming into leaf, which delays the emergence of the caterpillars, which will in turn defer the breeding of such birds for up to four weeks if necessary. Conversely, if the previous winter has been too mild caterpillars can emerge earlier and become too large so that the hatchlings can still die of starvation.

Thus, the number of oak woodlands in the county are of major importance, supporting summer migrant populations of warblers such as Blackcap, Chiffchaffs and Wood, Garden and Willow warblers as well as the tit family. Woodpeckers, Nuthatch and Redstart are typical tree-nesting birds, the latter two preferring old holes, either natural or woodpecker in origin, but both will accept nest-boxes. Another woodland and hole-loving bird is the Pied Flycatcher, a trans-Saharan migrant, formerly found to the west and north of the county – then their most easterly range. Since the introduction of the Herefordshire Nature Trust nest-box scheme in 1963 its distribution has been extended well into eastern parts of the county from Bromyard Downs south to Ledbury.

The nest-boxes are situated in Trust woodland reserves or in the woods of interested landowners. Now there are well over 900 of which 60% are taken up by eleven species. Some 160-180 are used by Pied Flycatchers and the majority by Blue and Great Tits. Recording includes the number of nests made, eggs laid and young fledged, with the Pied Flycatchers ringed if possible. It is not unusual for woodmice to use the boxes or even dormice, although special boxes are provided for them – these in turn can be taken over by Blue Tits despite the rear opening with a small entrance angle.

Resident Woodcock nest in woodlands and can occur also as winter visitors – they are the only true forest-dwelling wader. In Woolhope Club records Dr Bull spoke of the rise of breeding numbers during the last century. However, sightings in 1996 were at only twelve locations. Being solitary, fairly silent and mostly active at dusk and dawn, their presence is often unnoticed. Kestrel and Sparrowhawk are both common woodland breeding residents today.

Some of our deciduous woodlands have been re-afforested with foreign conifer species. These make up dark, dense banks and wedges of trees giving heavy shade with little or no understorey except around the edges. However, it does not represent a complete loss of habitat to birds but does give a paucity of species. The Goshawk, still a scarce breeding resident, prefers to nest high in the trees, so too will Ravens in lieu of rock ledges. The tiny Goldcrest favours conifers, especially in summer, and Coal and Long-tailed Tits also occur in numbers. The Common Crossbill, with its beak adapted to the extraction of cone seeds, can be a late summer migrant or a winter visitor arriving in irruptions if the cone-seed crop is poor in north and east Europe – otherwise it is a scarce resident breeder.

ORCHARDS

Herefordshire is a traditionally important fruit tree-growing area. However, the extent of old orchards has declined by 50% since the last war and the new commercial ones consist of dwarf species intensively managed and subjected to frequent applications of chemicals, consequently severely limiting sources of unpolluted food for birds. As the trees are not allowed to over-mature there is also a loss of shelter and nest-holes which were more abundant in the older orchards. Bullfinches, so hated by fruit-farmers, appear to maintain their numbers across the county although declining elsewhere. With unwanted apples left on the ground during winter good feeding can be obtained for large flocks of visiting winter thrushes such as Fieldfare and Redwing with a mix-in of our resident thrushes.

AGRICULTURAL AREAS

It is in the agricultural areas, both arable and stock-rearing, that the greatest reductions of bird populations has occurred. These are due to the demand for increased productivity often with monoculture and larger field size resulting in:

(a) The drainage of wet areas with consequent loss of habitat particularly for Curlew and Lapwing, so causing a severe drop in numbers.
(b) The more efficient removal of cereals and the destruction of stubble coupled with early winter sowing, which has resulted in a loss of winter feeding for flocks of birds, both residents and winter migrants.
(c) The use of insecticide spraying, which has reduced the numbers of insects and their predators – both important food sources for birds.
(d) The increasing loss of hedgerows and their random trees as fields become larger again reducing food sources, nesting sites and shelter.
(e) The earlier cutting of grass for silage has destroyed both the nests and young of birds such as Corn Bunting, now a very scarce resident breeder, Skylark and, above all, the Corncrake.

The winter flocks of 150+ Skylarks so generally seen over farmland, when augmented by winter migrants, have virtually disappeared, although 1996-97 showed a possible improvement. Record numbers of c750 were seen in the Shobdon industrial estate but resident breeding numbers are now very low. The voice of the Corncrake has not been heard for several years and none have been known to breed during that time.

The Corn Bunting's decline has accelerated throughout the 1980s both countrywide and in northern Europe with local extinctions. Preferring spring-grown cereals for nesting, crops of winter wheat are not suitable, especially as it needs earlier harvesting. The decline of the Corn Bunting is mirrored in other farmland bird populations such as the Linnet, Grey Partridge, Tree Sparrow and Turtle Dove.

Research by the British Trust for Ornithology (BTO), the Royal Society for the Protection of Birds (RSPB), and the Institute of Terrestrial Ecology has shown that set-aside management has proved of value to farmland birds as well as other forms of wildlife. Lacking the disturbance of crop maintenance Skylarks will obviously raise more young. The monitoring of bird populations by the BTO has shown the decline of some species, such as the Linnet, has slowed down since the scheme began in 1992.

The management regimes imposed by MAFF were not wildlife-friendly at first, allowing farmers to cut or plough at any time during the breeding season. Updated rules were introduced to prevent this until after nesting in mid-July. Originally the scheme was not designed for the benefit of wildlife but to reduce the 'food mountains' of the 1980s and 90s. As this has been achieved, the policy ceased by 1999. A new scheme called Arable Stewardship has been set up by MAFF to reward farmers for creating habitats on cropped land with conservation headlands, uncropped wildlife strips for wild flowers to seed, and leaving winter stubbles. It is hoped that it will be available to all farmers by the year 2001.

PARKLANDS

Parklands were originally created by wealthy landowners from late medieval times and managed as wood pasture for both deer and stock. Many parks are remnants in size today. Herefordshire is fortunate in still retaining so many; among the best are Kentchurch, Eastnor, Brampton Bryan, Croft, Brockhampton by Bromyard and Moccas Park. The latter is ranked amongst the five most important areas of relic wood pasture in Britain and is now a National Nature Reserve.

In these parks trees survive into large specimens with little ground flora or shrub cover below. Their importance to birdlife lies in the old pollarded trees and undisturbed fallen branches which provide niches for rich communities of lichens and invertebrates so providing abundant food for birds and nesting sites for Redstart, Nuthatch, Woodpeckers, Hobby, Raven and Buzzard. The open aspect gives more space for the hunting birds.

CHURCHYARDS, GARDENS & OTHER AMENITY AREAS

Churchyards, urban parks and golf-courses, especially when well wooded, provide an oasis and refuge amid towns or agricultural land for other wildlife apart from birds. Although often 'well-manicured', the short turf can provide the right habitat for the larger insects fed upon by the Little Owl while the roughs give the longer grass suitable for rodents, especially voles, a primary food source for Barn and Tawny Owls.

Gardens abutting each other with their trees, shrubs and hedges help to counterbalance loss of habitat elsewhere, with the added bonus of nest-boxes for breeding and as winter dormitories for Wrens, as well as providing food and water during winter. The decline of the Mistle and Song Thrush seems to be largely associated with the gardener's desire to keep slugs and snails at bay so poisoning those that feed upon them – both thrushes and hedgehogs. Song Thrushes show a dramatic decline since the mid-1970s and are now birds of conservation concern.

The BTO has been running a garden bird survey for several years to monitor the number of species that visit when food is provided. The top ten vary in different parts of the country and county but in 1998 in Herefordshire they were, on average, the Blackbird, Blue Tit, Robin, House Sparrow, Chaffinch, Greenfinch, Great Tit, Starling, Song Thrush and Dunnock in that order.

Collared Doves, unknown here before 1963, frequently appear in pairs and Siskins are increasingly visiting nut-feeders. This helps to counterbalance loss of alder seeds as alders are being damaged or killed by a fungal root disease in the county. Great Spotted Woodpeckers can make inroads on such feeders and during a winter influx of Bramblings they too will visit food tables in even the smallest garden. Sparrowhawks also benefit from the prey available.

Magpies used to be regarded as the farmers' friend – a devourer of grain pests. With game-keeping interests they became feathered vermin, so the population plunged by the end of the century. Since then numbers have been regained and a BTO study over the last fifteen years has shown a steady increase of 4% in farmland with more than 8% in suburban habitats. Despite this, the study has shown no evidence that they have reduced song-bird numbers because of their predation of nestlings and eggs. All corvids have a varied diet which can include robbing nests – with Crows observing the comings and goings of the parents while Jays systematically search through hedges. Jackdaws seldom pillage nests while Rooks are mostly insectivorous and the Raven is primarily a scavenger. Of all the crow family the Rook nests in the largest colonies moving these at intervals and re-using the sticks. In 1995 the Herefordshire Ornithological Club (HOC) carried out a Rookery Census, as part of a wider BTO survey, which showed a rise of 35% in their population since the last survey in 1975.

COMMONLANDS & ROUGH GRASSLAND

Many of the original commons were enclosed in the eighteenth and nineteenth centuries but some escaped and survive today. Herefordshire has some 250, ranging from tiny village greens to upland grasslands of several hundred hectares, the largest being Hergest Ridge, the Malverns, Bringsty and Garway. Ewyas Harold Common, although smaller, provides a rich habitat. But these habitats are not unchanging, if commoners no longer maintain their rightful grazing levels then natural succession leads to scrub development and an increase of bracken and ultimately to woodland. Commons provide a refuge for wildlife generally giving abundant untainted invertebrate food, seeds and berries, where birds from the open country, scrub and woodland can all thrive. Linnets and Yellowhammers, which both prefer scrub, are spread equally throughout the county.

Nightingales are losing ground nationally apart from in S.E. England but have never been abundant in Herefordshire. Nightingale habitat is in woodland with thick undergrowth or in scrub, preferably dense or impenetrable for one to two metres above ground level amid bare patches of ground or short turf, to give good foraging for insect prey. Once active coppicing in woodland ceases, increased shade diminishes suitable habitat. Increasing populations of roe and muntjac deer make a severe impact on this lower vegetation so coppice regeneration is prevented. However, scrub habitats may hold more Nightingales than managed woodlands. Herefordshire has been a breeding borderland for Nightingales but the few recorded pre-war have abandoned the sites and moved to the extreme south of the county. One or two have been heard with no evidence of breeding except over the border in Gwent. Again the BTO is conducting a national survey relating numbers to the variety of habitat. Gains could be made elsewhere such as in willow scrub or in disused gravel pits. The loss of the Nightjar in the county could be due to the same reduction of dense scrub in woodlands and elsewhere – they are in national decline, and this county is at the edge of their range so most likely to lose the peripheral population first.

OWLS

In the late 1980s there were believed to be some forty-eight pairs of Barn Owls in the country, a reduction of 75% over the last fifty years. They are under severe stress from road accidents, loss of barns and nesting sites, the poisoning of their prey and the reduction of unimproved grasslands. Loss of nesting sites alone is not a major factor as some are still abandoned. Their population levels coincide with those of their primary prey, the short-tailed vole. When these are low in number the alternative prey of rickyard rodents has been lost. Research has shown that if there is snow cover for more than twenty days, hunting is further limited and they are unable to withstand prolonged food shortages as their fat reserves are too low to keep their weight/flight ratios in balance.

In 1991 a Barn Owl rehabilitation scheme was introduced in Herefordshire using young owls bred in captivity from injured adults. The numbers released were carefully monitored in suitable areas of rough grassland with back-up feeding in the early stages. Their survival and breeding were successful at first but continued road deaths have counteracted this latterly.

The Tawny Owl is still a common breeding resident in wooded areas but is nevertheless not as common as hitherto, so the erection of owl nest-boxes could prove helpful. The Short-eared Owl, a rare winter visitor, has been seen occasionally, also the Long-eared Owl which is resident but breeds in neighbouring counties further north. The Little Owl was introduced to Britain in 1879-89 gradually spreading up the valleys, preferring riverside grasslands and the edge of woodlands. It is now a fairly common resident breeder.

RIVERS, WETLANDS AND FLOOD MEADOWS

The main rivers of Herefordshire have upstream tributaries providing fast, well-oxygenated water remaining unfrozen, which provides feeding throughout the year for Kingfishers, Dippers and Common Sandpiper, a summer visitor. Kingfisher numbers have risen again with the improvement of water purity in many rivers and the milder winters. Further downstream the slower moving waters provide feeding grounds for Mute Swan, Mallard, Teal, Wigeon, Tufted Duck, Moorhen, Coot, Little Grebe and Water Rail. Snipe are now rarer. The numbers of Mute Swan have increased by one-third over the last few years so vindicating the ban on the use of angler's lead weights.

The Wye provides a corridor for migratory birds each spring and autumn. Single sightings of the Osprey and their juveniles en route to and from Scotland are becoming more frequent. The river also provides a routeway for Cormorant from the South Wales coast and for Goosanders. In the early fifties Cormorant were seldom seen as far inland as Herefordshire but by 1986 some seventy-eight used Carey Island, Hoarwithy, for roosting. During the nineties there were about forty-five as their numbers fluctuate yearly. The Goosanders are tree-nesting ducks moving further upstream to breed and were first recorded in the 1960s-70s. The numbers of both birds have increased sufficiently to cause concern to anglers and fishery-owners and, despite both being protected, a growing number of licences to shoot a limited quantity have been issued by MAFF to 'prevent serious damage to fisheries'.

In 1995-96 the Wye Winter Bird Survey was carried out by HOC to try and estimate numbers. This was in collaboration with other ornithological groups in adjoining counties through which the Wye and its tributaries flowed from Llangurig to Chepstow, where the main Cormorant roost is at Piercefield cliffs. Previous tag-marking could provide information on the origin and movement of the birds. It is by no means proven that Cormorants and Goosanders do make a serious impact on fish-stock – other factors could be responsible such as field run-off containing excess chemicals and silt, or human over-fishing at the river mouth. The survey was repeated at the same sites in the winter of 1996-97. The results show more than twenty-eight species recorded in Herefordshire only and in particular were as follows:

	Cormor-ant	Goosan-der	Heron	King-fisher	Little Grebe	Mallard	Mute Swan
1995/6							
26 Nov.	57	134	64	31	22	1689	322
4 Feb.	85	179	31	13	14	1413	252
31 Mar.	98	175	14	14	6	462	303
1996/7							
8 Dec.	49	203	30	7	18	1477	192
20 Feb.	47	232	50	9	40	1619	272
6 Apl.	31	234	23	6	0	715	290

(The lower numbers of Heron in the spring are because many are nesting.)

Herefordshire has few large lakes so the Great Crested Grebe does not reproduce abundantly. Breeding pairs are found at Titley Pool, Bodenham Pool, Wellington gravel pits and Berrington Pool. Berrington also has a large permanent heronry amid the oak trees on the island with up to twenty-seven nests in the early nineties. Breeding fluctuates according to the hardness of the winter but it is still one of the largest in the county. Other smaller heronries are at Leach Pool, Clifford; Weston Farm, Bredwardine; and Brampton Bryan. A few random ones occur elsewhere.

Where river gravels have been worked pits and lakes remain, such as at Stretton Sugwas (on the pre-glacial course of the Wye), at Bodenham and Wellington on the Lugg plain. The latter two are particularly rich in bird life for both nesting, over-wintering and passage migrants. Bodenham Pool is one of the best bird-watching sites in the county with a large extent of standing water and varied shorelines flanked by grassland and woodland. Seventy breeding species have been recorded with 130 species overall. At Wellington gravel pits 152 species have been recorded. The numbers will increase further once the gravel workings are finished.

Stretton Sugwas gravel pits have the steep cliffs which are ideal for nesting Sand Martins. Although numbers are generally in decline a strong colony has returned to breed each summer with 80-100 nest holes there in 1998. At Wellington gravel pits 100 nest holes were dug out of a pile of worked sand also in 1998; work was suspended until the birds finally departed. Sand Martins prefer to nest in such sites rather than river banks as the holes there can be subject to winter wash-out, but small colonies occur on the banks of the Monnow near Kentchurch and on the Wye near

Clifford. Their decline is estimated to be down nationally to one-tenth of the breeding figures of 1960 largely due to the effects of the Sahel droughts.

The river plain of the Wye floods regularly giving food to wetland birds. In 1989 mixed flocks of twenty-three Whooper Swan and fifteen Bewick Swan were recorded in association with Mute Swan and geese. The Lugg Meadows in particular flood regularly. Many parts to the north of the Lugg Bridge have been drained but the old Lammas lands of the Upper and Lower Meadows and the Hampton Bishop Meadow are undrained and still farmed traditionally, giving food and forage for winter flocks. So rich are they that they have SSSI status.

MIGRATION

After breeding, waders and water birds return southward and many come to Britain in search of wetlands and water, but the number of sites is diminishing due to drainage. Britain is one of the most important staging posts for millions of migrating species. However, Herefordshire is a poor county for winter wildfowl and waders. Some birds, such as Siskins and the winter thrushes, migrate westward from northern Europe. Blackbirds and Starlings come in large numbers from Scandinavia and Russia respectively. The latter gather in flocks, though the huge numbers seen over the countryside at dusk ten years ago are becoming a rarer sight. By March the visitors return to their breeding areas and it is possible to distinguish these from our resident starlings as the latter have golden-yellow beaks ready for breeding whereas the Russian visitors still retain brownish beaks.

October is the main migration month. The mid-September equinoxial gales are often followed by a stable period so, if the autumn is mild and there are no mountain ranges to cross, many smaller birds benefit from late departure using the later autumn plant re-growth and seeds for feeding *en route*. Occasional mass movements or irruptions can occur every few years in winter if food supplies in Europe are low. For example, the westward irruption of Waxwings if the berry-crop is poor, or that of Bramblings if the beechmast crop fails, or the Crossbills if the cone supplies are inadequate. There was an influx of Long-eared Owls in the winter of 1986-87, the largest for ten years. Most remained in S.E.England but one was recorded at Dinmore. An influx of Quail was recorded in 1989 – they are difficult to see being only 18cm long but their distinctive calls at dusk and dawn were heard by many. They would be more abundant but for the twice-yearly slaughter when passing over France.

Many birds, such as Crows, Jackdaws, Starlings, Lapwings, Skylarks and mixed gulls, come together in winter when territorial behaviour has been abandoned, feeding daily in flocks in the countryside. Others in mixed flocks of thrushes feeding on fruit, chaffinches on seeds and berries, or Siskins with Redpolls on alder cones. Many make a movement back to sheltered, warmer areas of conifers or towns and gardens by evening. Nightly congregations of Pied Wagtails have been collecting in Hereford city and around Belmont Tesco over the past few years with flocks close to 1,000 in High Town in December 1991. After 1995 they moved to the Bulmer's/Sainsbury's site and hundreds were recorded on the rooftop of Hereford Safeway's in 1997.

Summer migrants reach Britain in waves from mid-March to mid-June with the warbler males arriving first to establish territories by singing to define their boundaries. Swallows and House Martins need damp mud for nest-building, so a dry spring affects them. Among the last to arrive are the secretive Nightjars, flying at night to trawl for insects over heathlands. None breed in Herefordshire now but it is hoped that they may recover in areas of newly-felled and replanted forestry.

The numbers of migrants returning have to run the gauntlet of bird-shooting in W. Europe as well as adverse winds and poor weather *en route*, and the trans-Saharan migrants suffer that extra hazard. In addition they can be affected by conditions in their winter quarters. For several years there has been severe drought in the Sahel region south of the Sahara, accompanied by over-grazing, so winter feeding has been poor, giving reduced numbers returning. Once rainfall returned in 1995-96 increases in the locust population then defoliated plants and insecticide spraying further affected birds' food supplies.

Thus bird populations, with their widespread movements, are affected by many factors beyond our immediate control so reduction in the loss of habitat variety within the country and county is vital for both residents and migrants if they are to maintain their present numbers or to return to those of the past.

SOME CHANGES SINCE EARLIER WOOLHOPE CLUB RECORDING

Since the early days of the Woolhope Club attitudes have greatly changed towards the rare visitor, which is no longer shot on sight and stuffed. Changes in some bird sightings and numbers were cited by Dr Charles Walker in the centenary volume of the club (1951) recording the loss of the Honey Buzzard, Black Grouse and Wryneck – last seen and heard in Breinton in 1945 but since reappearing occasionally. The Stonechat was becoming rare, having succumbed to the extreme winter of 1947. Dr Walker hoped that its numbers would return, as had the Goldcrest and Long-tailed Tit from a similar eclipse during that great frost. Today the Stonechat has returned in small numbers to upland areas especially where there is good gorse cover.

The Black-headed Gull was rarely seen then but a widespread increase has occurred generally in this century. Herefordshire was colonised in the early thirties by over-wintering birds in the wet areas of the Teme valley. Today they are recorded throughout the county all year with thousands more streaming in from Europe to over-winter with the resident population increasing it fourfold. Some have been breeding in the Shenmore area in recent years.

The Common Gull is mainly a winter visitor, feeding in flocks of up to 3,000 in the Lugg meadows, with some non-breeding birds occasionally seen in summer. The Little Gull is a rare vagrant but seen in 1991 and 1994 and again from 1996-98 at Wellington gravel pits. The Lesser Black-backed Gull was a rare visitor a century ago but today it can be recorded in flocks of 3,500 – also at Wellington. The only breeding record is on the Inco factory rooftop in Hereford since 1992 where the site is aggressively defended against any incursions by maintenance men.

As already mentioned, the Pied Flycatcher has been encouraged further east and the Little Owl introduced since those Woolhope days. The Willow Tit was unknown then as its differences from the Marsh Tit had not been recognised; however, its numbers are in decline by 50% countywide. Dr Bull referred to the scarcity of the Marsh Warbler which has only since been recorded nesting in 1953. The Reed Warbler is a scarce summer breeder but the Sedge Warbler is fairly common.

With progressively milder winters some summer migrants are remaining, singles of Chiffchaff and several Blackcap are now seen and heard in gardens throughout the year. Some of the Blackcaps may be those migrating west from Germany. The Mandarin Duck is an escapee now breeding in small numbers and the Canada Goose, another introduced species, is well established. Dr Bull recorded the Hoopoe but its striking appearance was its death-knell. Today this summer visitor from Africa can be seen in open countryside and there was one breeding record at Lyonshall in 1955.

Single sightings of the Golden Oriole, also a summer visitor to woods and gardens, have occurred since early Woolhope days when most were shot. Records show no return for many years then random sightings, the last being 1986, 1991 and 1996. The Little Egret is appearing more frequently as far west as Herefordshire. If the climate continues growing warmer perhaps more of these three and other species will be seen. Rarities occur occasionally, westerly gales have driven in Puffin, Manx Shearwaters, Kittiwakes and other seabirds in an exhausted condition. Other recent rarities in 1995 include a Desert Wheatear – the first, and a Collared Pratincole, for which there is one record last century. In 1996 there was a Red-throated Diver, not seen since the last century, and a Black-throated Diver in 1956 for which there are no previous records.

Generally, the quantity of bird life in Herefordshire, as in the country overall, presents a depressing picture with many species diminishing in numbers. Farmland birds especially are losing habitat and feeding as well as facing nest destruction. Only public awareness of their plight and consequent public opinion can bring the much needed changes if their numbers are to survive through to the next millennium.

ACKNOWLEDGMENT
My thanks to Keith Mason of the Herefordshire Ornithological Club for checking the accuracy of various figures.

SOURCES
H. G. Bull, *Notes on the Birds of Herefordshire* (1888).
C. W. Walker, 'Herefordshire Birds' in *Herefordshire: its natural history, archaeology, and history* (1954).
C. W. Walker & A. J. Smith, 'Herefordshire Birds' in *TWNFC*, XLI (1975).
Conservation Potential of Herefordshire, Herefordshire & Radnorshire Nature Trust, 1977-78.
Annual Reports Herefordshire Ornithological Club, 1971-97.
Reports by the British Trust for Ornithology, 1985-98.
Reports by the Hawk & Owl Trust, 1985-95.
B. H. Harding, Ornithology Recorder Reports in *TWNFC* 1984-98.

Life on the River: Some Aspects of the Navigation of the Wye 1770-1855

JOHN C. EISEL

BACKGROUND

Looking at the peaceful scene on the river Wye today, it is difficult to imagine that once it played an important part in the economy of the region. In the following essay a look is taken at the life of the users of the river, and some of the personalities who played a part in its story. It is limited to the period 1770 to 1855 for several reasons. In 1770 the first Hereford newspaper styled *The British Chronicle or Pugh's Hereford Journal* started publication, and a careful study of the local news contained in its pages, together with the advertisements, sheds some light on conditions then pertaining. Unless otherwise stated, all advertisements and news items referred to are taken from its pages. Also in the same year the Reverend William Gilpin journeyed down the river, and subsequently published a book on his observations, particularly relating to the picturesque beauty of the river Wye, starting the cult of the picturesque; this book went through several editions.[1] The year 1855 marks the end of the river Wye as a serious navigation up to Hereford, as will become apparent, although the section below Monmouth continued to be used as such for some time longer.

In the *Transactions* of the Woolhope Club the late Isaac Cohen more than adequately dealt with the history of the navigation of the river Wye,[2] and he also published a paper on ship-building on the river Wye at Hereford.[3] This essay is supplementary to those papers, and deals with matters of more human interest, but I shall inevitably refer to matters dealt with by Cohen.

The late eighteenth century was a great period for topographical works, generally illustrated by copper engravings. One of the greatest of these was Grose's *Antiquities* which covers the counties of England and Wales in eight volumes, with supplemental volumes on Scotland and Ireland. The section covering Hereford includes a plate, engraved from a drawing now in the Hereford Museum, showing a view of the cathedral taken from the south bank of the river, more or less where the new bridge now crosses. On the north bank of the river can be seen two barges complete with masts, and the mast of a further vessel appears above the south bank.[4] A similar view of the cathedral was published in 1797 in Samuel Ireland's *Picturesque Views on The River Wye*, where a nice aquatint shows a barge with a keel and a tall mast, and a smaller vessel without a keel. The river trade was conducted by such vessels, of varying size, flat-bottomed because the river is generally very shallow in places, and with a single sail which helped to propel them, the mast which supported the sail being rigged such a way that it was easily lowered in order to go underneath a bridge.

Goods were brought up the Wye from Chepstow and the Forest of Dean, the main item being coal, of which about 20,000 tons were used annually in the vicinity of Hereford at the turn of the last century.[5] Barges were loaded with coal at Lydbrook for the upriver trip. Manufactured goods from elsewhere were trans-shipped from larger boats to the smaller barges in the tidal part of the river for transport upstream, Brockweir being the upper limit of this section of the river. The larger sea-going vessels were commented on by Gilpin:

> In many places also the views were varied by the prospect of bays and harbours in mini-ature, where little barks lay moored, taking in ore and other commodities from the moun-tains. These vessels, designed plainly for rougher water than they at present encountered, shewed us, without any geographical knowledge, that we approached the sea.[6]

The journey upriver must have been a trial for the bargemen, very much dependent on the vagaries of the weather. The sail was not a very efficient means of propulsion, and navigation was impeded by several weirs across the river. The idea of these was to hold the water back in order to help navigation, but they also formed an obstacle to the barges, with the rapidly flowing water through the constriction. The barges needed help to negotiate them, and this was generally supplied in the form of manpower, with gangs of men helping to pull the barges past the weirs and rapids. Ireland, talking about the lower part of the river near New Weir, close to Symonds Yat, has the following to say:

> The river here receives a considerable degree of agitation from the huge masses of stone, either swept down by the stream, or hurled from the summit of the neighbouring rocks. Here the Wye increases in width, and its current is so strong, that it is with extraordinary labour and difficulty the barges are towed up. I have seen eight or ten men throw them-selves on the earth on every pull, to give force to their exertions.[7]

Unless it was a case of artist's licence, the view of 'Simmonds Rocks' given by Ireland provides evidence that horses were also used on occasion at that period to supply the necessary motive power to pull the barges upstream, for a barge is depicted being pulled by four horses (Pl. 1).

A hundred years later, the situation below Monmouth was little different, even though the navigation above the town had ceased at that time. An interesting description is given in H. A. Gilbert's book *The Tale Of A Wye Fisherman* (1929).

> I have spoken to a man who earned his living as a youngster in pulling the barges up to Monmouth. This man is old Parry, who is now in the service of the Wye board as a netsman, and who made the record catch of salmon in 1913. He tells me that the crew of a barge used to be one man for every ton of load, and that twenty men were needed to take a big coal barge upstream. When the barge got to a stream, tackle was got out and every man har-nessed to pull. It was hard work. He told me that very often 'we were pulling half an hour before the blanky blank moved an inch'. I gather Parry prefers his present trade as a netsman to that which he followed in his youth. As he tersely said: 'I earned my money in those days - every penny of it'.[8]

Plate 1. A barge being towed upstream at 'Simmonds' Rocks. From Samuel Ireland's *Pictur-esque Views on the River Wye...*(1797).

All this labour was only possible if there was enough water in the river to float the barges – and often there was not, particularly in summer. In that case, all that could be done was for the barge to be moored in a suitable place and wait for rain higher up the river. This is illustrated by an advertisement of 3 December 1788 publicising casks for sale, which stated that they 'will arrive at Hereford by the very first barge-water in the Wye'.

When the barges arrived at Hereford, they were unloaded, and coal and other materials were stockpiled against times of shortage of water when coal could not be brought upriver. The extent of the wharfage is best seen on the map of the city, published on 1 April 1806, which was drawn for Britton and Brayley's *Beauties of England and Wales*. There were wharves on both banks on either side of the Wye bridge. On the north bank, downstream of the bridge, there was a series of ware-houses running down from Pipe Lane (now called Gwynne Street) to the river, while upstream there was a large wharf at the Friars, to the west of the area marked as 'Tenters' on Taylor's map of 1757. On the south bank, upstream was a coal yard, while downstream a wharf was marked with buildings on three sides. Some of these survive and were known until recently as the Sack Warehouse. To the east of these is a building near to where the Dorset Ale Store now stands, and further east still timber yards are marked. This building is not shown on the plan of Hereford that was surveyed by H. Price in 1802 and published on 1 January 1803, although it may just be an omission. The buildings of the coal wharf just to the west of Castle Cliffe (the Old Bridewell) are shown on the 1806 map, but not marked as a wharf. There was also another coal wharf further downstream at Eign, where the Eign brook discharges into the Wye.

Not all the barges were unloaded at Hereford, and some continued upstream above Hereford. There was a serious hindrance to navigation at Monnington where wind-lasses were used to help haul barges over Monnington Falls. When a bill to enable a toll bridge to be built at Whitney was presented to Parliament in 1774, provision was made that barge owners using the river were to be answerable for any damage caused to the bridge by their boats.[9] Ireland seems to consider that the limit of navigation was just below Hay, where the Dulas Brook joins the Wye:

> On quitting Hay, the Wye receives a considerable body of water from the river Dulas, across which is a stone bridge of one arch. Thus assisted, our river becomes a copious stream, and has been long rendered navigable in the winter seasons.[10]

However, it would appear that the river was navigable on occasion as far as Glasbury, about four miles upstream as the crow flies but somewhat more by water, as when some timber was advertised for sale in the *Hereford Journal* of 23 April 1772, it was said to be '14 miles from Glasbury Bridge, where the River Wye is navigable'. This is reinforced by Clark in his *General View of the Agriculture of the County of Hereford...* (1794), in which he states, '...even the counties of Brecon and Radnor derive some little benefit from the Wye, as it is in floods navigable six miles above Hay'.[11]

For the return journey down the Wye, the barges were loaded with produce of the area. Ireland lists the main products as timber, grain and bark.[12] Oak bark was important in the tanning industry, and considerable quantities were used. When two tanhouses at Ross were advertised for sale on 27 June 1782, it was stated that there was upwards of 100 tons of bark on the premises. Timber for sale was regularly advertised, and care was taken to point out if the timber was near the river so that it could be transported that way. It was either transported by barge, or floated down river. When the barge *Valiant* of 32 tons burden was advertised for sale on 22 June 1808 she was said to be '...well worth the attention of Timber Merchants, being capable of taking in heavy Timber'.

One important product of the region that was overlooked by Ireland was cider – usually spelled cyder at this period – a rather different product to that of today, very much stronger and the better varieties of which were considered a vintage drink. For example, on 22 March 1787 Peter Dickins, a cider merchant of High Town, was advertising cider of the growth of 1784. The export trade was conducted down the Wye. Cider was stored in bulk by the merchants and shipped when there was demand. On 19 November 1788 warehouses at Pearce's Wharf, near Wye bridge, were advertised as being to let 'capable of holding 2-300 hogsheads of cider'. We can imagine the cider being loaded into barges for transport down the river. There was the occasional disaster. On 8 March 1809 we read:

> Same day (28 February), a barge, belonging to Owner Crompton, of this city, laden with cider, for Bristol, sunk in the River Wye, (from what cause is not known), about five miles from Ross. Very providentially another barge was so near as to enable them to save the crew, five in number, from a watery grave.

Advertisements about seagoing vessels appeared periodically in the *Hereford Journal*.

Thus on 10 April 1777 a vessel was advertised as sailing from Chepstow, to take ciders and other goods to London. Two months later, there were two similar advertisements concerning vessels sailing from Chepstow to London.[13] Evidently the merchants shipped their cider down the river to take advantage of this, the state of water permitting, and usually plenty of time was allowed between the advertisement appearing and the proposed sailing date in order to enable this to happen.

Life on the river was hard and dangerous. There were a number of fatalities recorded. On 10 January 1782 it was stated that 'Yesterday a man fell over a barge, near Bredwardine-bridge, and was drowned', while on 26 October 1791, it was reported that a man stepping onto a barge moored at a wharf a little below Wye bridge fell into the river and was drowned. Over two years before a 13-year-old lad had been drowned jumping from a barge in the same part of the river.[14] The methods used were also hazardous, and in December 1806 a float of timber near Ross went disastrously wrong and three men were drowned. In the same issue it was reported that a barge had sunk near Monmouth and three men had been drowned.[15] The hard physical activity also took its toll, but the consequences were accepted in a rather fatalistic way. When an inquest was held at the *Dog* in St Martin's parish on William Jones, a bargemen who died from a rupture caused by unloading a barge, the verdict was the usual one of 'Death by the visitation of God'.[16]

Employment must also have been very uncertain, with the traffic depending on enough water in the river. The frantic activity when trade resumed was highlighted by a report of 13 July 1791: 'The river Wye has experienced a considerable encrease during the late rains; the craft have again been put in motion, and the boatmen now labour incessantly in loading, and delivering, their cargoes of corn, coals &c'.

It is clear that there was friction between the bargemen and riverside dwellers, manifesting itself in complaints and notices. The behaviour of the bargemen was not always above reproach, and on 29 August 1792 there was a report of drunken behaviour by bargemen in a public house in Monmouth. There are occasional notices aimed at the river traffic. Thus on 27 May 1779 there was a notice about bargemen trespassing at Hentland, and on 24 April 1805 Thomas Moore put in a notice requiring barge owners to desist from bringing barges onto any part of Bartonsham estate.

With this background, the proposal to establish a horse towing path received support. On 29 August 1804 it was announced that the survey of the river Wye was to commence the next day, while a fortnight later there was a notice of application for an Act of Parliament, together with a comment on the '…Scarcity of Men to navigate the Barges and the exorbitant Wages demanded by the few remaining on this river...'

It was not until early in 1811 that the towing path was completed, the first journey being reported on 23 January:

On Thursday last two barges belonging to Mr. Crompton, of this city, completed their voyage from Lidbrook by means of the newly made Towing-path on the Banks of the Wye. The whole voyage was performed with facility and expedition, with the aid of two horses to each barge. – Their arrival was announced by the ringing of bells, a band of music, &c.; but the general rejoicings are deferred until, by this or some other mode, the price of coal shall be brought within some *reasonable* limits.

PERSONALITIES
Along the waterfront there was a complex web of relationships, both business and

personal. At this distance it is only possible to outline these and occasionally put further detail. At any one time there were several active businesses, but it is difficult to follow them as they passed from one owner to another, except for what appears to have been the major firm. In a trade directory for 1793 the name of James Biss, bargemaster, appears.[17] He was a cornfactor and carrier then operating from the Castle Quay and clearly in a good way of business. His name first comes to attention on 22 October 1778, when it was advertised that 25 bundles of Rind Hoops had been delivered at his warehouse at Mr Bird's Quay, one of the quays near to Wye Bridge. On 17 November 1785 he advertised:

> JAMES BISS, takes this method of returning his most sincere thanks to his friends in general for all past favours; and informs them, that he is removed to the Castle Quay, where all sorts of goods are taken up and forwarded with the greatest care and expedition to Chepstow, Bristol, London, &c. &c. by their obedient humble servant...

In 1800 James Biss, with other proprietors of trows, advertised that it was necessary to increase freight charges, and in March 1812 he advertised again to the same effect. He died in 1813, and two of his trows (*Friends* and *Prudence*), both of which he had bought in 1805, were transferred to his widow Susanna who evidently carried on the business, at least for a short period.[18]

Another figure became prominent at this period and on 22 April 1815 it was announced that the proprietors of the Chepstow boat were declining the same in favour of Mr John Easton. On 23 August 1815 it was announced that Mrs Biss had declined the carrying concern from Bristol in favour of Mr Easton, and she subsequently sold the trow *Friends* to him.[19] John Easton was both carrier and timber merchant and clearly in a good way of business. Although barges and trows had been built along the river for many years, in 1822 the major boat building phase at Hereford began, with Evan Hopkins constructing the sloop *Hereford* for John Easton on a site on the south bank of the river opposite the garden of the college of vicars choral. Subsequently a number of other sea-going vessels were built there under the supervision of John Easton. From 1824 to 1826 he built boats at a yard in Chepstow and then transferred his activities to Brockweir for at least another seven years. During this time he was running a carrier's business between Hereford and Bristol from the Castle wharf, using the sloop *Hereford*, built in Hereford in 1822, for the sea-going leg of the trip. In 1835 he advertised that he was declining the business of carrying goods weekly to and from Bristol in favour of Mr William Bunning.[20] This was the usual phrase, but has been incorrectly interpreted as implying financial difficulties: whilst this may have been so, it is an inference that cannot be drawn from the advertisement.

William Bunning was a schoolmaster with a slightly chequered career. He came to Hereford to teach at the Cathedral School, but in June 1826 advertised that he intended to open a school the following month. In March 1829 he advertised that he intended to resign from the Cathedral School and devote his time exclusively to the school that he had recently opened in Wyebridge Street. In December 1829 it was announced that the school had been moved to Widemarsh Street, while in July 1830 it had been moved to Bridge Street. Bunning's Academy was successful as it offered commercial subjects and charged half the fees of the Cathedral School, which until 1836 was purely classical. Consequently the number of pupils at the Cathedral School declined and by the mid 1830s there were only about twenty-nine pupils there, consisting of one boarder, twelve choristers, four dean's scholars and twelve private pupils.[21]

When Bunning took over the business of John Easton he appears to have closed his school and on 17 June 1835 his residence in Wyebridge Street was advertised as being to let and '...may be viewed by applying to Mr Bunning at the Castle Quay...'. As part of the carrier's business Bunning bought the sloop *Hereford* and the barge *John and Mary*.[22] In 1836 he bought the barge *Liberty* from William Cooke, a merchant of Hereford, and this was registered in his name on 21 November 1836.[23] Cooke went bankrupt in 1838[24] and Bunning bought the barge *William*.[25] Curiously, the advertisement regarding Cooke's effects still mentioned a barge *Liberty*. The approach of the Hereford and Gloucester Canal obviously affected the business on the Wye, and in 1843 an advertisement appeared for Bunning and Wilson as carriers on the canal.[26] However, what little profit there was in transport on the Wye was clearly diminishing, and in 1845 Bunning sold the barge *Liberty*, the following year he sold the barges *William* and *John & Mary*, and finally, on 15 March 1847, he sold the sloop *Hereford*.[27] At that time he was described as being a farmer, of Holmer, Herefordshire.

Another name that is much associated with the river is that of Crompton, but the complexities of the family make it difficult to sort out the relationships. The name of Jonathan Crompton appears in the 1793 trade directory as a barge-master, and Crompton's wharf, where cider was advertised for sale at Mr Jones's Cider House in April 1794, was probably his wharf. The firm of J. Crompton and Co. was one of those which advertised an increase in freight charges on 22 January 1800. He was clearly involved in the porter trade from a warehouse in Pipe Lane - now Gwynne Street - and on 26 December 1804 he advertised that he had received a large quantity of porter, also that his barges and trows continued to carry goods. On 1 December 1813 he advertised that he had moved from Pipe Lane to a wharf situated 'over Wye bridge', where he had a coal business. However, this did not prosper, and notice of his bankruptcy appeared on 22 November 1815. His premises were advertised as being to let on 27 March 1816 and a dividend was paid to his

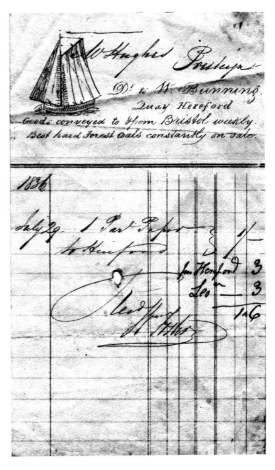

Plate 2. A bill issued by William Bunning just after he took over the carrier's business.
Reproduced by courtesy of Mrs J. O'Donnell.

creditors more than two years later.[28]

William Crompton, a contemporary of Jonathan Crompton, also had premises in Pipe Lane, his being based on the *Star Inn*. On 29 January 1800 he advertised a barge for sale as he was going into another line of business. This barge was of 25 tons burden, two years old and was priced at £100. However, since his name continued to appear in connection with the river it seems likely that he changed his mind. The Hereford Iron Warehouse at Crompton's Wharf may well have been part of his business[29]. He also dealt in coal, lime and timber.[30] Crompton's death at the age of 50 was announced on 6 October 1819 and a fortnight later it was stated that his widow and eldest son were carrying on the business. On 11 April 1821 Mrs Jane Crompton of the Coal Wharf in Pipe Lane advertised the inn known as the *Star* in Pipe Lane to be let. She had financial difficulties; in 1822 there was a notice that she had assigned her goods for the benefit of her creditors (24 April) and a notice to her creditors appeared on 19 March 1823. It is not known who took on the tenancy of the *Star Inn*, but in 1826 the landlord was David Davis, by which time the name had been changed to *The Bell*.[31] A few years later, the inn was in the possession of Richard Crompton. On 21 September 1831 it was reported that two bargemen, labouring servants to Mr Richard Crompton, had deserted his barge *William* on a voyage to Chepstow with a cargo of bark, so that the remainder of the crew could not proceed without them. They were hauled into court and sentenced to two months imprisonment with hard labour. On 13 June 1832 it was reported that Mr Richard Crompton had died at the age of 28, and on 25 July his property and effects, including the barge *Martha* and a pleasure boat, were advertised for sale.

The Pearce family was another much connected with the river. Perhaps the most prominent member was Daniel Pearce. His wharf was described as being near Wye bridge, and was probably on the south side of the river. He married Ann Symonds on 3 November 1786 and his son Daniel was baptised on 20 August 1787. Both of these are recorded in the St Martins' registers.[32] On 4 November 1795 it was advertised that a cider mill at his wharf was to be removed, and that four barges, *Valiant*, *Daniel and Anne*, *Sally*, and *Thomas* were to be sold. Almost three years later (25 July 1798) the *Valiant* and *Dan and Anne* were again advertised for sale. An inference of financial problems is justified, for on 15 July 1801 it was stated that Daniel Pearce was bankrupt. His name appears twice more: on 19 September 1810 it was reported that Daniel Pearce had saved from drowning a girl who had attempted suicide below Wye bridge, and his death in his 68th year was reported on 15 April 1829.

THE DECLINE OF THE NAVIGATION

The difficulties of the navigation were such that it was not surprising that alternatives were seriously considered. In 1801 there was a proposal to build a tram road to Hereford through the Forest of Dean, and a revised plan submitted on 30 September 1802 showed a tramroad starting from the opposite side of the river to Lydbrook and terminating at Wye Bridge, Hereford, but this came to nothing. However, the opening of the Brecon to Abergavenny canal in 1800 and the benefit of the cheap coal brought by it, stimulated two proposals to link the canal to Herefordshire. A proposal to build a tramway from Brecon to Eardisley was first mooted in 1810, and the necessary funds were raised and acts of Parliament obtained: the first section from Brecon to Hay was completed in 1816, and the section to Eardisley was opened on 11 December 1818. The approach of the Hay tramroad stimulated a proposal in 1818 for a connecting railway to Kington and beyond, the section from Eardisley to

Kington being opened on 1 May 1820. Naturally this had an adverse effect on the river trade, and the transport of coal by river above Hereford must be presumed to have ceased.[33] The second proposal made in 1810 was for a tramway to link the Brecon to Abergavenny canal at Llanwenarth to Llanfihangel Crucorney and this was more successful. A bill was passed in 1811, while the following year a bill for a further construction from Llanfihangel to Monmouth Cap was also passed. It is rumoured that meetings were held from time to time with a view to stimulate interest in extending the tramroad to Hereford, but that these were broken up by persons with vested interests in the failure of the project. However, in 1825 a series of public meetings were held and an application made to Parliament for an Act. This was passed the following year, and the construction put in hand. The tramroad was opened for traffic on 21 September 1829 and at 10am the first consignment of coal arrived at the terminus in Hereford, which was the old coal wharf to the west of the south end of the Wye Bridge. It had been estimated that about 6,000 tons of coal would be transported annually, but it is suggested that the peak tonnage transported in the mid 1830s was rather more than this. The subsequent decline was attributed to the increased price of South Wales coal, which made Forest of Dean coal more competitive.[34]

It is inevitable that the trade on the river was affected by the coal coming from South Wales. It must have been further damaged when the Gloucester and Hereford Canal reached Hereford in 1845, and the final blow came when the Newport, Abergavenny and Hereford Railway, which used part of the old tramroad, was opened for traffic on 2 January 1854. With this the navigation effectively ceased to function. Until this period the half-yearly general meetings of the proprietors of the River Wye Horse Towing Path Company were advertised regularly, and on 15 June 1853 it was reported:

We hear that the proprietors of the River Wye Towing-Path, at their half-yearly meeting at the City Arms, on the 1st instant, were able to make a dividend of 35s. per share upon the shares of the company, which is the largest they have been able to make for some years and the trade on the Wye would have been much larger if there had been a better supply of coal in the Forest.

This forecast was optimistic. The last general meeting of the proprietors was advertised on 28 November 1855, and it is assumed that the company then became inactive. With this the navigation to Hereford effectively ceased to function.

REFERENCES
[1] W. Gilpin, *Observations on the River Wye* (1770).
[2] *TWNFC* 1956, 83-101.   [3] *TWNFC* 1958, 75-9.
[4] The drawing was made in 1775. F. Grose, *The Antiquities of England and Wales*. (New edition, n.d.), 244.
[5] *TWNFC* 1947, 66.   [6] 5th edition (1800), 47.   [7] Ireland, 97.
[8] Page 38.   [9] *TWNFC* 1935, 121.   [10] Ireland, 35-6.
[11] Page 12.   [12] Ireland, 58.   [13] 8 May 1777.
[14] 24 June 1789.   [15] 22 December 1802.   [16] 22 February 1804.
[17] *Universal British Directory*, n.d. (c.1793).   [18] G. Farr, *Chepstow Ships* (1954), 70-1.
[19] ibid., p.71.   [20] 4 & 11 March 1835.
[21] W. T. Carless, *A Short History of Hereford School* (1914), 42.

[22] Farr, op. cit., 110 & 119.   [23] ibid., 136.   [24] 30 May 1838.

[25] Farr, op. cit., 125.   [26] 1 & 18 January 1843.

[27] Farr, op. cit., 136, 125, 119, 110.   [28] 6 January 1819.   [29] 23 January 1805.

[30] 22 April 1815, 22 April 1818, 14 April 1819.

[31] R. Shoesmith, *Gwynne House and 19-22 Bridge Street, Hereford*. Hereford Archaeology Series 263 (1995).

[32] International Genealogical Index for St Martin's parish.

[33] A full history of the Brecon to Kington tramroad is given in *TWNFC* 1935, 127-131; 1937, 76-87; 1964, 16-26.

[34] Summarised from *TWNFC* 1947, 65-72.

The Care of a Herefordshire Church: Winforton 1685-1728

E. D. PAUL

The parish of Winforton lies on the road from Hereford to Brecon, about fifteen miles W. of Hereford and close to the Welsh border. The nearest towns are Hay-on-Wye, about five or six miles to the S.W. and Kington about eight miles N. The area of the parish as given in the 1841 census is 1,240 acres and its southern boundary on the Wye is about 56m above sea level. The northern boundary, at its highest point on the N.W., just reaches 90m. Isaac Taylor's map of 1754 shows that then, as now, there was a village on either side of the main road. A lane led northwards out of the village as it still does and there was a track leading down to a ferry on the Wye.[1] The population in 1801 was 179, but in the late seventeenth century it was probably higher, as rough estimates based on the hearth tax returns of 1671 and the Compton Census of 1676 indicate a figure somewhere between 251 and 321.[2] If, in Winforton, as elsewhere, the population level remained fairly static until 1710 and then began to rise slowly, in spite of higher death rates between 1720 and 1730, it had probably not changed much by 1728.[3]

The hearth tax of 1671 indicates that the social and economic hierarchy within the parish took the form of a pyramid with a broad base and a narrow apex. Although the assessment includes the tiny parish of Willersley to the east, it is unlikely that this distorts the picture much, since the latter only contains one minute hamlet. The tax return records fifty-nine houses of which twenty-nine were exempt from tax on account of poverty. A further twenty-one had one hearth each, while four boasted two hearths. Of the rest two had three hearths, one had four, one had five and the fifth, the property of the Holman family who were lords of the manor, had eleven.[4] A militia assessment of 1663 confirms this structure. The Holmans' property was valued at £211. Then there was a big drop to Edmund Greene of Weere Lesey (probably Willersley) at £100 and another to Thomas Dowsing, the rector, at £45. The properties of Thomas Higgins, gentleman, and Thomas Hunt were valued at £26 and £13, with eighteen other properties in a band ranging from £8 down to £1.[5] Most of the population were farmers, smallholders and labourers. There were also a few craftsmen and the incumbent was resident.

THE PARISH CHURCH

Winforton church, which stands in the village, is built of local sandstone rubble and consists of nave, chancel, a north transept or chapel, a west tower with a timber-framed upper stage and a south porch. The nave and chancel together are nearly 80ft long and just over 19ft wide. The tower is 19ft 3ins square and the north transept measures 16ft 3ins by 14ft 9ins. The building was very heavily restored in 1895, when much of the south wall and the porch were rebuilt and new windows were inserted in the north walls. The timber-framed bell-chamber is thought to date from the sixteenth century and the east wall of the chancel was rebuilt in 1698, but the fabric is otherwise medieval with some windows and the roofs attributed to the fourteenth century.[6] Sir Stephen Glynne, who visited the church in 1869, commented on the lack of a chancel arch and recorded several features that have now gone: most notably a coved ceiling, a single very tiny lancet in the north wall of the nave and a priest's door in the south wall of the chancel. He also condemned the box pews made in 1707.[7]

Financial responsibility for the fabric and furnishings of the church at this period was divided. The rector, as recipient of the great tithes, was responsible for the chancel; the Holman family, as lords of the manor, continued to maintain the north transept; while the owners of property in the parish were responsible for the rest of the fabric and all the furnishings, apart from most of the seating. The property owners' share of the work was paid for by a church rate levied annually at about 4d in the pound. This produced an income of approximately £3 a year to cover all the expenses of maintaining and running the church. In a normal year about one quarter of the money was spent on the building, one quarter on fees and expenses for visitations twice a year, one quarter on bread and wine for the communion and the remaining quarter on a variety of smaller expenses. But, when restoration or any other exceptional work was carried out, the rate could rise very steeply.

The major responsibility for the church in practice lay on the churchwardens, who arranged for maintenance and restoration work to be done on behalf of the ratepayers and represented the parish at visitations, when they had to report on the state of the entire church and its furnishings, not just the parts which they maintained. If work needed doing, time would be allocated by the authorities for its completion and the churchwardens were expected to submit a certificate from the incumbent confirming that it was finished. If the diocese thought there was cause for concern, perhaps because of the extent of the work and the cost, those responsible would be cited in the consistory court. This does not necessarily imply negligence, since there were many reasons why a church might be out of repair. No one was normally punished or fined because a church needed repair, since the ecclesiastical courts were primarily courts of correction and their concern was to see that problems were put right. But they sat every four weeks and could monitor progress in the interval between visitations.[8]

The main evidence for the care of Winforton church from 1685 to 1728 is to be found in the parish book in Herefordshire Record Office, which was bought in 1685 to record the parish officers' accounts. In addition to the accounts it contains a variety of minutes, notes and lists, including the rector's notes of all the restoration work done and all the new furniture acquired from 1693 to 1708.[9] This evidence can be extended and checked against evidence from the diocesan records and also from the fabric of the church itself. All the evidence is incomplete and the building itself has to be regarded with extreme caution, since it was so drastically restored by the Victorians. In 1895 they rebuilt the porch and much of the south wall, installed new windows and removed the ceiling and the priest's door. They replaced the stone floor with wood blocks and stripped plaster from the interior and probably from the exterior too, since churches built of rubble were generally plastered and painted outside as well as inside. It is likely, too, that the alterations made to the furnishings date from this time. The pulpit was moved to the N.E. end of the nave, the box pews replaced, a wooden chancel arch installed and the eighteenth-century communion rails adapted so that they were straight and not three-sided. Some old materials were put to new uses. Old floor slabs were used to pave the porch, including two ledger stones for relatives of Joseph Guest who was rector from 1691 to 1721. In addition the eighteenth-century panelling slotted between the modern pew ends and the walls is probably all that is left of the old box pews.

PROPERTY OWNERS AND PARISHIONERS

Itemised churchwardens' accounts were copied into the parish book from 1685 to 1695 and from 1705 to 1728, after which only totals of income and expenditure were entered. The accounts show that work was carried out fairly regularly on the roof, plasterwork, windows and bells, while the clock, acquired in 1699, needed attention almost every year. Some of the work consisted of routine maintenance and repair, but it is clear from the accounts and the rector's notes that a great deal of time, money and effort was invested in restoration and new furnishings. In 1693 the porch was partly taken down and rebuilt. In 1699 and 1700 the roof of the nave was stripped and restored in two stages and in 1700 the tower was repaired. In 1704 paving was laid or (more probably) re-laid. In 1708 the walls were painted white and the programme of restoration was completed in 1710 with the enlargement of a window to give better light to the new seats.

In the meantime a number of other changes had been made. In 1699 a clock was bought from Mr Bannister of 'Norton' and in 1707 the parishioners presented a new communion table. Six years later, in 1701, the furniture in the nave was completely rearranged. The pulpit and the rector's pew were moved to a position near the south door and 'a new regular, uniform frame of Seats' was installed. These were box pews, made by William Parlar the younger of Pembridge, which were placed E. and W. of the pulpit and probably on the N. wall as well.

The restoration work was paid for out of the rates, the clock and the furnishings out of donations and small charges levied on those who had a right to seats in the church. The subscription lists show that lay people at all levels of society contributed and not just in the parishes where they lived. The list of 'benefactors' for the pews is headed by the Barnesleys, who owned the manor of Eardisley, and concludes with 'Walter, son of Walter Lewis of this parish a London apprentice' and the rector's servant maid, Susanna Nicklas.

After 1710 no more major work was done until 1722 when the bells were recast. The peal was enlarged from four bells to five and the work was done by Abraham Rudhall of Gloucester. The casting and hanging of the new bells was carried out successfully, but there were problems over accounting for the money involved, as a memorandum in the parish book in 1725 explains.

> A Law suit depending in the spiritual Court about paying for the new Bells, occasioned the continuance of the same officers in the Parish, the Principal of which being illiterate caused some confusion in the Accounts from the year 1722.

At this date it was nothing unusual for churchwardens to be illiterate. We have no means of knowing how well they could read, but at least four of the eleven men who served as wardens at Winforton from 1710 to 1728 could not write their own names.

What the memorandum does not explain is that the rector, Joseph Guest, who had written up the parish accounts since 1705, had died in October 1721 and this undoubtedly contributed to the confusion. As well as copying the accounts he had looked after the parish records and the church plate, which were listed and handed over by his executor, together with a sum of just over £5. To keep the plate and the records safe in the church a new chest was made in 1722 which is still there.

The court case referred to in the memorandum appears in the diocesan acts of instance as *The Churchwardens of Winforton v. Fewtrell.*[10] It ran from 4 October 1723 to 8 April 1725 and was almost certainly a means of ensuring that the confusion over the accounts was officially resolved once and for all. The act books do not give Fewtrell's first name, but he was probably Richard Fewtrell who was churchwarden in 1726 and he had probably been asked by the parish to collect and account for the extra money needed to pay for the bells. He deposited £14 with the consistory court in 1723 and a further £22 0s 11d in 1725, together with money for the proctor's expenses which were assessed at £10 10s. There is also a receipt for a 'lewn' or rate in 1723 for which the amount is not specified, but it may have been the rate of £3 16s 10d recorded in the parish book for that year.

The income and expenditure for the four years from 1722 to 1725 have to be reconstructed from several different places in the parish book and the acts of instance, in both of which some entries are difficult to interpret. But it seems that a total of approximately £87 9s 2d was collected and approximately £88 7s 9d was spent, leaving a deficit of 18s 7d. How this was met is not clear; but to find sums of £22 a year for four years was a considerable achievement for a small parish which normally levied a church rate of about £3 a year.

CRAFTSMEN AT WINFORTON

Most of the craftsmen employed to work on Winforton church were local men, a number of whom served as churchwardens. Several came from the Higgins family, who were prominent in the parish in the seventeenth and eighteenth centuries both as landowners and craftsmen. The earliest reference to them is on the pulpit. This was partly rebuilt in 1707 but incorporates two panels from a pulpit given in 1613 by Thomas Higgins, gentleman. His namesake had one of the most valuable properties in Winforton in 1663 and in 1682 Richard Higgins repaired the north chapel of the parish church.[11] When the clock was acquired in 1699 nine of the family contributed to the cost, including four married men, Thomas Higgins the elder, Thomas Higgins the younger, Roger and Richard. Thomas Higgins the younger made the 'clock house' for the new clock; and he and Roger and Richard were all employed on the church in the first two decades of the eighteenth century, generally as carpenters. Thomas Higgins the elder and Thomas Higgins the younger between them served as church-wardens for at least nineteen years during the period from 1693 to 1725, and in 1721 the younger man was sent to consult the Glasbury bellfounder Henry Williams, who did some work on the bells the year before they were recast. He served as second warden to Edmund Mason, the principal warden, for five years from 1721 to 1725 and their names are carved together on the parish chest.

Another name which appears regularly in the accounts from 1687 to 1722 is that of John Collins, a blacksmith. He was most often required to repair the bells or the clock, and he did a large amount of work when the bells were taken down and rehung in 1722. He also supplied small items like hinges and nails and he made the locks and keys for the new parish chest.

The craftsman most frequently employed during this period was undoubtedly John Houlds or Howles, the mason whose name is on the datestone on the east wall of the chancel. He was churchwarden in 1704 and was one of those who could not write his own name. His work as a mason was varied. He helped rebuild the porch, repaired the roof and walls and relaid the paving slabs in the nave when people were buried there. He restored the chancel for the rector in 1698 and it was probably he who restored the roof and floor of the nave between 1699 and 1704. The subscription list for the clock shows that he had two namesakes in 1699, John Houlds junior, who was probably his son and John Houlds 'de Court', but the name disappears from the parish book after 1718.

THE HOLMAN FAMILY

The Holman family who owned the Winforton estate at the turn of the seventeenth and eighteenth centuries were recusants. They lived at Warkworth in Northampton-shire, about two miles E. of Banbury, and their Herefordshire estates, mainly in Kington, Huntington, Brilley and Winforton, were registered as papists' estates in 1717. The register includes Winforton Court, let to David Price for £245 8s a year, and a number of cottages in the parish whose tenants are named.[12] David Price, as lessee of Winforton Court, was the most substantial farmer in the parish and was principal churchwarden from 1705 to 1709 and again from 1711 to 1720.

The subscription list for the clock in 1699 was headed by Sir John Holman, who died shortly afterwards. By 1701 the estate, the advowson and the responsibility for repairing the north chapel were vested in his widow, Lady Jane Holman, who, before her death in 1703, restored the north chapel and made several gifts to the church. In 1701 she gave communion rails and in 1702 a cover for the communion table, made of green broadcloth with a silk fringe 4ins long, and a new cloth and cushion of green shag for the pulpit. But her biggest outlay was undoubtedly on the chapel. This was being used at the time as a house by Jone Higgins, who was a widow and unable to meet the cost of repairs. Lady Jane Holman rebuilt the roof, put in a ceiling, glazed the windows and repaired the floor.

By 1705 Lady Anastasia Holman, widow of Sir George Holman was patron of the living. She sent a donation of £5, of which £3 10s was spent on remaking the pulpit. The balance of £1 10s was put towards the cost of a new surplice at £2 5s. This is the last recorded gift from the Holmans to the church, but they probably continued to maintain the north chapel until they sold Winforton in 1749.

JOSEPH GUEST

Joseph Guest, who was rector of Winforton from 1691 to 1721, came from a clerical family that served the diocese of Hereford for at least four generations. He was about 24 when he was presented to Winforton and about 54 when he died. When he came up to Oxford in 1684 his father Benjamin, a clergyman, was living at Claverley in Shropshire and was probably curate there. Two of Joseph's sons, Joseph and John, followed him into the ministry, each holding several different livings in Hereford-shire and Radnorshire.[13] His grandson, another Joseph, who died in 1804, was perpetual curate of Titley when the church there was rebuilt in 1762.[14]

The chancel at Winforton had been repaired in 1682. The roof was tiled, windows glazed, the walls plastered and the floor paved with stone.[15] But by 1698 it was 'dangerously overhanging' and Joseph Guest carried out a thorough restoration. He rebuilt the E. wall, glazed the E. window and had the roof stripped and reconstructed.

A few years later he completed the replacement of the paving. He also contributed to the restoration and refurnishing of the nave. In 1707 he paid for a new window near the pulpit after it had been moved. A year later he gave two benches, one of them being for people who had no right to a seat of their own and he had 'a whole, warm, decent Pew' made for himself, after what he describes as 'A Winter's Experience of the Inconveniency of an open Pew so near the great Door'.

There seems little doubt that Joseph Guest was the moving spirit in the restoration and refurnishing of Winforton church in the early eighteenth century and there were probably several reasons for his success. Firstly, he cared about the state of the church: 'nothing' as he says in his notes 'pleasing me more than Safety and Decency in the House of God'. Secondly, he led by example, although the living of Winforton was not a rich one and it is unlikely that he was personally well-off. He restored the chancel before the parish embarked on the restoration of the nave, with which he helped, and he contributed to the clock. Thirdly, he was appreciative. He took great pains to record all the work done and all the donations made, however small. He listed gifts of money and materials, gifts of furniture and gifts of time. When the pulpit was moved and partly rebuilt William Parlar of Pembridge, the joiner, gave four days labour and John Houlds, the mason, one. And, characteristically, when the chancel was restored, the rector placed a datestone on the E. wall carrying not his own name, but that of the man who did the work.

In his notes there are clear indications that Joseph Guest faced difficulties and that his patience was sometimes sorely tried. He writes of the new clock that it was 'an Enterprise sufficiently difficult in the Prosecution, yet more abundantly satisfactory to myself and others when accomplished'. A few years later, in reference to Lady Jane Holman's death, there is a slightly wistful comment that 'I hope she is reaping an everlasting Reward in that eternal Temple that needs no Ornament or Repair'.

CONCLUSIONS

Winforton is unique in Herefordshire in having such a full record of the restoration and refurnishing of its church from 1693 to 1708. But it is not the only parish for which itemised churchwardens' accounts survive during the century after the Restoration. Detailed accounts are available for twenty-six other parishes and, although some of them only cover a few years, they all show that money was being spent on the maintenance of parish churches. The longer series also confirms that other parishes, like Winforton, spent regularly on roofs, plasterwork, windows and bells, as well as on clocks if they had them. In addition it is possible to establish that they too undertook restoration work extending over a period of years. At Whitbourne, for example, a considerable amount was done during the seven years from 1677 to 1683, with a two-year break in 1680 and 1681.[16] Similarly, at Pipe and Lyde, the church was restored during the years from 1749 to 1755 with a break in 1754.[17] Elsewhere parts of the fabric were restored individually. Roofs, for example, were stripped at Stoke Edith in 1674 and at Edwyn Ralph in 1748.[18] But it is unfortunate that itemised accounts survive for so few parishes, since they provide only limited evidence for a county in which there were more than 200 medieval churches. However, they do suggest that repair and restoration were a normal part of parish life.

Chancels were usually the responsibility of individuals: the incumbent in about one-third of the parishes, and in the rest impropriators, who might be senior clergy, lay people or (more rarely) institutions. Of the parish clergy who were responsible for chancels in Herefordshire, just under a quarter had livings worth less than £50 a year in 1707, when livings were valued for Queen Anne's Bounty.[19] These men therefore earned less than the minimum considered adequate for a clergyman at the time and chancels might be vulnerable when the poverty of the clergy was compounded by the frailties of old age or illness, since most of them died in office. At Pixley (worth £18 a year) the rector died in 1680 and the diocese proposed to sequester the tithes to repair the chancel.[20] Yet there is little indication in the diocesan archives that chancels were not well cared for and much restoration and maintenance undoubtedly went unrecorded. Winforton was worth at least £50 a year, but probably not much more, and Joseph Guest wrote that he 'undertook a charge above my Capacity' in restoring the chancel, although he does not give the cost. A comparable restoration appears to have taken place at Byton (valued at £21 a year) in 1716 when the parish stated that '...our Rector since he came to ye place hath been at ye Charge of building up ye one side of ye s^d chancel and hath new tiled ye s^d Chancel at his own cost and charge'.[21] The living was very poor and yet the work was done.

By the late seventeenth century few chapels in parish churches were maintained by individual families and their condition probably varied. Winforton clearly needed attention in 1703 and the 'aisle' belonging to the Baskervilles at Eardisley was cited as 'ruinous' in 1675 before it was put in good order.[22] But there is no evidence of disrepair at Hope-under-Dinmore, where the Coningsby family had a chapel on the north side of the chancel. It was quite possibly restored at the time when the church was rebuilt about 1707 or about ten years later when Lord Coningsby paid for its redecoration.[23] Similar generosity was shown by the Hopton family, who built a private 'aisle' and vault and repaired and beautified the church at Canon Frome between 1717 and 1723. This work included repairs to the porch and belfry, glazing old windows, making new seats and painting and gilding the font and the royal arms.[24]

During the century and a half that the Woolhope Club has been in existence, ecclesiastical historians and others have generally taken the view that churches were seriously neglected from at least 1689 until the 1820s. This belief has only recently been questioned, most notably by Yates and Humphreys.[25] Yet it is usually based on very selective use of the evidence and an assumption that disrepair inevitably implies neglect. No allowance is made for the age of the buildings, the long-term effects of climate or the short-term impact of thunderstorms and gales. In Herefordshire detailed examination of the records of the diocese and its peculiars shows that neglect was rare; while parish records and family papers record conscientiousness, generosity and good care. Inevitably there were problems, but most of the people responsible for the care of churches did their best to see that they were kept in good order and they were well aware of the implications of what they did. As the churchwardens of Tretire put it in 1708, their church was 'well amended and may hold good to future generations'.[26]

All this was achieved at a time when there were no grants from public bodies like English Heritage or from voluntary organisations like the Historic Churches Preservation Trust. Nor did the lotteries of the day offer building grants. There is considerable evidence that regular attention was given to the restoration and maintenance of churches, as well as occasional evidence of failure. To accuse those concerned of neglect, without considering the evidence in full, is to do them a great disservice. Without their efforts many medieval churches would not have survived.

REFERENCES
1 Isaac Taylor, *A New Map of the County of Hereford* (1754).

[2] M. A. Faraday, 'The Hearth Tax in Herefordshire', *TWNFC*, XLI (1973), 84; *The Compton Census of 1676: a critical edition*, ed. E. A. W. Whiteman (1986), 254.

[3] E. A. Wrigley and R. S. Schofield, *The Population History of England 1541-1871: a reconstruction* (1981), 161-162.

[4] M. A. Faraday, loc. cit. in note 2.

[5] *Herefordshire Militia Assessments of 1663*, ed. M. A. Faraday (1972), 88.

[6] RCHM, England, *An Inventory of the Historical Monuments in Herefordshire*, vol. I, South-West (1931), 212-213.

[7] Sir Stephen Glynne's church notes, vol. 90, p. 63. These notes are in St Deiniol's Library, Hawarden and may be seen by appointment at the Flintshire Record Office.

[8] Cases relating to church maintenance appear in the acts of office, HRO HD4/1 Vols. 99-125.

[9] HRO F83/4 Winforton Parish Book 1685-1799. This volume is written up in various hands from both ends. There are a number of different chronological sequences and no page numbers.

[10] HRO HD4/1 vol. 47.

[11] *Herefordshire Militia*, loc. cit., in note 5; HRO HD4/1 vol. 124, Weobley Deanery, p.17.

[12] HRO Q/RP/2, pp. 9-10.

[13] J. Foster, *Alumni Oxonienses. The Members of the University of Oxford, 1500-1714*, vol. I (1968), 167.

[14] HL *Herefordshire Collections, Historical, Biographical and Topographical. Volume 12 containing an Account of the Visitation of Parish Churches*, p. 26. (Unpublished ms. compiled by the Rev. C. J. Bird); HRO AB56/21 Titley Parish Book.

[15] HRO HD4/1 Vol. 124, Weobley Deanery, p. 17; HRO HD7/22/159.

[16] HRO AL92/1 Whitbourne Parish Book 1677-1756.

[17] HRO G20/4 Pipe and Lyde Parish Book 1678-1834.

[18] HRO J72/9 Stoke Edith Churchwardens' Accounts 1675-1834; N20/2 Edwyn Ralph Parish Book 1708-1749.

[19] HCL, Dean and Chapter's Archives, Book of Bishop Humphrey Humphreys, 1711-1818, pp. 224-249, 477-493.

[20] HRO HD4/1, Vol. 120, pp. 102-103.

[21] HRO HD7/42 Diocesan Registrar's Files, October 1716.

[22] HRO HD4/1 Vol. 119, p. 56v.

[23] HL James Hill's Mss. Vol. I, p. 333; HRO HD4/1 Vol. 107, p. 57v.

[24] HRO R93 LC8351.

[25] N. Yates, *Buildings, Faith and Worship. The Liturgical Arrangement of Anglican Churches 1600-1900* (1991), 23-123; S. C. Humphreys, *Churches and Chapels of Northern England* (1991), 30-31.

[26] HRO HD7/36.

Medieval Houses in Herefordshire

J. W. TONKIN

For the purposes of this paper I have taken medieval as being the period 1066-1485, i.e. up to the coming of the Tudors. Changes in plan and construction begin to take place about that time and as far as houses are concerned the next period could well be Tudor and Stuart.

The boundaries of the county of Herefordshire have changed very little since the coming of the Normans. Geologically it is a ring of hills, some red sandstone, some Silurian Limestone, some very early pre-Cambrian surrounding fertile valleys which have given the county its agricultural importance and wealth. Oak is the natural vegetation of this area and if left to its own devices most of the county would revert to a forest of hardwood, mainly oak. It is drained almost completely by the river Wye and its tributaries and was almost entirely in the diocese of Hereford, only a small area in the south-west having been in the diocese of St David's until 1856. The diocese itself covers much of the Wye basin, roughly the area of the pre-Roman Celtic kingdom of the Silures and of the western part of the Dark Ages kingdom of Mercia.

MATERIALS

The natural building material of much of the county is hardwood, oak for houses, chestnut being used in a few cases, and elm for poorer quality buildings and farm buildings. A few examples have been found of the use of black poplar and it can be seen growing in a few places. In the south-west of the county and in one or two other areas Old Red Sandstone is quarried and used for buildings and roofing. It is the underlying rock of most of the area, but in the Aymestrey/Wigmore, Woolhope and Eastnor areas, there is Silurian Limestone and there are the Cambrian and pre-Cambrian rocks of the Malvern Hills. The Silurian Limestones are used for poorer quality rubble buildings. Sandstone is the superior stone used in such places as the cathedral and Goodrich Castle, and is cut into squared ashlar blocks and used for doorways and windows in buildings of Silurian rubble. The Malvernian rocks are very little used for building, and then only for rubble walling. The clays of the river valleys make good bricks and there is evidence of these being used as early as 1190.[1]

ROOFING

Roofing can be of stone, tile, thatch, shingles and in a very few cases slate. A pile of neatly stacked stone slates each with its peg-hole for securing it on the rafters can still be seen outside a number of houses in the county. After a time, three hundred years or perhaps more, the stone gets 'tired' and begins to split. This is when the stone roofs have to be replaced. Almost all the stone 'slates' or 'tiles' are of the red sandstone and the weight required substantial timbering in the roof. The quarries for this stone are in the Black Mountains area of the county, the south-west , and a few small ones in the west and in the north-east. Tiles were made from the local clays from very early times, but need replacing more often than stone. Thatch was very common. A good reed thatch will last sixty or more years, but there seems to have been little of this used in this area. Wheat straw will do thirty years, oat straw twenty; so there was plenty of work for the thatchers. Little slate was used in medieval times; it was not until the coming of the canals and railways that it was used much in this area. Oak shingles were used for roofing, but it is difficult to know to what extent. Certainly, they were used on church spires, and there is evidence of them in the roof of the bishop's palace. There was one house in Castle Street, Hereford which had a modern shingle roof when I first looked at it some twenty-five years ago.

CONSTRUCTION

Timber, stone and brick can all house the different types of construction inside them. Today only the better quality houses of the medieval period survive and of these, the earliest types are the aisled construction, the base-cruck and the stave type. These are followed by the cruck and the box-frame. There must have been a lot of poorer quality timber-framed building which has disappeared and been replaced, in many cases more than once. The bishop's palace at Hereford dating from *c*1180-90 is one of the great buildings of medieval Europe still surviving. It is just over 60ft long and 45ft wide and of three bays, the aisles being about 10ft wide. The eight great pillars are each about 30ft long and 3ft in diameter with a clerestory some 7ft high above the arcade plate. To have found trees of this size and quality the builders must have thoroughly searched the bishop's forest.[2] Two other buildings of about the same age partially survive. One is the bishop's palace at Stretton Sugwas of which one well-preserved late twelfth-century arch and some Norman walling survive, all in stone.[3] The other is part of Wigmore Abbey in Adforton parish, which dates from 1179.[4]

Plate 1. Longitudinal arch, Bishop's Palace, Hereford, 1180-90, aisled hall.

The other early type of building which survives is the first-floor hall built over an undercroft. Some fifteen examples of these can still be seen in a recognisable form. One of them is the hall of Clifford Castle, which could well mean that some of the other castles had similar halls in the thirteenth century. At least four of the others, the abbot's lodging at Wigmore Abbey, the old hall of the vicars choral in Hereford, Upper Hall at Ledbury and Sugwas Court have religious connections, while the Booth Hall and the remains behind 54 Broad Street, Hereford, have an institutional background. The earlier hall at Hergest belonged to the Vaughan family and the best surviving example, Brinsop Court, to the Torell family. These were the homes of men of some considerable importance and wealth in the society of the day.

One rare survival is the stave type of construction found encased in early seventeenth-century brick at Gatley Park and although it is early in style it is a late example as dendrochronological evidence indicates that it dates from no earlier than 1525, and possibly later.[5] It is basically the same type of construction as that used in the belfries at Pembridge and Yarpole and the church towers at Orcop and Mamble. Other examples outside Scandinavia are Brooklands in Kent, Burstow and Newdigate in Surrey, and several in Essex.

The well-off yeoman verging on gentry status in the fourteenth century built the base-cruck halls, nine of which still survive.[6] A base-cruck truss is a pair of curved timbers rising from a sill at ground level, but instead of going up to meet at the apex as crucks do, stop at collar-beam level and carry a separate roof structure above this. It appears not to be derived from the cruck construction and most examples are earlier than the cruck buildings. Seven of these appear to have been of manorial status, but Peg's Farm at Wellington Heath and the house in Bell Square at Weobley appear not to have been. Perhaps it is significant that Peg's Farm is the only base-cruck house that has crucks as its other trusses instead of box-frame. All except the one in Weobley have a spere truss.

Plate 2. Peg's Farm, Wellington Heath, base-cruck hall, sixteenth century and seventeenth-century added wing.

This last named, spere truss, is found also in cruck and box-framed houses and is an aisled type of truss forming an entrance into the hall from the screens-passage. It can be thought of as a ceremonial entry into the hall. There was a doorway in the 'aisle' at each side and the wider central part may originally have had a movable screen such as still exists at Rufford Old Hall in Lancashire.

The biggest of the base-cruck halls is Eaton Hall in Leominster parish which is 38ft x 24ft and was the home of the Hakluyt family, having been built by Leonard Hakluyt, who was one of the knights of the shire for the first time in 1385, sheriff in 1400 and fought at Agincourt in 1415.[7] The lower purlin is set square and moulded in the manner of an arcade plate in an aisled hall and the house has an aisled truss at the solar end. Amberley Court in Marden parish also has the purlin set in the form of an arcade plate, but is probably a little later in date. Wellbrook Manor in Peterchurch and Swanstone Court in Dilwyn parish each has its elaborately foiled aisled-truss remaining at the solar end of the hall and probably date from the late fourteenth century. Lower Brockhampton became the property of the Rowden family late in the fourteenth century and the house appears to be early fifteenth-century in date. Upper House at Preston on Wye probably dates from the fourteenth century while Court Farm at Preston Wynne is more likely to be fifteenth century. The former has two cross-wings while the latter has a parlour cross-wing and a bay at the service end.[8]

Plate 3. Wellbrook Manor, Peterchurch, base-cruck and aisle-type gable, fourteenth century.

The cruck construction in which two curved timbers rise from sill to apex and carry the roof on these 'blades' is prominent in some of the county's villages. These crucks are normally cut from the trunk and lowest bough of a tree, which gives a naturally curved shape. Sometimes a knot can be seen at the elbow of the cruck indicating where the branch had taken off from the trunk of the tree.

Plate 4. Behind Red Lion, Weobley, cruck.

Freestanding oaks can be seen growing in fields in many parts of the county with the good crucks still available. Sawing these huge timbers in a pit must have been quite an experience; the 'underdog' in the pit would have had an unpleasant job. About fifty of these houses have only a central cruck, but about seventy have two or three crucks, about fifteen four crucks and four have five crucks. Those with a single cruck often have a cross-wing at each end with a box-frame construction, but the social importance of the open hall with its central hearth and a louvre above made the cruck desirable in that position. Most of the cruck houses are probably of fifteenth-century date, but about twenty are fourteenth century, at least one of them, Upper Limebrook, the home farm of Limebrook Nunnery, having been built quite early in that century.[9]

The normal English way of building was the box-frame, a rectangular box with a triangular roof on it. However, in Herefordshire and much of the Marches the cruck, not found in the S.E. and S.W. of England nor in the east midlands, East Anglia, Yorkshire, east of the Pennines and very rarely in Northumbria, was common and the preferred type of building among the yeomen and husbandmen in the fifteenth century. Thus in the medieval period the box-frame is comparatively rarely used in Herefordshire, there being about forty remaining examples, again mainly dating from the fifteenth century, but with a few surviving from the fourteenth and one or two from the late thirteenth.

Many of the parlour wings of the medieval houses have a cellar beneath. This ensured that the parlour, the master's room, had a wooden and, therefore, warmer floor. This end of the house often had its own fireplace as opposed to an open hearth. In the city, a number of cellars from this period still survive, bearing little relationship to the present buildings above them. In the towns the existing cellars are often under the modern room back from the street, the present room in front being a little later and, having replaced the old selda or stall in front of the original building.

PLAN TYPES

So far, this paper has dealt with materials and types of construction. The various plans of these buildings are also of considerable influence and a pointer to the social status of the builder.

The aisled hall is a mark of high social class and the bishop's palace has only two other similar contemporary buildings in England, viz. the bishop's palace at Farnham in Surrey, not nearly as complete as that at Hereford, and the great hall of Leicester Castle, a stone building. A fourteenth-century aisled hall survives in Shropshire and a later aisled barn in this county, but aisled domestic or agricultural buildings are rare in this part of Britain.

The tower type of house does occur in the county at Kinnersley, but that is not medieval. Some of the castles seem to have had tower accommodation in them, e.g. Goodrich, and there is the medieval tower at Kentchurch Court, but the best examples are over the county boundaries at Holt in Worcestershire, Hopton and Stokesay in Shropshire, Penhow in Gwent, the canonry at Brecon and at Tretower. Closely related to the tower is the first-floor hall over an undercroft, some of which were no doubt intended to be defensive against a small band of rustlers rather than a military attack.

The most common type of house remaining today from medieval times is the open hall with a cross-wing or wings. In the wealthiest of these, there is a wing at each end with a cross-passage at the lower end of the hall. 'Lower' in this case signifies socially lower. The wing at the upper end of the hall would be the solar or parlour wing. In most cases, this consists of a parlour with a fireplace and a chamber over with a little parlour or inner room beyond and a smaller chamber above. The upper floor would be reached by a stairway from the hall or by a circular stairway in a corner of the parlour sometimes in a projecting turret at the corner of the wing. Sometimes there are two rooms only over an undercroft or cellar. Outside the building, either at the rear of the wing or at the side, is a barrel-run into the cellar, down which the pipes or hogsheads or half-hogsheads would be run. In some cases the parlour was heated by a brazier, but the fireplace, one on each floor was more common.

The hall itself was open from the floor to the ridge of the roof with a central open hearth from which the smoke escaped through a louvre in the roof. These sometimes had a wind vane on them to help suck up the smoke from the hearth. At the upper end there was usually a low platform or dais on which the master sat at high table. In some cases, quite probably most, he had a bench against the parlour wall and evidence of this can sometimes still be found. In a few cases, the canopy over it to protect the master of the house from anything dropping from the roof still survives. Sometimes there was a tall window the full height of the wall on the south side at the dais end, and a big window in the same wall at the centre of the hall.

Across the centre of the hall was the main truss, base-cruck, cruck, or post and truss. In the last type, this would be a tie-beam across the hall with decoration above, often a quatrefoil in the centre and a trefoil either side. In the bigger halls there would be an intermediate truss either side of this, again with decoration above.

At the low end of the hall, there was a doorway in each lateral wall opposite each other making a cross-passage. Sometimes the hall was shielded from the draught from this passage by a screen, often with a gallery over the passage. In earlier houses, this screen was sometimes moveable, but no examples remain today in this county. In a number of houses, a post rises from each end of the passage about a door's width from the external wall. These posts go up to a tie-beam above, which has decoration similar to that over the central truss. This was known as a spere truss and was often the intermediate truss at the low end of the hall.

Beyond this passage was the other cross-wing. Usually there were two rooms in this, often a buttery and a pantry, i.e. a serving room for liquid and a serving room for other food. In many cases, one of these became a kitchen, but in earlier houses, the kitchen was usually external as a safeguard against fire. An excellent example of an external kitchen still survives at Swanstone Court in Dilwyn parish. Sometimes these were approached from the low end of the cross-passage, sometimes from a central passage between the buttery and pantry with a doorway in the gable wall.

In the not quite so well-off houses there would be a service end instead of a service cross-wing, the walls just carrying on beyond the passage in line with those of the hall. In some cases there was simply a long rectangular building with a parlour and chamber above at the high end, an open hall with cross-passage and a service room or rooms beyond this with a chamber or chambers above.

Similar in plan to this last-mentioned type is the long-house. This is a dwelling in which people and cattle use the same cross-passage and is found in Cornwall and Devon as well as the Marches. Normally it occurs in hilly areas with the domestic end up the hill and the cattle down the hill. The cross-passage is wider than that in a purely domestic building and the domestic part of the accommodation is normally a step up from the passage. These houses are found both with cruck and box-frame construction and as they are mainly in the W. of the county many of them are of stone. Socially they are not of a lower status, Olchon Court in the Olchon Valley in the S.W. of the county and the old vicarage at Burrington in the N. of the county both having been long-houses, though the latter has been demolished and a new house built in its place in the last twenty years. Generally speaking, they are built up and down the slope of the hill, but Lower House at Staunton-on-Wye was built along the hillside. Black Daren and Great Turnant in the Olchon Valley had cattle in them within the last thirty-five years. Lower House at Burrington is built almost along the hillside, but there is a slight slope. White Haywood in the Black Mountains, modernised in the 1630s, has a cross-wing at the upper end. As a plan type the long-house dates back to the Dark Ages, and the writer has seen similar houses in Norway, Austria and Nepal. The houses of the Outer Hebrides and a few in the Orkneys are closely related in type. There is an unusual example at Adforton where the cross-passage is on the ground flour with a byre beyond and a barn over it. Access to the dwelling area is from another doorway as well as the passage; perhaps in strict terms not a long-house, but very closely related to it.

Medieval houses surviving today of the types discussed above were those of the better-off, the more important members of society both civil and clerical, who could afford to build reasonably substantial houses which have been adapted over the centuries to meet changing ideas and means of heating and lighting.

The majority of houses were of a two-room plan, frequently one heated room and a smaller room with a chamber above. Some of the smaller of the cruck and box-frame dwellings were of this type and would have been the homes of the lesser husbandmen in the local communities.

Even smaller were the single cell houses, those with one room down and a room or loft above. There must have been many of these, the homes of the landless labourers.

Very few exist today and where they do survive are virtually lost in later additions. Probably the best guide to the standard the poorer person expected are the few surviving 'hospitals' or almshouses dating from medieval times. In Hereford some of the almshouses occupy medieval sites but date from the seventeeth century in their present form. The college of the vicars choral was moved in 1473 from its earlier site in Castle Street, Hereford, to its present site around a quadrangle S.E. of the cathedral. Each of the houses has a living room with a bedroom above with an open roof with collar-beams on curved arch braces, with a trefoil above and foiled wind-braces with cusped points. The earlier hall of the vicars choral dates from the fourteenth century and although much altered has a nine-bay roof with moulded wall-plates in each bay between the purlins, two tiers of wind-braces with cusped arches and decoration on the cusp-points, and in one bay an additional purlin with a range of quatrefoiled panels between the two purlins.

At St Katherine's Hospital in Ledbury the master's house in the centre of the court-yard and the hall at the S.E. corner are both of fourteenth-century date. In the former the central truss of the hall has curved braces to the tie-beam with arch braces above to the collar, and a spere truss at the E. end of the hall with curved braces to the tie-beam in the central opening, queen posts to the collar and above this two posts foiled on the inner face. The W. truss is similar except for the spere posts. The hall and chapel have a fine fourteenth-century roof with two tiers of curved wind-braces.

MOULDINGS

Something not easy for present-day man to envisage is the actual appearance and atmosphere inside a medieval house. The main timbers of the principal rooms in a house in the very late fifteenth and early sixteenth century were heavily moulded, but there seems to be no evidence of this form of decoration earlier than this, other than the simple quarter-round moulding in the wealthier houses of the early fourteenth century, of which good examples include Swanstone Court in Dilwyn parish, Brinsop Court and Old Court, Longtown.

The capitals in the bishop's palace are good examples of the scalloped type so often found in stone in contemporary churches, but in the other houses there is no attempt at this or similar decoration.

PANELLING

The four-bay ceiling in the chapel at Hampton Court is very low pitched with a tie-beam and king post with tracery above and curved bosses beneath. In each bay, it is divided into eighteen panels with curved bosses at the intersections. At Shelwick Court the dividing wall has four giant quatrefoils as braces very much like a similar hall and parlour at Swanstone Court.

Some late medieval panelling survived in one Shropshire house, but there seems to be none in Herefordshire. Much survives from only a few years later in early Tudor times.

PAINTED BEAMS

In the medieval period colour played quite an important part in the principal rooms of houses, but little trace of it remains today. A number of painted beams and some painted timber-framing survives from the sixteenth century, but the only decoration of this type remaining today that is certainly medieval is the decoration on the arcade plate in the bishop's palace.

MURALS

Hangings, and in wealthy cases tapestries, were used in the more prosperous houses, but once again few survive from pre-Tudor times. A few painted cloths stretched over the timber-framing survive from the sixteenth century, but the chances of such fragile items having survived 500 years is very small.

The same applies to murals: they survive from the sixteenth century, but even those at such places as Swanstone and Old Sufton do not seem to date back to medieval times.

SCREENS

Some early screens remain and in one or two cases they are an essential part of the structure of the house. That at Swanstone Court in Dilwyn parish probably dates back to the fourteenth century and that at the Booth Hall in Hereford certainly dates from the second half of the fifteenth century,[10] and a number of post-and-panel screens survive from the fifteenth century. These consist of alternating posts with thinner panels inserted between them. Excellent examples survive especially in the W. of the county as at Upper Gwerloddyd in Newton parish, Upper Limebrook, the old home farm of Limebrook Nunnery in Wigmore parish, and Middle Trewern in Longtown parish. The last still has the painting on the screen, a series of vine-like patterns trailing up and down the alternating posts and panels and still preserving its medieval colour quite well. There must have been many more of these, which were probably 'cleaned up' in Puritan times, though some sixteenth- or seventeenth-century colouring remains on some timbers.

Further colour was provided by tiles in some of the wealthier houses. Good examples remain at the abbot's lodging at Wigmore Abbey and in the chapel of St Katherine's Hospital in Ledbury.

FIREPLACES

From a period when the central hearth was the main source of heat few actual fireplaces are likely to remain, but there is at Lodge Farm, on the western edge of Wigmore parish, a Norman fireplace built into one of the chambers of the late sixteenth-century house, probably brought there from Wigmore Castle when the house was built, the Harley family of Brampton Bryan owning both at that time. In the solar in the cross-wing of Wellbrook Manor in the Golden Valley is a very good example of a fourteenth-century hooded fireplace with its original hood and corbels. The first-floor hall at Hergest also has a fourteenth-century fireplace with a hood.

WATER SUPPLY AND SANITATION

Essential for any house was an assured water supply, and a good well close to, or even in, the house is a standard feature. Many houses had a well in the kitchen and at least one house of the period in Cornwall has a stream flowing through the kitchen. Sometimes a stream or a leat taken off it was used to carry away the human excrement from the garderobe. This is the case at Wigmore Abbey abbot's lodging. Often the garderobe is situated in the master's chamber screened off or in a small room off it, and the waste was collected from an opening in the wall at ground level. Good examples exist at Penrhos in Lyonshall parish, at Wigmore Castle where it empties into the moat, at Kentchurch Court and at Gillow Manor. In most cases, there would have been a 'necessary house' somewhere in the house compound.

The house was normally at the highest point on the yard or enclosure, and in really wealthy examples there would be a gatehouse at the entrance as at Bosbury and Lower Brockhampton. Originally these may have had a defensive element in them, but they were more for show and acted as a lodge rather than to keep out armed men. Eight of them still survive in the county, though in the case of Yarpole the house seems to have disappeared.

The majority of those houses are in their own yard or grounds a little distance away from the nearest settlement, but those surviving in the towns or bigger villages tend to be parallel to the street or road rather than at right angles to it, as in most of the remaining town houses, and a little distance away from the centre of the settlement.

DOCUMENTARY EVIDENCE
Documents are the surest method of dating, but few of these survive from medieval times. In this county the records of the Hellens estate in Much Marcle date from *c*1190, but all they tell one is that brick was being made.[11] How much, if any, of that survives is up to one's judgement when examining the house. With the estates of the bishop the records are such that with some knowledge of building materials and methods of construction it is possible to put a fairly close date on most of the palaces and what remains of them.[12] Probate records for the diocese, the deanery and the peculiars give a date when a house existed on a certain spot and again an examination of the building can often help connect building or parts of it with a will, administration or inventory. These had to be prepared for all property valued at £7 or over from 1261 but it was not until 1529 that the law of the country ordered that this should be done. For this diocese, the earliest surviving is from 1428 and a more or less complete run exists from 1465. A good inventory gives a list of the rooms in a house and inspection of the building can confirm how much survives.

A few later building accounts survive and some of these are for additions or alterations to existing houses and again give some clue as to construction and what survives.

DATING
After one has spent some time studying the houses of an area, carpenters' assembly marks can normally be dated within about a generation, and in this period are scratched marks several inches long usually in Roman numerals with sometimes an additional mark to denote the level in the house, first or second floor.

Mouldings and chamfers are also reasonably closely datable. In this early period, the quarter-round moulding of the first third of the fourteenth century is a very useful one. Other than that, they tend to be a plain chamfer or a hollow (cavetto) which can be up to about 6in deep. This requires quite sizeable timber.

Within the last decade or so tree-ring dating has become popular. It is a skilled task and the timber has to be suitable to take a sample. Comparatively little has been done in Herefordshire, but those that have tend to confirm the dates already assigned by the earlier methods.[13]

Often the least altered part of a house is the roof. Many of these were the roofs of open halls or fine chambers and in these the decoration, which was intended to be seen and to show the master's wealth, can be seen above the inserted ceilings.

These open halls had floors inserted after the end of the medieval period and so the two or three-storey house we see today was built as a single storey open hall with two-storey cross-wings.

Herefordshire is one of the best counties for timber-framed building in England with some very good stone building in a few areas. This wealth of timber-framing is due to the good timber available and to the wealth of the farming in this county.

APPENDIX

Parish	House	NGR(SO)	cent.	walls	RCHM	TWNFC
AISLED HALL						
Hereford	Bishop's Palace	509397	12	T	I,1	XLII,60-1.
FIRST FLOOR HALL						
Adforton	Wigmore Abbey	410742	12	lime	III,1	
Brinsop	Brinsop Court	446457	14	sand	II,2	
Clifford	Clifford Castle	245457	13	sand	I,4	
Hereford	29 Castle Street (Old Vicars Choral)	511398	14	sand	I,99	XLII,198.
	41 Bridge Street (Building at rear)	508397	14	t.f.	I,49	XXXIX,164. XLV,772,778.
	54 Broad Street (Carpenters' Hall)	499399	15	t.f.	I,39	XXXIX,164.
	City Arms, Broad St.	509399	15	sand	I,33	XLI,261.
	20 Church Street	510398	14	t.f.	I,106	XLV,772-3,778.
	Booth Hall	510399	14	sand	I,21	XXXVI,266-9. XXXIX,378. XLIII,302-3. XLV,796-7.
Kington	Hergest Court	281554	14	lime	III,2	XXXIX,180.
	Hergest Court	282554	14	lime & t.f.	III,2	do.
Ledbury	Upper Hall	713378	15	sand	II,5	XLV,521.
Marstow	Marstow Court	555192	15	sand		XXXVIII,266
Stretton Sugwas	Sugwas Court	454408	12	sand	II,5	XLII,58
Whitchurch	Old Court	553174	15	sand	I,3	XLII,106.
BASE-CRUCK OPEN HALL						
Brockhampton	Lower Brockhampton	688560	15	t.f.	II,2	
Dilwyn	Swanstone Court	441531	14	t.f.	III,5	
Leominster, Out	Eaton Hall	508580	14	t.f.	III,5	
Marden	Amberley Court	546478	15	t.f.	II,4	XXXIX,379. XL,128,248. 250-1,258-61.
Peterchurch	Wellbrook Manor	352386	14	t.f.	I,8	XXXIX,486.
Preston-on-Wye	Upper House	382423.	14	t.f.	I,2	XLI,306-11. XLVII,250-1.
Preston Wynne	Court Farm	557470	15	t.f.	II,2	XXXIX,377.
Wellington Heath	Peg's Farm	703411	14	t.f.	II,2	XL,169.
Weobley	TudorHouse	401517	14	t.f.	III,21	XXXIX,377.
CRUCK OPEN HALL						
Adforton	Old Hall	399711	15	t.f.	III,11	XXXVIII,264.
Almeley	Castle Frome	332513	14	t.f.	III,42	
	Summerhouse	332526	15	t.f.	III,6	
Ashperton		644416	15	t.f.	II,10	
Aymestrey	Upper Lye	394657	15	t.f.	III,28	
Bishop's Frome	Green Dragon	662484	15	t.f.	II,12	
	Lower Vine Tree	662471	15	t.f.	II,26	
Bredwardine	Bottrell Farm	322433	15	sand	I,9	
Breinton	Warham Court	486392	15	t.f.	II,2	
Bridstow	Ashe Farm	581258	15	sand	I,11	
Brilley	Fernhall	277515	15	t.f.	III,4	

Parish	House	NGR(SO)	cent.	walls	RCHM	TWNFC
Brilley (cont'd.)	Little Pentre Coed	280496	15	sand	III,10	
	Llanhedry	276501	15	t.f.	III,6	
	The Wern	243486	15	sand	III,28	
Brimfield	Lower Drayton	537674	15	sand		XXXIX,481.
Brockhampton	Much Fawley	590296	15	sand	II,4	
Byford	Fallsbrook Farm	398428	15	t.f.	III,5	
Cradley	Upper House	724481	15	t.f.	II,36	
Craswall	Middle Blackhill	296329	15	sand	I,15	
Cusop	Blaenau	261400	15	sand		
Dilwyn	Bytack	427558	15	t.f.	Mercer, 1975	
	Middleton House	427557	14	t.f.	III,22	
	Yew Tree Cottage	427557	14	t.f.	III,23	
Docklow	West End Farm Cott.	556577	14	sand	III,5	
Eardisland	Knapp House	418585	15	t.f.	III,15	
Eardisley	Broadlands	310496	14	t.f.	III,9	
	Little Quebb	299517	15	t.f.	III,32	
	Old Crow Farm	316475	15	t.f.	III,62	
	Forge	311495	15	t.f.	III,6	XL,287.
	Great Quebb	302519	15	t.f.	III,33	
	Eardisley Wootton	308505	14	t.f.	III,29	
Eaton Bishop	Wormhill	432395	15	t.f.	I,11	XLII,198.
Elton	Elton Hall	458710	15	t.f.	III,2	XXXIX,484
Ewyas Harold	W. of Lower House Fm	389282	15	sand		XXXIX,375.
Eye	Burns Croft, Moreton	503648	15	t.f.	III,18	XLIII,363.
Fownhope	Cottage	581351	15	t.f.	III,15	
	Nupend Cottage	579350	15	t.f.	III,14	
Goodrich	Whitehall	572188	15	sand		XLIX, 139-40
	Main Oaks	571176	15	sand	I,16	
Hampton Bishop	Cottage	555383	15	t.f.	II,14	
	Farm	557379	15	t.f.	II,20	
Hentland	Great Treaddow	541239	15	sand	I,4	
	Treseck	542296	15	sand	I,8	
Hereford	Putson Cottage	514386	15	t.f.	I,123	
Hope-u-Dinmore	Middle Hill	472538	14	t.f.	III,4	
Huntington	Burnt Hengoed	265522	15	t.f.	III,8	
	Great Penlan	273520	15	t.f.	III,10	
	Little Penlan	272517	15	t.f.	III,9	
	Penlan	252527	15	t.f.	III,11	
Kilpeck	Dippersmoor Court	447297	15	t.f.	I,5	
King's Caple	Forge	562289	15	t.f.		XLVII,360.
Kingsland	House on A4110	438614	15	t.f.	III,53	
	Malthouse Farm	438615	15	t.f.	III,54	
King's Pyon	Black Hall	438505	15	t.f.	III,3	
Kington	Apostles Farm	285524	15	sand	III,10	
	do	285524	15	sand	III,10	
	Maholland Cotts.	270543	15	t.f.	III,6	
	Lilwall	302545	15	t.f.	III,15	
	Old House	307583	15	t.f.	III,29	
	Pound Farm	289542	15	t.f.	III,12	
	13 High Street	296567	14	t.f.		XLVII,98-9
	Woodbine Cottage	275553	15	t.f.		XLVII,249.
Kinnersley	Cottage	344494	15	t.f.	III,12	
Ledbury	Homend	709382	15	t.f.	II,40	
	Wood House	690412	15	t.f.	II,32	
Leinthall Starkes	Marlbrook Cottage	437698	15	t.f.	III,2	
Leominster	Broad Street	496591	15	t.f.	III,45	
		495593	15	t.f.	III,56	
Leominster, Out	Stagsbatch	465583	14	t.f.	III,17	

Parish	House	NGR(SO)	cent.	walls	RCHM	TWNFC
Lingen	Tudor Cottage	364673	15	t.f.	III,10	XLVIII,355-6
	Mortimer Cottage	364673	15	t.f.	III,10	XLVIII,356-7
Linton (Ross)	Pinford Farm	659248	15	T	II,14	
Little Dewchurch	Court Farm	531317	15	t.f.	I,2	
Llancilo	Upper House	354264	15	sand	I,8	
Llangarron	Langstone Court	533221	15	sand	I,3	
	Ruxton Court	540195	15	sand & t.f.	I,5	
Llanveynoe	Black Daren	296304	15	sand	I,11	
	Great Turnant	305288	15	sand	I,19	
Longtown	Belpha	357296	15	sand	I,34	
	Celyn	337308	15	sand	I,44	
	Great Bilbo	359293	15	sand	I,7	
	Llanwonnog	324297	14	sand	I,40	XXXIX,379.
	Middle Trewern	326317	15	sand	I,45	
	Old Court	338303	14	sand	I,5	
	Ty Mawr	322266	14	sand	I,6	
	Welsh Hunthouse	335262	15	sand	I,27	
Luston	The Hollies	486631	15	t.f.	III,17	
Lyonshall		330562	15	t.f.	III,8	
	Penrhos	317561	14	t.f.	III,18	XL,289,XLI,68-76
	The Wharf	336555	15	t.f.	III,3	
Marden	Wisteston Court	518488	15	t.f.	II,5	XXXVIII,266 XXXIX,376.
Michaelchurch Escley	Oldhay Farm	310381	15	sand	I,27	
Monkland		459577	15	t.f.	III,4	
Much Dewchurch	Church Farm	482312	15	sand	I,8	
	Ridby Court Farm	466311	15	t.f.		
	The Forge	482312	15	t.f.		XXIX,106-7
Much Marcle	Cottage	658326	15	t.f.	II,10	
	Cottage	658327	15	t.f	II.13	
Newton	Carelau	341316	15	sand	I,6	
	Upper Gwyrlodydd	349324	15	sand	I,3	
Pembridge	Bruton	360532	15	t.f.	III,90	
	Bolton	356556	15	t.f.	III,89	
	Bridge Cottage	390584	14	t.f.	III,47	XXXIX,168.
	East Street, North	392582	15	t.f.	III,10	
	East Street, North	392582	15	t.f.	III,12	
	East Street, North	392582	15	t.f.	III,14	
	East Street, South	391582	14	t.f.	III,20	
	The Smithy	392582	15	t.f.	III,22	
	Upper Broxwood	366534	15	t.f.	III,91	
	West Street, North	388581	15	t.f.	III,29	
	West Street, North	382581	14	t.f.	III,35	
	Lowe Farm	370583	15	t.f.	III,60	
	West Street, North	388581	15	t.f.	III,34	
	West Street, North	388581	15	t.f.	III,36	XLIII,365.
	Moorcot Farm	355555	15	t.f	III,81	XLIV,254.
Pencombe	Lower Marston	569552	15	t.f. & sand	II,3	
	The Maidenhyde	568548	15	t.f.	II,13	XXXIX,486.
Pencoyd	Netherton	523267	15	t.f. & sand	I,3	
Peterstow	Little Peterstow	545245	15	t.f.	I,7	
Preston-on-Wye	Hacton Cottage	387417	15	t.f.		XLVII,250
Putley	Lacons	642379	15	t.f.	II,22	
Rodd	Upper Nash	307624	15	t.f.	III,6	

Parish	House	NGR(SO)	cent.	walls	RCHM	TWNFC
Rodd (cont'd.)	Cottage	322626	15	t.f.	III,2	
Rowlestone	Lower Mill	375265	15	sand	I,4	
St Devereux	White Hse Fm, Didley	454321	15	t.f.	I.7	
Stapleton	Carters Croft	327654	14	t.f.	III,3	
Staunton-on-Arrow	Highland	339619	15	t.f. & sand	III,2	
Stoke Edith	Perton	597405	15	t.f.	II,8	
Tarrington	Alders End	622398	15	t.f.	II,29	
Thornbury	Freeth	627608	15	t.f.	II,8	
	The Wooding	617596	14	t.f.	II,2	
Tyberton	Eynons Farm	381397	15	t.f.	I,3	XXXIX,377.
Upton Bishop	Woodhouse	655290	15	sand & t.f.	II,11	
Walterstone	Court Farm	343247	15	sand	I,5	
	Upper Goytre	351248	15	sand	I,6	
Weobley	Dairy Farm	400518	14	t.f.	III,14	
	Red Lion	402517	15	t.f.	III,22	
Weston-u-Penyard	House	639220	15	sand & t.f.	II,14	
Whitbourne	Bradbournes Farm	723572	15	t.f.	II,7	
	Cottage	724569	15	t.f.	II,4	
	Finchers Farm	721574	15	t.f.	II,9	
	Huntlands	718558	15	t.f.	II,36	XXXIX,487.
	Lower Poswick	709571	15	t.f.	II,27	
	Upper Poswick	710572	15	t.f.	II,28	XXXIX,487.
Whitchurch	Old Court	553175	15	sand	I,3	XLII,109
Wigmore	Upper Limebrook	375665	15	t.f.	III,21	XLII,149-64
Winforton	Cross Farm	297470	15	t.f.	III,5	

OPEN HALL BOX-FRAME

Parish	House	NGR(SO)	cent.	walls	RCHM	TWNFC
Abbey Dore	Grange Farm	404311	14	t.f.	I,6	
Allensmore	Little Cobhall	451359	15	t.f.	I,14	
Almeley	Manor House	331516	15	t.f.	III,5	
	Upper Stocks	347529	15	t.f.	III,19	
Aymestrey	Shirley	385653	15	t.f.	III,29	XLI,154-5
Bishop's Frome	Court Farm	664485	15	t.f.	II,13	
Bosbury	Old Court	694435	15	sand	II,4	XL,286.XLII, 56.
	Lower Townend	711431	15	t.f.	II,34	XLIII,75.
	Bell Inn	695434	15	t.f.	II,13	
	House W. of Bell Inn	695434	15	t.f.	II,12	
	Temple Court	692433	15	sand	II,3	
Bredwardine	Old Court	335448	14	sand	I,4	
Brilley	Brilley Court	259488	15	t.f.	III,20	
	Pentre Jack	280502	15	t.f.	III,7	
Brimfield	Nun Upton	543666	15	t.f.	III,2	XLI,155
Bromyard	55-7-9 High Sreet	654607	15	t.f.		XLI,66
Byford	Lower House	397427	15	t.f.	III,6	
Byton	Court House	370640	15	t.f.	III,2	
Clifford	Priory Farm	253446	14	sand	I,5	
Cradley	Parish Hall	737471	15	t.f.	II,4	
Eardisland	Nun House	417589	15	t.f.		XLI,156.
	Burton Court	573572	14	t.f.	III,3	
	Staick House	421587	14	t.f.	III,4	
Eardisley	Bank House	312494	15	t.f.		XLV,520-1
	Eardisley Wootton	308505	13	t.f.	III,30	
Grendon Bishop	Westington Court	589567	15	t.f.	II,5	
Hatfield	Old Hall	592593	15	t.f.	III,4	XXXVIII,265

Parish	House	NGR(SO)	cent.	walls	RCHM	TWNFC
Hentland	Gillow Manor	532253	14	sand	I,3	
Hereford	Pool Farm	507392	15	t.f.	I,116	XXXVIII,162-3.
	24 East Street	510399	15	t.f.		XL,165.
	5 Harley Court	511398	14	sand & t.f.	I,101	XL,166
	6 Castle Street	512397	15	t.f.		XLV,126.
	25 Commercial Street	512401	15	t.f.		XLV,520.
	Coningsby's Hosp.	511404	13	sand	I,10	
	3 St John Street	511398	14	t.f. & sand	I,102	
	Black Friars	511404	14	sand	I,9	
	50A Commercial St.	512401	15	t.f.		XLVI,329.
Holmer	Shelwick Court	527430	15	t.f.	II,12	XLIV,127. XLVII,358-9.
Hope-u-Dinmore	Hampton Court	521524	15	sand	III,2	
	Winsley House	483527	14	t.f.	III,3	
Kentchurch	Court	423259	14	sand	I,5	
Kingsland	St Mary's Farm	449613	15	t.f.	III,23	
	Vartry House	446614	15	t.f.	III,16	
	Black Hall	462629	14	t.f.	III,3	
Kington	39-40 Duke Street	299567	15	t.f.	III,27	
	45 Bridge Street	298565	15	t.f.		XLVII,360-1.
Kinsham	Lower Court	360645	15	t.f.	III,2	
Knill	Knill Court	291603	15	sand	III,2	
Ledbury	St Katherine's Hosp.	711377	15	t.f.	II,2	
	Junction Church Lane	711377	15	t.f.	II,65	
	Old Grammar School	712377	15	t.f.	II,67	
	Massington Farm	740395	15	sand	II,41	
	Old Plaistow	692397	15	t.f.	II,34	XL,167.XLII, 288.
	Upper Hall	713378	15	sand	II,5	XLV,521
Leominster	Corner School Lane & Corn Street	497591	15	t.f.	III,114	
	21-25 Bargates	494590	15	t.f.	III,163	
Lingen	Limebrook Cottage	371659	15	t.f.	III,4	XL,156.
Linton (Bromyard)	Old School Hse., Bringsty	692546	15	t.f.		XLV,779
Linton (Ross)	Priest's House	660253	15	sand	II,3	
Llangarron	Little Trewen	539187	15	sand	I,12	
Llanrothal	Farm	468189	14	t.f. & sand	I,7	
Lyonshall	Maidenhead	336555	15	t.f.	III,6	
Monkland	Manor House	461575	15	t.f.	III,2	
Mordiford	Old Sufton	575384	15	sand & t.f.	II,3	XLV,552-3
Much Dewchurch	Black Swan	483312	15	sand	I,6	
Much Marcle	Hellens	661333	15	brick	II,5	
	Chandos	643345	15	t.f. & sand	II,7	
Pembridge	Grub Court	367541	15	t.f.	III,92	XLI,457.
	Swan House	388581	15	t.f.		XLIV,439
	Old Wheelwright's	393582	15	t.f.	III,18	XLVI,98.
Ross	36 Broad Street	598241	14	sand	II,33	
Rowlestone	Court Farm	376272	14	sand	I,2	
St Weonards	Caerwendy	466251	15	sand	III,15	
Staunton-on-Wye	Church House Farm	375448	15	t.f.	Mercer, 1975	
Sutton St Michael	Freens Court	520459	15	t.f.	II,3	
Sutton St Nicholas	Ivy Cottage	535454	14	t.f.	II,4	
Tarrington	Sollers Court	618404	15	t.f.	II,4	

Parish	House	NGR(SO)	cent.	walls	RCHM	TWNFC
Tarrington (cont'd.)	Cottage	617408	15	t.f.	II,14	
Wellington	Old Parsonage	497482	14	t.f.	II,5	XXXIX,486.
	Bridge Farm	498482	15	t.f. & sand	II,2	XXXIX,486.
Weobley	Aroha	400518	15	t.f.	III,16	XXXIX,169 & 386.
	Chamberwell	402515	15	t.f.	III,51	XL,269
	Old Vicarage	401518	15	t.f.	III,19	XLI,127.
	Birches	374525	15	t.f.	III,6	XLI,156
	2 High Street	403515	15	t.f.	III,44	XLIV,128
	Red Lion	402517	14	t.f.	III,22	
	N.W. Corner, Broad St.	402517	15	t.f.	III,23	XLIV,255
	E. side Broad Street	403516	14	t.f.	III,32	
	E. side Broad Street	403516	15	t.f.	III,33	
	Mayfield, Hereford Rd.	404515	15	t.f.		XLVIII,152.
	S.E. Corner, Broad St.	403515	15	t.f.	III,35	
Whitbourne	Whitbourne Court	725569	15	sand	II,2	XLII,59-60. XL,169.
Wigmore	Chapel Farm	394684	15	t.f.	III,3	V,181-3,VI,1I -12.XLI,159.
	Court Barn	413691	15	t.f.	III,10	XL,169.

CELLARS
Under Later Buildings

Parish	House	NGR(SO)	cent.	walls	RCHM	TWNFC
Hereford	89 Eign Gate	508400	13		I,68	
	15 St Peter's St.	511399	15		I,18	
	20 High Town	510400	15		I,24	
	21 High Town	510400	15		I,25	
	2-5 Widemarsh St.	509400	15		I,70	XXX,v-x
	51-4 Commercial St.	512410	15		I,88	
	3 & 4 High Town	510400	15		I,27	
	3 High Street	509400	15		I,31	XXXVIII, 49-61
	4 High Street	509400	15		I,32	
	46 Broad Street	509399	15		I,35	
	White Hart Inn	509398	15		I,37	
	53 Broad Street	509399	15		I,38	
	Spread Eagle, King St.	509398	15		I,41	
	Grapes Inn, West St.	509399	15		I,63	
	18 Widemarsh Street	510403	15		I,76	
	6a Commercial Street	512410	15		I,87	
	6 St Owens Street	514398	15		I,91	
	133 St Owens Street	516397	15		I,97	
	Harley House, Harley Ct	510398	15		I,100	
	24 Church Street	510398	15		I,108	
	2 Offa Street	510399	14			XXXIX,63, 165
	Putta's Close	510399	13			XXXIX,68-70
	47 Broad Street	509399	15		I,36	

NGR	National Grid Reference		TWNFC	*Transactions of the Woolhope Naturalists' Field Club.*
RCHM	Royal Commission on Historical Monuments, England: *Herefordshire*, vols I, II & III (1931-4).			
lime	limestone		T	Timber
t.f.	timber-framed		sand	sandstone

REFERENCES
[1] Seen in Norman/French document in HRO *c*1981.
[2] C. A. Ralegh Radford, E. M. Jope and J. W. Tonkin, 'The Great Hall of the Bishop's Palace at Hereford', *Mediaeval Archaeology*, XVII (1973), 78-86; H. J. Powell, 'The Bishop's Palace, Hereford', *TWNFC*, XXXVII (1963), 320-4; J. W. Tonkin, 'The Palaces of the Bishop of Hereford', *TWNFC*, XLII (1976), 53-64.
[3] Ibid., J. W. Tonkin, 58-9,64.   [4] R.C.H.M.E., *Herefordshire*, III (1934), 1-3.
[5] J. W. Tonkin, 'Buildings', *TWNFC*, XLVII (1991), 96-7.
[6] J. W. Tonkin, 'Social Standing and Base-Crucks in Herefordshire', *Vernacular Architecture*, 1 (1970), 7-11.   [7] Ibid.
[8] R. Bond, 'The historical development of Court Cottage, Preston Wynne, Hereford and Worcester', English Heritage, (1998).
[9] J. W. Tonkin, 'The Nunnery of Limebrook and its Property', *TWNFC*, XLI (1974), 149-64.
[10] G. Boswijk and I. Tyers, *Tree-ring Analysis of Booth Hall and 16-18 High Town, Hereford*, Ancient Monuments Laboratory Report 101/97 (1997). ML report.
[11] op. cit. in note 1.   [12] J. W. Tonkin, op.cit. in note 2, 53-64.
[13] See *Vernacular Architecture*, 11 (1980), 34; 20 (1989), 46; 23 (1992), 45; 24 (1993), 47.

In the Footsteps of Timothy Curley:
towards the 'Modern' City of Hereford

GRAHAM ROBERTS

One consequence of the Roman invasion was the introduction to Britain of a system of town and country planning. Where previously patterns of human settlement and communications had been random products of widely varying local circumstances, from around AD 43 the Romans applied themselves to schemes of organised and cohesive development. Sites for new towns and forts were competently selected and there was for the first time a system of well constructed roads. Locally the walled town of Kenchester (*Magnis*) became established towards the end of the first century, served by routes leading to all parts of the Midlands and the Welsh border. When in time the legions withdrew, Kenchester was abandoned and later avoided by the Saxons, who in due course arrived to establish their own district centre. They selected a new site five miles to the east, typically by a river. A drained gravel terrace – mainly above flood levels – it was well suited for timber-built structures and enjoyed ample sources of wholesome water. Close to an important ford across the Wye linking not improbably with the remains of the Roman main road network, it commanded one of the main approaches to central Wales. The site stood at the centre of rich countryside and, in spite of periodic troubles created by the recalcitrant and covetous Welsh, it turned out to be a good choice for the Saxons – indeed for all who have followed during the ensuing twelve centuries.

By the year 1000, after periods of great activity, a fortified urban framework had evolved to a regular grid system; it had grown to form a planned royal town and was designated a *burh* – one of the principal Saxon towns of Mercia – although hardly any bigger than abandoned Kenchester. As the setting of a cathedral, Hereford was a city and it also contained St Guthlac's monastery but notwithstanding the prominence of the church, its primary standing was that of a royal foundation. During the eventful first hundred years of the second millennium it was fortified with 'one of the fairest, largest and strongest castles in England', a royal castle later compared with that at Windsor. There were city defences of equal stature, and within the walls rights were being acquired to hold all-important markets. The consequent prosperity of Hereford was apparent in Domesday in 1086 where it was named as one of sixteen English shire towns ranked as cities.

The main street pattern was firmly fixed by 1200: it was unchanged when mapped by Speede in 1610, in 1757 by Taylor and in 1856 by Curley. And after eight centuries it was virtually still the same in the city centre, but straining to cope with the huge assaults of late twentieth-century motor traffic. By the end of the thirteenth century, Hereford had reached the highest point of its medieval development and a strong trade current flowed for another three centuries before the city lost its political and strategic importance. Great economic and social damage occurred upon the destruction of corn and cloth mills in the reign of Henry VIII and the aftermath of the Civil War compounded the resulting physical decline of Hereford. In 1724, John Macky, a visiting traveller, wrote of 'the dirtiest old city I have seen in England', and a year later Daniel Defoe – described as 'the keenest observer of economic growth of his time' – found 'truly an old, mean built and very dirty city'. Much of this was at the time put down to 'a lack of transportation'. Connecting roads and bridges were impassable for many months each year, except by foot or on horseback, whilst the Wye was unreliable, due either to a lack or an excess of water. Hereford, substantially isolated from the rest of the kingdom, was largely denied the benefits of the Industrial Revolution until much later.

Its people were still mainly walled in within 93 acres and signs of crowding were evident by the twelfth century. In 1757, of a total population of 5,592 within the walls, there were 3,816 inhabitants in 812 houses, in addition to the cathedral, bishop's palace and castle site. By 1851, when the Woolhope Club was founded, the city population was 12,128 with nearly 2,500 houses – many of them cramped, badly built and rundown cottages in the courtyards and 'stews' created by infilling. This was an unhealthy situation in unhealthy times. Overcrowding meant that typhus, smallpox and other epidemic scourges became a part of everyday life and bad drainage brought typhoid. Surprisingly cholera, a disease from contaminated water which had devastated poor and congested parts of most other towns since 1831, did not arrive – a mystery debated by the Woolhope Club in 1852 and more recently argued as one more consequence of the city's telling remoteness from the outside world.

Cures were difficult and prevention was the only real control. A Public Health Act was passed in 1848 giving powers to create local boards of health where the mortality rate exceeded twenty-three per 1,000 population (about double the 1990s level). In Hereford this had averaged twenty-seven per 1,000 over the seven years to 1851 and so a sanitary commissioner, Mr Rammell, was appointed to examine the sewerage, drainage, water supply, state of the burial grounds, number and sanitary condition of the inhabitants and other matters. He delivered his list of recommendations in May 1853. The complexity of the required technical work was beyond the scope of the city surveyor, Leonard Johnson, a very talented architect who had held office since 1840, but it was not necessary to look far for professional assistance.

As civil engineering agent for Messrs Dennis & Logan, contractors for the advancing railway from Abergavenny, Timothy Curley was already involved in a process which would begin to remedy Hereford's 'lack of transportation' (Pl. 1). In 1853 the town council appointed him as its consulting engineer 'to make plans and estimates for the construction of a new cattle market, a cemetery, water works and drainage'. He rapidly presented an exhaustive report, which left no doubt as to the need for action. 'During one of my visits', he wrote, 'I witnessed such scenes of filth and uncleanliness in this city as I did not believe could exist in a civilised community. The back streets and courts are in a most filthy state, the floors of several privies being inundated by the semi-fluid contents of the cesspools; in some cases they are too filthy to be entered'. He also condemned the polluted well water supply and endorsed common opinions about the inadequacy of the burial grounds and of the stock market – 'the best provincial market in the kingdom, but much to its demerit the very worst accommodation'. After some controversy an enabling Act was passed by Parliament in 1854, hailed as 'the instrument by which a new Hereford has been created'.

Plate 1. Timothy Curley

Curley was authorised to proceed with his proposed £43,225 programme of works, and after detailed survey and preparation a £25,000 drainage and sewerage contract was let. In 1867 further sewers were laid in the Broomy Hill and Whitecross districts and many others were to follow in the suburbs. Instead of raw sewage passing into cesspits, ditches and open pools, pipes serving different parts of the city fed large volumes of partially settled or untreated effluent straight into the Wye – until 1890. Not until the 1970s was pollution by untreated sewage finally stopped. Disposal became a major preoccupation for the council and their second city surveyor, George Cole. By 1881 an 81-acre site had been bought at 'Corporation Farm', Hampton Park, and the old Eign Mill, for use as a sewage farm and pumping station site. Unfortunately the £15,000 scheme turned out to be unworkable, but much later the city housing authority was to be very glad of this 'white elephant' land.

Curley started a £35,000 water supply scheme in 1856, the year of his admission to the Woolhope Club, and followed with many additions and improvements to cater for new suburbs at Whitecross, Aylestone Hill and Hampton Park. In 1886 (four years after his death), a water tower costing £7,725 was completed at Broomy Hill to supply higher and more outlying districts and to provide adequate supply and pressure in the event of a fire in the city. He also drew up plans for the new market and this opened at Newmarket Street in 1856, heralded then as 'The foundation of the city's future prosperity'. Thenceforth animals were no longer sold 'by hand' in King Street and Aubrey Street, although until the middle of the twentieth century they continued to be driven on foot to market through the streets. The site had been chosen to allow for expansion and for convenient service by rail – arranged with the GWR in 1914 on the Worcester Sidings, Edgar Street. The nucleus of 1856 expanded to 12.5 acres and by the end of the century the annual 'throughput' had reached over 150,000 animals, increasing in 1955 to 267,491 and peaking in the 1990s at over 400,000.

One aspect of the Rammell Report took a long time to achieve. Back in 1847 a committee tried to provide for a general cemetery but only in 1909, after much prevarication and ill will, was the new cemetery at Westfaling Street eventually opened. In 1851, coaches and other horse-drawn vehicles still clattered along the cobbled streets – although most people just walked. Hereford was almost the last place of its size to be served by rail but when trains finally arrived in 1853, the increased mobility and improved communications soon started to tell. Combining with the new market, benefits from piped water and sewerage and a general Victorian boom, it was to signal the dawning of a 'New Hereford'. As this entered first gear, the population-count in twenty years surged by over 50% – from 12,128 in 1851 to 18,347 by the 1871 census. Unprecedented needs and great responsibilities were being imposed upon local authorities. These included the provision of roads, footpaths and bridges, drainage, disposal of sewage and household refuse, street cleansing, water supply, street lighting, parks, housing, public toilets, municipal buildings, building bye-law control, forward planning and all the amenities required to enrich the lot of the town dweller.

It fell to a new breed of 'municipal' engineers to serve such diverse needs. General practitioners in the civil (rather than the erstwhile military) sense, they also required extra-professional sociological and administrative skills and were normally members of the Institution of Civil Engineers. This is a learned society which in 1828 received its first royal charter for service in 'the Art of directing the great sources of power in Nature for the use and convenience of man'. A more specialised Institution of Municipal and County Engineers was founded in 1873.

John Parker, (Pl. 2) a chartered civil engineer, succeeded George Cole as city surveyor in 1881. Inheriting the sewage disposal topic, by 1885 he was immersed in the scheme at Bartonsham. After many difficulties the storage and precipitating tanks, filter beds, sludge presses and other equipment were commissioned in 1890 at a cost of £36,000, nearby residents being reassured by medical and sanitary officers that the works would act as a tonic to their health!

Plate 2. John Parker

Seven years later Parker erected a refuse destructor, which burned 5,000 tons of separated refuse per annum. This reduced the need for 'tipping' space, produced clinker for road foundations and created steam for the pumping engines – saving significantly on the annual coal bill. As the population continued to increase, new houses appeared along the main radial routes, the railway industry creating a considerable demand – as the dates on the house-plaques testify. New roads, sewers and building sites were laid out by the Freehold Land Society at a 30-acre site purchased at 'Above Eign'. The slopes of Aylestone Hill, Hafod Road, Hampton Park and Broomy Hill provided more spacious dwelling sites but there remained great housing need in the traditionally poor parts of the city. All the recent legislation had done little to eliminate suffering in the unhealthy and congested quarters of Bewell, Friars, Cross, St Owen and Eign Streets, Turk's Alley and other unwholesome areas (Pl. 3). The Public Health Act, 1875 consolidated previous Acts and created mandatory powers, enforceable by medical and sanitary inspectors, and it fell to Hereford town council, for the first time, to provide better homes for the needy.

The 'garden city movement', pioneered by Ebenezer Howard in 1898, inspired a special collaboration between the city council and 'Hereford Co-operative Housing Limited'. At Barr's Court they provided eighty-five cottages for over 400 people

Plate 3. Back of the 'stews' in Bewell Street.

and, from this beginning, the local authority eventually built or acquired some 8,700 dwellings in the city. Parker was fully involved in this programme until his retirement soon after the Great War; he also had many other projects, such as police cottages at De Lacy Street, Holmer and St Peter's (Girls) schools, St Owen's Gate model dwellings and the cemetery chapel. There was also the Electricity Supply Works at Widemarsh Street (Pl. 4). Opened in 1899, the buildings were later described as 'totally bereft of architectural features; an uglier pile could not be imagined'. Inwardly however the works was said, rather extravagantly, to 'almost surpass the wit of man to describe'! They were enlarged during the First World War to cope with heavy demands at the government munitions factory at Rotherwas and again afterwards.

Plate 4. The electricity supply works.

Parker's Victoria Bridge was rather different. Replacing a short-lived ferry, financed by public subscription, it cost £1,200 and was presented to the city in 1898 as a memorial of the Queen's Diamond Jubilee. Although not ranking with the many major works of spectacular art created by the Victorian civil engineers, the bridge was considered to be 'artistic in design, elegant in form, light in construction and beautiful in effect', a judgement which time has endorsed.

Parker and his predecessors were not lavishly accommodated for the additional work expected of the local authorities and their staffs. For twenty years council business was conducted from a few small rooms adjoining the Guildhall Chamber at Widemarsh Street, and then across the road at the Mansion House. Parker produced plans and elevations for a new town hall at the Guildhall site, but eventually a gift of land in St Owen's Street was accepted instead and a competition was mounted for suitable designs. Over fifty architects applied for particulars but, by a not unfamiliar process, the recommendation of their independent professional assessor was rejected by the city fathers. They chose instead the plans of architect Mr H. A. Cheers of Twickenham and his building was opened on 9 June 1904, the civic rejoicing dampened only by a 30% increase in the final reckoning, in respect of 'extras', from the local builder, Mr Bowers. The eventual expenditure of £24,000 produced a structure then described as massive and commanding and 'probably a little out of harmony with its surroundings' and, recently, as 'A most flamboyant design characteristic of its date'. Among its many novelties was electricity. This was supplied from the new works at Widemarsh Street but it was not to be used for public lighting for many years.

Parker, also a Woolhope Club member, would probably have owned one of the early cars in the city, doubtless putting it to much use on his rounds as Hereford continued to spread. However the 'motor car age' was not to create a problem until after he retired, although by 1910 the surfaces of some roads, Ledbury and Whitecross Roads especially, were showing signs of breaking up. Relying on his steamrollers and carts and seventeen horses he tackled the necessary repairs, having no inkling of what lay ahead as travel by horse and shanks's pony gave way to lavish employment of the internal combustion engine. As he drove around upsetting horses he could hardly have foreseen that before very long they would all disappear – to be replaced by 'the all-in-one benefactor and despoiler of modern quality of life' – the motor vehicle.

William M. Shimmin took over as city surveyor soon after the war. The city population had reached 23,000 and housing schemes at College Hill, Bryngwyn, Bartonsham and Hunderton produced a surge in growth, requiring many added services. The Buttermarket (Pl. 5) was rebuilt in 1925 after a fire and in 1929 a new refuse incinerator was constructed at Edgar Street. Linked to new public baths by a pipeline proposed by city councillor A. E. Farr, head of the nationally renowned civil engineering company, it generated steam in its boilers to heat the 75ft x 30ft pool, baths, showers and laundry. All remained in use, along with a controlled refuse tip at Belmont, until the 1970s. In 1976, the baths were superseded by new ones at St Martins Avenue and the building reopened in 1979 as the Nell Gwynne Theatre, to be demolished in 1998 for its successor the Courtyard Theatre and Arts Centre.

As the 1930s progressed so did development of the motor car. Numbers doubled by 1939 and 'traffic jams' on main roads and junctions started to become a problem. By 1938 the daily traffic volume across the narrow Wye Bridge was almost 5,500 vehicles and the Ministry of Transport, in consultation with the city, considered a by-pass as a means of saving the city centre from havoc. Studies showed that as the

Plate 5. The Buttermarket – opened in 1860.

county town and focus of ten trunk and major roads, Hereford attracted some 80% of the total movement. As a first step an inner relief road approach was preferred and in 1939 a final line was agreed.

The 1939-45 war created special problems for Shimmin and before it ended he was engaged in a vigorous programme building 'prefabs' in the College, Eign Mill, Hinton and Westfields areas. Much bigger developments involving some 1,500 dwellings followed at Hinton, Hunderton, Newton Farm, Crossfields, Putson, Redhill and Whitecross with their roads, sewers and other services. From July 1948 the city council was granted delegated powers by the county council under the Town and Country Planning Act, 1947 and the city surveyor became also the planning officer to advise on planning matters. A statutory town plan was stipulated to secure: (a) provision for the needs of a population of 45,000 up to 1971; (b) co-ordination of development to obtain maximum benefit from land used and proposed public services; (c) provision for the needs of Hereford city as an administrative, business and shopping centre of increasing importance and (d) assistance in the relief of traffic congestion.

As Shimmin's successor in 1948, it fell to Frank Margerison to work with the county planning officer on the preparatory research and survey. Among the attempted predictions was the extent of traffic growth. By 1954 the daily movement across the Wye was over 9,300 vehicles, increasing at compound rates, consistent with the national total on the roads of about 3.5 million. Also the Ministry of Transport had planned an arterial road scheme that would connect the South Wales ports with the Mersey through Hereford...!

By 1951 the population had reached 32,490 and soon afterwards growth accelerated due to the concentration of manufacturing activities from Glasgow and Birmingham by Henry Wiggen on a 65-acre site at Crossway Farm, Holmer. After considerable discussion with the planners, the plant opened in 1954. It was subsequently extended and largely as a consequence the city population by 1967 was nearly 50% above that of 1951. By then Hereford's small country town character had gone forever.

Of some 4,700 council houses built since the end of the war, many were for industrial 'key personnel'; they required roads, paths and sewers totalling several miles and the need also arose for a widening and improvement programme for existing highways. These included Yazor Road, Plough Lane, Venns Lane, Belmont Road and railway-bridge, and Roman Road. The amount and variety of work for the city surveyor and staff was prodigious, covering also the need to build main foul and surface water sewers, public conveniences, a crematorium and chapel, a modern parks nursery, improve the state of the baths and modernise the cattle market. In 1963 a £43,000 privately financed experiment to produce a soil conditioner by mechanically composting sewage sludge and household refuse was supported, but this early 'green' initiative did not catch on.

In the meantime agreement was finally reached for work to proceed with the 1939 relief road scheme. Traffic across the 23ft 8in wide fifteenth-century Wye Bridge had risen to over 25,000 vehicles a day and the medieval city centre street system was continually blocked. Throughout the 1960s there were constant grumbles from near and far by those who had 'got stuck in the traffic at Hereford' (Pl. 6).

Plate 6. 'Stuck in the traffic' – High Town in the 1960s. *Photo: Derek Evans*

Frank Margerison retired in 1964 to be succeeded by the author just as work was commencing on the new Greyfriars Bridge and approaches. The design caters for the highest known flood of the Wye, recorded in 1960 at 19ft above normal summer

Plate 7. Greyfriars Bridge under construction 1965.

level. The main span is 290ft, the clear height at the centre is 32ft above normal summer level and 12ft above the maximum recorded level. There are two anchor spans of 85ft and the total length of bridge and approaches is 1,800ft with a total road width between parapets of 68ft (Pl. 7).

In 1945, George Cadbury had published his *Hereford Walls* booklet supporting the use of the site of the old surrounding moat as a by-pass route and making Hereford a 'precinct city'. This process eventually commenced in Bath Street South in 1964 and continued from 1968 with the construction of the north-south and east-west relief roads at Victoria Street, Edgar Street, Newmarket Street, Blueschool Street and Bath Street North (Pl. 8). Archaeologists and antiquarians were continually on hand at a time when Hereford was at the forefront of research on Anglo-Saxon and later defences. The fruits of their work have been widely published and their example has paved the way for a great deal of effort from those caring about the conservation of the city's historic fabric.

Plate 8. Victoria Street before the Ring Road, c1965.

At the official opening of the ring road in December 1969, a long procession of motor vehicles, from a 1897 Daimler to a 1965 Rover/BRM turbine car, were able to 'beat the bounds' outside the opened-up wall line. But it was now time to attend to conditions within the city centre. The statutory Town Map and Written Statement had become operative in October 1963 and in the previous year county and city councillors published a 'Statement of Principles' upon which an eventual plan for the central area would be based. Read in conjunction with a map showing the relief road, the principles meant that if it was followed there would be almost complete segregation of pedestrians and vehicles within the walled area. In 1964 a town centre map was prepared by the officers of the two councils and the Taylor Woodrow Group. This applied the principles and recommendations produced by the county planners and Development Analysts Ltd. for an additional 300,000 sq. ft. of shopping floor space by 1981. The working party agreed that the best location was the area of land at the rear of Eign Street, High Town and Commercial Street – afterwards known as sectors A, B and C. The team also supported the urgent provision of 8,500 extra car parking spaces and the segregation of pedestrians from vehicles.

Eign Street (within the gate), part of the medieval street system, had carried an average of 7,500 vehicles per day by 1965, and in stages all were diverted. By 1970 the street had been relieved from the chaos of its former fume-filled and noisy state to become a tranquil and prosperous shopping precinct, (Pl. 9) and Church Street was re-paved soon afterwards. In 1973 the daily 'road-rage' of 15,000 harassed pedestrians and 9,500 fuming motorists at the infamous zebra crossing in High Town was ended and the pedestrianisation of Commercial Street and St Peter's Street completed the programme in 1988.

Throughout the 1960s and 70s Hereford was vulnerable to 'comprehensive developments' which destroyed the intrinsic character of so many other towns and cities. Major threats occurred but they were mostly overcome, leaving a few 'carbuncles' to represent the era.

Against a 1964 special short-listing of Hereford as one of fifty-one towns in Britain regarded as 'so splendid and precious that ultimate responsibility for them should be a national concern', fitting conservation policies have been developed. In not seeking to leave everything as it is, often a recipe for neglect, they have encouraged design flair and intelligent change for the better – in harmony with the essential nature and 'grain' of the city.

The joint city council/Norwich Union 'Maylord Orchards' shopping and housing scheme was a reasonable example of this for the 1980s, being four times commended – regionally, nationally and in Europe – for 'the imaginative redevelopment of Hereford's City Centre, providing traditional shopping, parking and residential facilities'.

In the rest of the city, renewed attention was paid to improvements at the market, including the conversion of the 7.5-acre Merton Meadow as a paved car and lorry-park and twenty-bay lorry wash. A new abattoir was built at Westfields and leased to a local operator, and partly because of the concentrated effluent from these establishments and from new industrial concerns, a £1.32m sewage disposal extension scheme was carried out, divided between sites at Eign Works and Rotherwas.

As a corollary of pedestrianisation, extra car parks were provided, many temporary spaces being later replaced by permanent ones in the Tesco and Maylord Orchards developments. These were located chiefly underground to make the most of the sites and also as a move to preserve the roofscape of the historic core. Hereford's first multi-storey car park was built just outside the crowded 93-acre central area, and surface spaces were provided at St Martins and Wye Streets, Greyfriars, the market area and Edgar Street, Blackfriars, Bath Street and the bus-station. A charge tariff was drawn up which recognised the short, middle and long term value and appeal of the sites, making special provision for disabled drivers. Later on, three further supermarket developments provided parking not only for their own customers but also for those able and prepared to walk the relatively short distance to the centre.

In 1853 improved 'comfort and health' of citizens was mainly to be gained by various 'sanitary arrangements', although Curley's proposals were endorsed by local clergy with added moral, social, mental and religious bonuses. 'Healthy minds live in healthy bodies' they wrote – but in the council brief refreshment of mind and body had not extended to calls for leisure and recreational ideas. However, people walked a lot more in those days. They could soon be out in the countryside, enjoy the elegantly laid out Castle Green or take cheerful trips on, or a dip in, the Wye, play cricket or football at Widemarsh Common and attend the races – among simple

Plate 9. Eign Gate in the early 1970s.   *Photo: Derek Evans*

pleasures freely available. As new building took the city out into the fields some of these opportunities became less available and many more new amenities were required for the growing population. During 140 years, Curley's successors had a hand in establishing over 400 acres of public parks, open spaces, play areas, walkways and cycle-ways, to which have been added three local nature reserves and 26 acres of woodland. An early river bathing station was built at Bartonsham followed by the 1930s public baths at Edgar Street and the leisure pool complex at St Martin's, opened in 1976. Policies recognising the high importance of sport and recreation have since added a leisure centre, floodlit athletic track and 'all weather' sports area, golf course – all of them much used in the 'modern' city of Hereford.

Towards the end of the century Hereford was bursting from its meagre 5,031 acres. In 1998, after centuries of special corporate privilege, tenaciously preserved and atified by many royal charters, it became – as a cathedral city, borough community, county and assize town and market, shopping and employment centre – part of a unified administrative Herefordshire.

And since 1991, Timothy Curley's final successor has been left wondering how, during another 140 years, changes in the shape and character of the city of Hereford will compare with the magnitude of those witnessed by the four city surveyors who have followed in the engineer's footsteps, ever since the distant earliest days of the Woolhope Club. Much of the great responsibility for the answer and for the guardianship of a great heritage will, from the very beginning, rest with future citizens, with successive mayors and councillors of the city and, not least, the members and employees of the Herefordshire Council.

BIBLIOGRAPHY
Books
  M. D. Lobel, *Historic Towns*, volume 1: Hereford (1969).
  J. Macky, *A Journey through England in Familiar Letters* (1714-23).
  D. Defoe, *A Tour through the Whole Island of Great Britain* (1724-6).
  G. Cadbury, *Hereford Walls* (1945).
  City of Hereford, *Official Guide* (1969).
Papers and texts
  J. Taylor, *Map of Hereford* (1757).
  TWNFC, (1852-1865), 20-24.
  J. Ross, *Hereford and Cholera – Why did we escape it?* (1990).
Reports
  National Census, from 1801.
  T. W. Rammell, *Report to the General Board of Health...City of Hereford* (1853).
  T. Curley, *Hereford Sanitary Improvements* (1854).
  Dean of Hereford, other clergy. William Aldridge, other Ministers. *Letters* (1854).
  W. Collins, *Modern Hereford*, Part 2 (1911).
  W. Collins, *Short History of Hereford* (1912).
  Herefordshire County Council, *County Development Plan, Town Map No1* (1960).
  Special Central Redevelopment Joint Sub-Committee, *Statement of Principles* (1962).
  Joint Working Party, *Report-City Central Area Redevelopment* (1964).
  City of Hereford, City Surveyor's Department surveys and reports (1965–91).
  Cement and Concrete Association, *Greyfriars Bridge, Hereford* (1966).
  Department of Environment, *List of Buildings of Architectural...interest* (1973).
  Hereford City Council, *Hereford Local Plan* (1987).
  Royal Town Planning Institute, *Award for Planning Achievement* (1988).

Herefordshire Field-Names

RUTH E. RICHARDSON

Field-names may include the oldest documentary information available to us. Although most names were first written down in the eighteenth and nineteenth centuries, field-names are mentioned sufficiently often in manorial and estate records to show that they were in common usage. An early famous example is in the peace treaty of 1215 between King John and the barons, later known as Magna Carta, which was signed in 'the meadow that is called Runnymede' (from Old English *runieg*, council or assembly island). The location 'between Windsor and Staines' on the banks of the river Thames is given but no map was attached. Indeed, probably the earliest English village plan known which shows named fields is of Boarstall in Buckinghamshire dated 1444.

Names provide a simple and practical method for referring to a particular area of land. This is only necessary if the person involved is recording information about it, or discussing it with another party. While you are standing, or working, in a field then its name is irrelevant. If you have one patch of land to work then again a name is unnecessary, but when a farmer has two or more areas of land then differentiation will become important. Place-names came into being in exactly the same way, for if you are living in a place you do not need to allude to its name. In fact, place-names result from population mobility even in a small area. As the oldest place-names and most field-names are descriptive, it is artificial to categorise them separately. However, place-names have been in the written record for far longer and have therefore been studied more thoroughly. It is possible to find changes in spelling and to propose meanings from the earliest version of the name. Field-names are an impressive oral tradition of great antiquity, probably dating back to the introduction of farming in the neolithic period, but are far more difficult to study as we cannot always easily trace which names are original and which have evolved.

This situation has resulted in field-names either being largely ignored academically, or regarded as fanciful folklore, the latter somewhat reinforced by ill-informed guess-work that can masquerade as interpretations of the names. Conversely, there have also been notable efforts made to use what is an invaluable resource but generally, as access to the information has proved difficult, the results have tended to examine the field-names of a single parish, or part of a county, or examples from several counties. What has been lacking has been a systematic examination of all the parishes in a county published in a way that could facilitate their use in checking their location on the ground and the frequency of individual names. This was the aim of the Herefordshire Field-Name Survey 1987-1993, the details of which are available in several Woolhope *Transactions*, particularly the 1996 edition. As this was the first time field-names had been made available for research in this way, and on this scale, the group won a British Archaeological Award in 1994. We were delighted, but the reason we had entered for an award at all was to try to publicise the use of field-names. They are an undervalued resource and a direct link with people who farmed the land in the past.

GREAT AND LESSER TITHES

Herefordshire has an almost complete set of tithe apportionments, or schedules, and accompanying maps (Fig. 1). These surveys were the consequence of the Tithe Commutation Act of 1836 which altered the collection of the clerical tenth from goods to a rent charge based on the value of the land.

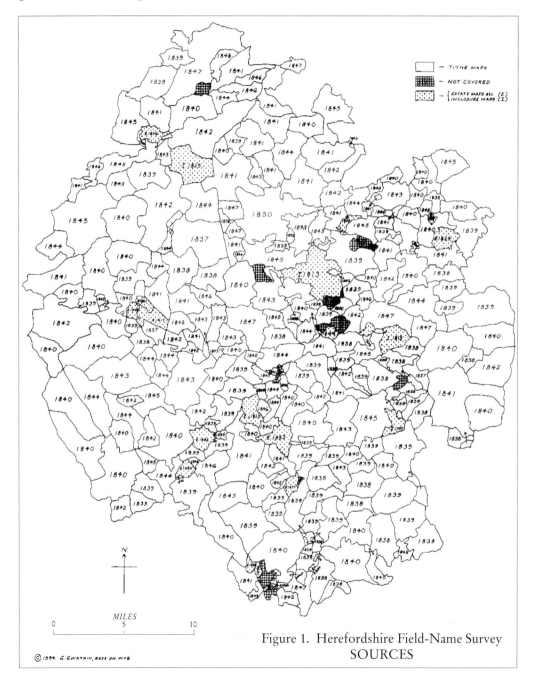

Figure 1. Herefordshire Field-Name Survey
SOURCES

Most of Herefordshire's apportionments have a short introduction but that of the parish of Brimfield gives considerable detail:

We the undersigned Tithe Commissioners for England and Wales by virtue of the Power to that Effect given to us by the Act for the Commutation of Tithes in England and Wales Do hereby assign the Parish of Brimfield in the County of Hereford to be a District within which the extraordinary Rent Charge in lieu of Tithes upon Hop Grounds shall be after the rate of Four shillings and six pence for every Imperial Acre to be paid according to the provisions of the said Act. In Testimony whereof We have hereunto set our hands and caused our Official Seal to be affixed this eighth day of August in the Year of our Lord One thousand eight hundred and forty three. signed Wm. Blamire. Rd. Jones.

Therefore, in order to deduce the amount each occupier had to pay, a survey was necessary for each parish.

The system of tithes (from Old English *teothe*, a tenth) had originated in the need to pay the clergy. In the Saxon period churches were often served by a group of priests working from a central minster, but by the thirteenth century churches were an established part of manors and the local lord was the patron. If the patron appointed a priest then he would grant him glebe land to use and the congregation would pay offerings on feast days, weddings and funerals as well as great and lesser tithes. If the patron ceded the church to a monastic institution then the monastery became the rector and had the right to claim the great tithes on corn, hay and wood. If the monastery then appointed a priest to the church he was known as a vicar and he had the right to collect only the lesser tithes arising from other crops, young animals and activities such as fishing and milling. A parish priest who was a rector was clearly in a superior financial position to a vicar. These rights were a survival from the feudal dues and they continued even when the official English church became Protestant.

Brimfield provides details of tithes still in use in 1843 and they illustrate not only the wide ranging nature of the system but also the incredible difficulties of collection:

In lieu of tithe of Hay, Corn, Grain, Fruit, Hemp and Flax growing and increasing in that part of a Meadow belonging to the Estate or Farm called Drayton...and also instead of all the last mentioned description of tithes arising from Lamberls Close and the Lower Grove...a composition real of twelve sheaves of Wheat, or Six Pecks and twelve sheaves of Oats, or Six pecks of Wheat at the Election of the Minister.

In addition, the incumbent, referred to as 'the Perpetual Curate', was entitled to the following customary payments and Easter offerings 'payable throughout the parish':

CUSTOMARY PAYMENTS
For each Cow and Calf – One penny halfpenny
For each Barran Cow – One penny
For the fall of a Colt – One shilling
Smoke [i.e: a chimney] – One penny
For a Cock – Three Eggs
For a Hen –- Two Eggs
Garden – One penny

EASTER OFFERINGS
Each Householder – Two pence
Each Child – Two pence
His Wife – Two pence
Man Servant – Six pence
Maid Servant – Four pence

Other variables included milk yield, the parson's pig, wild duck decoys, windfall apples, cherries, garlic and turnips. The glebe terriers provide a fascinating collection of items. Income depended on the personality of the minister with some, who did not wish to add to the hardship of their parishioners, not collecting all their entitlements, whilst others wanted everything. Some ministers carried out the collection personally but others used a tithe gatherer who would take 25% to 40% as payment depending on distance and difficulty of collection. The system was uneven, inefficient and could cause resentment. Rent charges seemed to provide an answer.

The surveys for the Tithe Commutation Act covered 79% of England and Wales. Many counties already had useable surveys from parliamentary enclosure awards, which had proliferated after 1760, and here the commissioners only had to record those areas not previously examined. According to M. Turner's 1980 survey in *English Parliamentary Enclosures* Herefordshire's enclosures had amounted to less than 10% of arable open fields and less than 5% of common and waste. This suggests that the medieval open-field system was not widespread in the county and that older systems of small irregular fields had survived alongside the mediaeval closes, strips, commons, meadows, woods, and tofts or burgage plots. In Herefordshire, useful parliamentary enclosure awards were only available for part of Much Marcle 1797, Bodenham 1813, Stretton Grandison 1815 and Shobdon 1829, so the tithe commissioners had to arrange surveys for nearly the whole county. A small proportion of the county remained unsurveyed but these were mainly extra parochial areas such as Haywood, a royal forest until the late sixteenth century, and Treville, also a royal forest for centuries and never tithed. Fields, and by implication field-names, in these areas are likely to be late in date, perhaps post-mediaeval except for *assarts* (irregular clearings) in the woods.

Treville provides a good example of the appearance of such an area in the medieval period. By 1213 a thousand acres of Treville, or Trivel Wood, had been acquired by Dore Abbey and Gerald of Wales criticised their timber felling, saying the monks had changed 'an oak wood into a wheat field', though he did concede that the wood brought an excellent price in Hereford market. Despite this, the wood was allowed to recover, indicating land management not wholesale clearance, and by 1398 there were enough mature trees for the abbot to complain to King Richard II that four local lords had felled ninety-four 'great oaks of the best'. The abbey's grange at Morehampton, in the Golden Valley, had also been raided and thirty beef cattle killed, presumably in fields.

THE PARISH OF MUCH MARCLE
Interestingly the 1797 Much Marcle enclosure award covers a part of that parish that was re-surveyed when the rest of the parish was surveyed for the 1839 tithe map, and this does allow for a forty-two year comparison of the area. The field numbers on the two maps are different. The enclosure award includes all of Much Marcle, while the tithe omits the northern third, Kynaston township, but includes Yatton in the south-west. Therefore, two thirds of Much Marcle, the townships of Marcle and Wolton, are covered on both maps and both apportionments. The enclosure award has 908 fields composed of a patchwork of large fields with small, narrow, rectangular fields, many of which, where the narrow side fronts a road, were probably mediaeval tofts. By the tithe map there had been some consolidation and there were now 743 fields, the pattern showing far more large fields, though with some survivals of small fields.

Actually the loss of small fields is even more startling. Although the general pattern is for amalgamation on the later tithe map, there are five areas where the trend was reversed. An example was the encroachment made on to the hill named *265 Wheelers Knowl* in 1797 which, by 1839, had become seven fields: *442 Upper Knowl, 443 Lower Knowl, 444 Barn Meadow, 445 Barn field Cottage and Garden, 446 Thirty Acres, 447 Lower Acres*, and *450 New Inclosure*. The only changes that had been made were to add the internal boundaries, except to the west and south of *450* where irregularities were smoothed out. It is interesting to be able to date this *New Inclosure* so exactly. None of the 1797 field-names for the other four large areas, *319, 369, 382, 803*, were lost as they became attached to a new field, or became an area name shown on the map. Half the new field-names were multiples of acres. If these five areas are removed from the calculations then 195 small fields were lost as independent units between 1797 and 1839. As most seem to have been in single occupation a comparison with population figures would probably reinforce this apparent movement of people to towns and larger villages.

Between 1797 and 1839 some roads vanished in areas like *Careswall* and *Oatleys*, though the former road alignment was preserved in field boundaries. Another example was the road that ran from *Arnolds* west to *Bodnam* past 'Hom House', which by the 1839 tithe had been closed while the fifteen quite large fields, to the east of the house, were turned into a park. Incidentally, *Bodnam* was now written as *Bodenham*, though even today still pronounced as *Bodnam*. Unless specific contrary instructions were given much of the material was verbal. Spelling could depend on pronunciation and on the understanding, or even whim, of the scribe when recording what he was told. Other roads were also closed but conversely, by the tithe, a new three-and-a-half mile road had appeared running from the crossroads west of 'Hellens' south, following the stream, to *Gamage Ford* (Fig. 2). Halfway along it provided the access to the new drive to 'Hom House'. This road is now part of the A449. It provides a concrete example of a method of dating a road. If field boundaries appear to continue across a road then a check of the field-names adjacent to the road can be of use. In this case this is demonstrated by the enclosure *207 Lower Bartons* which is subdivided by the road to become tithe *322 Upper Bartons* and *327 Lower Bartons*, preserving the field-name.

Many other names apparently changed slightly, though in fact pronunciation may not have been very different. The area names of *Walton Brook* and *Huntliss* became *Wolton* and *Huntleys* respectively. An interesting survival is in the *-dine* names, possibly denoting an original *-wardine* name, which may indicate an enclosure. These all change to *-den*, which could give an indication of dialect. The boundaries do not change for enclosure *613 Boyardine* to tithe *221 Boyarden, 643 Millerdine* to *102 Millerden*, and *838 Nordine* to *108 Nordens*. However, *862/863 Nordines Pens* became *103 The Pens*, and *373 Harsadine* became *167 Hasarden*. These survivals are all the more surprising in that they are the only examples of these names except for a second *614 Boyadines*, which was lost on the tithe as the subsequent larger field became *222 Little Normandy*, taking its name from another component field.

The greatest chance for a name to be lost is if it only applied to a single field, such as enclosure *624 Cinderbury*, which also became part of a larger field. The name indicates the possibility of Roman finds, as discussed in the Woolhope *Transactions* 1996. Another probable Roman site is easier to locate as the four enclosure *Streetsend* fields amalgamated into the one *240 Streets end* field on the tithe and the name was retained. The Iron Age hillfort of Oldbury was known as *349 Camp Field Allotment*, with each field on the side of the hill being known as *Oldbury Hill Allotment* in 1797. By 1839

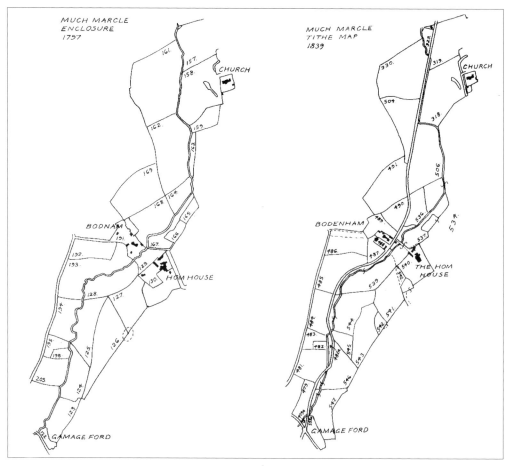

Figure 2. A comparison between the 1797 enclosure map of Much Marcle and the 1839 tithe map showing the new names and the new road.

a name change has apparently occurred. *Camp* survives but *Oldbury* fields have changed to *Woburg*, (Fig. 3 and Pl. 1) which could reflect pronunciation, or could be a deliberate translation perhaps in compliment to Queen Victoria. It would be interesting to investigate further.

The unusual *Beargains*, which was two fields, *277* and *264*, in 1797, survived in the one field *455* in 1839. Indeed, most distinctive field-names did survive though the chances were maximised if several fields in an area were involved. The group of thirteen 1797 *Puredine* fields all became part of the three fields with the same name in 1839, though one had become *Purden*. Exactly the same pattern occurred for the 1797 *Normandy* fields, though these too were reduced in number but not in area (Fig. 4). Such field-names, which appear to have altered relatively little, may be traceable in earlier documents, so proving their age as the first use predates the earliest document.

In Much Marcle a group of about 150 deeds for the thirteenth and fourteenth centuries has survived and is housed in the Herefordshire Record Office (G/37/11) where Sue Hubbard has translated them. These are transactions between the lord of the manor and his tenants, later called copyholders, and between the tenants themselves.

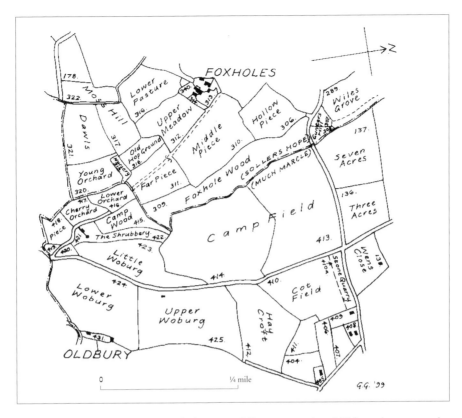

Figure 3 (above) and Plate 1 (below). Oldbury Iron Age hillfort shown on the Much Marcle tithe map and as an aerial photograph, where the ditch can still be seen as a cropmark on the south, while on the north it is marked by a hedge. The photograph was used as the backdrop when the British Archaeological Award was presented to the Herefordshire Field-Name Survey at York in 1994.

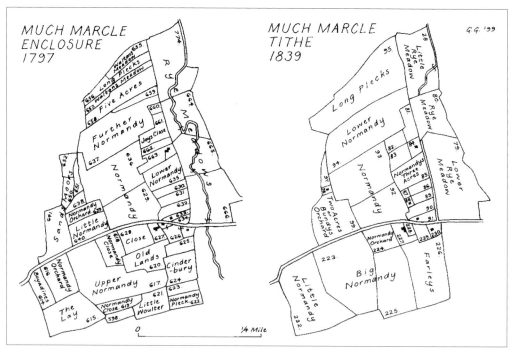

Figure 4. A comparison between the 1797 enclosure map of Much Marcle and the 1839 tithe map showing the *Normandy* fields. The original medieval field area can be deduced.

They were designed to facilitate exchanges of land in the common fields, which in some instances also allowed block holdings to be formed. Names of fields are given. In a deed dated 'At Marcle, the morrow of the Assumption. B.V.M. 2 Edward II' (16 August 1308) Walter, son of William le Taylur sold, for 30s – though subject to the chief lord in fees by usual services – to Adam Grimle and Agnes his wife, one acre of land 'in the field called *Normondi'*. This is spelled *Normandy* on the back.

The name recurs in 1335 (*Normandie*), 1337 (*Normandie/Normade*), 1339 (*Normandie/Normandi*), 1340 (*Normandie*), another in 1340 (*Normandie/Normandi*), 1346 (*Normandye*) and 1491 (*Normandie*). In each deed strips are being referred to and their positions are given. The 1491 deed refers to 5 acres and *Joys Green* that are in the field called *Normandie*, which shows that at least some of the strips within the larger fields had their own independent field-names. *Normandy* can therefore be traced back 489 years to 1308 and it had evidently been in use for far longer.

Linedown occurs in an area defined by roads and illustrates very clearly that it is advisable to find the earliest spelling of a field-name before trying to deduce its probable meaning, though if none is available pronouncing the name can suggest – and it is stressed, no more than that – various possibilities. In fact the Much Marcle deeds include an undated deed referring to land called *La Lynde*, in 1333 (*Le/La Lyndens*), 1354 (*Le Lyndende*), 1359 (*Lyndemedowe*), and 1395 (*Lyndens*). The name could have meant hill with flax, or lime-trees, growing on it, but the earlier spellings show the derivation is from lime-trees. Lime-trees, even more than oak, are indicators of ancient woodland. Felling probably started as early as the neolithic, as farmers knew that limes grew on fertile soil. This survival in Much Marcle is likely to have been because the site is on a hill. The ancient woodland lasted into the medieval period, long enough to give the field its distinctive name.

The 1797 award included *288 Linedown*, a narrow strip-shaped field, though the name was also attached to the irregularly shaped field to the west as *282 Linedown Field Allotment*. By 1839, *288* and part of *282* had become *470 The 4 acres*, while the rest of *282* had become *459 The Great Harp*, from its new shape. The only boundary changes were internal. Adjoining these fields, in 1797, was *283 The seven acres* and north of this was *284 Upper Linedown Field Allotment* which were amalgamated by 1839 to become *460 The 8 acres*. North of *284* was *259 Upper Linedown Field Allotment*, which became incorporated into two other fields and lost the name. In the same area was *258 Linedown Field Allotment* which became subdivided into two fields by 1839, the southern of which was *466 Lying Down Piece*. Part of the 1797 field *256 New-house Homestead and Home Close* became *473 Lying Down Orchard*. West of *283* was the larger *278 Little Marcle Field Allotment* and this retained the same boundaries in 1839 becoming *456 Lying Down*. The *287 Smiths Forge Slingate and Orchard* became *468 The Lying Down* and *286 A Close* became *46 Lying Down Piece*.

Linedown had become *Lying Down* because this was the more easily understood by the occupier or by the scribe. Perhaps this is simply what the scribe thought he heard. Reference to the published maps of the Herefordshire Field-Name Survey will clarify the above. It is clear that in 1797 there were five fields called *Linedown*, and in 1839 there were five called *Lying Down*. Of these only one half of one *Linedown* field became a *Lying Down* field. This does make the point that a field-name can originally be attached to a larger area and that when a field was subdivided, or changes made, the name can become attached to the 'wrong' portion or even to an adjacent field. Therefore, it is useful to examine a group of fields rather than just one field. However, the name *Linedown* was not forgotten but became attached to an adjacent area. On the modern OS map *Lyne Down* is now an area name south-east at the old *Gamage Ford*.

Some names change because they were so common and yet the term went out of use, an example being *messuage* which proliferates on the enclosure award. The tithe has *cottage* in great numbers. The two fields, *531, 549*, called *Monkfield* became *277 Walk Field*, while *571 Windmill* became *252 The Stocking lands*. Of the fifty-five *Close* names in 1797 only one survived when *721 Green Close* became *47 The Close and Homestead*. For the first time *America* appeared, in 1839, for a field at a distance from the farm; it took a long time to reach. Some names changed for economic reasons so the several *stone pits* of 1797 disappear, presumably worked out, while new, more formally named, *quarries* are found in 1839. An interesting example of the way names changed can be seen in *202 Public Stone Pit*, which was next to *201 Island Meadow*, three roads forming these into a triangular island. By 1839 the former stone pit was only separated by a dotted line on the map from, and so incorporated into, *477 The Island and Garden*, the latter name persisting even though the road now only ran on two sides, not three. Similarly the 1797 *49 Stone Pit* and *48 Barn and Yard* had become, by 1839, *614 Barn and Fold*. The three 1797 fields of *The Ship and Castle*, *219, 220* and *221*, had become, by 1839, one field and while it was still a public house the name had changed to *325 Wallwyn Arms Inn Garden and Paddock*, preserving the three original components. The new name commemorated Edward Wallwyn, owner of *Hellens*, and the prime mover behind the enclosure.

A name that, if it survives, changes little is *Old Lands*, which refers to newly ploughed land and is considered a name for the medieval strip. This can suggest the presence of open-field farming which can be deduced from names such as *North*, or *Upper, Field*;

Middle Field; South, or *Lower, Field*; or from fields which retain the shape of an open-field and have a joint name. However, there are three *Old Lands* on the 1797 enclosure award and three on the 1839 tithe map. Of these only the enclosure *190 Old Lands* remained exactly the same becoming *493 Old Lands,* and *38 Old Lands Orchard* became *605 Old Lands Orchard.* The *704 Old Ground* also remained the same becoming *242 Old Ground.* The enclosure *620 Old Lands* lost its name when it was divided, half becoming *225 Big Normandy,* a group name which in itself is of interest. The other tithe *436 Old Lands* name is far more inexplicable as in 1797 it was *271 The two Acres.* The name may have been an alternative because it is strange that such a name came into use at such a late date. Nevertheless, this does demonstrate that even an apparently early name can only serve as a possible indicator and that other evidence needs to be found before reaching concrete conclusions. Researchers need to be cautious in interpretation.

FIELD-NAMES DENOTING SIZE

Most field-names are descriptive of the quality of the soil, type of vegetation, agricultural practice, shape or size. Of these the least examined are those reflecting size. In 1797 Much Marcle had *467 The four Lands* which was a very specific name. This does suggest far more definition than just a vague term for cultivated land. Although prehistoric fields did survive, and it is possible that even 'celtic' fields can be seen on the Wigmore and Orcop tithe maps, medieval farming especially in the midlands was organised into the open-field system. Each of the large open-fields was divided into strips which were worked using ridge-and-furrow, probably to facilitate drainage and to save at least the half of the crop on the ridges if the soil became waterlogged. Ridge-and-furrow was the agricultural method, not the size, and was not restricted to the open-fields. Excavations at Hen Domen in Montgomeryshire (reported in the paper by P. A. Barker and J. Lawson, 'A pre-Norman field system at Hen Domen, Montgomery', in *Medieval Archaeology XV*, 1971, 58-72) have shown ridge-and-furrow to lie underneath, and therefore to be older than, this Norman motte-and-bailey. So the local people subjugated by the Normans would seem to have continued farming in their traditional way.

By the thirteenth century the open-fields were established and it was probably on the central plain of Herefordshire where villages used the system. The divisions within the open-fields can be hard to find as the strips could be separated by marker stones, or by undug paths called baulks. These were necessary because a villager's strips would not be together, to share the better quality soil, and in some places could be allocated differently in different years. Boundaries were the subject of complaints in the manorial courts. When the open-field system ended, some strips were preserved by becoming hedged fields. There were several names for strips, *land* was one of them, and a field-name such as *The four Lands* suggests a hedged field comprising four strips. A name given to a holding of about 30 acres, or 12 hectares, was *yardland* and it is possible that some *old lands* fields are corruptions of this name. Parallel strips in the open-fields were in blocks called *furlongs*, meaning that the area was bounded by the length of a furrow, which became defined as a furrow in a 10-acre field. This survived at Much Marcle, in 1797, as *386 Furlong below Harrolds Allotment.* However, by 1839 this field was divided into two and only one half, *356,* continued to retain the name, showing that the measurement no longer applied. A *fall* was a fortieth part of a *furlong.* Another possible size name in 1797 was *119 Farthingdown* (*down* meaning hill). This name may be concerned with copyhold descending to a youngest son, or daughter, but it also seems to have been a considerable measure of land. By 1839 this field became half of *548* and the name was lost.

Strips varied greatly in length and some up to a mile have been recognised. However, a plough team was considered to be able to work an acre strip measuring 220 yards by 22 yards in width in one day. Although an English acre was first defined in 1305 as being 160 perches, terms such as *furlong, fall, acre,* and other similar names, continued to be measured differently in different parts of the country being based as they were on the area of land that could be worked in a day. However, a standard size of each acre containing 4,840 square yards (yard here bearing no size relation to *yardland*) was enshrined in law in 1878. The tithe commissioners surveyed to a standard measure but it is interesting that the measurement of a field does not always correspond with its field-name. *Twelve acres* is not necessarily that size.

The Herefordshire tithes show evidence of an unsuspected conservatism. The secretary hand which was presumed to have died out can still be found in a number of the parish tithes, as in the court rolls. In the same way local measurements persisted. *The Court Rolls of Ewyas Lacy, 1729–1858* I (HRO J 91/1) provide examples in the agreements:

1750, Michael Church Eskley –
…Rough piece or parcel [another name for a strip] of pasture and wood and a little meadow now in the possession of James Thomas as Tenant to the said Lord abergavenny Containing in the whole by Estimation Sixteen English Acres be it more or less…

1767, Michael Church Eskley –
…All the said Twelve Acres of Customary Lands Welsh Measure with the Appurtenances…

1770, Crasswell –
…All those Nine Acres of Customary Land Welsh Measure Situate lying and being Juxta Keven (Welsh cefn) bach in the Township of Crasswell in the parish of Clodock…

According to Jowitt, customary acres could be the Irish Acre of 7,840 square yards, the Scottish Acre of 6,150 and two-fifths square yards, and the Welsh Acre of 9,680 square yards. This is a generalisation as there were considerable variations, the area being the land ploughed in a day. The Welsh acre is pertinent for Herefordshire. In Breconshire the acre was a quarter of an English acre, in Merionethshire and Montgomeryshire it was 2,430 square yards, while in Anglesey and parts of Caernarvonshire it was as much as 3,240 square yards. The Welsh word for acre was *cyfair* and appears first in 1200. However, *erw*, which sometimes seems to have equated with the English *bovate*, the amount one ox could plough in a year (about 10 to 18 acres), later became equated with acre too. Such difficulties of translation, together with variable plough-time being taken on different soils, could explain these huge discrepancies. They could also explain the need for the term the larger Welsh acre which can be found, and which was considered to be more than the English acre. Herefordshire's customary Welsh acre is certainly different from the standard tithe measurement. It is possible that Herefordshire, like Cornwall and other parts of England, also had its own local customary acre, which could be revealed by a survey showing which numbers appear regularly as field-names. An analysis of acreage field-names, comparing them to the specified tithe measurements, could provide evidence for both the Welsh customary acre and the existence of a local customary acre.

CONCLUSION

Field-name analysis can provide a wealth of evidence about life in the past. Individual field-names can be analysed (as in the 1996 Woolhope *Transactions*) to suggest meanings. This paper has suggested further ways field-names could be examined. In Herefordshire, the extent of Welsh influence could be determined by acreage size and by recognising the anglicised spelling of Welsh field-names given verbally. Dialect is demonstrated by field-names such as the distribution of *plock* versus *pleck,* a small field near the farm; few parishes have both spellings and this could indicate connections with neighbouring counties. Topographical field-names can show evidence for the changing landscape. Indeed, field-names provide a wide research base precisely because they were so useful in the past, giving a reliable method of recording information and passing it to future generations. All the evidence points to a high proportion being early in date and continuing in use even if no longer understood. The reason for a field-name must always predate its first use for that particular field so it is advisable to try to trace the earliest record, remembering that the area around a field could be involved in the designation.

Field-names are a 'first step', an indicator that an area is worth further investigation and, therefore, the fields need to be located. Although the modern loss of hedgerows

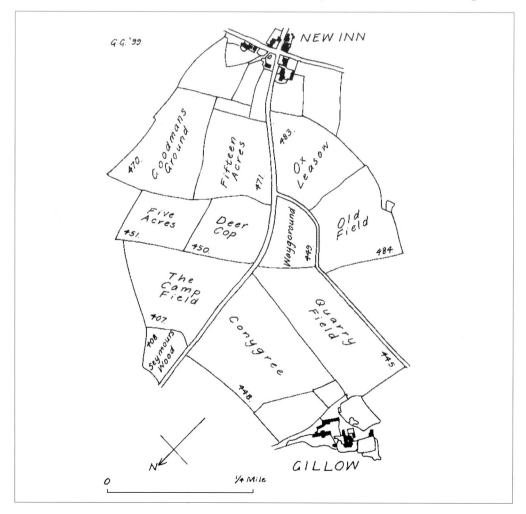

across England and Wales has been enormous, with 119,000 miles disappearing between 1984 and 1993, it is usually possible to see where hedges used to grow. The sites show as dark lines which can be seen on aerial photographs and from higher ground. Also by looking along the base of any existing boundary hedge it is possible to see the rise in the ground level where another hedge used to meet it at right angles. In early thirteenth-century grants to Dore Abbey fields were laid out by building a dyke around them to enclose them. The ditch was the important boundary mark as the internal hedge took a little time to grow and thicken. In time the hedges would extend into some of the ditches, but a ditch or a hole is a permanent feature as it will never have the same fill as the ground on either side. The size of field is governed by the method of agriculture and the type of equipment employed but even in modern prairie fields the sites of former hedgerows can often be discerned. In this way the pattern of fields not only provides evidence of early use, but can also be compared to early maps and the sites of particular fields located.

Figure 5 (left) and Plate 2 (above). Gaer Cop, Hentland, shown on the Hentland tithe map and on an aerial photograph (reference 99-MB-0930) taken facing south, on 15 March 1999. The photograph reveals the defensive enclosure of the Iron Age hillfort with traces of a possible second line of defence in the foreground. The tithe map shows the field-names of *Old Field*, *Deer Cop* (a corruption of *Gaer Cop*) and *The Camp Field* (very common for hillforts). The central *Way go round* is bounded by the curved road in the hillfort ditch. *Coneygree* shows this is another hillfort used to breed rabbits in the medieval period. The photograph was taken as part of the Millennium Air Survey of Herefordshire.

A researcher can, therefore, examine a particular field-name to find if it is always attached to a field with the same topography. Features of significance could help to suggest the meaning of some names. Areas can be examined. Such research is viable in any country where names have been used. Indeed, a data base of such information, that could be easily augmented by other individuals, would be invaluable. There is still an incredible amount of information to be learned from field-names. They have all been important to farmers in the past and some are even indicators of archaeological and historical remains. Field-names are a direct link with the past and as such are an invaluable resource.

ACKNOWLEDGEMENTS

I am most grateful to Sue Hubbard and the staff of the Herefordshire Record Office and to Raymond B. Davies, assistant librarian of the National Library of Wales. I am also grateful to Geoff Gwatkin for re-drawing the tithe maps and to Howard Dudley for the aerial photograph of Oldbury Iron Age hillfort, and to Chris Musson for the aerial photograph of Gaer Cop. (Fig. 5 and Pl. 2)

BIBLIOGRAPHY

The Herefordshire Field-Name Survey, general editor and co-ordinator, Ruth E. Richardson, published transcripts of the tithe maps and field-names, copies available in HRO.

TWNFC, older field-names are given from XLV (1987), 752-760 and in succeeding *Transactions*. The *Transactions for* 1996 gives an analysis of field-names.

R. E. Richardson, 'The Herefordshire Field-Name Survey', *Current Archaeology*, no.145, Nov., 1995.

R. E. Richardson, 'Field-names: An Underused Resource', *Local History Magazine*, no.52, Nov.-Dec., 1995.

H. D. G. Foxall, *Shropshire Field-Names* (1980).

S. Beckensall, *Northumberland Field Names*.

R. & N. Muir, *Fields* (1989).

M. Aston, 'Shapwick', *Current Archaeology*, No.151, Feb.1997.

A. T. Bannister, *The Place-Names of Herefordshire* (1916).

B. Coplestone-Crow, *Herefordshire Place-Names*, BAR British Series 214 (1989).

J. Field, *Place-Names of Great Britain and Ireland* (1980).

M. Gelling, *Place-Names in the Landscape* (1984).

E. Jowitt, (ed.), *The Dictionary of English Law* - N.B. the number of sq. yds. in an acre is mistakenly given as 4,480.

R. Shoesmith and R. E. Richardson, *A Definitive History of Dore Abbey* (1997).

NB: *The Millenium Air Survey of Herefordshire* arose as a direct result of *The Herefordshire Field-Name Survey* and the aerial photographs, taken by Chris Musson, can be seen in HRO.

Herefordshire Archives:
the Clerks and Custodians

BRIAN S. SMITH

In an illiterate society the testimony of the spoken word before witnesses is taken as sufficient proof of authenticity. The practice lingers on. To this day a verbal deal may be completed with a handshake and the minutes of the Woolhope Club are not signed until they have been read aloud and approved by those who witnessed the proceedings. Yet well before the Norman conquest royal and ecclesiastical clerks were producing writs, tax records and land-charters to collect their masters' dues and protect their rights, like the sixteen charters of Herefordshire, the earliest dating from between 510 and 540, relating to properties of the church of Llandaff.[1] However, it was not until the twelfth century that the superiority of the written record over the spoken word became widely recognised.[2] Charters of bishops Robert de Béthune (1131-48) and Robert Foliot (1173-86) specifically refer to the need to confirm grants by committing them to writing owing to the failings of human memory.[3] In order to deal with the growing complexity of diocesan bureaucracy the bishops were by the end of the century establishing a regular chancery of their own scribes to replace the cathedral clergy they had previously employed.[4] At that date even the greatest baronial magnates did not have chanceries. They either expected a monastery receiving a grant of property from them to write the charter or they employed any available chaplain or scribe. In the twenty-two years between his coming of age about 1121 and his death in 1143 Miles Earl of Hereford issued at least ten such charters.[5]

The surviving local records from such feudal sources are almost entirely conveyances of property, usually sought by the recipients as evidence of their rights. The dean and chapter accumulated deeds of the endowments of St Ethelbert's hospital from c1225 and deeds of the Scudamores of Kentchurch and Walwyns of Much Marcle survive from the late thirteenth century.[6] More unusual are the scattered letters written by Bishop Gilbert Foliot (1148-63) but this correspondence is more a literary compilation put together in his own lifetime as an opponent of Becket than an archive of letters dispatched.[7] With laymen of all ranks illiterate and unable to sign their names deeds were authenticated by applying seals, a practice that filtered slowly down from the Norman royal chancery. The dean and chapter were using a seal by c1190 and the mayor of Hereford's seal is listed in the first inventory of the city's treasures in 1475, its earlier existence being implicit in Henry III's grant of return of writs to the city in 1256.[8] By then seals were owned by quite modest freeholders, including women, and it was sufficiently unusual in 1291 for a man of substance not to have a seal for John de Mosewell's need to borrow one to be recorded.[9]

If both ecclesiastical and lay feudal landowners demanded written record of their property rights the Crown's priority was for evidence to assist the collection of taxes and the administration of justice. Post-conquest financial bureaucracy began in the royal exchequer with Domesday Book and the annual pipe rolls from 1129-30, though an experiment in the 1160s, probably by Thomas Brown, the king's almoner and a considerable Herefordshire landowner, to bring the Domesday Book up-to-date did not proceed beyond Herefordshire.[10] Royal control over the kingdom's finances extended to checks on money-lending and therefore from 1194 upon Jewish scribes and their loan-agreements.[11] Similarly, it is no accident that the earliest surviving Hereford city archives are the murage rolls of 1263, recording the collection of the local tax for the upkeep of the city walls, and the bailiff's account rolls from 1272. From 1276 these include payments for the parchment on which the accounts were written.[12] The cathedral's earliest surviving account rolls begin in 1273, shortly before Bishop Thomas de Cantilupe introduced controls over his official revenues.[13] Personal accounts, like those of Cantilupe's last journey to Rome in 1282 and the fine household accounts for 1289-90 of his successor, Richard de Swinfield, are more unusual.[14]

If the twelfth century had been the era for creating records the thirteenth century was that of preserving them safely. Leominster priory copied its charters into a cartulary about 1260, Bishop Peter d'Aigueblanche codified the dean and chapter's record-keeping in the first statutes of the cathedral c1262 and Thomas de Cantilupe began recording his principal episcopal documents in the first of a series of bishops' registers in 1275 and a volume of estate surveys in 1285.[15] The county records remained the responsibility of the principal royal official, the sheriff, and such few records as were not transmitted to the exchequer in London would therefore have been kept at Hereford castle. The records of the royal justices in eyre were similarly kept in London but the records of the lower courts were retained locally. The rolls of Hereford's mayor's court begin in 1275, the bishops' consistory court in 1407, the borough courts of Pembridge in 1433 and Leominster in 1524; and among manorial court rolls Pencombe's from 1303 are some of the earliest.[16] The burgesses of Hereford, who took opportunities to extend their privileges from financially hard-pressed monarchs, had these recorded with increasing sumptuousness and expense in royal charters and they were careful to record their rights, precedents and treasures in a custumal and inventories which were kept up-to-date.[17]

The protective merits of bound books and registers encouraged the compilation of cartularies, especially among monastic houses in the fourteenth and fifteenth centuries. The earlier cartularies of Leominster priory and its parent house, Reading abbey, were imitated in the early fourteenth century by St Guthlac's and Wormsley priories from the early fourteenth century as well by St Katherine's hospital, Ledbury and the Mortimer family c1300.[18] The Mortimer cartularies, two rolls and the great Black Book of Wigmore cataloguing some 2,000 deeds, were particularly skilfully arranged and indexed with references to the leather bags, baskets and wooden chests in which the archives were stored.[19] Chests, the usual storage for a quantity of documents, had been placed for security in the cathedral's chapter house since at least 1276, and one thirteenth-century and two later medieval chests remain on display in the south cloister, and, by contrast, by Hereford's Jewish community from at least 1220.[20]

The records were valued and used for the practical purposes for which they had been created. The bishops' registers were scrutinised for evidence, for example in 1419 to prove to the exchequer which churches in the diocese were exempt from

enth.[21] Thefts occurred, Bishop Thomas de Cantilupe threatening
municate anyone who had taken away charters or other muniments,
re made, sometimes 'officially' to provide written evidence which
ad gone missing.[22] Hereford city's charter of 1399 from Richard II
l contemporary forgery of a genuine document which is otherwise
n its enrolled text on the chancery charter rolls.[23] Bishop Thomas
e precaution of examining, handling and carefully inspecting a papal
to him by Richard Clifford, abbot of Dore, to ensure its authenticity
transcribed.[24] Although little is known about the men who wrote
ome medieval scribes at the cathedral have been identified and it is a
where the last witness to a medieval deed is described as a clerk that
r.[25] The fees paid to Hereford's town clerk appear in the bailiff's
d of the thirteenth century.[26] The qualifications of William Bourdoun
ted to his office by presentation of pen, ink and parchment, were set
f appointment by Bishop John de Trilleck in 1345.[27]

trative reforms, the effects of the Reformation and the spread of
l an immense proliferation of new records. Documents which had
rarely in the bishops' registers now accrued in separate series, for
ory court papers, probate records and clerical and other licences and
sociated with the Elizabethan church settlement. The dean and
ng series of act books begins in 1512 but perhaps the most familiar
urred at the lowest administrative level of the parish.[28] Stoke Edith
eformation churchwardens' accounts from 1533, Madley's accounts
d among seventeenth-century accounts are those of Hentland, All
rd and Leominster.[29] The introduction of parish registers in 1538
gorous requirements of the 1598 ordinance for their maintenance,
ekeeping are reflected in the registers of many parishes. Pencombe
the only original paper parish register in Herefordshire surviving
ing, although its first three folios of entries before 1542 are missing.
pied from the beginning in 1598, for example at Bromyard and
t Colwall the first register, which was copied only from 1553, is
decorative initial letters.[30] The well-known but rarely published
8 was written out at Ledbury, where the paper register survives from
e, however, no early civil parish records created under the Highways
Poor Laws of 1597 and 1601, and Herefordshire's small towns and
he later voluminous poor law papers commonly found in more
; these survive in quantity only in Bromyard.[32]

oration of minutes, accounts and jurisdictional records evolved among
Hereford city, incorporated in 1597, and Leominster borough, incor-
as it emerged from the control of the priory.[33] Private archives
eeds and manorial court rolls, but estate records, accounts and
remain relatively scarce in Herefordshire before the civil war, the
tion being that of the Harley family of Brampton Bryan.[34] The
ngton school, dating from 1632, are noteworthy.[35] Such great
attached to written evidence in this period of massive social and
nge that deeds were commonly called 'evidences'. Consequently, the
d early seventeenth centuries were a peak of good archive keeping. It
ic of the period that Sir John Prise, visitor to the monasteries, book-
istorian, should maintain a careful rental of his Herefordshire

BOOK SIGNING

Cambridge-based Dr Roger French, much the furthest flung of our contributors, is caught up in a busy academic term as a lecturer at the university and, despite a strong wish to come to Hereford for the signing of *A Herefordshire Miscellany*, has found it impossible to get away in the time frame between receipt of the books from the printer and the commencement of their distribution. Lapridge Publications regret the lack of his signature and hope that subscribers will understand that it was always going to be difficult to assemble twenty-one busy people at precisely the time they were needed, particularly someone based as far away as Dr French.

property from the date of its acquisition.[36] On a grander scale Swithin Butterfield, deputy surveyor to Bishop John Scory, spent three years in researching and compiling his splendid survey of the episcopal estates, running to some 250 well-written folios completed in October 1581. He inserted practical advice and exhortations to his successors to keep his work up-to-date, claiming proudly of his own research:

> If that I have erred, Correct me with skyll:
> Before you amende me unto your wyll,
> See Courte Role, & Rentrole, which warranted mee:
> And th[e]n doe I thinck, small error wilbee.[37]

The cathedral's Elizabethan statutes of 1583 required the appointment of a keeper of the archives, a duty which in the parishes was laid upon the churchwardens but in practice fell to the parish clerk.[38] At Pencombe the churchwardens noted in 1561 that they wrote the entries in the register; at Hentland in 1633-4 the churchwardens 'paid for writing a Copie of the Register booke in parchment, xiid.' (the annual bishop's transcript); at Yarkhill the inhabitants agreed in 1629 on an assessment to pay the parish clerk's wages and at Yarpole in 1635 John Lugger, a former yeoman of the guard at the Tower of London, was paid to copy the old register book beginning in 1561.[39] Like many other registers, the initial copy and succeeding entries are neatly written in a good secretary hand but the quality of the handwriting deteriorates later in the seventeenth century.

Hereford's charter of incorporation had required the appointment of a town clerk, a post held with that of custos rotulorum. In the county the importance of the medieval royal office of sheriff declined as the Tudors enlarged the administrative duties of the magistrates sitting in quarter sessions. But the magistrates were not a corporate body, so their sole official, the clerk of the peace, became responsible for the growing quantities of quarter sessions archives under the remote supervision of the lord lieutenant, who was also custos rotulorum of the county records. These archives, however, did not survive the civil war.

Accompanying these changes were improvements in storage. Parchment continued to be preferred over paper for all formal records, like deeds and court rolls and for such new ones as parish registers and bishop's transcripts. Paper came into use from the early fifteenth century for less formal business and personal documents, such as accounts and letters. Exceptionally, a letter among the archives in the case for Bishop Thomas Cantilupe's canonisation was written from Avignon on Spanish paper dating from 1308 or soon afterwards, and perhaps the earliest surviving paper document written in Herefordshire is a letter from the prior of Wormsley to the bishop in 1385.[40] Paper is, of course, more convenient to make and use than parchment but less durable. Butterfield had noted in 1580 that the bishop's White Book of rentals made c1517 'beinge wrytten but in paper, is now almoste worne in peeces'.[41] When the Reverend Richard Wynter appointed trustees for his charity to relieve the poor of Stoke Edith, Tarrington and other parishes in 1599 he endorsed the deed 'I have sent to you on[e] part of my deede, hoping that you will have a care that it be saffely kepte, and also desiring my good frindes to take copies thereof that if this deed be lost, that then the poore be not deprived of this my smale gifte'.[42] Chests remained the most suitable storage for small quantities of records in both private houses and parish churches, the inventory of All Saints, Hereford in 1638, for

Plate 1. The fourteenth-century parish chest of All Saints, Hereford. (The Vicar and Parochial Church Council of All Saints, Hereford). *Photo: Derek Foxton*

instance, including 'One Register booke of parchment, One blacke boxe to putt writinges in, Three old Chestes all havinge lockes and Certaine old evidences of the church in one of them'[43] (Pl. I). Bishop Matthew Wren's visitation articles of 1635 asked parishes whether they had a chest for the church books and ornaments, whether in it they had both a parchment register of christenings, marriages and burials, written and kept in all points according to the canon, with a transcript sent annually to the bishop's registry, a paper register of preachers, and also a glebe terrier with a copy sent to the registry 'there to continue for a perpetuall memory'.[44] Leominster borough also kept its archives in a chest at this period.[45]

Larger collections demanded more elaborate arrangements. Hereford corporation had, most unusually, since at least 1533 been bundling its annual accumulation of records in sheepskin sacks which cost only a few pence.[46] Inventories from 1475 reveal that the city's valuables, including the custumal and other volumes, were checked as they passed from mayor to mayor.[47] The failure of the master and wardens of the Tailors' Company to hand on archives at the end of their term of office brought threat of a heavy fine in 1610.[48] At the cathedral after the Reformation the chamber over the north transept was used as a muniment room for the dean and chapter's archives (and perhaps much earlier for it possesses the characteristics of medieval muniment rooms) and the Booth porch housed the diocesan archives from at least 1615. About 1630 the dean and chapter augmented the old chests in the chapter house by constructing in the muniment room the first of two presses of eighty

Plate 2. The capsules or archive cupboards, *c*1630, at Hereford Cathedral. (The Dean and Chapter of Hereford Cathedral).
Photo: F. C. Morgan

archive cupboards, remarkable early archival furniture probably derived from examples at Oxford[49] (Pl. 2).

The civil war led to losses, revealed more by the absence of pre-Restoration records, like the county quarter sessions archives, than by specific known instances of destruction. The dean and chapter's archives were confiscated by Parliament and despatched to London, the current chapter act book being lost in the process, perhaps because it remained concealed in Hereford. The antiquary and Parliamentarian officer, Silas Taylor, is reputed to have ransacked the cathedral library, but there is no firm evidence that he did more than make his own extensive research notes.[50] Both the register and commonplace book of Bishop Charles Booth were in the hands of collectors by *c*1700, the latter volume through the agency of the bishop's registrar, David Walker.[51]

At the Restoration the cathedral archives, recovered from London, rearranged and catalogued, were used to regain the dean and chapter's control of their property and affairs.[52] The parish clergy were reinstated and their registers renewed in the old style, though many Herefordshire parish registers continue relatively uninterrupted through the Commonwealth period, even at Pencombe where the parishioners had got themselves in a tangle over the appointment of a civil 'register' in 1653-4. They had somewhat hastily selected Philip Andrews 'haveinge not much choise of men able & capable of that place' before they knew the terms of the Act of Parliament for the appointment. So then they chose Thomas Burghope, who was sworn into office by a magistrate. But again they were mistaken in their choice and 'because neyther the said Phillip Andrewes nor the said Thomas Burghope are clarks sufficient for that worke, We have intreated Thomas Eaton thelder gent to keepe the Register booke in his hands; And to assist the said Thomas Burghope in the Certifyinge and registeringe', a task which he performed neatly until his death in 1657.[53]

The Crown's administration of justice in assize and county quarter sessions was also resumed. The quarter sessions archives were housed within the remains of Hereford castle, the only crown property available for their storage. The gatehouse was to be made fit for the purpose in 1674, though four years later the magistrates were still ordering 'That the Old gate of the Castle be repayred and fitted for the publicke Records of the County'[54] (Pl. 3). The rebuilt house was broken into in 1690

Plate 3. Castle Cliffe House, Castle Green, Hereford, the repository for the county archives from *c*1680 to 1817.   *Photo: Derek Foxton*

and in 1709 the clerk of the peace employed 'Workmen and paid for Boardes & other necessaries for the preventing the boys from breaking into the Record Room'.[55] The magistrates' intermittent concern for the protection of their archives surfaced in 1753 when the clerk of the peace and three magistrates were ordered to 'look over & inspect the Papers Parchm[en]ts &c in the County Court House' and report back at the next sessions; but there is no further reference to the matter.[56] Hereford's charter of re-incorporation of 1682, like those of other towns, ceded to the crown the right to confirm the appointment of steward, aldermen and town clerk, a loss of freedom recovered in 1697.[57] The corporation bought an expensive but secure iron chest for its valuables in 1737, probably for monies and plate but also for the custumal and other treasured volumes, and seems to have kept archives in the Tolsey until its demolition in 1770-1.[58] At Leominster the arrival of Charles II's charter from London was hailed in a triumphal procession through the streets, with John Stead, the town clerk, 'sitting on horseback and carrying the charter opened on his breast'.[59] The town's archives were in the custody of the town clerk, who was scrupulous in recording when a document was removed and returned to the archive chest.[60] In the early eighteenth-century disputes with Lord Coningsby the charters were sent to London in 1721 to support the borough's case and then remained in the hands of Edward Harley who, as recorder, had successfully led Leominster's defence of its privileges. His letter returning them to the town in 1733 was still tucked in the chamber book, undisturbed, in 1998.[61] The chamber book from 1665-80 also fell into private hands, being returned to the borough in 1743 and placed in the press or cupboard that had been fitted in the council chamber in the Court House (Forebury Chapel) in 1724.[62]

The pace of change and inexorable increase of official records accelerated in the last decades of the eighteenth century, driven by the statutory requirements to register a growing variety of documents with the clerk of the peace – for oaths of allegiance, window and land taxes, alehouses, parliamentary electors, inclosure awards, friendly societies and public schemes for canals, turnpike roads and, later, railways. From the turn of the century the clerk of the peace began keeping precedent books, memoranda books and all sorts of lists to guide him through this documentary jungle.[63] Unsurprisingly, therefore, when the new Shire Hall was planned in 1814 one of the requirements was 'A Building for the Archives of the County'; Smirke's design of 1817 duly incorporated a records room of 24 x 12 feet.[64] There is, of course, a corresponding increase of official records in the Public Record Office and House of Lords Record Office that relate to local affairs but which, like the medieval archives of chancery and exchequer, lie outside the scope of this survey.[65] But it was parliamentary concern for the proper conduct of marriages in 1754 and the recording of baptisms and burials in 1812 that brought new printed forms of parish registers and, in 1812, the order for every parish to have an iron chest in which to keep them. Several of these heavy, airtight and fireproof chests survive in Herefordshire churches, for example at Bromyard, Monkland, Thruxton and Vowchurch. The chest at Kimbolton was made at Coalbrookdale and the one at neighbouring Middleton-on-the-Hill cost £6 16s 8d, more than one-fifth of the parish's expenditure for that year.[66] Similarly, parliamentary reforms of the poor law in 1834 and municipal government in 1835 began the whole process of change in local government and its archives, which has continued remorselessly ever since.

The archives of corporate bodies and private individuals mostly lay outside such statutory control and their survival in Herefordshire has been haphazard. The dean and chapter gave up appointing a keeper of archives in 1783 but their records reflect changes in the management of their estates until they lost control of some of them to the Ecclesiastical Commission appointed in 1835.[67] Records relating to the nonconformist churches in Herefordshire are scanty before the mid-nineteenth century with the notable exception of the Quakers, always careful to record their sufferings and proceedings; the Almeley meeting's accounts and sufferings date from 1678 and 1692 respectively.[68] By the end of the seventeenth century Herefordshire landowners, like Dunne of Gatley, Foley of Stoke Edith, Harley of Brampton Bryan, Knight of Downton, Scudamore of Holme Lacy, had begun keeping their estate papers to add to the older muniments of title and manorial court rolls. The quantity increased considerably throughout the eighteenth century. Among these archives the business papers of the Foley family's ironworks in Worcestershire and west Gloucestershire are exceptional. The archives of the Brydges family's extensive estates acquired by Guy's Hospital fortunately remained intact after the sale of the estates in 1961. Less happily the archives of the Harley family were dispersed in 1742, many eventually going into public ownership by purchase and acceptance in lieu of tax.[69]

The larger country houses had their own muniment rooms and estate offices to hold this accumulating quantity of business documents. Personal papers such as family correspondence, diaries and antiquarian notes were usually kept in writing desks and cupboards within the house, perhaps in the library if they were bound volumes. At Hampton Court Lord Coningsby devised an evidence room to contain his mass of transcripts of documents relating to Leominster. According to William Stukeley in 1724 the room was approached by 'two new stone staircases of the geometrical method, with a view, I suppose, of security from fire. The Record room is at the top of a tower arched with stone, and paved with Roman brick'.[70] By contrast, the Scudamore family papers consulted by Duncumb at Holme Lacy in 1805 were to be found in the library.[71] The archives of the Cotterell family at Garnons were arranged in lettered trunks by 1823.[72] More recently those at Stoke Edith survived the fire which destroyed the mansion in 1927 and were kept in an undamaged service wing; whilst the Somers-Cocks family papers remain in a muniment room within Eastnor Castle.[73] The estate stewards, agents and solicitors who compiled so many of these muniments and estate records were themselves becoming established in dynastic partnerships from about 1800, accumulating and storing records in black-painted tin deed boxes embellished with the names of their clients (Pl. 4). The bill books of Bodenham & James of Hereford reveal much about their business and the records they created from 1810.[74]

Plate 4. Nineteenth-century archive boxes and containers for privately owned papers. (HRO)
Photo: Derek Foxton

Later in the century the growing number of public offices became concentrated in certain firms of solicitors. Frederick Bodenham was clerk of the peace for the city and John James the clerk to the magistrates of the Hereford division and to the commissioners of income tax; Symonds & Son acted in similar capacities for the county. In Ross Henry Minett of Minett & Piddock held a clutch of official posts, as did Anthony Temple of Temple & Philpin in Kington.[75]

From the time of Sir John Prise in the mid-sixteenth century there had been antiquaries and collectors of manuscripts in Herefordshire.[76] A widening national interest in archives led the government to print public records from 1704 and to appoint parliamentary committees and Records Commissions from 1800 to investigate and publish public records. These uncovered many deficiencies in the safekeeping of the public records that were reflected in conditions locally. Sheer administrative necessity had driven the clerk of the peace of the county to compile rudimentary lists and to index the quarter sessions order books. His memoranda books note some of his fees, as on 5 August 1820, 'Attending at the Record Room searching for Willersley inclosure Award from 1779 at 1s.4d. a year …£2 14s. 8d.' and the more exasperated entry in 1830, in response to an enquiry from the government about the cost of furniture for the county gaol, 'Attending the Record Room at the Shirehall Searching for the Treasurers Accounts and for the Vouchers to supply the information for those Years in which the Accounts were deficient Viz from 1813-1819…£1 1s. 0d.'.[77]

If the county archives lacked finding aids they were at least secure in their new records room. The city archives were both disordered and insecure. In 1829 a cleaning woman at the Guildhall, Esther Garstone, sold William Beniams, a grocer in Eign Street, a quantity of documents as waste paper. The corporation acted swiftly. They recovered the minute books of the corporation 1472-1529 and 1543-89, known respectively from their original binding as the Lesser Black Book and the Great Black Book, but succeeding volumes are missing. The Red Book, compiled in 1477 in connection with a dispute with the bishop over payment of fees, has also been lost, though perhaps not on this occasion.[78] The incident alerted the corporation to the state of their archives. The charters were listed in 1831 and, if not then at some other time early in the nineteenth century, the contents of the sacks were examined[79] (Pl. 5). A later town clerk, Richard Johnson, also went through the sacks and in 1868 published *The ancient customs of the city of Hereford*, in which he warned that 'It is to be greatly regretted that access to the numerous and valuable papers stored in the archives at the Guildhall, Hereford, is not rendered more convenient; they are at present deposited in a vault, deficient in ventilation and devoid of all light except that afforded by one gas-jet, to which persons must carry every book or paper they wish to consult'.[80]

Progress in the safekeeping of archives was slowly made in the nineteenth century. The Record Commissions between 1800 and 1831 culminated in the Public Record Office Act 1838 to house the public records. In the second half of the century scholarly and antiquarian interest in privately owned historical papers led to the appointment of the Historical Manuscripts Commission in 1869 and to many local improvements. In 1892 the Reverend W. D. Macray inspected the city archives for the Historical Manuscripts Commission, his published report of seventy-four pages being the first scholarly description of the papers in the iron chest (perhaps the one bought in 1737), oak boxes, sacks and parcels in which they were gathered. He commented on the interest shown by Joseph Carless, the town clerk, and of the

Plate 5. The sheepskin bags for 1744-45 and 1777 and wooden caskets for deeds from Hereford corporation's archives. (HRO) *Photo: Derek Foxton*

voluntary work of R. Paterson in sorting, cleaning and arranging the vast mass of dirty and crumpled papers. These were bound up in nine great guard books which Macray catalogued and it was probably about the same period that the Black Books and eight volumes of the common council minutes 1693-1835 were rebound.[81] Earlier at Leominster two of the commissioners appointed to inspect the charters, accounts and other records of municipal corporations prior to the Municipal Corporations Act expressed themselves perfectly satisfied with their visit in 1833.[82]

The diocese, under the energetic leadership of Archdeacon B. L. S. Stanhope, carried out a survey of parish registers in 1895-7. This revealed a far from satisfactory situation. Although twenty-six registers notified as missing in the returns to the 1831 population census had surfaced, twenty-one others had been lost.[83] The Elizabethan register from Eastnor is a fortunate survivor; it was returned to the parish after being picked up on a dung heap in Upton upon Severn in 1791.[84] The stained and tattered state of many Herefordshire parish registers bear witness to their storage in damp country churches, one incumbent noting: 'The Register-Book belonging to the Parish of Brinsop having been much injured by the dampness of the Church, it has been thought expedient to insert a Copy of it, faithfully transcribed, from the Year of our Lord 1758 to that of 1787 inclusive'.[85] Losses of vestry minutes and other parish records since the early nineteenth century can also be traced from the reports of the Charity Commissioners between 1819 and 1837.[86] At the cathedral the archives had been moved out of the muniment room in 1869-70 to a less suitable room above the bishop's cloister. Despite the dean claiming in 1902 that this room was fireproof and dry, Canon W. W. Capes found the archives neglected and damp on his arrival in 1904 and immediately set about sorting and selecting the most important for publication.[87]

The state of local records was by then attracting national concern. A Treasury committee reported in 1902 on the case for establishing local record offices. Witnesses were generally in favour, except where their own archives were concerned. In evidence the clerk of the peace for Herefordshire considered that records relating to the county might be deposited with the county council but saw no need to deposit the quarter sessions archives. The dean paid tribute to the activities of the Woolhope Naturalists' Field Club, stated that it was desirable to establish a local record office, but held that the episcopal, chapter and parish records should be exempted. He went on to say that he very much doubted whether landowners would be willing to deposit their deeds with a local authority.[88] A Royal Commission on Public Records, reporting between 1912 and 1919, found that the county records had overflowed from the records room and were not properly arranged or classified, the older lieutenancy and coroners' records were missing, the city archives remained unlisted as did the wills at the probate registry. The registry's small staff were obliging but not very competent and had allowed one frequent searcher to endorse the wills in indelible pencil and transfer some from one bundle to another incorrectly; there had also been a case of unauthorised access and forgery.[89]

No legislation followed these enquiries and in the inter-war years progress in the care of local records was largely the result of private initiative. A handful of county councils opened record offices and municipal libraries enlarged their longer established collections. Hereford City Library had been given the Pilley collection of deeds in 1913 by a former mayor and, after he became librarian in 1925, F. C. Morgan accepted gifts and loans of private archives almost every year. The British Records Association, formed in 1932, assisted this flow and was quick to support Mrs C. C. Radcliffe Cooke of Hellens when in 1932 she pressed the county council to set up a county records committee. Despite the immediate response that this was 'not opportune time for the expenditure of any money in this connection' the council did appoint a subcommittee to investigate. Having found from other counties that Herefordshire was by no means alone in doing nothing, they recommended only minor improvements to the storage and arrangement of the county archives at a cost of £11 10s 0d, but 'in view of the cost...do not recommend that any attempt be made at the moment at...indexing, cataloguing or printing the records'.[90]

The situation was changed materially by the wartime and post-war public interest in local records. The dean and chapter's archives were evacuated to the National Library of Wales for safekeeping and cataloguing in 1943, but their return to the cathedral delayed until a new muniment room could be constructed in 1955.[91] The city library and National Library of Wales continued to acquire Herefordshire archives of the nature that elsewhere, with the active encouragement of the Historical Manuscripts Commission and the British Records Association, were going to newly-founded county record offices. By the mid-1950s only Herefordshire, Rutland and the West Riding of Yorkshire lacked a county record office, the last two simply on account of their exceptional size. The county librarian, A. Shaw Wright, though handicapped by the indifference and limited resources of the county council, supplied the Historical Manuscripts Commission with lists of Herefordshire archives for the National Register of Archives, most notably the family papers at Eastnor Castle in 1956 and Kinsham Court in 1957. This connection gave the Commission's secretary, R. H. Ellis, an opening in October 1957 to ask Lord Cilcennin, the newly appointed lord lieutenant and custos rotulorum, 'to bring the matter up in the biggest possible way' with Herefordshire county council. The clerk, R. C. Hansen, was sympathetic and despite some residual opposition by two or three members the council decided in July 1958 to proceed with the appointment of an archivist under the overall direction of the county librarian. Ellis then alerted Shaw Wright to the possible candidature of Meryl Jancey who was offered the post after open competition on 30 September 1958.[92] Thereafter the story of record keeping in county, city and diocese becomes interwoven in the history of the county record office, its donors and depositors.

ACKNOWLEDGEMENTS I have had much assistance from the archivists and librarians of the repositories cited in the notes. Among these I have, of course, drawn most heavily upon the Herefordshire Record Office, whose staff has been supremely helpful and patient in guiding my research. Especially am I indebted to Miss D. S. Hubbard for also critically reading the draft of this paper.

REFERENCES

[1] H. P. R. Finberg, *The early charters of the west midlands* (Leicester 1961), 136-146.

[2] M. T. Clanchy, *From memory to written record* (London 1979), 39-42.

[3] J. Barrow ed., *English episcopal acta VII. Hereford 1079-1234* (Oxford 1993), lxxiii.

[4] Barrow, ibid, liv-lv, cii-cx.

[5] Clanchy, op. cit. in note 2, 41; D. Walker, 'Charters of the earldom of Hereford, 1095-1201', *Camden Miscellany Vol. XXII*, Camden 4th series, I (1964), 13-16.

[6] HCA, 305-4000 *passim*; HRO, AL40 and G37.

[7] A. Morey and C. N. L. Brooke, eds., *The letters and charters of Gilbert Foliot* (Cambridge 1967)

[8] B. S. Smith, 'The Archives' in G. Aylmer and J. Tiller, *Hereford Cathedral, a history,* (London, 2000), 545; HRO, BG11/17/9; E. M. Jancey, *The royal charters of the city of Hereford* (Hereford 1973), 12.

[9] *Reg. Swinfield*, 277. For seals of women c1240-3, see K. Morgan, 'An edition of the cartulary of Leominster priory up to the mid-thirteenth century', Cardiff MA thesis, University of Wales 1973, 170, 179-80, 235-6 [BL, Cotton Domit. A. III, fos. 80v, 83, 97].

[10] V. H. Galbraith and J. Tait, *Herefordshire Domesday circa 1160-1170* (Pipe Roll Society 1950); E. M. Hallam, *Domesday Book through nine centuries* (London 1986), 38, 41.

[11] J. Hillaby, 'Hereford gold: Irish Welsh and English land. The Jewish community at Hereford and its clients, 1179-1253', *TWNFC*, xliv, pt 3 (1984), 364.

[12] HRO, BG11/22.   [13] HCA, R1-212; *Reg Cantilupe*, 108, 261, 262.

[14] HCA, R745/1; J. Webb, ed., *Roll of the household expenses of Richard de Swinfield, bishop of Hereford*, Camden Soc., 2 vols. (1855).

[15] K. Morgan, op. cit., in note 9; HCA, RS/1/1; *Reg. Cantilupe*; HRO, AA59/A/1, published, but not fully, in A.T. Bannister, 'A transcript of the "Red Book"...of the Hereford bishopric estates in the thirteenth century', *Camden miscellany*, xli (1929), pp. v-ix, 1-36.

[16] HRO, BG11/2/1-71; HD 4/1; A63/I/1-23 [Pembridge]; S67/2; A63/I/24-33 [Pencombe].   [17] Jancey, *op. cit,*. in note 8.

[18] G. R. C. Davis, *Medieval cartularies of Great Britain* (London 1958), nos. 311, 448, 552, 801-8, 1081, 1292-4.

[19] BL, Egerton Rolls 8723, 8724; Add. MS.6041; MS Harl 1240 (microfilm copy in HRO, X146).

[20] *Reg. Cantilupe*, 41; J. Geddes, 'Decorative ironwork', *Hereford cathedral, a history,* op. cit. in note 8, 336; F. C. Morgan, 'Church chests of Herefordshire', *TWNFC*, xxxii, 133;

Hillaby, op. cit. in note 11, 364.

[21] *Reg. Lacy*, 30.   [22] *Reg. Cantilupe*, 133.   [23] Jancey, op. cit. in note 8, 20.

[24] E. N. Dew, *Diocese of Hereford. Extracts from the cathedral registers A.D. 1275-1535* (Hereford 1932), 111-2.   [25] Barrow, op. cit. in note 3, cii-ciii.

[26] HRO, BG 11/22.   [27] *Reg. Trilleck*, 53.

[28] HCA, 7031/1-6 and RS/2/1-18, continuing.

[29] HRO, J72/8 (Stoke Edith); BK52/34 (Madley); N13/1 (Hentland); BC63/1 (All Saints, Hereford); G.F. Townsend, *The town and borough of Leominster* (Leominster [1866]) contains extracts from the Leominster churchwardens' accounts.

[30] HRO, AB84/2 (Pencombe); AH21/2,3 (Bromyard); AG24/1 (Lugwardine); AK99/1 (Colwall).

[31] G. H. Piper and C.H. Mayo, *The registers of Ledbury, co. Hereford*, Parish Register Society (London 1899), v-ix.

[32] HRO, E38/14, 23-6, 42-5, 65-8.

[33] W. D. Macray, 'The manuscripts of the corporation of Hereford', Historical Manuscripts Commission, *13th Report*, App. Pt. IV (1892), 283-53; Townsend, op. cit. in note 29, *passim*. The archives of both towns have been deposited in the HRO; the Hereford city charters remain at Hereford town hall.

[34] BL, Harleian MSS (scattered entries) and Add. MSS. 70001-70523 (Portland papers, especially 70057-93). See C. Jones, 'The Harley family and the Harley papers', *British Library Journal*, 15, no.2 (autumn 1989), 123-33; R. J. Olney, 'The Portland papers', *Archives*, xix, no. 82 (October 1989), 78-87; Historical Manuscripts Commission, *Portland II-IX*; T. T. Lewis ed., *Letters of Lady Brilliana Harley, wife of Sir Robert Harley, of Brampton Bryan* (Camden Society 1854). Other estate papers remain at Brampton Bryan Hall.

[35] HCA, D853.   [36] HRO, BH53/1.   [37] HRO, AA59/A/2.

[38] HCA, RS/1/2.

[39] HRO, AB84/2 (Pencombe); N13/1 (Hentland); AD56/1 (Yarkhill); AD55/1 (Yarpole).

[40] HCA, 1443 and 3220.   [41] HRO, AA59/A/2, fo. 170v.

[42] HRO, K14/75 (Tarrington); the wording of the Stoke Edith copy has minor spelling variations.

[43] F. C. Morgan, op. cit. in note 20; HRO, BC63/1.

[44] K. Fincham, ed., *Visitation articles and injunctions of the early Stuart church. Volume II*, Church of England Record Society, 5, (1998), 131, 133. The visitation was not carried out.

[45] HRO, S67/4/2/18 (1555-6); S67/3/5/7 (1665). In 1998 the chest was in Leominster Museum.

[46] HRO, BG11/23. The sacks are also in the HRO.   [47] HRO, BG11/17/9.

[48] HRO, City misc. papers 12.v.v.   [49] Smith, op. cit. in note 8, 547-9

[50] J. Williams, 'The library', *Hereford cathedral, a history*, op.cit. in note 8, 521-2; J. Cooper, 'Herefordshire' in C. R. J. Currie and C. P. Lewis, eds., *English county histories, a guide* (Stroud 1994), 176-7.

[51] *Reg. Booth*, xvii. Elias Ashmole bequeathed the commonplace book to the Bodleian Library in 1692 and Thomas Tanner had the register by 1707.

[52] Smith, op. cit. in note 8, 548-9   [53] HRO, AB84/1

[54] HRO, Q/SO/2, fos. 23v., 89v.-90, 97v.-98, 121v.-122.

[55] HRO, Q/SO/3, fos. 3v.-4; Q/SO/4, fo. 120.   [56] HRO, Q/SO/6, fo. 202.

[57] Jancey, op. cit. in note 8, 26-8.   [58] HRO, BG11/24/2, p. 64; BG11/24/3, p. 48.

[59] Townsend, op. cit. in note 29, 138-9.

[60] HRO, S67/3/1/1, 4 Feb 1720, 6 Jan 1721, 6 Oct and 12 Nov 1722.

[61] HRO, S67/3/1/1, 17 Feb 1724, 1 Jan 1733; Townsend, op. cit. in note 29, 172, 175-6.

[62] HRO, S67/3/1/1, 21 Nov 1724; S67/1/2, 4 Apr 1743. In 1998 the press was on display in Leominster priory church.

[63] HRO, Q/CE/1-2; Q/CM/1-4.   [64] HRO, Q/AS 5/15; A84/1-5.

[65] See W. B. Stephens, *Sources for English local history* (Cambridge 1981) and P. Riden,

Record sources for local history (London 1987).

[66] Information from incumbents and churchwardens; HRO, AH61/32 (Middleton-on-the-Hill).

[67] Smith, op. cit. in note 8, 550-2   [68] HRO, A85/1a and /4.

[69] Most of the collections named here have been deposited in the HRO. The Scudamore papers are in the British Library and Harley papers in the British Library, Nottingham University Library and Nottinghamshire Record Office. For Harley, see *Principal family and estate collections: family names A-K*, Guides to sources for British history 10, Royal Commission on Historical Manuscripts, London 1996, 27-9. For lists of Herefordshire private papers in both public and private hands consult the National Register of Archives at the Royal Commission of Historical Manuscripts, Quality House, Quality Court, Chancery Lane, London WC2A 1HP (e-mail nra@hmc.gov.uk or on-line access at http://www.hmc.gov.uk).

[70] Townsend, op. cit. in note 29, 167, citing W. Stukeley, *Iter curiosum. Iter IV* (London 1724), 72. The collections had been dispersed by 1861.

[71] J. Duncumb, *Collections towards the history and antiquities of the county of Hereford*, I (Hereford 1804), 259-65.

[72] HRO, D52.   [73] Personal knowledge.   [74] HRO, BH69/1-7.

[75] *Kelly's directory of Herefordshire* (1885).   [76] J. Cooper, op. cit. in note 50, 176-85.

[77] HRO, Q/CM/2 and /3.

[78] R. Johnson, *The ancient customs of the city of Hereford* (Hereford 1868), 58-9; Historical Manuscripts Commission, op. cit. in note 33, 283, 288-9; HRO, BG11/17/10 and 11, memoranda inside front covers of each. Esther Garstone was found guilty at the spring assizes 1830 but her case was not reported in the *Hereford Journal*.

[79] Historical Manuscripts Commission, op. cit. in note 33, 283; HRO, City misc. papers, vol. IV.

[80] Johnson, op. cit. in note 78, 59. The Guildhall was successively in the Market House in High Town until its demolition in 1862, on the west side of Widemarsh Street adjoining the Butter Market 1862-82 and on the opposite side of Widemarsh Street 1882-1904. The Town Hall in St Owen Street was built in 1904.

[81] Historical Manuscripts Commission, op. cit. in note 33, 283-353; W. D. Macray, *Catalogue and index to manuscript papers, proclamations and other documents, selected from the municipal archives of the city of Hereford* (Hereford 1894).

[82] Townsend, op. cit. in note 29, 201.   [83] HRO, AL59/15.

[84] *Report of the committee appointed to enquire as to the existing arrangements for the collection and custody of local records and as to further measures which it may be advisable to take for the purpose. Presented to Parliament* (London 1902), 200.

[85] HRO, AP33/2. Inspections made under the Parochial Registers and Records Measure 1978 show that high levels of relative humidity in Herefordshire church vestries continue to imperil parish records.

[86] *The reports of the Commissioners...appointed to enquire concerning charities in England and Wales...the county of Hereford 1819-1837.*

[87] *Report on local records* in note 84, 112; 'Memoir of the Rev W. W. Capes' in *Reg. Poltone*, xx-xxii; W. W. Capes, *Charters and records of Hereford cathedral* (Hereford 1908).

[88] *Report on local records* in note 84, 18, 146, 200-1.

[89] Royal Commission on Public Records, *Minutes of evidence to the second report...England and Wales*, 1914, ii (pt II), 151 and ii (pt III), 42-3, 47; *Third report*, 1919, (pt II), 36, 45, 76, 102 and (pt III), 23, 87, 104-5.

[90] HRO, A49/1   [91] Smith, op. cit. in note 8, 553-4

[92] PRO, HMC 8/34; HRO, T38/13, E100 and HRO files O17.

Plate 1. Hereford Free Library, 1874. Drawn by Worthington G. Smith.

The Hereford Free Library 1871-1912

JEAN O'DONNELL

One building in Broad Street shines forth as an architectural gem of the Victorian age standing between the mediocre concrete buildings of the 1960s that jostle it. It is the engaging Hereford Free Library and Museum where the riot of wildlife on its façade captures the eye and compels the pedestrian to linger and inspect the menagerie. It received scant attention until recently and was thought to be pretentious by such writers as Pevsner.[1] In its time it was the repository for the new treasures of the arts and sciences that were becoming accessible to the public through museum collections and reference libraries, and its exterior proudly emblazoned the riches to be found through its portals.

The establishment of a public free library in Hereford was part of a national enthusiasm for public education and literacy which emerged in the middle of the nineteenth century and which resulted in the opening of free libraries. In 1855 an act of Parliament empowered municipal corporations to raise money for them and this was adopted in Hereford in 1871, when it was proposed by Dr Henry Graves Bull and seconded by Alderman Bodenham, at a public meeting. The resolution of 7 February endorsed the concept of a library in conjunction with a museum, together with premises for the Woolhope Club, offering rate support for the enterprise (Pl.1).

There had been earlier moves to open free libraries. Charles Anthony, who owned the *Hereford Times*, and Hugh Watson had both tried in 1833. In Church Street in 1855 there was the Hereford Athenaeum and Mechanics' Institution which had its own newsroom and library. A working-class library was attached to St Peter's Literary Institution in Commercial Street, which had opened in 1836 for young men and where Reverend John Venn fostered education and literacy by means of lectures and books. For the middle-classes at this time there was the Hereford Permanent Library that had been founded in 1815 by Benjamin Fallowes. It had about '7000 books by modern English authors; mostly comprising history, biography, travels and fiction'. The annual subscription was £1 10s. Adjoining the City Arms hotel and on the corner of High Street in 1856 was the Hereford Antiquarian and Philosophical Institution, where on the ground floor was the news-room with London and local journals, and upstairs a museum containing 'a large number of stuffed wild animals'.[2]

In the 1860s the Hereford Penny Readings were held. They were started in 1864 when it was said that there was nowhere of equal importance 'which is more destitute of the advantages which citizens are supposed to possess over their friends in the country, no comfortable and well-lighted reading room, supplied with newspapers and periodicals, stands invitingly open, and no good public library exists within reach of persons of moderate means.'[3]

The penny readings provided an evening's recreation at a modest cost. Extracts were read from various authors in prose verse and they proved extremely popular. The first reading of the 1866 session was given in the Corn Exchange on a Friday evening in November, with the mayor in the chair, and 378 people present. The committee decided to devote the profits to a fund for the provision of books when a free library was established.

The vision to build such a library came from James Rankin in 1870. He had been President of the Woolhope Club in 1869 when he became keen to establish a museum for the club and let it be known that he was willing to put up the required capital. After an unsuccessful approach to the Literary and Philosophical Society on Castle Green where the club had been in the habit of meeting and where there was an existing museum, a committee of the Woolhope Club was set up at the annual meeting to investigate the establishment of a museum. It was decided that a preferable institution would have a free library attached to it. Dr Henry Graves Bull was chairman of this sub-committee which then put forward their scheme to the Hereford town council where it was supported. Two weeks later, the Woolhope Club adopted it at their meeting on 23 February 1871 (Pl. 2).

James Rankin (1842-1915) was both a scholar and a wealthy man. He was the son of a partner in a Liverpool shipping firm which had made a fortune from the North Atlantic timber trade. After studying at Cambridge, where he took a degree in natural sciences, he married and settled at Bryngwyn on the estate his father had given him. To design a new house he had engaged the young Frederick Kempson as architect. Over the years he acquired 3,300 acres of land, Lyston Court and numerous farms. A man

Plate 2. James Rankin. (Woolhope Club coll.)

of standing, he was also philanthropic and scholarly, donating the generous sum of £4000 for the library and museum with the following objects for his foundation:

(1) That the Free Library was to be open at all hours it was likely to be used; the same to be provided with books of an instructive as well as an amusing character.
(2) To provide a museum where objects of natural history and scientific interest, arranged in systematic order, might be preserved with a view to popular instruction; and where scientific meetings might be held and lectures on literary and scientific subjects delivered.[4]

After a public meeting in July 1871, when the Public Libraries Act was adopted, a resolution of the city council appointed a management committee to oversee a library to be established in temporary premises at 3 King Street. One of the first acts of the management committee was a request to the trustees of the penny readings fund to purchase books to furnish the temporary library.[5] In August of that year Rankin bought the site in Broad Street for £1,750 ready for the new building, then occupied by Hewitt's, a shop retailing wine, spirits, tea and coffee.

The first librarian was appointed on 23 October of the same year. He was Richard Paden who, at the age of 23, already had ten years experience of working in Liverpool Free Library. His assistant was a young boy of eleven, Thomas Reid, whose duties would have been to fetch and carry books. The newsroom opened on Monday, 4 December with some daily papers: *The Times*, the *Daily News* and the *Birmingham Post*. By the first report the committee had purchased the library of the Working Men's Institution and the valuable collection belonging to the St Peter's Literary Institution. The library now contained about 4,000 volumes. The daily average attendance was 108 persons. The committee had prepared a catalogue of 1,000 books for the lending section which was due to open in January 1873. It included rules and regulations for their use. Lack of space meant that the reference library could not be used until it was housed in the new building which by now was in the course of erection.

Adult education in King Street began with evening classes; the first was a drawing class carried out under the auspices of the science and art departments at South Kensington. Once the new building was operating the programme was extended to include physical geography, magnetism, electricity and animal physiology. These were held in the Woolhope Room. By 1878 the extra-mural department of Oxford University was holding evening lectures on 'The First Stuarts and the Puritan Revolution'. From 1887 Oxford, then later Birmingham University, with the WEA, provided academic courses for men and women. The Woolhope Club continued to read and publish papers for its gentlemen members on all their latest research into the natural history, geology and the archaeology of Herefordshire. James Rankin's ambition for the institution was fulfilled and many Herefordians over a century have benefited.

In March 1872, at a meeting of the Woolhope Club, the first report from the Hereford Free Library and Museum committee was read and adopted. It mentioned the success that attended the opening of the free library and reading-room at the temporary premises in King Street and urged members of the club, one and all, to use their best endeavors to provide specimens of the various branches of natural history so that the new museum should be a credit to the scientific men of the county.[6]

It is interesting to see the composition of the library and museum committee at this early stage. The trustees were the mayor, aldermen and citizens of Hereford and, although the bishop was chairman, the real guiding hand was that of Dr Bull who usually took the chair. The committee was all male and some of the prominent citizens who served on it were Charles Anthony, editor of the *Hereford Times*, Thomas Llanwarne, solicitor, Thomas Cam, physician, and J. F. Symonds, clergyman.

The young architect selected by Rankin and recommended by him to the library committee was Frederick Robertson Kempson (1838-1923). He came to Hereford in 1861 to start a practice at 18 St Owen's Street after two years in Gordon Square, Bloomsbury. He had finished Bryngwyn, Rankin's country mansion at Wormelow, in 1868, and was beginning to gain a reputation.[7]

Kempson was the fifth child of William Brooke Kempson, the rector of Stoke Lacy from 1838-59. His grandfather, a London druggist, had purchased land in Stoke Lacy in the 1830s but lived with his family at Birchyfield near Bromyard. On his death in 1851 the Stoke Lacy lands, rectory, house, advowson, tithes and glebe had all passed to William, Frederick's father, while the Birchyfield estate went to the eldest son, John.

After attending Cheltenham College, Frederick Robertson Kempson was articled to two partners with a practice in London and Cardiff who were to influence his work and introduce him to a wide circle of artists and craftsmen. They were John Pollard Seddon (1827-1906) and John Prichard (1817-1886) who worked on the restoration of Llandaff cathedral, as well as designing the modern post office building in Cardiff in 1857.

Seddon was a follower of Ruskin and greatly admired his ideas without abandoning his own. He was part of the Pre-Raphaelite set and his brother was a minor painter who died accompanying Holman Hunt to the Middle East in 1856. In 1862 Seddon commissioned the William Morris firm to produce a piece of office furniture for his Whitehall chambers. This was the famous 'King Rene's Honeymoon' cabinet on which Burne-Jones, Brown and Rossetti painted four panels while Morris and Webb decorated others. Seddon's own masterpiece is University College, Aberystwyth. His Herefordshire work was limited, but he is best-known for his Italianate design of St Catherine's, Hoarwithy.

John Prichard was the son of a vicar-choral of Llandaff cathedral and trained under Pugin. He was responsible for much of the rebuilding and restoration of Llandaff cathedral during the middle years of the nineteenth century when he was diocesan architect. For this work the influence of his partner, Seddon, meant that commissions were given to members of the pre-Raphaelite school in glass, painting and carving. These included a triptych by Rossetti and porcelain panels by Burne-Jones. Only one Herefordshire church was his design: Ganarew, built in 1849.

The association of Kempson with these two architects ensured that he was familiar with Ruskinian ideals as well as those of Pugin. In addition, artists and craftsmen from the William Morris firm became well known to him during his training. The association with his mentors continued, for it was Seddon who proposed him as a fellow of the Royal Institute of British Architects in 1870, and when Prichard died in 1886 Frederick Kempson was his natural successor as diocesan architect.

One new building that caused a stir in the 1850s was the controversial Oxford Museum, which was under construction after a stiff competition won by Benjamin Woodward. Prichard went to see it as 'a true disciple of Pugin' and it surely made an impact upon him. Kempson probably accompanied him; he must have been anxious to see such a new landmark in architecture. This building was influential because it was to house the natural sciences at Oxford and Ruskin himself had imposed his views on the design. The skilled carving of flora and fauna on the exterior by two Irish brothers, the O'Sheas, excited comment and discussion about the amount of free expression to be given to sculptors when carrying out architectural work, and they set the pattern for the use of natural forms. Prichard was engaged upon Ettingham Park at the time, an imposing country house in Warwickshire, when he brought Edward Clarke, a master craftsman from Llandaff, to carry out carved panels on the front in line with this current trend for exterior decoration. Kempson was working in their office and must have been party to discussion on the project and the use of carving. This included the principle that the function of a building should be reflected in the design and decoration as in the Oxford Museum.[8]

When Kempson began his practice in Hereford he prepared plans for many of the parish elementary schools and the restoration of several churches, including Bishop's Frome. St Paul's church, Tupsley (1865) was one of his best early buildings.[9] His most notable work in Herefordshire is the County College for Boys on Aylestone Hill (1880), now the Royal National College for the Blind. This was in Ruskin's gothic revival style with a central tower over a façade that made full use of brick and polychromy. It remains an impressive example of Victorian building. Kempson worked on some notable projects in South Wales after he succeeded Prichard as diocesan architect, including St Michael's Theological College in Llandaff (1905) constructed from Prichard's own uncompleted house.

The commission the young Kempson was to carry out for James Rankin and the Hereford Free Library committee, with his assistant William Martin, must have been an exciting challenge and vastly different from the numerous churches and parish schools that he had worked on since starting his own practice. The mansion he had designed for Rankin had met with approval and at last he was able to create a building in the modern gothic about which Seddon had enthused.

The library building designed by Kempson combined the latest ideas on Ruskinian gothic with an iconography designed, like the Oxford Museum, to convey its function. Its appearance, like other institutional buildings of the 1860s and 70s, suggested a palace from one of the mercantile and medieval cities of Italy about which Ruskin wrote so avidly. The Venetian gothic style which Kempson chose allowed for plans with continuous floor-space so suitable for a library building. The exterior arcade-like sequence on either side of the entrance gained support from heavy square columns and allowed for the four large ground-floor openings, which were glazed with rose windows with six lights in the upper part; the remaining centre arch was the main entrance. Radyr stone, used for the columns, clearly shows the bedding of the various sediments, making a geological statement about the rocks which support the living world carried on the capitals above, just as the Oxford Museum had done. The front walling was entirely of bluish-grey stone from Pontypridd, while the dressings were a light brown Campden stone. The window shafts were from quarries at Bridgend and Mansfield. Brick was used for the rest of the structure as may be seen at the side and rear of the building.

The nature of the site dictated a high narrow frontage on to Broad Street as it was sandwiched between a three-storied shop on the N. side and a two-storied house to the S. Opposite was the stately mass of the Norman cathedral behind a group of eighteenth-century houses removed in the 1930s. This site must have posed a problem, for the design had to convey its importance to the existing streetscape without being diminished by the cathedral. The challenge was tremendous and Kempson resorted to a Gothic echo of a nave in the two upper stories of his building which are reminiscent of a triforium with columns supporting the pointed window openings. The balcony above the main entrance gave an emphasis to the main room of the building; the Woolhope Room and library. The seven Gothic windows light it well for the purposes of study and reading for which it was intended. The central grouping of three windows over the balcony give it extra boldness. Each is a casement that allows for opening and for access to the balcony. Above, the third floor, which was intended for living accommodation, has similarly grouped trefoil-headed windows. Over this floor is a parapet with machicolations and quatrefoil openings that brings the concept back to the Italian *palazzo*. The rainwater was carried away from the lead roof gutters behind the parapet by long stone spouts as in a mediaeval building. To use all available space more domestic accommodation was arranged in the roof space and lighted by three dormer windows which Pevsner hated but which provided access to the roof for the menagerie that runs along the parapet. These, in turn, were finished with three iron flowering stems as finials.

The influence of Darwin and his work *On the Origin of Species by means of Natural Selection* (1859) gave architects a new interest in the natural world. Ruskin himself had studied geology and collected fossils so that when the Oxford Museum of Natural Science was built just prior to Darwin's bombshell on evolution, immense emphasis was placed on realistic carving from nature according to Ruskin's ideas. Now there was new interest in animal forms for decoration. The subjects for the new free library and museum plus the activities of the Woolhope Club provided infinite possibilities for Kempson to decorate the façade with natural forms mixed with rebuses or puns on the names of personages connected with the enterprise, a Victorian as well as a mediaeval sense of humour, and to use the Campden stone with some subtlety.

The exterior had to suggest the purpose of the building as a museum, a library and a centre for science and art teaching. Two medallions with idealised heads of Science and Art were placed on either side of the entrance supported by the arms of the city of Hereford and those of James Rankin. The two fine heads were carved by a London sculptor, Milo Griffith. He executed the work from Kempson's own cartoons (Pls. 3 & 4). The square capitals of the four large pillars represent the

Plate 3. Head of Arts on Free Library front by Milo Griffiths from cartoons by F. R. Kempson.

Plate 4. Head of Sciences.
Photos: D. Foxton

squirrels of Europe, the monkeys of Asia, the crocodiles and water-fowl of Africa, and the cockatoo, toucan and opossum of America. Carved around the entrance arch is a Noah's ark of amphibians including the water-shrew, the mullagong, the beaver, the walrus, the hippopotamus, the sea-elephant, the rhinoceros, the tapir, the otter, the sea leopard and the water rat. On the inner side are a kingfisher, a frog, a butterfly and a kangaroo, which faces another marsupial, the duck-billed platypus. On either side of the façade are the projecting heads of larger animals that complete the four string courses. The peacock and the eagle symbolise majesty and sublimity, while the seal refers to Lord Saye and Sele, who was archdeacon, and the lion to the city arms. The third string-course terminates in the heads of a bull and a goat; the one being for Dr Bull (chairman of the library committee) and the other the crest of architects and therefore Kempson. The bull is playfully surrounded by mushrooms, an allusion to the doctor's mycological interests. The four string-courses are also highly decorative with the first entirely devoted to the signs of the zodiac and flowers of the months they represent, the second, to birds and animals of the chase including owls, fox, dog and rabbit (Pl. 5).

Plate 5. Monkeys of Asia by R. & W. Clarke on façade capital.   *Photo: D. Foxton*

The sculptors of this wildlife extravaganza were the brothers Clarke. Robert and William were the sons of Edward Clarke of Llandaff and had learned their skills from him. Kempson's connections with Seddon and Prichard at Llandaff meant that he knew the family well. Their close connection with Kempson continued in later years, for William continued to work for him when he practised in Cardiff and became diocesan architect. He was also employed by Burges to carve some of his designs at Cardiff castle which was being rebuilt for the Marquis of Bute at this time. Robert, the elder son, moved to Hereford, presumably when he was engaged on the library carving with his brother. By 1876 he was advertised as a builder at 21 Guilford Street. He specialised in carving and by the 1890s had his own premises, the Phoenix Works, in Commercial Road and was described as an 'architectural sculptor'. His later commissions were the reredos in Mansel Lacy church in 1912 and that of All Saints, Hereford, but by then he had completed many others including work at Hereford cathedral and Brinsop church. He then resided at North Villas in Barr's Court Road, near to the Phoenix works. Robert had six children, one of whom, William, was an architect and became partner to John Nicholson when he was Hereford diocesan surveyor *c*1913, and for many years they had offices over 1 King Street. Robert became a prominent member of the Woolhope Club committee in 1895, becoming assistant secretary in 1912 until his death in 1915, contributing papers and drawings on churches and archaeology. His son, William, then took over the post.[10]
These talented brothers brought the façade of the new library building to life and

gave it a unique appeal. The dazzling array of wildlife is carried out with youthful exuberance, for Robert was only 25 years old and William was younger when they came to Hereford.

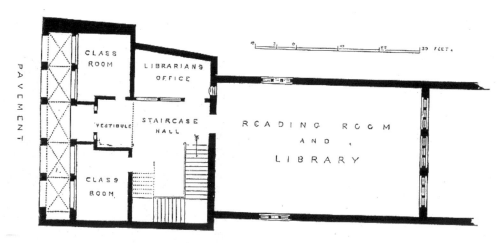

Figure 1. Plan of building - ground floor, 1874.

The interior plan for the Hereford library was simple. Through the inner porch lay a vestibule with a classroom on either side, then through to the hall where the staircase rose opposite the librarian's office door. These two front rooms had to be converted to shops before the opening so that the city corporation could be paid the rent towards an extra £1,000 that it had lent the library committee because of the escalating cost. Through the hall lay the reading room and library. On the first floor was the Woolhope Room occupying the dominant position at the front of the building. The position of the club at this time was a strong one, for James Rankin had been President in 1869 and was a worthy contributor to its *Transactions* for which he wrote papers on natural history. He was also a member of the editorial committee. Frederick Kempson was a member having joined in 1868, presumably at the instigation of James Rankin, for he was at this time engaged upon the plans for Bryngwyn. He would have been well aware of Rankin's aspirations for his club and shared his enthusiasm. With Dr Henry Bull as vice-chairman of the library committee and an ex-president it was natural that the provision of accommodation for their club should assume great importance. The room provided was large and airy, 44ft x 20ft, with open fireplaces at each end for heating. The tiled surrounds to these are particularly interesting as they mark Kempson's connections with the Arts and Crafts movement.

The N. fireplace is, like its counterpart, of black stone set into light-coloured surround with a chamfered edge (Pl. 6). Around the rim is a sunflower abstract design; cut into it and set into the surround is a complete set of original tiles specially designed for the room. There are twelve; all of them female faces carried out in a line drawing with an overglaze on a cream background representing various arts and sciences. On the left are Literature, Geography, Engineering, Natural History, Architecture and Sculpture while those on the right are Commerce, Painting, Astronomy, Music, Chemistry and Agriculture. The faces are distinctive and the hands well drawn so that the style is noticeably Burne-Jones in character.[11] There is

Left: Plate 6. Tiles depicting Literature (top) and Geography.

Below: Plate 7. Tile of Aquarius from fireplace at south end of Woolhope Club room.

Photos: D. Foxton

a certain irony that no women were admitted to the club until 1954 and yet two of the female faces enigmatically represent engineering and commerce. At the other end of the room is a similar fireplace, but set into it are twelve roundels of the zodiac signs similar to a later set decorated by the William Morris company. They are cream on terra-cotta. It is the quality of the drawing of both sets that distinguishes them from similar tiles. The hearth tiles in both fireplaces are Godwin's of Lugwardine in a typical geometric flower-shape and glazed[12] (Pl. 7).

Nine years after the library opened, in 1883, an evening reception was held to which the mayor and corporation were invited to mark the occasion when handsome new glazed bookcases were installed at each end of the Woolhope Room. James Rankin and Frederick Kempson were both present with their families as members of the club. There was also a series of glass cases for the display of fossils. On the walls were photographs of all the leading men of science, including Darwin, who were honorary members of the club, and others of notable members or presidents. This serious interest in science was shown by the presence of powerful microscopes through which virulent bacillii were examined with the help of George With, a renowned local chemist and honorary member.[13]

Up a short flight of stairs was the museum room, 50ft x 30ft. Planned like a mediaeval open hall, the roof beams were carried on ten corbels carved with foliage. The lighting was from five roof lights and glass roof tiles that diffused the light through a ground-glass panel. The cases for exhibits were wall-mounted with free-standing show cases added later when the Hereford Society for Aiding the Industrious gave a loan of £300 for furniture in 1892. These were in place for over one hundred years but were removed recently to make way for a modern display. By the 1890s the museum had acquired some fine collections from members of the Woolhope Club, including geological specimens from Reverend J. D. La Touche and insects from Dr T. A. Chapman.

The zealous gentlemen members of the Woolhope Club had collections of fossils and other geological specimens while the antiquarians had acquired archaeological items. The chairman of the library committee, Dr Bull, was a keen botanist and started the fungus forays as well as writing about subjects as diverse as hill-forts and apples. The retiring president of 1875, Reverend J. Davies had urged members to help the museum form the collections from their own work, and the proximity of the museum to the Woolhope Room allowed it to be a natural depository for all the club specimens. Much of the present collection is formed from this early fieldwork. By 1902 there was a museum committee formed of aldermen and councillors but the curators of the museum were honorary and were all members of the club. Botany, conchology, entomology, geology and ornithology were all covered between them.

The second and third floors were over the front of the building and were occupied by the librarian's apartments; one floor had a kitchen, scullery, sitting-room, store rooms, etc., while the bedrooms were in the roof space with the dormer windows. Here a succession of librarians must have climbed two flights of the narrow staircase to their drawing-room to gaze at a splendid view of the cathedral and close from the narrow second-floor windows (Pl. 8).

Plate 8. Dog on parapet guarding librarian's apartment by R. &. W. Clarke.   *Photo: D. Foxton*

The foundation stone of this remarkable new building was laid by the mayor, Edwin Bosley, on 11 March 1873. The builder selected by tender for the work was James Bowers who had accepted the contract for £4,700 but whose costs rose to £6,000. The final bill was for £7,600 including £1,750 for the site. The difference was made up by James Rankin and the city council who insisted that the two rooms on either side of the entrance intended as classrooms should be used as shops until the deficit was closed. They eventually became a ladies' reading room and the lending library.

The building was opened with a splendid reception on 8 October 1874 with the sound of bells and 'the people's glad acclaim'. It is difficult today to imagine the pleasure that was felt at this new institution, for libraries have become so much an accepted and essential part of society, that they are taken for granted: 'Never was a public gift received with more general or more hearty marks of gratitude; never was a public institution opened amid more enthusiastic, hearty and general wishes for its long duration and its usefulness.'[14]

It was a sunny autumn day, the city was decked out with banners, and there were festivities for the citizens. It was seen as a positive addition to popular education, the generosity of the donor was appreciated and the opening greeted with great enthusiasm. 'The Mayor, on behalf of the citizens, presented Lady Rankin [then Mrs] with a model gold key, jewelled with rubies and emeralds, and bearing the arms of the City. The Town Clerk read an address suitable to the occasion, which was artistically illuminated and handsomely framed. ...Sir James Rankin handed over the title deeds of the building to the Mayor.'

A *déjeuner*, with champagne, was given by the mayor and mayoress in the reading-room and all the magistrates of the city and county attended. Among the toasts given to the queen, bishop, mayor and other dignitaries was one to the Woolhope Club, proposed by Archdeacon Waring and responded to by the president, the Reverend James Davies, thus reflecting the importance attached to the club's part in the enterprise. Three thousand six hundred children of the Sunday schools were given a substantial tea with large amounts of cake and a medal with a view of the Free Library and Museum and the name of James Rankin on one side, and the city arms with the name of the mayor on the reverse. They then went to High Town to sing hymns. At the barracks in Harold Street there were athletic sports. The day concluded with fireworks on Castle Green.

The gift was acknowledged much later, on 27 January 1908, when a handsome bronze engraved plaque was erected in the entrance hall by the doors. It receives scant attention. Today James Rankin is barely remembered although he was a member of Parliament, representing North Herefordshire from 1880 to 1906, and from 1910 to 1912. He piloted the new education service of the county council, helped with low-cost housing and pensions. He donated schools, libraries and workers' houses. He was one of those many benefactors whose enterprise and money enriched Victorian communities. In his lifetime he was honoured with a baronetcy, made high sheriff of the county and chief steward of the city. He died in 1915 at the age of 73.

It was not long before the building was found inadequate. By the early 1890s it needed the space occupied by the two front shops. The repayment of the existing mortgage was achieved by a donation from the Hereford Society for Aiding the Industrious for £250 on condition that the shops were removed. The town council made up the difference from the High Town Improvement Fund, which had been started after the removal of the old town hall. As a result, the size of the lending library was increased on the S. side and on the other side of the entrance a committee room was provided. This was was turned into a ladies' reading-room in 1898 after a request with 250 signatures. Extra floor space was also provided for the main reading room. In 1893 an adjacent strip of land was purchased from Canon Palmer and the Ecclesiastical Commissioners to make a passage way from the entrance hall to the back premises. A legacy in 1898 from Mrs Meadows of £500 enabled this to be covered over and it was used for occasional exhibitions. More land was acquired later to widen the Aubrey Street frontage. At this time an open yard lay behind the reading room with a stable and a narrow walkway to Aubrey Street. The insanitary lavatories were situated in an outbuilding next to an outside stairway, which led to the museum.

This area was to prove useful when finally the plans were carried out for an extension. In 1898 the Museums and Gymnasiums Act was adopted and this allowed the city council to raise a halfpenny rate towards the upkeep of the museum which had been left several valuable natural history collections by Woolhope Club members. There was also pressure to commemorate the queen's diamond jubilee by such an improvement. In 1900 electric light replaced gas after the new electricity works had installed cables along Broad Street. This was a great advance both for reading and for the leather-bound volumes, which were attacked by the gas fumes. For a time, due to lack of space, the reference library was housed in the Woolhope Room, and the Hereford Society for Aiding the Industrious gave another £250 for printed catalogues to be available so that books could be requested 'by all classes of society'.

The new century began with a legacy of £1,000 from Sir Joseph Pulley, former MP for the City, for the library extensions, and to further the project his nephew, Charles Pulley, contributed the same amount. The committee managing the extensions requested permission from the dean and chapter to put in three new windows in the S. wall of the proposed reference library overlooking their property which would enable the planned art gallery above to be the same width and to be lit by a large window in Aubrey Street. By 1910 the final plans of architects Groome and Bettington had been approved and sent to the council. The extensions were to cost £3,000 and once more Mr Pulley furnished sufficient funds after an appeal to the Carnegie Fund had been turned down because there was a museum in the building. The work was carried out by Willis & Son and was opened on 12 April 1912 by Mrs Pulley who was presented with a key with the arms of the city in enamels.[15]

The result of the enlargement was that the reference library was removed from the Woolhope Room and restored to the main library area. Half of this was a lending library where the shelves had been lowered to allow access to the books for selection by the readers. The corridor housed the fiction lending section. By 1913 there had been a rapid increase in book issues of over 10,000 a year. The librarian, James Cockcroft, had his office situated in a strategic position between the reference library and the lending library. Plate-glass windows separated the magazine room from the newsroom. 'The combined rooms give a very commanding appearance viewed from the vestibule,' reported William Collins at the time.

The picture gallery, 58ft x 38ft, was built above the extended lending library with an elegant wooden arch over doors leading into it from the museum. A ladies' lavatory was installed between the stairs to the librarian's apartment and the Woolhope Room, with a door from the room into the stairs-passage. This was to prove a nuisance to later librarians who lived in the apartment and it was removed. The basement storage was also enlarged under the new addition.

The extensions had taken fifteen years to materialize and for the building to reach its final extent. Sadly, in James Cockcroft's later years as librarian his management had declined, so that no new books were added from 1910 to 1924 when a new and talented librarian, Frederick Morgan, was appointed.[16] He found a basement full of rubbish, unsavoury characters loitering around the reading room, while ladies from the country sat over their lunches in the ladies reading room. Changes were made.

F. C. Morgan, later to be chief steward of the city and a centenarian, became a distinguished secretary of the Woolhope Club. As curator he was able to re-organise the museum and added many new collections. Under his supervision, the library, museum and club prospered in harmony.

Today, the building, viewed with disfavour forty years ago, has achieved a venerable appearance in a street despoiled by modern fronts. The library has once more outgrown its space but Kempson's dream of a building to house the Arts and Sciences remains relevant. The Woolhope Club continues to flourish, contributing to knowledge in natural history, archaeology, vernacular architecture and geology as it has done for over 150 years.

REFERENCES

[1] N. Pevsner, *Buildings of England: Herefordshire* (1963), 187.

[2] J. Jones, *Hereford Cathedral and City* (1855), 119.

[3] W. Collins, *Builders of Modern Hereford* (1909), 27.

[4] *The Builder*, 13 February 1875, 140. This also gives a full architectural description but contains inaccuracies.

[5] Now the florists 'Daisy Chains'.

[6] *First Report of the Committee for the Free Library* (1871), 42. This is the first of a series of published annual reports (1871-1922) in the library local collection in five volumes, which chart the progress of the library and museum. Dr Bull was chairman for this first report. The third report gives the costs of the site, architect's fees, building and internal fittings. HL. 027.4. These reports have been summarised in T. G. Porter & J. F. W. Sherwood, *Hereford Public Library: the First Hundred Years* (1974), an unpublished typescript in HL. Fp LC 027.4.

[7] Pevsner called it 'Tudor, stone and institutional'.

[8] M. Brooks, *John Ruskin and Victorian Architecture* (1989), 169, contains useful details of Seddon's work.

[9] Other work by Kempson in Herefordshire included: Ullingswick, Little Cowarne, Hope-Under-Dinmore, Holy Trinity (1883), all church restoration or building, and the following schools: Allensmore, Bishop's Frome, St Peter's Bromyard, All Saint's Hereford, Holmer, St Paul's Tupsley, Mordiford, Stoke Lacy. There was also the convent of the Poor Clares and Kington market hall plus numerous country houses. His assistant, William Martin, trained in Dublin and worked with Kempson for ten years at 134 St Owen Street before setting up on his own. Kempson's work in Glamorgan and Llandaff is recorded in J. Newman, *The Buildings of Wales: Glamorgan*.

[10] This line of the Clarke family has died out but Robert's younger brother, William, who also worked on the library carvings, remained at Llandaff and carried on a family business of church furnishers and builders which continues today. I am indebted to Mr W. R. P. Clarke MBE, TD, for this information. There is an obituary of Robert Clarke in the *TWNFC* (1917), 293 and he is buried in the cemetery, All Saints' section.

[11] They may have been carried out by Kate Faulkner who often did commissions for Burne-Jones and Morris.

[12] Letter from C. Blanchett of 'The Tiles and Architectural Ceramics Society' who considers the tiles of great importance as examples of the Arts and Crafts period.

[13] George With had been a master at the Bluecoat School but was appointed chemist and then assistant secretary of the Hereford Society for Aiding the Industrious.

[14] Collins. *Builders*, 26. There are graphic accounts in the *Hereford Times* 10 Oct. 1874.

[15] Groome and Bettington papers and plans in HRO. K21/58. Bettington was assistant to Kempson and lived near him in Bromyard at Flaggoners Green – *Hereford Times* 2 August 1963. An account of the opening ceremony of the extensions is in W. Collins, *A Short History of Hereford* (1912), 106.

[16] James Cockcroft had been librarian since 1888.

Plate 1. Percy Pritchard in his First World War army uniform.

Plate 2. It is wartime (World War II) – notice the restricted headlights – but Percy Pritchard is proudly displaying his new Ford Prefect. The good quality overcoat is obviously available at 1 & 2 Commercial Street and is excellent protection against the winter-rain, which falls easily off the well-waxed bodywork of the car. The Herefordshire lanes are still quiet and ancient barns still serve their traditional function and are not threatened with demolition or conversion.

The Pritchards:
a Family of Hereford Photographers

DAVID WHITEHEAD & PAUL LATCHAM

Percy Pritchard enjoyed a certain celebrity as a photographer of the local scene but it is less well known that his father Walter and his uncle Frank were also keen. The extensive collection of photos left at Percy's death in 1996 includes examples of their work. The images stretch back over a hundred years and chronicle the enthusiasms of the individual photographers as well as the life of the family in their successive homes and places of business.

Like his father Walter and his grandfather William before him, Percy ran the family tailoring business in Hereford, as his son Edward continues to do in King Street today. William founded the business in 1836. Frank was the youngest of William's sons and did not go into the family business. Serving in the Great War, he lost an arm in France. He was fitted with an artificial limb and worked in a government recuperation facility at Rotherwas. Frank was a very keen photographer and died in the 1930s. Little else is known about him.

Percy served his apprenticeship in London and gained his qualification as a master tailor and cutter. In an interview he gave the *Hereford Times* in 1986, when 90 years old, he recalled how tailors sat cross-legged in the workshop at their work. Amongst their number were some of the flotsam and jetsam of society, men without families and sometimes without homes, prone to drink too much. Some of these were allowed to sleep on the premises. Wages were low and, looking back, Percy couldn't credit how some brought up families on between 18s 6d to 25s a week. The Pritchards were generous employers; Walter is said to have introduced the half-day closing in Hereford. The clergy, from gaitered bishops down, came to Pritchards, as did farmers and sportsmen riding their horses and traps to the shop door, and servants from the big houses for their liveries.

Walter and Percy were both Woolhopians, Walter from 1919 and Percy from 1934. Walter was friendly with Alfred Watkins who would come into Pritchard's shop in High Town and yarn about their common interests. They would excursion together like all good club members of their day and, although they both had businesses to run, they were not afraid to take time away from work to pursue their interests. Percy later continued the tradition of sometimes allowing his well-organised business to run itself without his presence.

Percy was still a young man when one day Alfred Watkins called in to invite Walter to join him on an excursion, which Walter was too busy on that day to do. 'Take the boy', said Walter, and Percy duly went. After a good day out Watkins suggested they stop at a pub for some bread and cheese (those were the days!) and, when seated in the hostelry, Watkins sent Percy outside to top up the water tank of his steam car. The young man unscrewed the cap he believed to be the location for water-filling and proceeded to flood the paraffin tank. He had to endure something of a telling-off. Percy, according to those who knew him, had a mystic streak in his character and one of its manifestations was implicit belief in the concept of ley lines. It is pleasing to think of Watkins instilling his theories in the head of his young acolyte while motoring round the Herefordshire countryside of the early 1900s.

Percy Pritchard lived to within a few days of his one hundredth birthday and was a familiar sight a few years ago strolling peacefully across the close feeding the birds. War took him to some exotic places and gave him exciting adventures but, that apart, he lived all his life in Hereford where he became something of an institution. As a young volunteer he saw service at Gallipoli where he was wounded and taken to Malta. When recovered he enlisted in the Imperial Camel Corps and served in the desert on the back of his camel 'Johnny'. He met and served with Lawrence of Arabia. Later he was seconded to the Royal Flying Corps at Middle East Brigade HQ in Cairo. When the 1939-45 war came round he was commissioned into the Royal Air Force as flight-lieutenant and was engaged in training glider pilots.

An enthusiastic recreational glider, Percy regularly took to the air from the Lugg Meadows and the Long Mynde. He had a passion for motor cars and motorcycles which manifested itself in his ownership of an early Brescia Bugatti. Percy was one of the earliest amateur radio enthusiasts in Hereford and when the family lived at Blenheim House in Broad Street (one of the houses that stood in front of the cathedral at the top of King Street) he obtained permission to string an aerial lead across the street to the top of the library building in order to facilitate his transmissions. He was a man of many enthusiasms (boating on the river, fishing and bee-keeping were others) but perhaps the hobby that lasted the longest was photography - Percy was very proud of his ARPS (Associate of the Royal Photographic Society) qualification.

The purpose of this article is to record the work of these three Hereford photographers who loved photography and photographing their county. None of them would have made any claim to be other than amateur in status but what shines through is their enthusiasm. Much of their work is creative photography, exploiting the artistic possibilities of camera images, for both Frank and Percy belonged to photographic societies nationally and locally, regularly entering their work competitively.

They did not see the camera exclusively as a tool for recording the changing scene or the picturesque elements of the life around them, although their work includes images that admirably perform that function. Nowadays the camera is so often used to record what is left to us of times gone by and more rarely for artistic effect. Our preoccupation is with the chronicling of the lives and developing physiognomy of those we love and the recording for posterity of those things we find worthy and beautiful, particularly if they are in danger of disappearing. In times gone by these aims were also present but amongst amateur photographers there was often a commitment to composition, to images that pleased because, like paintings and drawings, they were artistically conceived. Frank Pritchard was particularly interested in the compositional aspects of photography, and Percy may have been encouraged in that direction by him.

The selection of photographs that follows results from several hours sorting through a large accumulation. Percy was often approached for photographs and was generous in allowing copying and reproduction. Many photographs taken by him and by Walter and Frank have appeared in print over the years but we hope these have not.

ACKNOWLEDGEMENTS Very many thanks to Elizabeth Patrick and Edward Pritchard for allowing the photographs to be reproduced here and for providing much help with biographical information on their family. Thanks also to Basil Butcher for memories of the Pritchards and to Derek Foxton for comments on the proofs.

Plate 3. The bike in the front is a Douglas and was apparently registered on 19 January 1921 to R. Morgan of Broxwood, Pembridge. That behind is a Harley Davidson with a Birmingham registration number. It was built in 1919. The women in front – dressed like Eastern European peasants but presumably in fashionable gear – look very purposeful although the passenger, perched on the pillion, seems overtly vulnerable. The machines look powerful enough but presumably the lanes were empty and the occasional spill into the ditch was part of the fun. Motorcycling was middle class and sporty but even Walter or Frank, one of whom probably took this photograph, thought the two girls mounted up front looked a little risqué. Such were the results of female emancipation!

Plate 4. Possibly the Herefordshire Hockey Club – captain, Allen Jenkins – who are mentioned in Jakeman and Carver's *Directory* of 1902. Fourth from the right with the cap is Will Pritchard, Walter's and Frank's brother. The photograph is perhaps by Frank. The exact position of the ground is difficult to identify but the cathedral is closer to the spot than St Peter's (?) spire, suggesting that it is south of the river. A fine collection of young men, wonderful moustaches – notice the ball balanced on the crossbar.

Plate 7. The second edition of the 6in OS plan of 1904 depicts the Blackfriars' monastery besieged by allotments. The photograph is by Alfred Watkins but Walter Pritchard frequently went on photographic excursions with Watkins. The ruins are peculiarly domesticated by the rows of neat cabbages, potatoes etc; the result, no doubt, of the excellent local response to the Smallholdings and Allotment Act of 1908, which made it mandatory for local authorities to provide plots for their citizens. The preaching cross had been restored by George Gilbert Scott in 1864 and neatly hedged around, but the remains of the cloister, albeit cleared of ivy at the same time, is once again about to succumb to the Victorian's favourite parasite. Beyond the gardens are the engine sheds of the Barrs Court station and above, the bosky skyline of Venn's Lane, terminating with the park-like grounds of Penngrove House and, across Aylestone Hill, the aptly named The Elms.

Plate 5. Opposite top: This looks like fun! An encounter in a Herefordshire lane in c1890 of some Pritchard ladies – Auntie Ada, Auntie Jessie and Auntie Hetty – photographed presumably by their brother Frank – with a couple of rustic characters who probably come with a safety warning. There is immunity in numbers. Lovely straw hats, trimmed blouses and full skirts – nice smiles too. Classic chaps – bowler hats, moleskin trousers with spats and wayward beards. How we have changed.

Plate 6. Opposite bottom: Any minute now Ella Mary Leather and Vaughan Williams will appear on the scene seeking a rendering of one of those ancient songs, which lay untainted by the music hall and phonograph in the hearts of Herefordshire's travelling folk. The setting appears to be the Lugg Meadows and a pile of wool (or some such material) has been laid out on a cloth. Are the bags nearby being stuffed with it? The patriarchal figure with the top hat appears to be whittling a stick. There is much dignity in this photograph and, perhaps a yearning by Frank Pritchard for the freedom and independence portrayed here.

Plate 8. The Woolhope Club *c*1925, smoking and resting after a hard morning of antiquarianism. Hats are obviously part of the uniform and tweedy clothes to get in amongst the brambles and nettles to investigate those fugitive relics of the county's past. On the right a piece of paper has been produced and a quick lecture – an hour at least, according to the earlier transactions – is about to be delivered. This is serious man's stuff, there are no women – presumably they are at home posing in front of their cottages for the like of Frank Pritchard. This photograph, however, is probably by Walter Pritchard.

Plate 9. Opposite top: A Herefordshire village – Bosbury – unassailed by motor vehicles, quiet and remote – approached by sticky roads with weedy edges. The scowling farm-boy has been asked to pose with his pony by Frank Pritchard who has set up his big black camera in the churchyard. The world depicted here, explored by early members of the Woolhope Club, connected so easily with times past, environmental change had been imperceptible for centuries, until the modern communications revolution broke the thread of continuity and destroyed 'localism' forever. On the positive side, however, the two houses depicted here have hardly changed, some slight variations in windows and doors, and a little more white paint. The lane in the fore ground leads to Catley, whilst the narrow opening opposite is called Mill Lane – a hop yard is just visible in the distance.

Plate 10. Opposite bottom: The river and the bridge at Hereford *c*1900 by Frank Pritchard. Plenty of activity and a pleasant strip of meadowland where the ring road was to crash through in the late 1960s. The stone quay of the Greyfriars is just visible on the left, a relic of its days as an important manufactory. In the middle distance the dignified late Georgian houses of Wye Terrace, their gardens full of burgeoning evergreens and the tip of the communal fountain just visible. How pleasantly they connect with the river and the surrounding landscape. The cathedral still displays Wyatt's west front – pinnacled and crenellated – so the date must be before 1902 when it was demolished and replaced with Oldrid Scott's feeble composition.

Plate 13. An unusual view, taken perhaps by Percy, from the new west front of the cathedral, looking towards Broad Street where the bulk of the city library overshadows the Residency. In the foreground the range of buildings which blocked the close until the 1930s. The large mansard-roofed house was occupied in 1902 by Henry Cecil Moore, surgeon, and a little later it was a boarding house. The buildings all look late Georgian but the houses are present on Taylor's plan of 1757 but not apparent – as far as it is possible to see – on Speede's plan of 1610. It is likely, therefore, that this piece of encroachment came during the 1650s when the administration of the cathedral was suspended. The fine cast-iron paling and the gateway with its lamp in an overthrow, probably date from the 1830s when the close was fenced.

Plate 11. Opposite top: Walter Pritchard looks out of one of the windows of Blenheim House – No. 24 Broad Street – upon scenes of devastation in the cathedral close. Several ancient elms, which had been a feature of the close since time immemorial, have been felled. The chapter act books refer to the planting of elms at various times in the eighteenth century, which were also regularly cropped for repairs to cathedral and canonical houses. The trees are marked on Taylor's plan of 1757 forming a series of alleys, which one commentator compared with St James' Park in London! As they became older the trees began to drop limbs and were condemned as dangerous in 1846. Following the tragic death of two children, crushed by a falling tree on Castle Green, in 1894 the chapter decided to replace them with better-behaved limes – some of which already appear quite mature in the background of this photograph.

Plate 12. Opposite bottom: There are many similar images of Broad Street in the early twentieth century but this one is distinguished by the wet weather and the viewpoint – out of the bedroom window of Walter Pritchard's house at the west-end of the close. It's Sunday and the Library is closed. Architecturally, the street has reached it apogee – the late-Victorian building boom has left it with a fine assemblage of gothic, classical and Italianate structures. The Modern Movement is simply a twinkle in the eye of a few members of the avant-garde and not until the 1960s did it begin to destroy the revivalist integrity of Hereford's finest street. The cars would indicate a date in the mid-1920s.

Plate 14. Frank Pritchard – mother and child doing the washing before a thatched cottage. Less posed than many similar scenes with the real world of grinding poverty tipping the balance against romanticism. But again, lots of good props – the ancient sieve; worn-out galvanised containers used as planters and two plaited bee skeps hanging from the door-case. Notice also how the whitewash on the cottage has covered the timbers – as it would need to, to act as a proofing medium.

Plate 15. Opposite top: The gardeners pause and brace themselves as Frank Pritchard – with an unerring eye for a good composition – captures another quintessential *fin de siecle* scene. The well-dressed child in the well-kept garden. It is early summer and the espalier pears on the wall are in full leaf; the strawberries have been strawed and on the left the soft fruit (raspberries?) have reached full height. Beyond, the asparagus has run to seed but the runner beans have yet to cover their sticks. The conic cloches – no longer in use – represent very desirable garden ornaments today.

Plate 16. Opposite bottom: A garden possibly located at Hunderton where young Percy used to spend his holidays. The Wye lies beyond the chestnut pale. The walled garden has seen better days, but the glorious hand-made bricks have an irreplaceable patina. Similarly, the wheelbarrow, which is not beyond some sensitive repairs. Most desirable are the ceramic pots – good sizes too – all round-rimmed in the traditional English manner (no thick French collars!) and, undoubtedly, the wares of Sankey & Co. of Nottingham, the ubiquitous flower-pot manufacturers of the early twentieth century. A great copper is being utilised for washing the pots – a winter chore for all serious gardeners before the advent of plastic.

Plate 19. The early morning mist rises from the tepid waters of the Wye, warmed by one of those halcyon summers of the 1930s. Percy Pritchard has borrowed a boat or donned some waders to get this low perspective shot of the cathedral, framed artistically in the medieval arch of the bridge and veiled in the trees of the bishop's garden. The river is low, showing the stone aprons (concrete?) protecting the bridge piers. The two historic phases of the bridge's construction are also revealed. In the foreground, the narrow fifteenth-century bridge, built of fine even ashlar, and beyond the widening of 1826.

Plate 17. Opposite top: Frank Pritchard – competition entry entitled 'Three Little Maids from School'. A wonderful evocative image, full of giggly self-consciousness and purposeful walks. The photographer is trying to compete with the sentimental prints and paintings of the late nineteenth century and comes up trumps. In the background the brooding backbone of the Black Mountains – innocence reflected against the sublimity of nature?

Plate 18. Opposite bottom: Frank Pritchard – competition entry entitled 'Sunlight in the old farmyard'. The photographic equivalent of a Helen Allingham painting but with a rather uncooperative hen, which refuses to stand still for the long exposure. Today every vernacular detail in this picture is a desirable object for the cognoscenti – including the woman stoically prepared to tolerate such an idyll. The building with its mixture of roof-cladding could well be in south-west Herefordshire. The tree – much beaten – appears to be a walnut.

Plate 20. Percy Pritchard's ploughman of January 1939 is an image replete with all the lyricism of the traditional winter countryside; a place worth dying for later in 1940 when this sort of scene was exploited to turn up the patriotic heat during the Battle of Britain. Herefordshire farmers were still ploughing in the late winter and planting in spring, which was so much better for the lapwings, skylarks and all the other arable birds that we took for granted in those days.

Plate 21. Late afternoon at Pritchard & Sons, tailors, 1 & 2 Commercial Street in the 1930s. Looking towards the back of the shop – the 'Tailoring Dept.' – the profile of an unknown figure just visible on the left. The traditional shop revealed – innumerable mahogany and glass display cases, lots of mirrors and bentwood chairs for the weary shopper or a prop for posing. It all looks so familiar but so remote.

Herefordshire Plants

PETER THOMSON

The Tees-Exe line is a simple way of dividing Britain into its highland and lowland zones. The highland zone to the north and west of the line is characterised by its relatively hard Palaeozoic rocks which form high ground, frequently with thin, hungry soils, whilst the lowlands are characterised by the English scarplands of limestone and chalk separated by clay vales and richer, more productive soils.

Herefordshire combines characteristics of both zones. The county is entirely underlain by Palaeozoic rocks. Some, as in the Malvern Hills and Black Mountains, are true to the upland type with high, steep land and hungry soil but in the central areas the Silurian Limestone scarplands are prominent in the Woolhope Hills, vale of Wigmore and the foothills between Ledbury and the Malvern Hills. The soils of the lowlands around Leominster, Hereford and Ross, where the easily eroded lower divisions of the Old Red Sandstone have been worn away, display the rich agricultural character of the lowland zone.

Agriculture is made possible because of the natural fertility of the deep soils, attributable in part to the widespread occurrence of lime in the hills of the scarplands, and in the cornstone bands at a number of levels within the Old Red Sandstone.

Soils and habitats are not only affected by the underlying solid geology, as this is obscured in many parts of the county by glacial and later deposits. Unlike many other areas within the highland zone Herefordshire displays little of the effects of glacial erosion. It is possible that the scarp in such sites as Moccas Park and below Merbach Hill were undercut and oversteepened by Devensian ice of the last major glacial advance pushing down the Wye Valley to its limit at Stretton Sugwas.

The most notable effects of the glaciation were the blanket of deposits left by the ice, the spreads of sediment left by meltwater streams, the disruption and diversion of drainage and the creation of inland water bodies. These latter take the form of small kettle-hole lakes or ponds amongst moraine in, for example, the Kington-Mortimer's Cross area. Larger water bodies were at one time present where water was impounded by glacial action and their traces now remain as wetlands such as Byton Moor, Wigmore lakes and Letton lakes. These features inherited from the glacial period are found mainly west of the River Lugg as its line marks the approximate limit of Devensian ice in the county. Evidence for a much earlier advance of ice is found further east where fragmentary gravel capped hills, such as Sutton Walls, are remnants of ancient terraces.

When considering the distribution of plants and habitats on a large scale the two most important factors are probably climate and the place of origin and mode of dispersal of the plant concerned. Local distributions are affected by other factors such as soils, relief, altitude, microclimates and land management past and present.

Within the county there is a wide range of habitats dependent on relief. The height of the land varies from about 20m where the Wye leaves the area near Monmouth to 703m on the border with Brecknockshire on the plateau of the Black Mountains. The county is almost completely surrounded by relatively high ground. The Malverns form an eastern barrier, the Forest of Dean to the south-east, Black Mountains and their foothills to the south-west, the north western uplands extend to Ludlow and the Bromyard plateau completes the circuit. The central parts are divided into three main lowland areas by two upland belts, which run more or less north-east to south-west. The steep-sided Dinmore and Wormsley hills separate the Leominster and Hereford lowlands and the Woolhope, Aconbury and Orcop hills divide the latter from the sandy soils of the Ross lowlands.

The rivers also form significant habitats especially as the Wye, Lugg and Teme are all designated as Sites of Special Scientific Interest (SSSIs). Their slower reaches with muddy beds contrast with the riffles of gravel and support contrasting plant life. The flood plains were traditionally used for hay meadows but few now remain in this management and several have been ploughed.

Climatically Herefordshire is more continental than its westerly position would lead one to expect. The hills which surround it place it in a rain shadow so that in the central parts rainfall is only about 28in (70cm) per year although this rises to over 50in (128cm) on the Black Mountains. The high margins also lead the area to become a frost pocket in winter.

Just as Herefordshire straddles the highland/lowland boundary with respect to its physical features so it does with its plant life, which ranges from species-rich ancient, broadleaved woodland to species-poor heathland on the summit plateau of the Black Mountains.

Several plants illustrate this contrast by reaching their limits of distribution in the area (F. H. Perring & S. M. Walters, *Atlas of the British Flora*, 1962). Characteristic of the lowland zone are: *Euphorbia amygdaloides,* wood spurge, which reaches its north-western limits in south Shropshire but is abundant in woods on rich soils and, some say, more common where there are former charcoal burning sites; *Cirsium acaule*, stemless thistle, is a plant of short limestone turf, being frequent in chalk and lime-stone areas further east but rarer in Herefordshire although it penetrates to Ewyas Harold common and even to a cornstone band at about 500m on the Cat's Back. Whether or not it produces viable seeds in these sites is not known; *Filipendula vulgaris*, dropwort, is a plant of limestone pastures but it maintains a tenuous foot-hold on the south-facing limestone of the Seven Sisters on the Great Doward.

The plants with highland affinities include *Huperzia selago,* fir clubmoss, which may no longer be a Herefordshire plant as our last sighting was on north-facing rocks at the head of the Olchon Valley in the late 1960s. *Asplenium viride*, green spleenwort, is now very scarce in the Black Mountains. *Trollius europaeus,* globe flower, remains in a few damp sites in the west of the county and *Saxifraga hypnoides*, mossy saxifrage, maintains a foothold on damp screes near our western border.

We have no endemic plants but for some species the county is a major centre. *Viscum album*, mistletoe, is found in all parts of the county and is common in Worcestershire and Gloucestershire to the east but only penetrates a little way along the Wye into Radnorshire to the west. The parasite grows on many host trees but is most frequent on apple, with hawthorn and lime following close behind. It is very uncommon on oak but Herefordshire can boast more records for mistletoe on this tree than any other county.

Colchicum autumnale, meadow saffron, often wrongly called autumn crocus, is another plant whose main centre of distribution is now in counties in the lower Severn region including Herefordshire where it grows in meadows, scrub and open woodland.

Campanula patula, spreading bellflower, is found sporadically in many parts of the county and rarely elsewhere. Its seeds will remain dormant in the soil for long periods, germinating when the ground is broken. It can be found on a few road verges, in open woods after coppicing or felling and on disturbed patches of soil on a few banks in pastureland.

Some nationally rare or scarce plants are present in the county. Rarities are described in the *Red Data Book 1 Vascular Plants* (F. H. Perring and L. Farrell, 1962) and Herefordshire has very few of these viz.:

Buxus sempervirens, box, reported from a few sites. In *A Flora of Herefordshire* (W. H. Purchas and A. Ley, 1889) it is described as 'planted in several places as a cover in game reserves' and 'only existing where planted'. Perhaps this explains the present records.

Epipogium aphyllum, ghost orchid, was first reported in 1854 in the Tedstone Delamere area and in 1881 near Ludlow – possibly in Shropshire (W. H. Purchas and A. Ley, 1889). In 1889 these were the only reports for the species and it has been found very rarely in the twentieth century, the last time being in 1982, when a solitary spike appeared.

Mentha puligeum, pennyroyal, was reported recently from a wet site near Ledbury.

Sorbus eminens, a whitebeam, is found on limestone rocks on the Great Doward.

Nationally scarce plants are selected as those occupying from 16-100km squares in the Atlas and are fully described in *Scarce Plants in Britain* (Compiled and edited by A. Stewart, D. A. Pearman, and C. D. Preston, 1994). Of a total of fifty-four scarce plants recorded in Herefordshire only twenty-nine (54%) have been recorded since 1970. Of these only the following have been seen in recent years:

Aconitum napellus, monkshood.

Campanula patula, spreading bellflower – occurs sporadically and sometimes in considerable quantities.

Cardamine impatiens, narrow-leaved bitter-cress – which may appear after felling in some woods.

Carex digitata, fingered sedge – grows mainly on limestone cliffs and shallow soils on the Great Doward.

Carex humilis, dwarf sedge, reaches its most northerly site also on thin limestone soils on the Great Doward.

Carex montana, soft-leaved sedge, grows in south facing wooded sites on the Great Doward probably where loess overlies the limestone.

Dianthus deltoides, maiden pink, survives on one hill in the north of the county.

Euphrasia rostkoviana ssp rostkoviana, an eye bright, is found in a few meadows in the west of Herefordshire, where it is at the eastern edge of its range.

Fritillaria meleagris, fritillary, occurs in the Lugg Meadows where, unlike most populations of this plant, the bulk of the flowers are white.

Gymnocarpium robertianum, limestone fern, grows on lime-rich screes in the Black Mountains.

Helleborus foetidus, stinking hellebore, is found in open woodland and hedgerows in some Silurian and Carboniferous limestone areas.

Hordelymus europaeus, wood barley, is a grass of limy woodland soils.

Hornungia petraea, hutchinsia, formerly grew in cracks and on limestone ledges on the Little Doward and has recently been re-found.

Meconopsis cambrica, Welsh poppy, is frequently a garden escape but is probably a native on some Black Mountain screes.

Oenanthe silaifolia, narrow-leaved water-dropwort, is a plant of unimproved wet meadows and one of the country's biggest populations is found in meadows beside the Lower Lugg.

Orobanche rapum-genistae, greater broomrape, is a scrub plant usually parasitic on broom or gorse and seen very infrequently.

Pilularia globulifera, pillwort, is a fern with grass-like fronds which creeps over the bare muddy margins of shallow winter wet pools at one site in the county. The plant is declining more on the continent than in Britain but is nevertheless increasingly rare here.

Potamogeton trichoides, hairlike pondweed, is known from one site in a stretch of restored canal.

Potentilla neumanniana, spring cinquefoil, is known from a site with skeletal limestone soil in the Woolhope Hills.

Sedum forsterianum, rock stonecrop, has been reported from several sites on rocks and screes in north-west Herefordshire.

Sorbus porrigentiformis, a whitebeam, is found in the woods on the Great Doward.

Tilia platyphyllos, large-leaved lime. Herefordshire has more records for this tree than other counties. It is found in several of our ancient woodlands where some large old coppiced specimens survive.

Truly natural vegetation unaffected by human activity now hardly exists except perhaps on inaccessible cliffs, whilst agricultural land can be almost completely controlled, but between these extremes there are a number of semi-natural habitats where intervention has been limited. Ancient woodland is one of these and Herefordshire is fortunate in having many small, and some large, areas of such woodland. Ideally an ancient woodland should never have been cleared and replaced by another form of land use since the area was colonised by trees in the post-glacial period. Even if such a wood existed it would be very difficult to prove its pedigree so a compromise definition is used. This allows a wood to be designated as ancient if it was deciduous, broad-leaved woodland in 1700 AD and has remained so to the present time.

In Herefordshire a number of such woods have been allowed to remain, particularly on steep slopes such as those rising above the Wye downstream from Symonds Yat where there are precipitous drops from the plateau surface to the river. Elsewhere they occur on the slopes of the Cornstone hills such as Dinmore and amongst the limestone scarplands where Paget's Wood near Fownhope, owned by the Herefordshire Nature Trust, is a good example. Larger areas of ancient woodland are Haugh Wood in the centre of the Woolhope hills and Queen's Wood, Dymock which straddles the Herefordshire-Gloucestershire border. In both these cases they occur on less fertile soils overlying Silurian/Llandovery sandstones and a low plateau of Downton Castle sandstone respectively. Both these large woods have been managed by the Forestry Commission who have introduced conifers, which reduce the amount of light reaching the ground and produce an acid humus. This has caused a decline of the deciduous woodland flowering plants but where the conifers have been cleared and the traditional coppice management has been re-introduced some of the former flora is returning. This has happened in Queen's Wood, Dymock, where some conservation areas have been established by co-operation between the Forestry Commission and a group of Ledbury naturalists led by Dr Michael Harper.

In a native, broadleaved, deciduous woodland, conditions on the woodland floor are strongly influenced by changes in the canopy. In winter, after leaves have fallen, sunlight can penetrate to ground level but also heat can be lost more rapidly on clear nights by radiation when there is little insulation above. In early spring, about April, with the canopy still open and the days warmer and longer, it is the time for most of the ground flora to bloom and set seed, before the incoming light is reduced by the canopy leaves.

The tree species found most frequently are *Quercus robur and petraea*, pedunculate and sessile oak, *Fraxinus excelsior*, ash, and *Prunus avium*, cherry. The oak and ash were formerly coppiced, the oak to supply timber and bark for the tanning trade, while the ash was valued for the strength and suppleness of its wood. This was used for tool and scythe handles and Herefordshire ash was used in the half-timbered Morris Minor Traveller. Until World War II coppicing was a major system of woodland management but with the coming of cheaper imported supplies the practice languished and the coppiced woodlands fell into decline. Results of this are that many present woods contain overgrown coppice and few, if any, large old trees.

The limes, both *Tilia cordata*, small-leaved lime, and *Tilia platyphyllos*, large-leaved lime, are two species which are indicative of ancient woodland and Herefordshire is fortunate in being well endowed with both. In Britain the small-leaved lime grows in more or less isolated areas within which it is relatively common. These concentrations are mainly in eastern England, a major exception being in Herefordshire and the Wye Valley. It is found, together with large-leaved lime, on many of the steep wooded slopes overlooking the Wye, as at the base of the slope below Capler Hill and on the lower slopes of Dinmore Hill. Some of the trees are very large such as one, on private land, on the edge of a wood near Vowchurch. This is an ancient pollard and lies on a parish boundary. In many places the trees have been coppiced along with the rest of the wood. Here the coppice regrowth is vigorous and the stools may be up to six metres across or even more. One, which has been allowed to grow, lies near a footpath between Ullingswick and Little Cowarne. This was left when the wood around it was cleared for pasture and now forms a magnificent feature with many sizeable 'trunks'. Some woods have large areas of small-leaved lime, examples being in Bear's Wood on the northern edge of Haugh Wood and in Skenchill Wood near Llanrothal. Dr Oliver Rackham in his book *Ancient Woodlands* states, referring mainly to limes in eastern England: 'Many stools are centuries old and some may even date from the first encoppicement of the woods' while Richard Mabey in *Flora Britannica* quotes Oliver Rackham and Donald Pigott's estimate of a clone's age as at least 2,000 years and quotes also private speculation that some clones may be more than 6,000 years old. In the 'Ancient Wildwood' over much of the Midlands and eastern England it is shown by pollen analysis that lime may have been the dominant tree.

Sorbus torminalis, the wild service tree, is another indicator of ancient woodland which is relatively abundant in Herefordshire. For example, it can be picked out easily in autumn on the south slope of Haugh Wood by its yellow to pink, or even red, foliage and the late Dr C. W. Walker claimed, perhaps with a little exaggeration, that the higher parts of this wood had been wild service coppice. It is also plentiful in Queen's Wood, Dymock, and on upper slopes of the Great Doward woodlands and in many other sites throughout the county. It is regarded as a rare tree nationally and was, at the time of preparation of the *Atlas of British Flora* in the 1950s, recorded more frequently in east and south-east England, but with more intensive botanical recording in Herefordshire over the last twenty years it is known to be very widespread here too. In some places large, almost pure, stands of the tree are found where it has spread intensively by suckers.

Both wild service and the limes occur occasionally in hedgerows and may indicate that the hedge has originated as a managed line of old woodland or that they were planted or that they colonised the hedge by seeding into it. As saplings of these trees are rare the latter option seems unlikely.

Other trees of the ancient woods include *Ulmus glabra*, Wych Elm, which has survived the onslaught of Dutch Elm disease better than its hedgerow relative *Ulmus procera*, the English elm. *Acer campestre*, field maple, which although better known as a hedgerow species, may attain the size of its neighbours in the woods. Likewise *Corylus avellana*, hazel, although most frequent as a coppiced shrub, may grow to become a small tree of 30ft or so in height.

Just as some species of tree are characteristic of ancient woodland so too are many plants in the herb or ground layer. The extent to which many of these plants are associated with ancient woods has not been studied in Herefordshire but G. J. Peterken has undertaken such a study in Lincolnshire and some of his findings are tabulated in Oliver Rackham's *Ancient Woodlands*. Although the situation in Herefordshire may well differ from that of an eastern seaboard county it will nevertheless be referred to where it seems appropriate.

Hyacynthoides non-scripta, bluebell, occurs as carpets in many woods in our area but on a world, or even European, scale it is relatively rare, being distinctly British in distribution. Outside Britain it is found only in neighbouring areas of northern France. Even though the plant is abundant in many of our woods it is nevertheless nationally facing many threats from woodland clearance, trampling, digging for sale in some nurseries, 'dilution' by hybridisation with the Spanish bluebell and possibly by global warming. The bulbs may be up to 25cms (10in) below the surface where they are vulnerable to long periods of waterlogging and it therefore avoids wet ground.

Anemone nemorosa, wood anemone, may also occur in carpets and having shallower roots it can tolerate damp sites better than the bluebell.

Mercuralis perennis, dog's mercury, is a third widespread species which may dominate the woodland floor. It prefers drier sites on limy soils than the previous plant and thrives in woodland shade.

All these species grow in some hedgerows and they may grow in unshaded places in damp, cool upland sites.

Some other plants of our woodlands which are described as having a very strong or strong association with ancient woodland in Lincolnshire, are as follows:

Galium odoratum, woodruff, frequently found in woodland rides on rich soils.
Paris quadrifolia, herb-Paris, grows locally in Britain on moist, limy soils and seems in many Herefordshire woods to grow in similar conditions to dog's mercury. As it is almost entirely green, it may easily be overlooked despite its very distinctive form.
Lysimachia nemorum, yellow pimpernel, *Oxallis acetosella*, wood sorrel, *Lamiastrum galeobdolon*, yellow archangel, and *Platanthera chlorantha* greater butterfly orchid, are also frequent ancient woodland plants found in the county.

The two grasses *Melica uniflora*, wood melick, and *Milium effusum*, wood millet, are both widespread in shaded woods, the former showing a preference for limy soils whilst the latter is more acid tolerant.

Two wood-rushes, *Luzula pilosa*, hairy wood-rush, and, *Luzula sylvatica*, great wood-rush, are both plants of acid soils and both are found on the upper slopes of Dinmore woods. The great wood-rush is particularly characteristic of ancient acid woodlands and dominates the ground flora of parts of the very steep north-facing woods above the Sned Wood Gorge near Aymestry.

Two sedges with strong ancient woodland associations in Lincolnshire and found in similar habitats in Herefordshire are *Carex pendula*, pendulous sedge, which grows abundantly in wet situations and is found in plenty in parts of Queen's Wood, Dymock, and parts of the Doward, and *Carex strigosa*, the thin-spiked wood-sedge, which seems to like the wet clay soils of woodland rides where competition is limited. Some rides in Credenhill Park wood are rich in this species.

A complete contrast to the woodland flora is found on the summit plateau of the Black Mountains. This area is covered in blanket bog which is species-poor and covered in low, shrubby, heath vegetation growing on acid, peaty, soils. Similar vegetation is found elsewhere on many flat or gently sloping upland areas such as the Millstone Grit moorlands of the Pennines, the North York moors and many Welsh uplands. In each of these the present vegetation has been shown to have developed since they were colonised by early agriculturalists. I know of no detailed study of such development on the Black Mountains but it seems reasonable to assume that the progression of events was similar to that found in similar sites elsewhere.

These areas were colonised in the post-glacial period by deciduous woodland growing on a Brown Earth soil and remains of hazel, birch and oak have been found beneath and in the lower layers of the peat. Tools of Mesolithic and Neolithic age have also been found, suggesting that early farmers occupied the area for at least part of the year. Trees were cut and land was cleared, in some cases at least by burning, with the result that soil was lost and removed as sediment to lakes and flood plains. Leaching was accelerated and soils were podsolised, losing their soil fauna, including worms.

After about 800-500BC increased rainfall in the sub-atlantic climatic phase stimulated the growth of bog-moss, *Sphagnum spp.*, which built up acid peat in which the present plants grow. The general appearance of the area resembles the Tundra but the plant species are different. The vegetation is dominated by *Calluna vulgaris*, heather or ling, *Vaccinium myrtillus*, bilberry, with a good deal of *Empetrum nigrum*, crowberry. Other associated species include *Molinia caerulea*, purple moor grass, in more sheltered and damper sites, *Galium saxatile*, heath bedstraw, *Trichophorum caespitosum*, deergrass, *Potentilla erecta*, tormentil, and *Juncus squarrosus*, heath rush.

Grasslands are probably all a result of land management as, if left unmanaged, they quickly revert to scrub, frequently dominated by hawthorn, *Crataegus monogyna*, and eventually woodland, the species composition depending on the available seeds. Birch and ash colonise quickly by wind-blown seed whilst oak is slower to join them being dispersed by jays and possibly squirrels. Tracts of grassland may have originated in woodland rides and open glades in the primaeval woods where tree growth may have been inhibited by grazing and browsing animals. As most of the 'woodland' flowers grow better beside rides where light can penetrate, the original glade flora could have been a precursor of the present day herb-rich meadows in which light-demanding plants predominate. Evidence of the origins of grassland comes from pollen analysis which shows in all areas a decline in tree pollen and an increase in grass and herb pollen coinciding with the arrival of pastoral farming. A decline in elm pollen heralds the change and this could have been brought about by the use of elm leaves as fodder. Significant among the herbs which appear about the same time are species of plantain, *Plantago spp.*, which grows well in cattle-poached and manure-enriched ground.

Grasses are very suitable plants for surviving a grazing or cutting regime as their meristematic tissue, where active growth takes place, is not at the tip of the plant. Instead leaf growth of both the blade and the leaf sheath takes place at the base of the blade whilst stem meristem is at the base of the stem which is protected by the sheath. As these meristems originate at or below ground level eating or cutting of the plant does not prevent further growth. If any weed patch is subjected to regular cutting then grasses soon become dominant.

Herefordshire has a number of grassland types on different soils, in different situations and with different management. The most widespread is certainly road verges and a few churchyards which are cut once or twice per year and display a great range of grassland plants. There is also land, particularly in the uplands and on common lands, which is managed largely or entirely by grazing. Hay-meadows usually enjoy a blend of cutting for hay combined with grazing. A few of these still remain unimproved, usually on traditionally managed farmland including the floodlands and former water meadows beside our rivers. There are also a few small areas of limestone grassland.

The most common grasses in the swards include the fescues, particularly *Festuca pratensis*, meadow fescue, which is a good fodder grass sown in many grassland mixtures. As it depends on seed for propagation it is more persistent in hay meadows than in pasture. *Festuca rubra*, red fescue, likes a lime-rich soil and is a useful fodder grass. It is also highly adaptable and forms tolerant of lead from car exhausts seem to have evolved beside some motorways. *Festuca ovina*, sheep's fescue, has a very wide tolerance of soil acidity and, as its name implies, is a valuable food for sheep on hill pastures where it is more palatable than *Nardus stricta*, mat grass.

Lolium sp., rye grass, is one of our most abundant grasses as its many hybrids are widely sown in leys for their nutritive properties. *Cynosurus cristatus*, crested dog's tail, survives better in pasture, where its wiry stalks may survive grazing, than in hay meadows, where competition from taller grasses limits it.

Meadow-grasses, *Poa trivialis and pratensis* – rough- and smooth-stalked meadow-grass respectively, are abundant and widespread. *P. pratensis* is the rather less frequent of the two and tends to grow and flower earlier. *P. trivialis* is found in a wide variety of niches from rich meadows to wasteland.

Dactylis glomerata, cock's foot, is again very common and palatable for stock but is most successful where it is not grazed too closely or frequently and can attain its full stature.

Holcus lanatus, Yorkshire fog, is not very tolerant of close grazing but can become abundant in hay meadows, road verges and waste ground.

Phleum pratense, Timothy, is frequently sown and survives well in hay meadows but is damaged by too much grazing and trampling.

Bromus hordeaceus, soft brome, is widespread on fertile soils and abundant in our meadows but not under a grazing regime.

Other grasses which are common but in more specialised habitats are *Anthoxanthum odoratum*, sweet vernal grass, which is early flowering, contains coumerin which gives the scent to hay, and prefers a slightly acid soil. *Agrostis capillaris*, common bent, similarly thrives on slightly acid soils. In hay meadows with very limited grazing *Alopecurus pratensis*, meadow foxtail, and *Arrhenatherum elatius*, false oatgrass, can grow, the latter being possibly the most common road-verge grass.

Lime-rich grasslands support *Trisetum flavescens,* the yellow oat grass, and on thin limestone soils *Bromopsis erecta,* upright brome, is characteristic.

In addition to their distinctive grass species the grasslands have an equally characteristic suite of wild flowers which not only add to their beauty but make them even more biologically diverse. Some examples suffice to illustrate the variety within the county.

In the Upper Olchon Valley beyond the enclosed areas the vegetation could best be described as *Nardus stricta,* mat grass, – *Galium saxatile,* heath bedstraw, grassland. This is relatively poor in species and much of it has been invaded by bracken but typical plants are *Agrostis capillaris,* common bent grass, *Festuca ovina,* sheep's fescue, *Deschampsia flexuosa,* wavy hair grass, and flowers such as *Campanula rotundifolia,* harebell, *Centaurea nigra,* knapweed, *Achillea millefolium,* yarrow, whilst beside the seepages and small streams *Pinguicula vulgaris,* common butterwort, and *Valeriana dioica,* marsh valerian, can be found. Also beside the stream, but not strictly grassland plants, are many ferns including *Oreopteris limbosperma,* the lemon-scented or mountain fern, and, usually among rocks in damp shaded places, *Cystopteris fragilis,* the brittle bladder fern.

A few traditional hay meadows further down the valley contain a much richer flora which includes *Trollius europaeus,* globe flower, and *Persicaria bistorta,* bistort, both plants of northern affinity, together with *Dactylorhiza fuchsii,* common spotted orchid, and even *Platanthera chlorantha,* greater butterfly orchid. Perhaps the best display of meadow flowers in the county is in Dulas churchyard where over a hundred species have been recorded, from *Narcissus pseudonarcissus,* wild daffodils, in spring through a profuse summer flowering of spotted orchids to *Colchicum autumnale,* meadow saffron, in the autumn. It also contains the limestone grass *Bromopsis erecta,* upright brome, and *Ophioglossum vulgatum,* the adder's tongue fern, an indicator of undisturbed old grassland.

In one of the Davies meadows at Norton Canon, *Conopodium major,* pignut, is abundant and meadows of this kind may at one time have been much more widespread on deep, slightly acid mineral soils. Where the lowland mineral soils tend to be waterlogged *Juncus spp.,* rushes, with *Lychnis flos-cuculi,* ragged robin, *Cardamine pratensis,* cuckooflower, and in even wetter parts *Iris pseudacorus,* the yellow iris, may be present.

Of the lowland meadows the flood and former water meadows near the rivers, such as the Lugg Meadows, are a special feature of the county. The Lugg Meadows are particularly known for their fritillaries, *Fritillaria meleagris,* growing here at almost their most westerly station and dependent on the quick draining of the gravel subsoil and the relatively late cut of hay in July after their seed has had time to ripen. In these meadows there is also a small amount of *Sanguisorba officinalis,* great burnet, a plant rare in Herefordshire, and *Oenantha silaifolia,* narrow-leaved water-dropwort, which is scarce and decreasing nationally.

Limestone grasslands on thin soils over limestone are rare but small areas remain on the Doward and within the Woolhope hills. The shortage of this habitat may be a result of the steep dip of many of the limestone beds which makes their outcrops both narrow and steep. This made them of little value as sheep walks which were found in more extensive limestone areas such as the Cotswolds or Chalklands. Instead their slopes have frequently remained in woodland. Where limestone grassland does occur the grasses upright brome, yellow oat grass and the aggressive tor grass, *Brachipodium pinnatum,* flourish along with many calcicolous plants such as *Helianthemum nummularium,* common rock-rose, *Pilosella officinarum,* mouse-ear hawkweed, *Leontodon hispidus,* rough hawkbit, *Lotus corniculatus,* bird's-foot trefoil, *Linum catharticum,* purging flax, *Rhinanthus minor,* yellow-rattle, a semi-parasite on grasses, *Blackstonia perfoliata,* yellow-wort, and a few species of orchid.

The rivers also have a distinctive flora. In slack water areas where muddy sediment accumulates *Sparganium erectum,* the branched bur-reed, and less frequently, *Butomus umbellatus,* flowering rush, grow together with *Stachys palustris,* marsh woundwort, and *Persicaria amphibia,* amphibious bistort. In the water and rooted in gravelly riffles is *Ranunculus fluitans,* river water crowfoot, which has declined greatly in recent years together with the less spectacular *Potamogeton spp.,* pond weeds.

Although this paper has dwelt on the variety of habitats and a few of the plants in the county it must conclude on a sadder note. All these habitats, with the possible exception of the bogs of the Black Mountains, have succumbed in varying degrees to decline in the last half century. Samples of many are safeguarded by being in reserves such as those owned by the Herefordshire Nature Trust in whose care they are managed for maximum diversity and remain as refuges from which the plants may spread again once conditions are favourable. Similarly some areas are afforded protection and sympathetic management by their owners, frequently in consultation with the Farming and Wildlife Advisory Group whose contribution to conservation in the wider countryside is vital and increasing. Despite the best efforts of these bodies economic circumstances are still leading to meadows being ploughed up and riverside cultivation is increasing sediment in the rivers with severe results for river life.

Finally there are diseases and invading plants which are devastating some areas. Dutch Elm disease has already removed virtually all the fully-grown English elms, *Ulmus procera,* which used to adorn the hedgerows. It still grows in them but when reaching about 6m or 7m in height is struck down again.

Insect-born fungal disease is also devastating the alders which line the river banks. *Impatiens glandulifera,* the Himalayan balsam, has spread with increasing speed along river corridors where it suppresses other vegetation whilst *Fallopia japonica,* Japanese knotweed, is making gradual inroads on riverside and waste places.

The future of our flora is largely in our hands, but if the predictable global warming comes to pass many species will certainly be lost leaving niches for newcomers to take their place.

BIBLIOGRAPHY
J. P. Grime, J. G. Hodgson & R. Hunt, *The abridged comparative plant ecology* (1990).
G. Halliday & A. Malloch, *Wild flowers: their habitats in Britain and northern Europe* (1981).
C. E. Hubbard, revised J. C. E. Hubbard, *Grasses* (1985).
J. R. Matthews, *The origin and distribution of the British flora* (1955).
F. H. Perring & L. Farrell, *Red data book I. Vascular plants,* The Society for the Promotion of Nature Conservation, with financial help from the WWF (1977).
F. H. Perring & S. M. Walters, *Atlas of the British flora.* (1962).
C. D. Preston & M. O. Hill, *The geographical relationships of British and Irish vascular plants.* Botanical journal of the Linnean Society 1997 No 124.
W. H. Purchas and A. Ley, *A flora of Herefordshire* (1889).
O. Rackham, *Ancient woodland* (1980).
C. A. Stace, *New flora of the British Isles,* second ed. (1997).
A. Stewart, D. A. Pearman and C. D. Preston, *Scarce plants in Britain* (1994).
A. Tansley, rev. M. C. F. Proctor, *Britain's green mantle* (1968).

Brampton Bryan Park, Herefordshire:
A Documentary History

DAVID WHITEHEAD

That a deer-park should emerge at Brampton Bryan in the middle ages comes as no surprise. Domesday Book shows that the N.W. corner of Herefordshire contained extensive woodland and waste, much of which was already being exploited for hunting in 1086.[1] At Lingen, to the south of Brampton Bryan, Thurstan, the tenant of Ralph de Mortimer of Wigmore, enjoyed 'three hedged enclosures (*haiae*) for capturing roe deer' whilst to the west at Stanage where the land was waste, Osbern fitz Richard of Richard's Castle also had 'three hedged enclosures'.[2] There was no sign of an *haia* at Brampton Bryan and like many neighbouring estates it had been waste before 1066 – perhaps as a result of the Welsh wars – but it was on the way to recovery by the time of the Domesday survey. It was a fairly typical lowland estate with land for six and a half ploughs, ploughmen, villeins and bordars but there was also a wood, half a league in extent, where we may presume the future park was to emerge.[3]

Brampton remained part of the barony of the Mortimers throughout the Middle Ages and by the reign of Henry II (1154-1189), it was tenanted by a Brian de Brompton. During the twelfth and thirteenth centuries this family assembled a substantial holding in the Welsh Marches, not only in the vicinity of Brampton but also at Kinlet, near Cleobury Mortimer. They were active in local and national affairs as benefactors of monasteries at Wigmore and Great Malvern and patrons of the Templars. Brian de Brampton (d.1287) accompanied Edward I on his crusade of 1270 for which a grateful king cancelled Brian's debt of £20 with the Jews.[4] The family also won other privileges from the Angevin kings such as a grant of free warren on their manors of Kinlet, Brampton, Buckton and Stanage. This allowed them to hunt small game and in the same year – 1252 – there was a grant of a market and fair for Brampton.[5]

This was a piece of commercial opportunism, probably designed to pre-empt the creation of a new borough at Knighton and, as at Knighton, this may have involved the re-location of the castle and the adjoining settlement, closer to the river and the thoroughfare into mid-Wales.[6] A low mound just inside the present boundary of Brampton Park may mark the site of the early Norman earthwork castle before it was removed in the mid-thirteenth century to its present site on a low cliff overlooking the Teme. When Brian de Brampton (IV) died in 1294 he was said to possess a tower with a curtilage of land, a garden and fishponds (*vivaria*).[7] The garden and fishponds would presumably have been located below the new castle on present walled garden where a canal garden was to be developed in the late seventeenth century. A stone castle – either a square keep or round tower – would require firm foundations and perhaps, rock-cut ditches. The process is paralleled elsewhere in the Welsh border, for example at Hay-on-Wye where an earthwork motte was replaced by a stone keep on a new site overlooking a new market place.[8] A foliated capital, re-set in the fourteenth-century gatehouse, suggests a mid-thirteenth century date for the building of the present castle, presumably by Brian de Brampton (III) who held the estate between 1262 and 1287. He was, as we have seen, a crusader and active in the Welsh wars.[9]

The re-location of the town and castle could have released land, which subsequently became the laund or lawn of the later park – a treeless and usually lowland area within a park where the deer could graze in the winter and where the hunters could be stationed to receive the driven deer[10] (Pl. 1).

Plate 1. A view across the laund or lawn, October 1995.

It seems, however, that in the late thirteenth century the de Brampton park was elsewhere. A series of inquisitions following the death of Brian de Brampton (IV), who left two young daughters, reveals that his principal park was at Kinlet, created on the fringes of Wyre Forest.[11] The earliest inquisition also mentions a park at *Ayston* (Weston) near Stanage, held from the Mortimers as a knight's fee for castle guard duty at Wigmore.[12] Slightly later a park is referred to at *Ambareslyth* which the local jury helpfully notes 'is not a manor but a park pertaining to the manor of Stanage' and, as this was held from the Mortimers for service at Stapleton Castle, it seems to have been distinct from Weston.[13] Finally, to complete this proliferation of de Brampton parks, an inquisition of 1304 notices a park at *Bocton* (Buckton) – about two miles from Brampton Bryan, across the Teme, and marked to-day by Buckton Park Farm.[14] On a survey of 1806 it was still surrounded by fields called Green Park, Park Leasow and Lawn Field.[15] Buckton seems to be an unusual situation for a park, the gently sloping lands above the Teme, are depicted in Domesday Book as a flourishing agricultural estate employing ten ploughs and with no woodland. We are led to believe that landowners like the de Bramptons with a variety of manors, usually emparked land, which did not impinge upon agriculture.[16]

It seems the de Bramptons were emparkers *par excellence* and we may suspect that the ownership of four parks was simply a means of exploiting demesne land for deer ranching, as O. G. S. Crawford suggests, and equally, a potent symbol of the position of the family in local society.[17] However, the uncertainties of dynastic inheritance ended the de Brampton reign at Brampton Bryan and soon after 1294 the estate was split between Robert Harley, the nephew of the king's 'beloved clerk' Malcolm de Harley, and Sir Edmund Cornwall. The latter secured Stanage and the property attached to the castlery of Stapleton; the former, according to a much later inquisition of 1507, acquired Brampton Bryan, Buckton, Pedwardine, Walford, Boresford and part of Kinlet Park.[18]

The architectural history of the castle suggests that Robert or one of his immediate successors improved the castle by adding the round towers and creating a new entrance[19] (Pl. 2). With the loss of Stanage Park, this may have been the moment when a new park, pivoted upon the town and the castle, was added to the Brampton demesne and during fieldwork carried out in 1995, it was possible to postulate an earlier enclosure in southern quarter of the existing park[20] (Pl. 3). Alternatively, the Harleys may well have been happy with the hunting at Buckton which certainly remained a park long enough to influence the surrounding field names. Sadly, for the modern historian, the success of the Harleys in producing male heirs meant that the estate makes few appearances in the public records of the late middle ages and we have to wait until the seventeenth century for estate records to fill the gap.

Plate 2. A picturesque view of Brampton Bryan Castle from Edward Kennion, *Antiquities of the Counties of Hereford and Monmouth* (1784).

Plate 3. Possible remains of an earlier park pale to the west of Broomy Hill Plantation (1995).

By the middle of the fourteenth century the first age of park formation was over; the decline in population and the inflation of labourers' wages made demesne farming unprofitable, consequently, many parks were leased to tenants for sheep runs or ploughed up.[21] Early parks were generally fairly small, no more than 200 acres – about the optimum size of Buckton, which would have been contained within the river Teme and the stream which runs down to Leintwardine from Bucknell. A river enclosing a park had the advantage of offsetting the cost of paling and also provided the additional opportunity for wild fowling.[22] Buckton also had another advantage as a park. Although it was in the honour of Wigmore – a well-defined unit in the late middle ages when it was frequently in the hands of the crown – it was within the 'Welshry' whereas Brampton Bryan was in the 'Englishry', i.e. subject to normal feudal law.[23] In the 'Welshry' the population lived under their own customs, which may have allowed the de Bramptons more room to manoeuvre in establishing a park. Stanage, it should be noted, was just outside the honour of Wigmore and not subject to Mortimer control. Significantly, there were five other parks in Wigmoresland – as the honour was frequently called – in the middle ages: Burrington (1360), Gatley (1301), Leinthall Earls (1301), Leinthall Starkes (1315) and Wigmore (1301).[24] All these parks were created by the Mortimers, which suggests, perhaps, that they restricted park foundation by their feudatories, just as the crown did within royal forests, e.g. the Forest of Dean.[25] Indeed, Buckton is the only park within the honour of Wigmore not in the hands of the Mortimers but it is also the only park in the 'Welshry'.

All this is rather conjectural, but there are a few further hints, which help to explain why Brampton Bryan Park was late in arriving on the scene. It seems possible that the site of the present park was common land for much of the middle ages, shared by the communities of Brampton and Pedwardine. The latter produced its own knightly family in the thirteenth century which on at least two recorded occasions was in dispute with the de Bramptons over rights of common in Brampton.[26] It is difficult to locate this common even with the aid of the tithe map, but it could have been within the present Brampton Bryan Park. Moreover, Pedwardine was a burgeoning community in the thirteenth century and the focus for considerable land clearance – Edmund Mortimer in 1331 received 5s 10d rents from his free tenants in Pedwardine but 26s 8d for assarts.[27] The intimate landscape of small fields around Upper and Lower Pedwardine which exists to-day is a typical product of assarting, reflecting the gradual nibbling away of woodland and waste on the fringes of Brampton Bryan Park or common. Pedwardine Wood, as it is today, seems to have been well protected from this process because of valuable pannage rights.[28] In this era of rapid population growth and high farming, the rights of common enjoyed by the population of Brampton and Pedwardine would naturally be an issue of contention, especially if the lord of Brampton tried to extinguish them by emparking.

There is further evidence for the agricultural use of the park in the thirteenth century in the faint signs of ridge and furrow close to the site of the suspected motte. It seems unlikely that this would pre-date the original castle and was probably the result of the expansion of arable once the castle had been removed and new land became available close to the existing township fields. Thus, it appears from a certain amount of circumstantial evidence that the site of Brampton Bryan Park may well have remained an extensive piece of common land, controlled by the lord of Brampton, but shared by the community at Pedwardine. The Harleys, when they took over in c1300, probably had no other alternative but to continue to enjoy the park at Buckton which survived, in name at least, until the present day.

Brampton Bryan Park makes its official debut as a paled enclosure on Saxton's map of Herefordshire in 1577. It is accompanied by parks at Stanage and Wigmore. Further confirmation of its existence comes in 1587 in a perambulation of the boundaries of the honour of Wigmore, which marches across country from Lingen Vallet, over Harley's Mountain and down to Boresford 'from thence downe the Brooke to the Pale of the Pke of Brompton. And soe downe by the pale side to a gate and soe over Reaves Way down Maisebrooke over Knighton's way'.[29] By this date the western boundary of the honour had become the national boundary of England and Wales and followed the park pale down to the Knighton road. Although this had officially been established by the Act of Union of 1536, two centuries before in 1349 Stanage was already regarded as being in Wales.[30]

The park probably came into existence in the late fifteenth century at a time when there was a retreat from arable farming, caused partly by population decline, when all over England land was being enclosed, put down to pasture or turned into new parks.[31] The Harleys by this date certainly had the political influence and the social standing to fulfil their desire for a new park. They were staunch supporters of the Yorkists and family tradition holds that they fought at the battle of Tewkesbury in 1461 – the battle which brought a Mortimer king to the throne as Edward IV. Indeed, the removal of Mortimer power from Wigmoresland and its replacement by remote and frequently inefficient state, may have provided the context for the creation of Brampton Park. From the late fifteenth century the Yorkists and, later the Tudors, relied increasingly upon the services of the local gentry as stewards and receivers to manage their estates in North Herefordshire. At first the Crofts were favoured, but later it was the turn of the Harleys.[32] In 1461 any restraint upon emparking which existed earlier in the Middle Ages was removed.

There are two local examples, which provide support for the scenario painted above. In 1460, Richard de Beauchamp, another staunch Yorkist was given a license to empark 1300 acres of land on the western slopes of the Malverns to surround his new hunting lodge at Bronsil.[33] Earlier in 1438, Roland Leinthall, a veteran of Agincourt, received a similar grant to empark 1,000 acres around his castellated mansion at Hampton Court, near Leominster.[34] These large parks are characteristic of the late Middle Ages and reflect the ambitions of the status-seeking gentry, thrown up by the inter- necine broils of the Wars of the Roses. Moreover, unlike earlier parks which tend to have oval boundaries, later parks have an arbitrary character, formed by the process of enclosure, having been squeezed into a landscape with existing features.[35] Brampton Bryan Park with its irregular six-mile boundary enclosing nearly 500 acres fits well into the category of later parks, albeit there is no sign of a royal license (Fig. 1). As it did not impinge upon a royal forest or royal hunting rights this is probably not to be expected. The park is, therefore, a suitable symbol of the arrival of the Harleys as one of the principal families in Herefordshire in the late fifteenth century.

Figure 1. Brampton Bryan Park on the 6in OS plan 1883, revised 1902.

Once the documentation for Brampton Bryan becomes plentiful in the seventeenth century, it appears the Harleys, like their predecessors the de Bramptons, enjoyed a variety of local parks. During his early life Sir Robert Harley (1579-1656) lived at Stanage Park, where there was a lodge.[36] He had been born at Wigmore Castle and eventually assumed his grandfather's role as Keeper of Wigmore Park. For this privilege he paid £2 2s to the crown in 1639, but as the park was tenanted it obviously had no amenity value for him. In 1650 he struck a bargain with Richard Walker of Bringewood Forge on the Teme at Downton for cutting 1,000 cords in the wood of the park at 4s 2d per cord.[37]

One of the earliest letters from Lady Brilliana Harley to her husband in 1625 – she was his third wife – reports with an almost perceptible sigh that 'the payling of the newe parke is made an end of'.[38] This new park is occasionally referred to in the late seventeenth-century rentals and can perhaps be identified with Heathy Park, adjoining Pedwardine Wood, which during some paling in 1664 is referred to as Heathy Banks.[39] Presumably, this was a sixteenth-century addition to the original park. During the siege of the castle in 1643, the park was seriously damaged. The royalists, in retribution for damage done to Viscount Scudamore's park at Llanthony near Gloucester, threatened to cut down the trees in Brampton Park. They also drove away the oxen grazing there – an interesting insight into the use of the park – killed 500 deer and destroyed the pale.[40] In July 1646 Sir Robert laid a claim for damages before Parliament which included a demand for £500 compensation for 'Two Parks wholly laid open and destroyed' and a further £500 for trees cut down and destroyed.[41] Sir Robert's estimate was based upon his own valuation carried out three months earlier in March 1646 which shows the park well stocked with trees:[42]

The timber trees and other woods	£1360
The copice in the Newe parke	
40 acres at £4 per acre	£ 160

The timber in Wigmore Park was also valued at £1,742, which seems to confirm that the second park referred to in the Parliamentary petition was Wigmore, as Robinson suggested in 1869.[43] There is a further undated but certainly late seventeenth-century valuation of 'Timbers in Brampton Pk':[44]

65 tuns of Cleft Timber at £2 per tun	£	130	
133 tuns of Rough Timber at 18s. per tun	£	119	14s
156 cords of 3 foot wood at 4s. 6d. per cord	£	35	2s
The Bark	£	19	15s
Total:	£	304	11s

Timber Trees	2510	£ 3565		
Best Saplings	2200	£ 275		
All Trees for cordwood	555	£ 282	6s	
Saplings for cordwood	260	£ 13	13s	
Total	5525	£ 4131	19s	

This valuation seems to post-date the great storm, which coincided with the death of Oliver Cromwell on 3 September 1658 and which wreaked great damage upon the park. Sir Edward wrote: 'I wish the devil had taken him any other way than through my Park, for not content with doing me all the mischief he could while alive, he has knocked over some of my finest trees in his progress downwards.'[45]

It is clear from these valuations that the trees in the park were regularly surveyed and a proportion felled either as standards or as coppice, much of it destined 'for the forge' at Bringewood. In April 1720 it was again calculated that there were 365 trees in the park which could be felled containing 192 tons of timber valued at £192 15s and 156 cords of coppice valued at £75. The bark was valued separately at £18.[46] An earlier document informs us that 'A corde of wood ought to be nine foote in lengthe and four and a half foote in height and the wood for the most pt. cutt four foote longer'. In 1722 all the wood had been cut and delivered to Mr Knight at Bringewood with a note that there was a further 105 tons which could be extracted from the Upper Park at Brampton.[47] The management of the woods on a rotational basis was still taking place in the late eighteenth century (as it is to-day) for Henry Skrine, a tourist with picturesque sensibilities, complained in 1795 that 'the rich groves of Brampton Bryan ...used to adorn the steep sides of its extensive park, but these have lately been despoiled of their grandeur by the ruthless axe, leaving naked territory to bewail the loss of its chief ornament'.[48]

To maintain the cycle of growth, the park was treated in separate compartments, each compartment had its particular name, most of which appear to have been forgotten to-day. A 'Particular' of trees drawn up in 1718 mentions:

> 177 trees in the copy (coppice) above the Lodge and Eading Hole (Hollow)
> 163 trees in Hern's (Heron's) Nest
> 261 upon the Ridge
> 76 in Utree (Yew tree) Hole
> 57 in the Lodge and Stony Hole
> 57 in Brick Kiln Hole
> 83 upon the Top of Utree, Lodge and Stony Hole.[49]

The Lodge referred to in this document is also mentioned in 1661 as being close to the 'Launds' or Park Meadow. Thus, the present Park Cottage overlooking the pasture land below the pool, appears to be in the same place and is presumably the building marked on several early nineteenth-century maps[50] (Pl. 4). This implies that the 'particular' cited above is concerned with the eastern side of the park.

In 1664 a paling account 'to divide Brampton park as directed by the Auditor Harley and Mr. Harley of Kinsham' deals with the same area and yet provides a different set of names (Pl. 5). It describes how the pale will run:

> From Whittings Brook Gate up by the waterside to ye head of ye parke meadow... across the head of the meadow to the-meadow gate... up the ditch to Ashhedd at the bottom of ye way ye leads into the coppy of saplings... along the upperside of the coppice to ye head of ye Hopyard hold... to ye poiynt of the Bank about 80 yds above the Swayling Shedd ...to a wich tree that groweth in ye upper end of the hollow of Greenod Hold... along the north side of Greenod Banks to ye Constableheald Gate which leads into Pedwardine Wood.[51]

It seems that this new pale is running from the fishponds below the Cottage, across the hill slopes above towards the sweet chestnut row which is still known as Greenold (*ex inf.* Christopher Harley), to the gate which leads into the woods. From this document we incidentally learn that there were ditches in the park indicating,

Plate 4. Distant view across the laund towards Park Cottage (1995), the site of the original 'lodge' first mentioned in 1661.

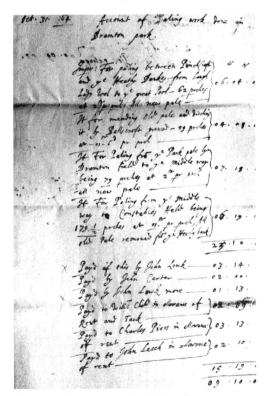

Plate 5. First page of a 1664 paling account

perhaps, disused boundaries. There was also an area of coppiced saplings and a 'hold' for growing hop poles (or perhaps the hopyard itself, although this seems unlikely). Ash and wych elm grew in the park and there was a Swayling Shed – *swale* according to the OED means a building made of pliant boards – probably the seventeenth-century predecessor of the nineteenth-century deer shed.

Paling work also took place along the western boundary of the park in October 1664 beginning at Laugh Lady Well, running down to the Great Pool, across Heathy Banks towards Constablesheld – confirming that this last landmark was located on the boundary of Heathy Park and Pedwardine Wood.[52] The account also included ditching but only on a short section of the boundary at Ballscroft ground. The pale on the west side of the park seems to follow the present-day boundary but clearly, from the evidence cited above, the priority of woodland management within the park, and especially the need to protect regenerating coppice from the deer, required constant fencing, ditching and embanking. This creates a considerable headache for the modern archaeologist, confronted with a variety of linear earthworks within the park. It seems safe to conclude, however, that the present boundaries of the park have remained fairly static since the mid-seventeenth century.

Paling was a constant chore. Lady Harley wrote to her husband Edward in January 1671 that a great storm had shattered the new windows in Brampton Bryan house but also 'blew down a great part of the palings in the park'.[53] The paling accounts indicate that old pale was often taken up, repaired and reused elsewhere at half the cost of new pale which was 2s per perch. Moreover, the work was done by tenants of the estate in lieu of rent or rights of pasture in the park.[54] The point of all this care and attention was to keep the deer within the park but they are hardly ever referred to in the documentation. In September 1726 Robert Harley wrote from his London house in Dover Street thanking Thomas Harley for the safe delivery of venison which 'proves very good'.[55] However, there is plenty of evidence for the exploitation of the park in other ways. The laund and pasture within the park was regularly valued for grazing. For example in 1640 when the estimated rent from 'The Parke and Laundes' was £60, the New Park - £2 and the 'grounde under the Parke' - £13 6s 8d.[56] In the late seventeenth century the pasture ground 'above the park pale commonly called Upper Park' contained 273 acres whilst adjoining it were a further 118 acres put down to coppice. A rental of 1661 also refers to part of the park being mowed.[57]

Sixteenth- and seventeenth-century parks were increasingly valued for amenity purposes.[58] Direct evidence for this at Brampton Bryan is elusive but we can assume that the park was integrated into the schemes of enhancement which repaired the damage inflicted upon the house and demesne during the Civil War. This work fell to Sir Edward Harley and his two sons, Edward 'Auditor' Harley and Robert, first earl of Oxford. The house was being rebuilt in June 1663 when a workman is recorded falling at 'the new building'. The architect is unknown but a few years earlier in 1655 Sir Edward corresponded with John Webb, the pupil of Inigo Jones and Assistant Surveyor of the King's Works about a house in Ludlow and it is possible, therefore, that Webb provided another design for the house at Brampton.[59] As Auditor Harley and his brother Robert moved in court circles, we should not be surprised to find that they sought elevated advice for their projects at Brampton. An account with a Worcester bookseller, Mr Rea, in 1657 includes Ralph Austen, *A Treatise on Fruit Trees* (1653) as well as a Greek Testament and a book on witchcraft. Austen, like Sir Edward Harley, was a puritan and connected gardening with godliness: 'God when he would make the life of man Pleasant unto him, he put him into an Orchard or Garden of delights, that he might labour therein with pleasure of mind'.[60] Father and sons took a considerable interest in the laying out of the grounds around the new house. In 1673 there is a correspondence about seeds for the garden including 200 'lecoris plants', asparagus seed, cauliflower seed and sweet marjoram. A stone roller was bought for the bowling green in 1686, the drive was levelled and gravelled in 1693 and a 'handsome pale' provided to prevent animals from straying into the garden.[61]

A year before in 1692 Robert Harley wrote to his father reporting the presence of the royal gardener George London at Stoke Edith in Herefordshire: 'If it were worth so much money he would go over to Brampton and see the situation, and could make a draught of what he thought the place capable of'.[62] George London was the most celebrated gardener of his age, whose signature was elaborate parterres and canals near the house, from which radiated avenues dissecting the surrounding countryside.

Several of these ingredients were to be found at Stoke Edith and Hampton Court, near Leominster – another local estate where London was consulted – but also at Brampton on a plan of the house and gardens, dated 1722, and attributed to Charles Bridgeman[63] (Pl. 6). The plan appears to be a survey of existing features and shows a T-shaped canal and two avenues – one running from the orchard, north towards the Teme and the other towards the west following the Knighton Road. We can only speculate upon whether London and Bridgeman gave advice on the development of the park.

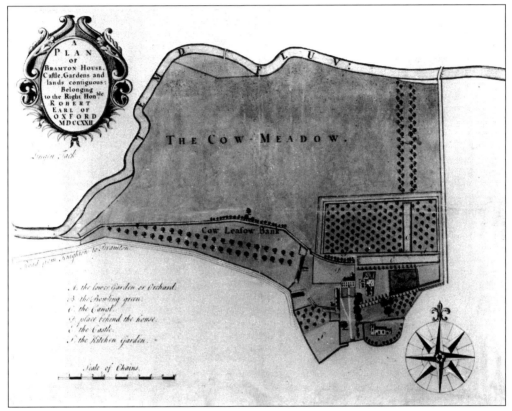

Plate 6. 'A Plan of Bramton House, Castle and Garden etc' (1722) (John Soane Museum).

This excursion into the gardening activities of the late seventeenth-century Harleys, may throw some indirect light upon the development of the park as a pleasure ground rather than as economic unit within the Brampton Bryan estate. The records naturally emphasise the importance of the park for forestry and only occasionally do we get a glimpse of any social or aesthetic appreciation of its amenities. We can assume that the concern shown for the setting of the house was probably extended to the park, which dominates the visual environment of Brampton Bryan. In several of his letters the Earl of Oxford, the busy politician, refers briefly but with warmth to Brampton as a summer retreat where he enjoyed walking the grounds with his brother Edward.[64] Notwithstanding his high office, Robert Harley remained at heart a countryman and, as his biographer notes, his correspondence is 'shot through with agrarian undertones'.[65] His brother Edward – who managed the Brampton Bryan estates – set himself up in a grand house at Eywood, near Kington whilst the earl's son was established at Wimpole in Cambridgeshire – where Bridgeman was also employed – but the earl himself retained a deep affection for his ancient home where he lived in retirement and died in 1724.

The principal addition to the park during this era appears to be the row of sweet chestnuts, which run up the central approach of the park to Greenold Bank where they form an alcove with a shorter line of chestnuts approaching from the east (Pl.7). The long row has a serpentine character and was clearly planted to accompany an existing – and perhaps, ceremonial – route into the park. Associated with the row is at least one quincunx-like group of chestnuts, halfway up the drive, slightly to the east. Local tradition associates these venerable trees with the Armada – as, indeed, are the chestnut avenues at Croft. It seems remarkable that none of the estate surveys – rich in topographical detail – refer to the row, which if Elizabethan, would have been a prominent feature in the late seventeenth century. It could, perhaps, have been introduced by George London, but its serpentine alignment is out of character with London's severely geometric schemes. Moreover, post-Restoration avenues are generally planted in elm, lime or horse chestnut – as recommended by writers such as John Evelyn.[66] Sweet chestnut avenues are generally earlier, for their picturesque indiscipline, irregular growth and tendency to drop limbs meant that they could not be trimmed into shape, a desirable feature for trees in a formal landscape. The sweet chestnut was a park tree *par excellence*, providing shelter for deer and nuts for swine. If the Brampton Bryan trees pre-dated the Civil War, we might expect such a regular feature to have been the first object of Royalist vandalism in 1643. Therefore, it would seem most likely that the row was planted in the 1650s during the first stage of the refurbishment of the estate. In March 1650 Sir Robert Harley was expected to

Plate 7. The sweet chestnut row (1995).

return to Brampton after a long stay in London, coal and beer were being laid in the house and the garden was being tidied. The steward, Samuel Shilton, added in his letter: 'The Col. thinks that it will be well to begin to pale some part of Brampton Park this autumn'. Was the row planted to mark the recovery and restoration of the park after the Civil War disasters? Alternatively, what a splendid way this would have been of marking the storm of September 1658 and the passing of the Lord Protector. As relatively young trees this would explain their absence from the park surveys. Moreover, sweet chestnuts achieve a venerable character quite quickly and trees in an avenue planted at Houghton in Norfolk in the early eighteenth century now have girths of over 22 feet.[67]

After the death of the earl of Oxford, Brampton Bryan was annexed to Eywood and the details of the management of the park were presumably lost with the records of that great house. Passing tourists like the Reverend Richard Warner in 1799 noticed the castle and the mansion house of the earl of Oxford 'capable of being converted into a desirable residence. The dilapidated state of the building, however, and the wild appearance of its extensive garden, evince that it has not been hitherto honoured with much of his lordship's attention.'[68] He failed to notice the park which two years before Henry Skrine saw being despoiled by 'the ruthless axe'.[69] *The Beauties of England and Wales* (1805) and *The Leominster Guide* (1808) both refer to the park 'nearly six miles in circumference, occupying a considerable portion of an extensive eminence' but are more interested in 'the largest and most flourishing oak tree in England' growing in the 'space called the Wilderness' near the castle.[70]

The park appears on several eighteenth-century maps, most clearly on Isaac Taylor's *Plan of Herefordshire* (1786) but with no discriminating features. The first edition of the 1in O.S. map in 1836 shows two parks – Brampton and Heathy – a hint of the Park Cottage and the row of chestnuts advancing from the park entrance. Both the latter features are shown on the tithe map of 1839 where the cottage belongs to the keeper and the upper park is dominated by blocks of formal plantations. A survey of the estate in 1852 records that the park is 459 acres in extent and the Park Meadow 28 acres; both are used for pasture.[71] A few years later in Shirley's *English Deer Parks* (1867) the park is said to be 500 acres, containing a herd of fallow deer and 'is a good specimen of a thorough English park, with well broken ground and fine oak timber'.[72] These details are repeated by Joseph Whitaker in 1892 but the park has been reduced to 489 acres and the deer to 250: 'The park is beautifully studded with fine oak, elm, larch, lime and other timber trees.'[73] The deer were removed soon after the First World War (*ex inf.* Christopher Harley).

The Woolhope Club made two excursions to the park in 1870 and 1882 and noted the fame of the park 'with varied scenery, and above and beyond all, perhaps, for the great number and variety of its picturesque trees'.[74] Some of these, the club decided, were the result of the storm of 1658. They examined the Laugh Lady Oak 'riven asunder...a hollow stem divided into three sections' and the Woodyard Oak, 17ft 9in in girth which 'may have lost its top and main branches in the Cromwellian hurricane'. Several other oaks 'grievously injured' and bearing 'grief scars' were also viewed in 1870 as well as the sweet chestnut row which they believed was probably 150-160 years old – planted, therefore, in the early eighteenth century. The young trees, they had been informed, 'are said to have been brought from Eywood'. All were measured and the beauty of their reticulated bark 'twisted, knotted and knarled' was admired before the party moved off to Coxwell Knoll. Here a glimpse of the castle produced a discussion about the general relationship of castles to deer parks. The author of the report commented on how strange it was that the castle was situated in the village and not in the park. Parallels were drawn with Windsor and Hampton Court. Significantly, there was no attempt at dating the park, the club members knew it was old and took pleasure in 'a ramble up its steep slopes [and] through its shady dingles' – scientific curiosity succumbed to the allures of picturesque beauty.

ACKNOWLEDGEMENTS: The research for this essay was commissioned by Tom Wall, site manager for the Marches National Nature Reserves, for English Nature in 1995. It formed part of a larger survey carried out by Dr Andrew Sclater of Landskip and Prospect, Landscape Consultants of Cambridge. I should also like to acknowledge the invaluable help of the late Christopher Harley who commented on the text and received with patience my many inquiries whilst I was delving briefly into the Harley Collection at Brampton Bryan.

REFERENCES

[1] H. C. Darby & I. B. Terrett, *The Domesday Geography of Midland England* (1954), 83-87.
[2] F. & C. Thorn, *Shropshire Domesday Book* (1986), f. 260a-b.
[3] Ibid. f. 260c.
[4] H. Hartopp, *Genealogy of the Brampton Family* (1924), 2-7.
[5] R. W. Eyton, *The Antiquities of Shropshire* XI (1860), 314, 328, 341.
[6] P. Woodfield, 'The Town Houses of Knighton', *Trans. Radnor Soc.*, XLIII (1973), 50-52.
[7] *Inq. Post Mortem (IPM)* III, 189-90.
[8] G. Fairs, *A History of the Hay* (1972), 10-12.
[9] RCHME *Herefordshire* III (1934), 20.
[10] O. Rackham, *Trees and Woodland in the British Landscape* (1990), 155.
[11] *IPM* III, 189-90; IV, 178; V, 57-8.   [12] Ibid. III, 189.
[13] Ibid. V, 57-8.   [14] Ibid. IV, 178.
[15] Brampton Bryan Archives (BBA), in the Library.
[16] DB. op.cit. in note 2, f.260c; L. Cantor, *The English Medieval Landscape* (1982), 81.
[17] O. G. S. Crawford, *Archaeology in the Field* (1953), 189.
[18] Hartopp, op. cit. in note 4, 9; *IPM* V, 57-8; *IPM* Henry VII III, 272-3.
[19] RCHME *Herefs.* III, 20. For a detailed study of the castle see Paul Remfry, *Brampton Bryan Castle* (1997).
[20] A. Sclater, *Fieldwork in Brampton Bryan Park* (English Nature Research Report, 1995).
[21] L. Cantor, *Medieval Deer Parks in England* (1983), 3.
[22] Cantor, op. cit. in note 16, 75.
[23] D.G. Bayliss, 'The Lordship of Wigmore in the 14th Century', *TWNFC*, XXXVI (1958), 43; D. Walker, *Medieval Wales* (1990), 59.
[24] Cantor, op. cit, in note 21, 36-7.   [25] Cantor, op. cit, in note 16, 81.
[26] Eyton, op. cit, in note 5, XI, 328.   [27] *IPM* VII, 279.
[28] *IPM* III, 261-2.   [29] PRO, Special Commission 2903.
[30] Eyton, op. cit. in note 5, XI, 315-16.
[31] C. Platt, *Medieval England* (1975), 126-37; Cantor, op. cit, in note 21, 77.
[32] C. Harley, *Brampton Bryan Castle* (1986); O. G. S. Croft, *The House of Croft* (1949), 40-3.
[33] *Cal. Charter Rolls* VI, 137.   [34] *Cal. Pat. Rolls 1429-1436*, 446.
[35] Cantor, op. cit,in note 16, 77.
[36] Hist. Mss. Comm., *14th Report, Mss. of the Duke of Portland* 1V, 6.
[37] T. T. Lewis (ed.), *Letters of the Lady Brilliana Harley*, Camden Soc., First Series, (1853), 229, 231; BBA. Parcel 68.

[38] Lewis, op.cit, in note 37, 2.   [39] BBA. Parcels 22, 102. 1

[40] J. Eales, *Puritans and Roundheads: The Harleys of Brampton Bryan and the Outbreak of the English Civil War* (1990), l64.

[41] Lewis, op. cit, in note 37, 230.   [42] BBA. parcel 22.

[43] C. J. Robinson, *The Castles of Herefordshire and their Lords* (1869), 8.

[44] BBA. parcel 102.

[45] A. Sidebotham, *Brampton Bryan Church and Castle* (1956), 21.

[46] BBA. parcel 68.   [47] Ibid.

[48] H. Skrine, *Two Successive Tours through the whole of Wales* (1798), 130.

[49] BBA. parcel 68.   [50] Ibid. 22.   [51] Ibid. 102.

[52] Ibid.   [53] Portland, op. cit, in note 36, III, 319.

[54] BBA. parcel 102.   [55] Ibid. 68.   [56] Ibid. 22.

[57] Ibid.   [58] S. Lasdun, *The English Park* (1991), 32.

[59] Portland, op. cit, in note 36, III, 274; H.M. Colvin, *A Biographical Dictionary of British Architects 1600-1840* (1995), 1030.

[60] BBA. parcel 68; Austen quoted in M. Hoyles, *Gardener's Delight* (1994), 125-6.

[61] Portland, op. cit, in note 36, III, 333, 396, 504.   [62] Ibid. 494.

[63] P. Willis, *Charles Bridgeman and the English Landscape Garden* (1977), 79, 176-7, Plate78a.   [64] Portland, op. cit, in note 36, V, 663.

[65] A. McInnes, *Robert Harley, Puritan Politician* (1970), 175-6.

[66] S. Couch, 'The Practice of Avenue Planting in the Seventeenth and Eighteenth Centuries', *Garden History* 20 (1992), 179, 182-3.

[67] Portland, op. cit, in note 36, III, 172; Couch, loc. cit, in note 66, 198 note 57.

[68] R. Warner, *A Walk through Wales, August 1797* (1799), 205.

[69] Skrine, op. cit, in note 47.

[70] *The Leominster Guide* (1808), 302; E. Brayley and J. Britton, *The Beauties of England and Wales* VI (1805), 551.   [71] BBA. Estate Office.

[72] E. P. Shirley, *English Deer Parks* (1867), 197.

[73] J. Whitaker, *A Descriptive List of Deer Parks and Paddocks of England* (1892), 69.

[74] *TWNFC* (1870), 302-4; (1882), 194-6.

❖❈❖❈❖❈❖❈❖❈❈❖❈❖❈❖❈❖❈❈❖❈❈❖❈❖❈❖❈❈❖

Numismatic Activities in Herefordshire

ALAN MORRIS

THE IRON AGE

Coins facilitate trade and the exchange of goods. They replaced the earlier time-consuming system of barter. By using the precious metals of gold and silver of standard weight and fineness, guaranteed by an established authority and bearing some effigy, symbol or emblem of that ruling body, then wealth could be concentrated in small portable objects and exchanged for whatever might be desired. Not only could coins facilitate trade within the market place (for which purpose silver was the usual medium) but the higher valued gold coins could be used as bullion for trading between tribal areas or between different countries.

Coins were first used in active trading in southern Britain about 125-100 BC. They were imported from the tribes of Gaul and used to purchase wine, plants, animals and other valuable goods. The British tribes exported raw metal (tin and iron), slaves or mercenary soldiers to Gallic tribes who, in turn, traded with the Romans established around Marseilles. Mount Batten (Hengistbury) and Selsey served as principal gateways into southern Britain, as did the Thames estuary. These first coins were Celtic copies of earlier gold staters of Phillip II of Macedonia that had been used by Phoenician traders. Gradually the designs were modified and 'disintegrated' to reflect Celtic art forms in a manner not unlike a Picasso painting (Picasso himself was strongly influenced by Celtic cave paintings in Spain).

Around 100 BC the tribes of southern Britain began to copy these Gallic coins themselves, a particular popular feature being the triple-tailed horse type of the Suessiones tribe in Gaul. At about the same time, the Cantii tribe of Kent began to manufacture its own coinage, consisting of low value cast coins of an alloy of tin and bronze. By 75 BC, six British tribes of southern Britain: the Durotriges, the Atrebates/Regni, the Cantii, the Trinovantes/Catuvellauni, the Iceni and the Corieltauvi were producing their own coins. Peripheral to these six was the Dobunni tribe which did not issue coins until after the Gallic War of 60-55 BC and indeed was the last British tribe to strike its own coinage. The Dobunni had traded directly with the Atrebates and were part of that network. It is thought that the Dobunni first issued coins about 35 BC. Their gold staters consisted of a branched emblem or corn-ear on one side and a triple-tailed horse on the other (Pl. 1). Silver coins were issued simultaneously consisting of a well-formed head facing right on one side and a triple-tailed horse on the reverse (Pl. 2). Over a period of some eighty years this head was

Plate 1. Dobunni gold stater.

Plate 2. Dobunni silver unit
(Ariconium).

gradually 'disintegrated' in the Picasso manner (drawings A to H). In about 30 BC the names of the Dobunnic rulers began to appear on the gold staters. CORIO was replaced by BODVOC in about 15 BC (Pl. 3) to be followed by ANTEDRIG, COMUX, EISU, CATTI and INAM in that order until about AD 45-50 when the Roman invasion brought the tribal coinage to an end.

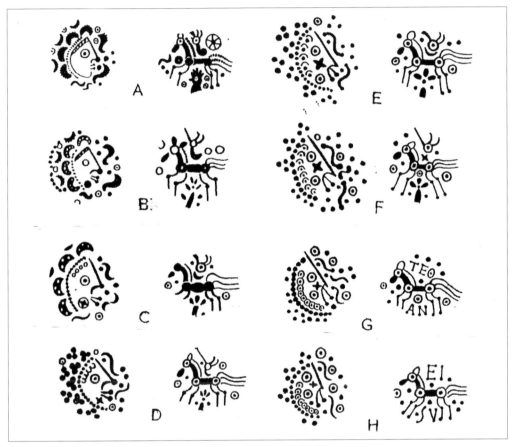

Drawings A to H. 'Disintegration' of Dobunnic silver.   *Source: Allen (1961)*

Plate 3. Dobunni gold stater of Bodvoc.

Just within the Herefordshire boundary, some three miles east of the Wye and some four or more miles north of the Forest of Dean, lies the site of Ariconium. The black earth in the fields around the village of Bromsash bears witness to the size of its economic activity in smelting iron ore from the Dean mines using the ample supply of timber to produce the necessary charcoal. Ariconium, as a source of Dobunni coins, is second only to the tribal capital of Bagendon, close to Cirencester. The Dobunni were an active, prosperous, trading people whose principal contacts were with the Atrebates immediately to the south and with whose coins there are striking similarities in design. The Dobunni coins conformed to exact standards and as such could only have been minted at the capital Bagendon. Nevertheless, gold- and silver-plated copies of these are not uncommon. Without doubt, many of these copies would have been produced at Ariconium, where the metallurgical expertise lay in abundance. The design of the gold staters was to remain unchanged throughout the whole period of 35 BC-AD 45 apart from a change of name of the ruler, evidence that the principal purpose of these staters was to act as bullion. During this period, in common with that of other tribes the gold content of these staters was gradually reduced, and it is this trend that provides us with the sequence of the rulers from Corio to Inam, rather than attempting to track the changing style or disintegrating imagery of the silver coins.

Despite the high concentration of Dobunnic coins within Ariconium, there is a dearth of finds to the west across the Wye and to the east. The odd find occurs along the Wye leading south which implies that the river rather than a track was the principal trade route. Similarly there is a void of finds between Ariconium and Bagendon. Van Arsdell and de Jersey have plotted the find spots of Dobunnic coins over several periods (Map 1) and it is evident that Ariconium appears as an isolated trading-centre or exchange-zone or 'gateway' remote from the main centre of Dobunnic

Map 1. Conjectural map of Dubonnic territory

territory. It would appear that Ariconium served as an exchange-zone for the trading routes into Wales just as Wroxeter served a similar purpose to the north where Dobunnic coins have also been discovered. Van Arsdell believes that this negative evidence, this no-man's land around Ariconium, is convincing evidence that, prior to the Roman occupation, Ariconium and indeed the whole of Herefordshire lay outside Dobunnic territory. In other words Ariconium and Dean were centres where the Dobunni had economic activity and nothing more. If it were otherwise, one would have to assume that the northern Dobunnic people were so very different from those of the south that they had no need of coinage. Recent detectorist finds do not distort the picture, but without proper recordings of their finds it is difficult to speculate further.

A separate identity for Herefordshire during the Iron Age had previously been advanced by Stanford. The densely populated hillforts of the Herefordshire basin, centred on Credenhill, have yielded no coins or wheel-turned pottery, unlike those of the Cotswolds around Bagendon. Hillfort density and pottery also distinguish this area from that of the Silures, and Stanford suggested that these people were the Decangi as in Tacitus, and that a stone inscription from Kenchester in the reign of Numerian (AD 283-284) with the enigmatic inscription RPCD might well refer to the Decangi rather than the Dobunni. Be that as it may, following the Roman conquest, the coinage of the Iron Age tribes was withdrawn and replaced by the Roman currency system. It may well be that, politically, the map was redrawn to include the Herefordshire basin within Dobunni suzerainty with its new tribal capital at Cirencester.

THE ROMAN PERIOD

The coins of the Iron Age tribes were rapidly demonetised shortly after AD 43 and the gold and silver melted down for bullion. They were replaced by Roman coins, but these were only thinly distributed and were probably used in the first place by the occupying legions to buy goods from the native inhabitants in the shanty towns (*canabae*) springing up beside the new military encampments. The standard coins were the silver *denarius* and the brass or copper *sestertius*, *dupondius* and *as* of Claudius. Before long counterfeit copies of these coins were being produced. The crudely produced copper coin *as* of Claudius recovered from Ariconium (Pl. 4) can be compared with the official issue (Pl. 5). Elsewhere, the technology was sufficiently well advanced to produce excellently plated copies of Claudian denarii such as the one illustrated (Pl. 6), part of a hoard recently recovered by the banks of the River Waveney. The coin-forger's lead mould recovered from Kenchester and used for plating base copies of a denarius of Titus lends support to this widespread practice (Pl. 7). Judging from the degree of wear of the host coin, the mould was probably in use around AD 100.

The principle mints for the supply of coins to the Roman Empire in the west were Rome and Lyons until the mid-third century, a time of rapid inflation. Silver was becoming increasingly scarce and its value rose dramatically such that the denarius became heavily debased, until by the time of the Gallic usurpers Postumus, Victorinus and Tetricus I and II (AD 260-273), the sole type of coin in circulation was a silver-washed bronze *antoninianus* or double-*denarius*, the larger base coins having long vanished from the currency. The purchasing power of this new double-denarius fell sharply, and increasingly more and more such coins were needed to buy such simple goods as eggs or wine. Supplies of these coins to Britain were very inadequate, and

Plate 4. Imitation *as* of Claudius from Ariconium.

Plate 5. Official *as* of Claudius.

Plate 7. Coin mould from Kenchester.

Plate 6. Silver-plated denarius of Claudius.

the opportunity arose once again of large-scale counterfeiting of the official coinage. The Gallic usurpers appear to have turned a blind eye to the practice, but it is clear from field finds that the forged coins probably outnumbered the official coinage at this time. The illustrations (Pls. 8 & 9) show a larger official coin of Tetricus I alongside its smaller barbarous copy (both coins from Kenchester). It would seem that every town in Roman Britain was engaged in the practice of copying the official coinage as so few die-duplicates are known. Those copies of very small module were of course very easily lost and presumably little effort made to recover them because of their low purchasing power. Britain was returned to the central authority of Rome in AD 273 and the barbarous copies ceased production.

Plate 8. Official coin of Tetricus I.

Plate 9. Forged copy of Tetricus I.

In AD 286 Britain and northern Gaul were again usurped by the naval commander of the Channel, Carausius, who quickly set about issuing his own currency from London and in addition from Colchester (or Colonia as it was known then). The earliest coins were overstruck on coins in circulation as the example illustrated in Pl. 10 illustrates. The inverted head of Claudius II is clearly visible on the undertype (from Kenchester). Barbarous copies once again make their appearance as the very crude example of Carausius from Kenchester demonstrates (Pl. 11). Much use was made of the reverse of these coins for propaganda purposes. Many novel designs and legends were used by Carausius, and Kenchester has yielded a number of unique examples such as that in Pl. 12. This bears the helmeted bust of the emperor on one side and what may be his flagship on the reverse together with the slogan PACATRIX AVG which has been interpreted as HMS PEACEMAKER. The exergual letters CANC have defied interpretation.

Plate 10. Overstruck coin of
Carausius.

Plate 11. Barbarous copy of
Carausius.

Plate 12. Unique coin of Carausius from Kenchester.

Kenchester has yielded a higher proportion of Carausian coins than any other site. A possible explanation may lie in the fact that Carausius withdrew his legions from Wales midway through his reign. Kenchester, being the most westerly civil settlement in this area, may have been deluged with the coins held by traders and others following in the wake of the withdrawal of the legions. In AD 293, Carausius was murdered by his finance minister Allectus, who for three years issued coins from London and Colchester of a quality greater than that issued by Rome (Pl. 13, recovered from Kenchester). In AD 296 Allectus was defeated by the central authorities under Constantius, and Britain was recovered by Rome. A new currency was introduced of both silver coins and large-sized, silver-washed bronze *folles* (Pl. 14, from the Llangarron hoard) which lasted virtually unchanged until inflation once again took a hold, the modules being steadily reduced in size, as their purchasing power fell. Again counterfeit copies become abundant, produced by all towns within the province. These and their larger official counterparts form the bulk of site finds today (Pls. 15 & 16, from Kenchester). After AD 388 the supply of coins to Britain from Gaul began to dry up. Copies of the earlier popular coins continued to be produced. Indeed to judge by the crudity of the designs, copies were clearly made of earlier copies. In the south-east of Britain official coins have been found of the mid-fifth century but it would appear that in Herefordshire, as elsewhere in the west, the Romano-Britons had reverted to barter.

Plate 13. Coin of Allectus from
Kenchester.

Plate 14. Large-sized follis of
Diocletian.

Plate 15. Unofficial coin of
about AD330.

Plate 16. Official coin of
about AD330.

THE ANGLO-SAXON AND NORMAN PERIODS

No post-Roman coinage appears to have circulated within Herefordshire until the time of Offa (757-796) and most of this would have come from his principal mint at Canterbury. It was not until the reign of Aethelstan (924-939) that Hereford had its own mint following the king's decree that every borough should be possessed of a moneyer. Indeed, Aethelstan met the Welsh princes at Hereford and exacted tribute (in gold and silver) from them. Moneyers were obliged to accompany military expeditions into Wales in order to strike coins to pay the fighting units. The name of the moneyer at this time in Hereford is not known, but during the reign of Eadgar in 973, his reformed coinage, now bearing his portrait, was struck by a single moneyer at Hereford named Gillys.

By the time of Aethelred (978-1016), Hereford had twelve moneyers (Pl. 17), London over ninety, whereas Gloucester merely had four. This sudden rise in minting activity reflected the need to pay Danegeld as much as any requirements for incursions into Wales. The Domesday Survey informs us that in Edward the Confessor's reign the number of moneyers in Hereford had been reduced to seven at any one time and one of these struck for the bishop. Both the king and the bishop received a fee for every £1 of silver struck and an additional fee when the design was changed, a frequent occurrence to defy the machinations of the counterfeiter. Among the moneyers striking at Hereford immediately prior to the Conquest were Aegelric, Aelfwig, Eadwig, Earnwi, Edric, Edwi, Leofnoth, Ordric, Raedulf and Wulfwine, but who struck for the bishop cannot be identified. Minting continued at Hereford, presumably within the castle, into the reign of Henry II and until his new coinage had been completed in 1180. Thereafter the number of operating mints was reduced from thirty-one to six and Hereford was among those closed. It was reopened during the reign of Henry III in 1247 to cope with the new long-cross coinage that replaced the very worn and clipped short-cross variety. The incorporation of a long-cross in the reverse design was to discourage clippers, such that if the ends of the cross were not visible, then the coin was not legal tender. Four moneyers – Henri (PL. 18), Ricard, Roger and Walter were needed at Hereford for this recoinage. It should be noted that throughout the whole of this post-Roman period the silver

Plate 17. Aethelred penny,
Hereford mint, moneyer Byrstan.

Plate 18. Henry III penny,
Hereford mint, moneyer Henri.

penny was the sole coin in circulation. Smaller denominations of halfpenny and
farthing were legally achieved by cutting the penny into halves and quarters along the
line of the long-cross. Once the recoinage of Henry III was completed, the
Hereford mint was closed and future coinage was contained in fewer mints. It was
not to reopen again until the time of the Civil War.

THE CIVIL WAR (1642-48)

The Tower of London was the sole mint for England from the time of Elizabeth I
until 1637, when Charles I ordered Thomas Bushell, the Master of the Mint, to set up
a separate mint in the castle at Aberystwyth so as to coin directly the silver being
extracted from the Welsh mines. It is possible that Charles foresaw the likelihood of
an imminent civil conflict and that he might lose control of London and the Tower
mint. A mint in royalist Wales would allow him to finance his own campaign and to
pay his own army. In January 1641/42 Charles established his court in York and later
on 22 August 1642, Charles raised his standard at Nottingham and then proceeded to
Shrewsbury to recruit an army from Wales and the Marches. Bushell was ordered to
move to Shrewsbury and to bring his silver, his dies and minting equipment from
Aberystwyth to set up a new mint in the castle at Shrewsbury. The Welsh silver was

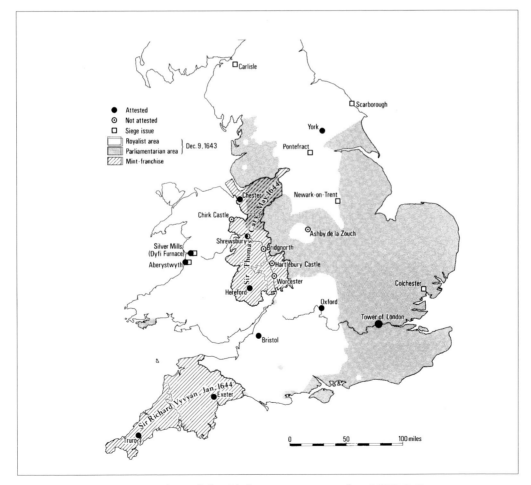

Map 2. Mints of the Civil War 1642-1648 after SCBI (33)

augmented by supplies of plate surrendered by the citizens of that town. Converting plate into coin had been common practice for centuries. Charles had the silver duly recorded with the promise that when victorious its value would be redeemed with interest. By December 1642 the king had moved his capital to Oxford and there it was to remain until its loss in 1646. Bushell transferred his mint to Oxford and immediately began striking large quantities of gold and silver, much of it surrendered by loyal citizens and the colleges. By 1643, further royalist mints had been established at York and at the important port of Bristol.

Elsewhere in the south-west, Sir Richard Vyvyan had been appointed mint master to coin for the king at Truro in 1642 and eventually at Exeter upon its capture in 1643. Along the Marches, Sir Thomas Cary was appointed mint master on 22 May 1644 and mints were opened at Chester, Worcester, and Hereford, and reopened at Shrewsbury by Royal Commission (MAP 2). Hereford had been in Royalist hands since May 1643 and was feeling very secure since the capture of Bristol. It remained in Royalist hands despite some minor skirmishing in April 1644, but by September of that year it had been fortified and its garrison increased with extra troops costing some £54 4s a week. This was the likely reason for the commission to set up a mint. The local antiquary James W. Lloyd of Kington had seen evidence of certificates and payments for the King's service. In a letter to the *Numismatic Circular* of 1898 he quotes this evidence and writes:

> In a MS of Certificates of receipts and payments for the King's Service, during the Civil War, in the city of Hereford, October and first week of November 1644, a time of comparative quiet, but really of active preparation for coming events, which culminated in the siege of the city in the following July, the following entries appear

RECEIPTS
Received of Mr Walter Kirle p.107 oz. Plate att Vs	26. 15. 0
of Melwyn p.80 oz. Plate att Vs	20. 00. 0
of Weaver p.50 oz. Plate and 7.10 in money	20. 00. 0
of Harford p. 40 oz. Plate at Vs	10. 00. 0

PAYMENTS
Paid Rude the Coyner for coyning	
277 oz. plate att IIIId. per oz.	4. 12. 4

> I shall be glad to know if any of the pieces so coined at Hereford are known, as so far I have been unable to trace the existence of any siege pieces which can be so assigned.
>
> James W. Lloyd

The halfcrown piece, the most common denomination struck by Royalist mints during the Civil War, had a value of 2s 6d and weighed 0.5ozs. Thus the amount actually coined at that time was under £80 and represented the cost of the additional garrison for little over a week. Presumably it simply supplemented what was already available unless other receipts have long since gone missing. The daily rates of pay for active militia ranged from 8d for a private soldier, 1s 6d for a sergeant, 15s for a captain to a top rate of £2 5s for a colonel acting as captain. The Ms that Lloyd witnessed can no longer be traced, nor has a search of Lloyd's correspondence to other antiquaries revealed just where he had located this information.

It had long been the custom to indicate on the Royalist coinage the place of mint-age by a letter or abbreviation of the mint's name e.g. OX for Oxford, Br for Bristol, Ex for Exeter and EBOR for York. Alternatively, some heraldic symbol drawn from the town or city's coat of arms had been used, e.g. three pears for Worcester. Research has identified the likely coins of Sir Thomas Cary's mints for the Marches, but apart from Chester, the identifying symbols remain an enigma. It is perfectly possible that a travelling mint moved from Hereford to Worcester to Shrewsbury, coining silver as the occasion demanded. The most likely candidates for this Hereford travelling mint are illustrated 3d, 4d, and 2s 6d. (Pls. 19, 20 and 21). Yet again, in 1645, a novel halfcrown with a garter reverse seems the most likely candidate for the Hereford mint (Pl. 22). In September 1645 the Scots siege of Hereford was lifted and Charles, in recognition of the heroic defence, augmented the arms of the city with Scottish crosses, supporters and a crest with the motto 'Invictae Fidelitas Praemium'. These coins are very rare and this may reflect the fact that Hereford was

Plate 19. Charles I 4d possibly struck in Hereford in 1644.

Plate 20. Charles I 3d possibly struck in Hereford in 1644.

Plate 21. Charles I halfcrown possibly struck at Hereford 1644.

Plate 22. Charles I halfcrown of Hereford dated 1645 and officially pierced in 1696.

lost to Parliament some three months later. The conundrum of which coins were actually minted in Hereford can only be resolved by the discovery of locally-buried hoards of this period. Even single finds of these rare coins might shed some light on the problem. One can only hope that metal detectorists will honour their obligations to report their finds to the museum or other authorities.

THE RECOINAGE OF 1696-97

Despite substantial issues of machine-made silver coins following the restoration of Charles II in 1660 and in subsequent years, considerable quantities of old hammered coins in very worn and clipped condition continued to circulate, often heavily discounted in trade because of their low weight. In 1695-96, in the reign of William III, Parliament decided to recall all old money at face value in return for new money. The cost of this exercise was to be recovered from the notorious window tax. Unfortunately, insufficient stocks of new money were available, nor could it be minted sufficiently quickly to satisfy the demand. There was also the difficult problem of speed of distribution to the various towns and cities throughout the realm. A simple expedient was resorted to, whereby old hammered coins could be brought in and weighed, and if they were within the tolerance permitted they were then pierced in the centre with a punch so as not to remove any silver, and returned to circulation to be traded or exchanged at face value. The Hereford 2s 6d of 1645 (Pl. 22) has been so treated. Any such punched coins would not then be redeemed at face value if they were subsequently found to be seriously underweight.

The Tower mint was still hard-pressed to cope with the recoinage and so it was proposed to set up extra mints which would also act as distribution centres. These were to be at York for the north, at Bristol and Exeter for the south-west, at Norwich for the east and at Hereford for Wales and the Marches. The initial letter of these new mint cities was to be placed beneath the bust of the king. Either Hereford was dilatory in setting up the coinage machinery or possibly one of the Grosvenor family of Chester was a member of the appointed committee to oversee this recoinage, but a sudden decision was taken to transfer the mint to Chester which already had an assay office for hallmarking gold and silver. Hereford thus lost this lucrative franchise, despite the fact that a Mr Batson had been nominated Warden of the Hereford mint, £100 being set aside and a 'fitt place having been found for it'. Thus silver coins of the Chester mint duly appeared (Pl. 23). The demand of the recoinage was met within two years and by 1697 all hammered coins had been demonetised and the auxiliary mints closed.

Plate 23. Chester halfcrown of 1696.

TOKEN COINAGE

The abolition of the monarchy by Parliament in 1648 led to a new-style coinage, in which the king's image and the royal arms were replaced by shields bearing the cross of St George and the Irish harp. In addition, English replaced Latin legends as the latter was thought to smack too much of Popery. The production of small copper farthings that had been introduced under James I and continued by Charles ceased.

This caused great problems amongst the poor, as within a year or two there was a great dearth of small change. Small quantities of silver pennies and halfpennies were still minted but their small modules caused great inconvenience as they were so easily lost. The city of Bristol, which, during the reign of Elizabeth had solved the problem by issuing its own token coinage, again repeated an issue of copper farthings in 1652. Parliament simply ignored the problem and within a year or two, practically every town and city throughout the country was doing the same. The Tower had always been reluctant to issue a base-metal coinage, partly because the intrinsic value of any such coin would lie beneath its face value. It could never serve more than a mere token coinage. This attitude persisted into the nineteenth century and indeed, within living memory there has been a limit to the amount of base metal coins that could be accepted as legal tender in any transaction.

Hereford, Leominster, Ledbury, Ross, Kington, Bromyard, Weobley and Pembridge all issued tokens between 1657 and 1671 to values of a farthing or a halfpenny. They were authorised by either the mayor or by wealthy merchants and other traders. Any customer could redeem the value of such tokens by surrendering them to the issuing authority in return for Tower silver. Most of these tokens bore the names of the issuer, their nominal values and usually a coat of arms representing the trade or guild of the issuer. Normally these tokens were round, but a few traders issued some that were square, octagonal or even heart-shaped, like those of 1668 of the glover Thomas Hutchins of Hereford (Pl. 24) and of the mercer John Breynton of Kington in 1667 (Pl. 25). In 1672 Parliament authorised a large issue of copper regal coins bearing the head of Charles II and trading in privately issued tokens was prohibited.

Plate 24. Hereford halfpenny token of 1668.

Plate 25. Halfpenny token of John Breynton of Kington

From 1672 until 1775 substantial quantities of copper halfpence and farthings were issued and the people were well satisfied, but the industrial revolution had drawn large numbers from the remote farms of Wales and the Pennines into the fast-spreading towns of the Midlands, Lancashire and Yorkshire. In addition, the size of the population was beginning to grow and there was greater prosperity. Inevitably the cost of commodities began to rise, and Parliament, forever disinterested in the copper coinage, refused to authorise any further issues, partly because of rising costs. In 1787 the Parys copper mine of Anglesey took the initiative and issued its own pennies and halfpennies, thus solving the problem of paying its workforce. Once again, this example was quickly copied by most boroughs throughout the kingdom. They were manufactured to order from expert die-sinkers in Birmingham. It gave rise to an extraordinary variety of designs and political slogans. Hereford was not exempt and C. Honiatt, a Birmingham warehouseman with a business in Hereford, had 3 cwts of halfpennies made, bearing on one side a cider-apple tree and on the reverse the slogan 'For Change Not Fraud' (Pl. 26). Other Hereford tokens were

issued for T. Gorton (a cider merchant) in 1794 and by J. Milton in 1796 (Pl. 27), the
latter showing a Hereford bull, representing Agriculture breaking free from its chains,
thus delivering a political message.

Plate 26. Hereford halfpenny token of 1794.

Plate 27. Penny token of 1796 by J. Milton.

Parliament's attention was riveted on the war with France and not only had the
Tower failed to deliver any copper coins, production of silver had also ceased in 1787.
In 1797, following a sudden fall in the price of copper, Matthew Boulton was authorised to strike copper coins. He produced the famous 'cartwheel' twopences and
pennies weighing 2 ozs and 1 oz respectively. This was followed in 1799 by a
substantial production of halfpennies and farthings. Again, the token coins were
declared illegal tender, and most of them disappeared into the hands of collectors or
were simply put aside. The cartwheel coins of 1797 proved unpopular because of
their size, and in 1806 and 1807 a new issue of copper coins was struck by Boulton at
his mint in Soho, Birmingham. Attention now focused on the dearth of silver. A
simple expedient was resorted to by Parliament. Tons of Spanish-American silver
dollars were bought from Spain and countermarked with the head of George III,
using the hallmark punch. By 1806, the Bank of England had softened them
sufficiently as to re-strike them fully. Because of their lower silver content, they
traded at 4s 9d rather than 5s. This did little to alleviate the crisis felt by a dearth of
smaller silver coins, so once again a token currency appeared in the towns and cities
of England between 1811 and 1812. But on this occasion it consisted not only of
copper tokens but also silver ones of values usually of sixpence or a shilling. Only
one issuer supplied tokens in Hereford and those were silver and of value 1s. They
were jointly issued by Carless & Co. and Wainwright & Co. (Pl. 28).
With the end of the war with France in 1815, Parliament was once again able to

Plate 28. Shilling token of 1811 by Carless and Wainwright.

focus on the state of the currency. In 1816 a new silver coinage was introduced in large quantity, and with few exceptions, silver was coined in all subsequent years. Token coins were once again prohibited. The silver coins were to remain as legal tender until decimalisation, after which they were duly withdrawn over a number of years. Regal copper coins were not minted again until 1821 and they then replaced the copper tokens of 1811 and 1812. Thereafter the Mint has ensured that sufficient coins are minted each year to meet demand. Mention should be made of banknotes. To alleviate the shortage of silver in the late eighteenth century, many private banks issued their own notes, usually guaranteed by the Bank of England. Finally, although supplies of coins were adequate during the latter part of the nineteenth century, many traders issued advertising or truck tokens.

It was common practice for cutlers who appear to have been possessed of the necessary punches to countermark foreign or obsolete coins. The example (Pl. 29) is one issued by Caswell who had his premises in the Old House in Butchers' Row. It bears no mark of value and is countermarked on an old cartwheel penny of 1797. It does not appear to have served as a token but may instead have served as a receipt for any tool or equipment left with the cutler. Likewise, in this century brass 'tokens' were issued by hop producers to pickers as a check on the amounts collected.

Plate 29. Cartwheel penny countermarked by Caswell, cutler, of Butchers Row.

BIBLIOGRAPHY
Iron Age
  D. F. Allen, 'A Study of the Dobunnic Coinage' in E. M. Clifford, *Bagendon: a Belgic Oppidum*, (1961).
  S. C. Stanford, *The Archaeology of the Welsh Marches* (1980).
  R. D. Van Arsdell, *Celtic Coinage of Britain* (1989).
  R. D. Van Arsdell with P. de Jersey *The Coinage of the Dobunni* (1994).
Roman Britain
  G. Askew, *The Coinage of Roman Britain* (1951).
  C. E. King *et al.*, *Studies in the Coinage of Carausius and Allectus* (1985)
  A. Morris, 'The Carausian Era at Kenchester' in Spinks *Num.Circ.*(1982), and 'The Enigma of the C mint' in Spinks *Num.Circ.*(1986).
  N. Shiel *The Episode of Carausius and Allectus* (BAR 40), (1977).

R. Shoesmith, 'A Roman Forger at Kenchester' in *TWNFC*, XLV (1986), 371-5.

Anglo-Saxon and Norman

D. M. Metcalf, *An Atlas of Anglo-Saxon and Norman Coin Finds* (1998).

The Civil War

E. Besley, *Coins and Medals of the English Civil War* (1990).

G. Charman, 'The Punched Hammered Coinage of 1696' in Seaby's *CMB* (1983 & 84).

G. Foard, *Col. John Pickering's Regt. of Foot* (1994).

J. J. North & P. J. Preston-Morley, *The John G. Brooker Collection*, SCBI 33, (1984).

R. Shoesmith, *The Civil War in Hereford* (1995).

The Recoinage of 1696-97

H. Farquhar, 'Portraiture of Stuart Monarchs', *BNJ* 1911, (1912).

E. J. & C. N. Moore, 'A Mint at Chester' in Seaby's *CMB* (1981).

Tokens

M. Dickenson, *Seventeenth Century Tokens of the British Isles* (1986).

J. Gavin Scott, *British Countermarks on Copper and Bronze Coins* (1975).

J. W. Lloyd, 'Herefordshire Tokens of the Seventeenth Century' in *TWNFC*, (1884) 183-209.

Windmills in Herefordshire

MURIEL TONKIN

Were there any windmills in Herefordshire and was there a need for them? As one remains, now converted into a house in the parish of Moccas, it can be presumed that there were others, which have disappeared (Pl.1). Herefordshire has always been, and still is, a county noted for its agriculture, especially for cattle-rearing and the growing of cereals. The Old Red Sandstone which is the predominant rock in the county produces a rich and fertile soil, which is valuable for rearing the various breeds of cattle and a variety of cereals. Straw and fodder were needed for the cattle and horses and the people required food of which flour was an important ingredient.

A number of rivers flow through the county, namely, the Wye, Lugg, Arrow, Teme, Frome and Monnow, as well as the many brooks which enter them. Along these

Plate 1. Moccas windmill, 23 July 1980, converted into a house with addition.

Copyright E. T. Price

rivers there were numerous watermills used for the grinding of corn to feed the population and the animals. Could these watermills provide for the whole of the county?
It would appear doubtful; so why not windmills in areas where the watermills were
not easily possible. Watermills whether undershot or overshot depended upon a
supply of water. The undershot type was found on an artificial watercourse, called a
leat, which diverted water from a river and then returned it by means of a tail-race.
The overshot type was used in hilly country where streams had good falls feeding the
water on to the top of the wheel so that the weight of water could turn the wheel.
The undershot was known from Norman times and the overshot developed in the
Middle Ages.

Common sense suggests that the watermills on the rivers could not have provided
for the whole of the county. It would not have been feasible to take the cereals long
distances to mill the grain into flour. Wind power must have been used in areas where
water power was impossible, hence the existence of windmills.

Windmills, according to Grigson,[1] arrived in England at the end of the twelfth
century and Richardson states that the earliest record of a windmill in England is at
Bury St Edmunds in 1191.[2] Recorded dates for windmills in Herefordshire will be
mentioned later in this paper.

Assuming that there were windmills in the county, where were they likely to be
found and what were their structures? They would need to be positioned on a high,
open site with land gradually sloping up to it from all directions in order to catch the
wind. In Herefordshire, the prevailing wind blows from the S.W. There were three
types of windmill, the post mill, tower mill and smock mill. Of these, the tower mill
became the most common.

The post mill consisted of a timber body containing the machinery and carrying
sails mounted on an oak main-post. The body of the mill was moved round to face
the wind by using a tail-beam. The oldest surviving mill of this type is that at Bourne,
Cambridgeshire, erected in 1636.[3] By the eighteenth century an automatic fantail
had been developed. The fantail was mounted on the structure to catch the wind and
with a system of gears and spindles turned the wheels at the foot of the mill ladder,
which then went along a track round the mill. A round-house structure often
covered the bottom part of the main-post. The mill was usually set upon an
artificial mound.

Tower mills developed in the mid-seventeenth century and most surviving
windmills are of this type. They have a brick tower containing the machinery, on top
of which is a moveable top or cap. The cap moves to face the wind. They also adopted
the automatic fantail. Smock mills also developed in the mid-seventeenth century
with a moveable cap and were usually a weather-boarded, octagonal structure
resembling a miller's flared smock. These were often found in areas where brick was
hard to acquire.

These mills needed sails, usually four, consisting of an open latticed framework
covered with canvas. They worked the grindstones. No attempt has been made, in
this paper, to describe the machinery or how the mill worked to grind the corn into
flour.

How does one set about discovering if and where windmills existed in Herefordshire? John Field suggests that field-names including the word windmill, such as
Windmill Close, Windmill Croft, Windmill Field, Windmill Furlong, Windmill Ground,
Windmill Hill, Windmill Meadow, Windmill Piece, Windmill Post could refer to 'land
beside, or containing, a windmill'.[4] Grigson states that often there are two indicators

for windmill sites: the name Windmill Hill on maps, and the remains of a small mound on which the mill was set.[5]

As the fields with the above names are likely to vary in size, it is not possible in many cases to pinpoint the spot where the windmill stood. Ploughing over the years since a windmill went out of use could mean that any mound would also have disappeared. It is reasonable to assume that a windmill stood somewhere in a certain field, but one must allow for the size of the field so that one could be within 50m of the site or as much as half a mile.

EVIDENCE FROM THE FIELD-NAME SURVEY

In recent years, members of the Woolhope Club and others have transcribed the field-names and their numbers from the tithe apportionments for all the parishes and townships of the county of Hereford. At the same time Geoff Gwatkin copied the tithe maps which were drawn as a result of the Tithe Commutation Act of 1836 and are dated approximately 1838-50. These have been published in pamphlet form.

Each parish and township has been searched for any reference to a field-name, which includes the word windmill. Also the size of the field, its land-use, the name of the owner and occupier have been noted. Of the 260 parishes and townships, the mention of the word windmill has shown up in thirty-eight parishes. The following table includes the grid reference and contour as far as it is possible to pinpoint the actual site. Allowance must be made for the field sizes and the passage of time.

PARISH	GRID REF.	FIELD-NAME AND NO.	Contour ft. Estimated	ACREAGE		
				a	r	p
Abbeydore	366308	706 Windmill Field	600+	5	0	11
Aymestrey	460697/8	320 Upper Windmill Bank		0	3	06
		321 Upper Windmill Bank with Rough	750 to 800	10	0	18
		322 Lower Windmill Bank		12	2	26
				23	2	10
Bosbury	708435/6	151 Windmill Hill		1	3	35
		152 In Windmill Hill	300	0	2	38
		152a In Windmill Hill Field		0	3	28
				3	2	21
Bridstow	375264	280 Windmill Field	200+	20	0	26
Brockhampton & How Caple	602304	72 Part of Upper Windmill Farm		0	2	10
		77 Windmill Piece	200-	3	0	18
		73 Part of Upper Windmill Field		1	0	30
		74 Do.		0	1	04
		78 Windmill Orchard		2	2	27
				7	3	09
Burghill	487451	659 Windmill Bank		9	2	18
		665 Under Windmill Bank		15	0	38
		799a In Little Windmill Field		0	1	26
		903 In Windmill Field		1	2	07
		905 do.	318 to 400	0	1	19

PARISH	GRID REF.	FIELD-NAME AND NO.	Contour ft. Estimated	ACREAGE		
				a	r	p
Burghill (cont'd.)	`	907 do.		0	2	09
		918 do.		0	1	22
		913 do.		0	3	22
		921 do.		0	2	37
		923 do.		1	0	15
		925 do.		0	1	23
		916 Windmill Field		0	2	38
		660 Windmill Bank		1	2	26
		904 In Windmill Field		0	3	18
		909 In do.		0	3	10
		917 Windmill Field Orchard		0	2	08
		920 In Windmill Field		0	1	32
		901 In Windmill Field		0	2	08
		926 do.		1	1	10
		799 In Windmill Field		0	3	08
		915 In Windmill Field		0	2	00
		323 Windmill Orchard		2	2	33
		919 In Windmill Field		0	1	29
		900 In Windmill Field		0	3	10
		906 do.		0	1	23
		908 do.		0	3	36
		924 do.		0	3	11
		902 In Windmill Field		0	2	10
		922 In Windmill Field		0	2	05
		928 Windmill Bank		0	3	22
				47	1	13
Clehonger	458386	256 Windmill Field	300+	40	1	10
Clifford	278442	818 Part of Windmill Park	500+	3	0	18
		829 Windmill Cottage & Garden		0	0	25
				3	1	03
Colwall	743406	773 Windmill Field		11	0	11
		776 Upper Windmill Field	c500	4	2	14
				15	2	25
Dormington & Bartestree	592394	415 Windmill Hill	600	7	1	14
Eardisland	422569	354 Windmill Coppice	300	0	1	18
		397 Windmill Field		8	0	13
		353 Windmill Bank		5	1	32
		398 do. field		9	1	28
				23	1	11
Eardisley	311482	864 Windmill Field	200	16	0	30
Eastnor	721385	186 Part of Windmill Field	500	3	1	12
	720381	146 Windmill Field	400	3	2	08
				6	3	20

PARISH	GRID REF.	FIELD-NAME AND NO.	Contour ft. Estimated	ACREAGE		
				a	r	p
Edvin Loach	660586	56 Windmill Hill	550	12	0	21
Eye, Moreton & Ashton	515644	220 Wind Mill Bank	400	43	3	20
Fownhope	586336	871 Windmill Piece	300	1	2	31
King's Caple	553291	159 The Windmill or Four Acres	200	4	2	13
		160 The Windmill or Four Acres		5	3	39
		154 Windmill		6	3	13
		157 The Windmill Field		0	3	30
		156 In the Windmill Field		0	3	10
		155 The Windmill Field		5	0	31
				24	1	16
King's Pyon	434497	241 Windmill Bank	c420	3	1	32
Ledbury	699361	1217 Round House Meadow	200	2	1	13
		1228 do.		6	2	34
		1472 Windmill Croft		1	3	06
	707365	1444 Windmill Croft	200	4	3	06
		1450 Windmill Croft		1	3	03
		1448 Windmill Fields		24	1	24
		1222 Round House Meadow		2	1	26
	722388	190 Windmill Field	400	2	3	32
		187 Windmill Field		1	0	03
		188 Windmill Field		3	2	35
				51	3	22
Leysters	558632	121 Windmill Piece	650	5	1	01
Llanwarne	522280	464 Part of Wind Mill Hill	400	11	2	10
Madley	411388	535 Windmill Fields	c275	8	2	00
Marden	519463	683 Windmill	c200	10	3	32
Moccas	360419	103 Orchard adjoining last & Windmill	c250	1	1	06
Moreton Jeffries	606488	60 Windmill Field Hopyard	400	2	3	04
		61 Windmill Field		14	3	33
		62 Far Wind Field		8	3	10
		47 Windmill Hopyard		2	0	08
		46 Windmill Croft		3	0	29
		44 Windmill Field		17	3	04
				49	2	08
Much Marcle (tithe 1839)	650305	557 Windmill Down	c380	4	2	09

PARISH	GRID REF.	FIELD-NAME AND NO.	Contour ft. Estimated	ACREAGE		
				a	r	p
Much Marcle (enclosure 1795)	650305	7 Wind-field		6	1	37
		60 Windmill Down		1	2	03
		62 Windmill Post		1	1	21
		571 Windmill Field		9	1	27
				18	3	08
Munsley	708435/6	193 Windmill Field	300	13	2	07
		183 Windmill Field		10	0	15
				23	2	22
Norton Canon	373478	223 In Windmill Field	300	9	3	32
		222 In Windmill Field		12	0	26
		219 In Windmill Field		0	2	08
		221 In Windmill Field		2	1	04
		218 In Windmill Field		0	3	14
		208 Windmill Field Gate		2	3	38
		220 In Windmill Field		3	0	35
				31	3	37
Pencombe	585522	155 Windmill Pit	675	15	3	11
Sellack	577280	37 Windmill Field	200	18	3	35
Thruxton	443345	33 Windmill Field	300+	7	0	25
		54 Windmill Orchard		4	2	30
		34 Windmill Field		13	2	10
				25	1	25
Upton Bishop	630263	675 Windmill Hill	250	8	3	20
Walford	576214	14 Windmill Hill	c110	12	1	20
Weobley	398515	419 In Windmill Field	c330	1	2	32
		429 In ditto		0	3	26
		429b In ditto		1	3	35
		430 In ditto		1	0	30
		434 In ditto		1	1	20
		443 In Windmill Field		2	0	32
		421 In Windmill Field		0	1	33
		422 In ditto		0	3	00
		436 In ditto		0	3	18
		431 In Windmill field		0	1	01
		433 In ditto		0	0	30
		408 In Windmill field		1	1	19
		425 In Windmill field		0	2	11
		426 ditto		0	2	01
		427 ditto		0	1	29
		409 In Windmill field		4	3	04
		411 ditto		0	2	15
		438 ditto		0	1	12
		413 In Windmill field		0	2	32

PARISH	GRID REF.	FIELD-NAME AND NO.	Contour ft. Estimated	ACREAGE		
				a	r	p
Weobley (cont'd.)		415 ditto		0	2	30
		418 In Windmill field		0	3	06
		428 In Windmill field		0	1	28
		445 In Windmill field		1	3	37
		416 In Windmill field		1	0	11
		432a In Windmill field		0	0	18
		432b In ditto		0	3	11
		420 In Windmill field		0	1	26
		432 In ditto		0	2	08
		437 In ditto		0	0	32
		406 In Windmill field		0	2	04
		412 In ditto		0	2	23
		423 In ditto		0	1	36
		424 In ditto		0	2	13
		444 In ditto		1	0	33
		429c In Windmill field		0	2	06
		410 In Windmill field		1	3	25
		414 In Windmill field		1	1	28
		417 In ditto		1	3	13
		440 In ditto		2	0	00
		441 In Windmill field		1	2	38
		407 In Windmill field		0	2	33
		435 In Windmill field		0	1	22
		442 In ditto		1	0	03
				43	0	24
Westhide	587440	84 Windmill Meadow	300+	2	1	12
Withington	568427	331 Farther Windmill Field	300	13	2	00
		332 ditto		11	0	22
				24	2	22
Woolhope	628378	1227 Windmill Field	800	6	1	34
		1226 Windmill Field		11	3	16
	612351	525 Windmill Hill	300	0	2	28
	600329	776 Little Windmill field	400	4	3	38
		777 In Windmill field		1	2	13
		778 In ditto		1	1	32
		779 In ditto		0	0	26
		523 In Windmill Hill		0	1	24
		524 Windmill Hill		4	3	17
				32	1	28
Yarkhill	616447	276 Windmill Hill	325/50	12	1	13
		278 Windmill Coppice		1	3	22
				14	0	35

An analysis of the field-names as indicators has produced the field-names Windmill with the additions of Bank, Coppice, Cottage, Croft, Down, Field, Gate, Hill,

Hopyard, Meadow, Orchard, Park, Piece, Pit and Post. The majority of these names agree with those mentioned by John Field. The use of the words Pit and Post are also significant indicating a post mill. Is this sufficient evidence to say that there were windmills in Herefordshire?

The following table shows the acreage of the fields in the thirty-eight parishes.

PARISH	ACREAGE			PARISH	ACREAGE		
	a	r	p		a	r	p
Abbey Dore	5	0	11	Llanwarne	11	2	10
Aymestrey	23	2	10	Madley	8	2	00
Bosbury	3	2	21	Marden	10	3	32
Bridstow	20	0	26	Moccas	1	1	06
Brockhampton and				Moreton Jeffries	49	2	08
How Caple	7	3	09	Much Marcle tithe	4	2	09
Burghill	47	1	13	enclosure	18	3	08
Clehonger	40	1	10	Munsley	23	2	22
Clifford	3	1	03	Norton Canon	31	3	37
Colwall	15	2	25	Pencombe	15	3	11
Dormington and				Sellack	18	3	35
Bartestree	7	1	14	Thruxton	25	1	25
Eardisland	23	1	11	Upton Bishop	8	3	20
Eardisley	16	0	30	Walford	12	1	20
Eastnor	6	3	20	Weobley	43	0	24
Edvin Loach	12	0	21	Westhide	2	1	12
Eye	43	3	20	Withington	24	2	22
Fownhope	1	2	31	Woolhope	32	1	28
King's Caple	24	1	16	Yarkhill	14	0	35
King's Pyon	3	1	32				
Ledbury	51	3	22				
Leysters	5	1	01	TOTAL	722	0	30

The total acreage of 722 acres 30 perches consisting of 164 fields gives an average field size of 4 acres 1 rood 24 perches. A further analysis of the field sizes is shown in the following table.

under 1 acre	= 64	4 – 5 acres	= 8	20 – 30 acres	= 2
1 – 2 acres	= 29	5 – 10 acres	= 19	30 – 40 acres	= 0
2 – 3 acres	= 11	10 – 15 acres	= 16	40 – 50 acres	= 2
3 – 4 acres	= 8	15 – 20 acres	= 5		
				Total	164

From these statistics ninety-three, i.e. 56.7%, are under two acres. In the parish of Burghill there are thirty 'strips' of which twenty-three are under one acre and four between one and two acres. Likewise the Windmill Field in the parish of Weobley has forty-three 'strips' of which twenty-seven are under one acre and thirteen between one and two acres. The two largest fields of over forty acres are in the parishes of Clehonger and Eye, but the ten fields in Ledbury parish have a total of 51 acres 3 roods 22 perches.

A significant factor is that of the 164 fields, 147 of them were arable land, three were woodland and the remaining fourteen were pasture and orchard. Can one assume that windmills were set up on the arable land for the grinding of corn?

Travelling around the county with a view to where windmills may have stood, it is noticeable that the probable sites were on high ground for the particular areas and well exposed to the wind from all directions. Again, because of the particular area, locations are at a variety of contour levels ranging from 200-300ft to about 800ft in Aymestrey parish, 600ft at Dormington and Bartestree, 650ft at Leysters and as low as 110ft at Walford. All contour heights shown in the table are approximate. Because of the large acreage of some of the fields the grid references also are estimated.

Apart from the remains of the windmill standing today in Moccas parish, one other site can be confirmed with some certainty. In Weobley parish on the O.S. map, there is reference to Windmill Knapp, and various persons who have visited the site say that there are the remains of a mound there. This spot is at SO 398515 at about the 330 foot contour in Windmill Field which was wholly arable. This area is still planted with cereals.

EARLY DOCUMENTARY EVIDENCE
Having discussed the possible locations of windmills using the field-name survey a random search has been made in other sources to prove the existence of windmills.

CLEHONGER: On 27 March 1828, Mrs Charlotte Elford and her trustees sold no. 231 Windmill field (40 acres 1 rood 10 perches) to Mr Thomas Woolcombe, the land being occupied by George Packwood and widow Packwood.[6] The acreage agrees with that in the field-name survey.

FOWNHOPE: The glebe terrier for Fownhope parish states:

11 May 1607
... Item one ochre (acre) in the same feeld at Wyndmyll haveing the lands of Thomas Scudamore gent one both sydes.[7]
10 January 1619
Item one other parcell of errable lande in the same fylde at a place there named Wynmyll Hill contyninge by estimacon one aker.[8]

The field-name survey gives Windmill Piece as 1 acre 2 roods 31 perches.

LEDBURY: In the Red Book of the bishop of Hereford c1285-90 under Ledbury borough it states: *'molendinium acque valet iijs iiijd molend venti valet xxvjs viijd'*, (watermill value 3s 4d, windmill value 26s 8d.)[9] (Pl. 2)

In the Ledbury Foreign manor court roll for 26 October 1759 a customary tenant is granted 'one acre of arrable land and pasture on which a windmill lately stood called Blanton's Windmill in Mitchel...'[10]

The Ledbury inclosure award, 1816, lists Somers with field nos. 177, 185, 186, 187.[11] These are probably nos. 190, 187 and 188 on the field-name survey. These are located in the N.E. of the parish and could refer to Blanton's Windmill.

No. 1442 on the award agrees in size with 1448 on the field-name survey ,and was in the hands of Biddulph. The Somers family of Eastnor and the Biddulphs of Ledbury were large landowners. Were there two windmills, one owned by Biddulph in the area of the Hazle Farm and the other by Somers near Mitchel Farm?

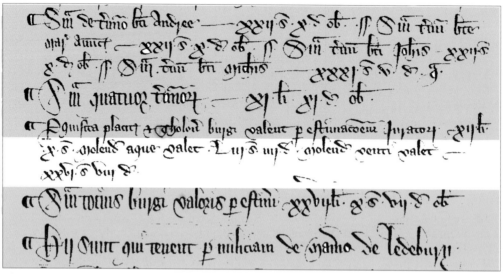

Plate 2. Bishop of Hereford's estates, Ledbury borough, 1285-90. '...molendinium acque valet iijs iiijd molend venti valet xxvjs viijd' (water mill value 3s 4d wind mill value 26s 8d). HRO AA/59/A/1

MUCH MARCLE: Three early deeds are interesting. The first one is undated between Robert Rutlan of Marcle and Walter Toperst of two 'doles' of land in the manor of Marcle one lying in the field called 'windmillmedow' between the land of the lord of Bickerton and that of Jordan Avechal.[12]

The second one is dated 20 March 1306 between Gilbert Bollock of Marcle and Phill Bollock, his son, of one acre of land with appurtenances within the manor of Marcle, situated in the field called Wyndmillfield at le Ferthygh next to the land of Roger de Westhaye and extending from the land of Galfred de Homme to the land late in the possession of Edmund de Mortuomar.[13]

The third is dated 4 October 1364 whereby John Hide gives to Richard Grene a plot of land with a windmill built on it called 'Warymille'.[14]

MUNSLEY: A map of the Callow Hills estate in Munsley parish dated 1828 shows 'No. 7 Windmill Field 13 acres 2 roods 25 perches'.[15] This is no. 193 on the field-name survey and is almost identical in size.

NORTON CANON: 25 November 1308 Walter Morewy of Norton (Canon) is to observe his covenant respecting two windmills 'in the vill of Norton and pay 30s'.[16]

On the field-name survey there are seven fields totalling over 30 acres and owned by seven different persons. The dean and chapter then owned no. 222 of 12 acres, the largest of the fields with the highest point, the 300 foot contour, in it.

STAUNTON-ON-WYE: A glebe terrier dated 1589 but in a very poor condition states:

'…of Staunton and Kilkington one other acre beneath the wyndmill at…southe and bounden with the Porteway…'[17]

There is no reference to a windmill on the field-name survey but the situation described in the terrier would be a suitable site for a windmill.

WEOBLEY: A close roll dated 1 November 1407 gives the following description:

…one acre…24 acres in Knavencastelfelde and Wyndmulfelde with a meadow… 2 acres together in the Wyndmulfelde between lands of John Oldecastelle knight and of Isabel Mayolkes and extending to heywey… 2 acres 8 selions together by the wyndmille between land late of Walter Brugge and land of the grantors and extending from land of the said Walter to the lord's land… 6 acres of land in Wyndmulfelde whereof 3 acres lie together above Holden between land late of Walter Brugge and land of the lord and Nicholas Dischewalle… ½ acre and two selions by the wyndmulle between lands of the prior of Crassewalle and of the grantors…[18]

A marriage settlement dated 30 March 1635 refers to four acres of land in Windmille Field…one and a half acres 'near where the windmill stand…'[19]

In the Garnstone estate records there are several references to Windmill Field. On 20 November 1651 William Davyes of Weobley, yeoman, bargained and sold one acre of arable land in 'Wyndmill Field' to Richard Davyes of Weobley, yeoman.[20] On 10 February 1674 Perkins sold two acres of arable in 'Windmill Field' to John Birch of Garnstone, Esq.[21] On 18 November 1684 John Birch sold two acres of land in 'Windmill Field' to Abell Lewes of Weobley, yeoman.[22]

On 2 September 1699 Richard Eckley exchanged a burgage of three acres 'adjoining a windmill belonging' to Birch with Upper Pound Meadow owned by Birch.[23]

John Probert of Weobley, cordwainer, in his will dated 29 September 1766 leaves to his youngest son William Probert, baker, his house called Wall's House with its barn, stable, and fold and 'two acres of land in the Windmill Field'.[24]

The close roll of 1407 shows evidence of the 'strips' and a windmill covering a large area.

WITHINGTON: A glebe terrier dated 17 December 1618 states:

…thre acres of glebe land arable whereof two lye inclosed in a Field there called Windmill Field between the demesne lands of the prebend of Church Withington aforesaid on the West side and on Common called the Oldgrove on the East side.[25]

Two papers by P. G. Barton in the Montgomeryshire Collections refer to windmills in Montgomeryshire.[26] He suggests that a field named Cae Post implies that the windmill was a post mill and that field-names including the words 'sail' 'sale' and 'sael' refer to the sails of the windmills. These names have not been noticed as field-names in Herefordshire although the word 'Post' does occur as No. 62 on the enclosure map (1795) for Much Marcle.[27]

Barton also suggests that windmills are depicted on church brasses, misericords and stained glass, and that there is one in St Laurence's church in Ludlow. In the chapel of St John the Evangelist in the annunciation or golden window, a windmill with three sails is shown in the right-hand lower panel. The window is said to have been given by John Parys, a rich merchant, who died in 1449.

CONCLUSION

Can it be said that there were windmills in Herefordshire? The use of the word 'windmill' has been found in 14.6% of the parishes searched. In five parishes out of the nine where pre-1838-50 references were found, seven mention the existence of windmills; in 1285-90 and 1759 at Ledbury, 1308 at Norton Canon, 1364 at Much Marcle, 1589 at Staunton-on-Wye and 1635 at Weobley. This proves that there were windmills in the county from the late thirteenth to the late seventeenth century. Some probably disappeared but could have been rebuilt on the same site or nearby, and then by 1838-50 have disappeared again or become derelict. It is suggested that windmills existed in parishes where water power was not possible and that they stood on arable land. No description of a windmill has been found but no. 62 'Windmill Post' at Much Marcle indicates a post mill type.

The use of the word 'windmill' in field-names in the mid-nineteenth century coupled with documentary evidence of windmills as early as 1285-90 shows that there were windmills in Herefordshire.

ACKNOWLEDGEMENTS

I am very grateful to the Herefordshire Record Office for being able to consult the various documents held there.

REFERENCES

[1] G. Grigson, *The Shell Country Book* (1962).
[2] J. Richardson, *The Local Historian's Encyclopaedia* (1974).
[2] N. Pevsner, *Cambridgeshire* (1954), 239.
[4] J. Field, *A Dictionary of English Field Names* (1989).
[5] Op cit. in note 1.   [6] HRO R8/1/13.   [7] HRO HD2/4/5.
[8] HRO HD2/4/6.   [9] HRO AA/59/A/1.   [10] HRO AF4/4.
[11] HRO Q/RI/25 and 45.   [12] HRO G37/II/76.   [13] HRO G37/II/98.
[14] HRO G37/II/179.   [15] HRO D96/94.
[16] B. G. Charles and H. D. Emanuel, *Calendar of Hereford Cathedral Muniments*, No. 3505, 25 Nov. 1308. Drawn to my attention by Dr A. Brian.
[17] HRO HD2/6/76.   [18] HRO AL2/15
[19] MBD/17/2. Copies of deeds held by Weobley and District Local History Society from originals at Longleat House, Wiltshire. Drawn to my attention by Brian Redwood.
[20] HRO F78/II/45.   [21] HRO F78/II/58.   [22] HRO F78/II/65.
[23] HRO L57/ bundle 66.
[24] HRO Hereford Diocese Probate, will John Probert, 28 Oct. 1766.
[25] HRO HD2/2/33.
[26] P. G. Barton, *The Montgomeryshire Collections*, 84 (1996), 61-6; 85 (1997), 51-62.
[27] HRO Q/RI/36.

Lammas Meadows in Herefordshire

ANTHEA BRIAN

INTRODUCTION

The word 'meadow' is used today very loosely for any pleasant grassy area, but in the past it had a very definite meaning understood by everyone. Meadow was permanent grassland on which a crop of hay was grown every year, hay that could be stored all winter and was essential for feeding stock when the grass stopped growing. The meadow was often grazed after the hay was cut. Pasture, in contrast, was permanent grassland that was grazed all the year on and off.

This article takes a brief look at the history and distribution of one sort of meadow, the Lammas meadow, in Herefordshire. Such meadows lay mostly beside rivers and various names are in use today for meadowland in valleys. Three of these are often confused with each other; 'Flood-plain meadow' is a fairly modern term and refers simply to the position of a meadow in the flood-plain of a river or stream. But 'flood-plain grassland' to ecologists tends to be one particular type of grassland, now very rare, classified as Mesotrophic Grassland Four (MG4) which grows in such situations.[1]

'Water-meadow' is a term often used wrongly as an alternative for flood-plain meadow. The name actually describes not the position of a meadow but the fact that the meadow has been adapted by man-made sluices and channels so that water can be diverted to flow over it thus encouraging early growth of grass. The meadows so watered were often flood-plain meadows but could also be valley-side meadows and the remains of them can be seen in many places in Herefordshire today.[2]

'Lammas meadow' and 'common meadow' are synonymous and ancient terms that refer to the type of tenure of owners and occupiers of the meadow. They do not refer to the position of the meadow, though in fact Lammas meadows always lay in a flood-plain. These meadows were sometimes described as lot meadows or dole meadows.

THE EARLIEST MEADOWS

Hay-making in England is thought to have started in Roman times because the earliest scythe, the essential tool for hay-making, has been found on a Roman site.[3] Before hay could be made all grassland areas would have been grazed by flocks and herds. Evidence for this in the lower Lugg Valley came from the excavation of Sutton Walls where large numbers of bones of cattle and sheep were found.[4] The Saxons increased the number of meadows and by the time of the Conquest and the compilation of Domesday Book hay meadows were well established in England. They were recorded carefully because they were the most valuable type of land, considerably more valuable acre for acre than the ploughland.[5] The value of the meadows was due to their fertility and this arose from their situation lying by stream or river and flooded regularly by water carrying fertile silt and lime which was deposited on the meadow every winter.

Figure 1 shows the distribution of the Domesday meadows in Herefordshire lying mainly in the river valleys. The largest were in the Lugg valley where they averaged 30 acres, those by the Frome averaged 15 acres, those in the Wye valley 9 acres and

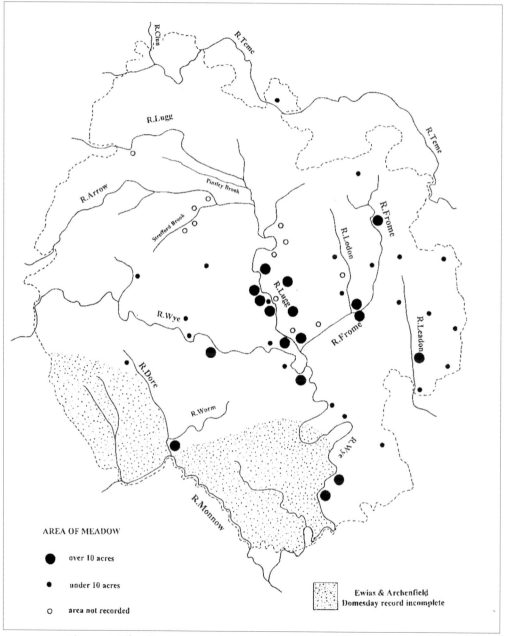

Figure 1. The distribution of Domesday meadows in Herefordshire.

the others only 7 acres. Some of the meadows recorded for upland settlements and therefore marked on the map in those positions may really refer to riverside sites, because settlements without flood-plains may have had rights in meadows situated several miles away. Certainly at a later date this was the case for Pencombe and Ullingswick, which both had rights in the Sutton meadows some 6 miles distant. This inter-commoning of animals from many settlements on one grassland is thought to be a very ancient practice dating back even to the Bronze Age.[6] It is thus of great interest that it continues today on the Lugg Meadows near Hereford where animals from Lugwardine, Hampton Bishop, Tupsley and Holmer all graze together in winter.

THE MEDIEVAL MEADOWS

The open field system of agriculture was widely spread in Herefordshire in medieval times and meadowland was one of the four basic elements of this system – the others being the common arable fields, the woodland and the rough grazing of the manorial waste. Under this system the meadowland, as well as the other three elements, was held in common and for this reason was often called the 'common meadow'. Common meadows were in fact well established before medieval times and probably the earliest reference to one comes in the Laws of King Ine, who was king of Wessex 688-694. Here it is stated that:

> If ceorls have common meadow or other gedalland (shared land) to hedge and some have hedged their share and some have not and if stray cattle eat their common acres or grass let those who are answerable for the opening go and give compensation to those who have hedged their share for the injury which may have been done.[7]

Not all medieval meadowland was held in common. The lord of the manor often had his own private demesne meadow and so did the church. The dean and vicars choral of Hereford Cathedral and the various prebendaries held meadows privately, as well as having rights in several common meadows.

The yearly cycle on the common meadow was, and still is, in two parts with the production of a crop of hay from Candlemas (2 February) to Lammas (1 August) and communal grazing by the stock of those having rights in the meadow from Lammas to Candlemas. Because Lammas Day was such an important date in the yearly cycle the common meadow often came to be called the Lammas meadow and that name is used in this article because it is so distinctive – the word 'common' carries too many other connotations nowadays and its use leads to confusion.

During the hay-growing part of the yearly cycle the meadow was no longer communal but was held in long, narrow, parallel strips, the width a man could cut with his scythe. The arrangement of these strips varied according to the shape of the meadow. Where this was long and thin the strips ran at right angles to the river. But where a meadow was of wide expanse it was often divided into several sections. These had individual names and were marked at the corners by stones or posts known as mere stones (from *mere*, a boundary) or dole stones because the strips were doled out. Figure 2 shows the sections into which the Wergins Meadow (Sutton) was divided. Each of the sections was subdivided into strips. In some meadows these were measured out afresh each year working from the stones but on others the strips as well as the sections had permanent markers. These rather complicated methods were needed because there could be no fences on a Lammas meadow, as these would

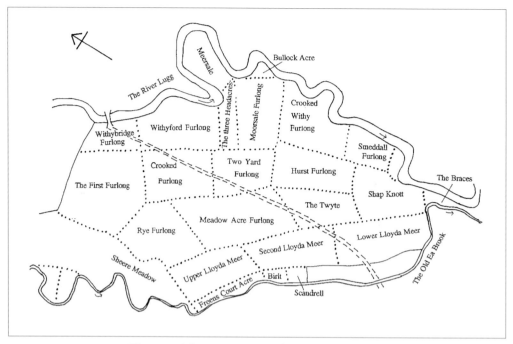

Figure 2. The Wergins Meadow, Sutton, c1720.

restrict the movement of grazing stock in winter.

On many medieval meadows the strips were allocated afresh each year by the casting of lots just before the hay was cut, a practice which continued on Pixey Mead near Oxford until the building of the Oxford bypass across the meadow in 1958 so disrupted the hay-making arrangements that sadly the ancient practice of lot-casting soon came to an end.[8]

In Herefordshire surviving evidence of lot-casting is widespread but patchy. The best documented Lammas meadow is the Wergins Meadow. Here the lots were originally named from local land owners, Walter de Freen, Richard de la Bere, the Master of Dinmore and the Crown, 'which brings out two lots'.[9] But later these were replaced by names such as 'moon', 'three holes', 'brandard', and 'trow', commonplace objects whose outline could be scratched onto a bit of stick or whatever served as the lot. However there were still two lots in each draw called 'crown'.[10]

Rather similar symbols may have been used on Astney Mead, which lies at the confluence of the rivers Frome and Lodon. This meadow is marked on a seventeenth-century map of Ashperton and Stretton Grandison on which most of the area of the two parishes is divided up into small enclosed fields, each marked by a symbol.[11] About twenty-eight different symbols are used and it seems likely that each of these represented a different owner. Astney Mead itself, however, is shown as unenclosed and is without symbols, which indicates that this was a Lammas meadow where the strips were in different ownership each year. If lots were indeed cast on the meadow then those taking part in the lot-drawing process would presumably have used the same symbols on their lots as those used on the map to mark their fields. In other parts of England it is known that marks were made on sticks, bits of arrow, apples or even bits of dock root which were then drawn out of a hat in random order by a child or other disinterested party.[12] Figure 3 shows that the basic marks used at

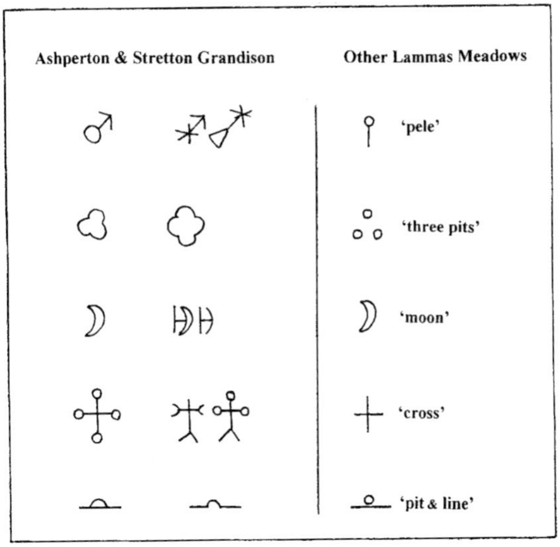

Ashperton were very similar to the lot symbols used elsewhere but that the simple marks have been elaborated, possibly to show divided inheritance. No names for the symbols have been found in Ashperton.

Great Ash Common Meadow (Goodrich) also gives evidence of past lot-casting. In a conveyance of 1715 three strips of meadow are described as 'moving and changeable as falleth out by lot'[13] while a second document gives indications of the symbols marked on the lots; 'hatchet', 'moon' and 'line'. Another meadow nearby called Little Homme probably had a similar system.[14] The strips on this meadow were marked out by stones in 1600 when the Goodrich Court rolls record that 'certain meere stones' were moved by three men to the damage of their neighbour. The men were fined and ordered to replace the stones.[15]

Figure 3. Some of the symbols used to mark fields in Ashperton and Stretton Grandison in the seventeenth century compared with symbols used elsewhere in England for casting lots in Lammas meadows.

There is evidence of the start of a breakdown in the process of lot-casting when in Great Meadow (Stoke Edith) in 1659 the vicars choral leased out two strips, one of which regularly changed position as it was 'allocated yearly by lot' while the other stayed always in the same place.[16]

At a later date on several meadows what was known as 'changeable land' probably evolved from lot-casting and came to replace it. Under this system only certain strips in the meadow were involved. The possession of these rotated yearly between the different owners in a regular sequence while the other strips on the meadow remained always in the same ownership.

A few examples will show how the system worked. On Upper Lugg Meadow (usually called Walney Meadow in the past) three strips were leased out by the dean and chapter in 1835 and the map on the deed shows one strip in a fixed position but two others as part of a block of three all described as 'changeable'.[17]

In the late eighteenth century the vicar of Lugwardine, in recording his glebe land, stated that this included two acres in Lugg Meadow but that his turn for the hay from these only came round 'but once in thirteen years as it is changed every year'.[18]

The commissioners, appointed in 1808 to enclose Marden, Sutton and the nearby parishes, a huge area which included over 1,000 acres of Lammas meadow, complained that 'changeable land' was a great complication to their work.[19]

In the twentieth century the system of changeable land persisted on the Lower Lugg Meadows (Hampton Bishop) into the 1980s when the owners of the strips involved decided to end the system and retain the same strips each year; even today one strip of changeable land still exists on Hampton Meadow.

The archaic practices described above that still lingered on in the county were survivals of the normal management of a medieval Lammas meadow. Figure 4 shows the distribution of Lammas meadows in the county in medieval times. This is based on a map drawn up by Dorothy Sylvester which covers the three Welsh Border counties.[20]   Her Herefordshire information came from the vast numbers of Hereford Cathedral muniments which deal with local land transactions all over the county. The distribution pattern is very similar to that of the Domesday map showing a concentration of meadows in the lower Lugg valley.

SEVENTEENTH TO NINETEENTH CENTURIES
THE SURVIVAL OF MEDIEVAL MEADOWS
Open-field agriculture disappeared early in some parts of the county, especially the west, but in other parts it hung on into the nineteenth century and beyond, with

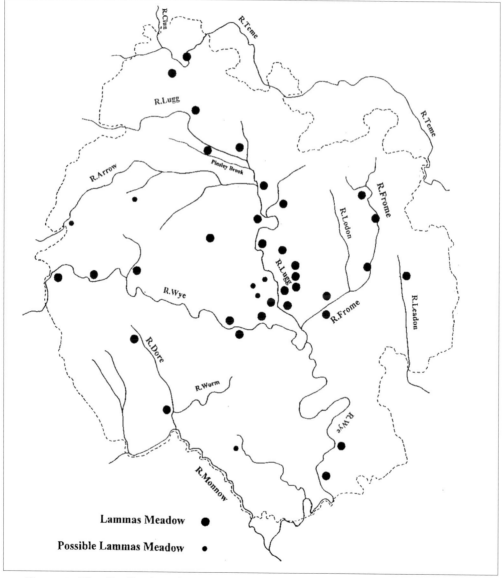

Figure 4. The distribution of Lammas meadows in Herefordshire in medieval times.

Lammas meadows sometimes still present in a parish when the open arable fields were long gone. The distribution of the surviving Lammas meadows over this period has been collated from a variety of sources and this is the earliest period for which it becomes possible to identify the actual position of a meadow within a parish with a fair degree of certainty. The two main sources from which this information has been drawn are the enclosure awards and the tithe maps.

The information about Lammas meadows given by enclosure awards is very variable; for a few parishes it is detailed but for the majority there is no information at all, probably because the meadow had been enclosed early, piecemeal by private arrangements.

The earliest Enclosure Act to affect a part of Herefordshire is of particular interest as it is only the second such Act for the whole country, having been passed in 1606.[21] The Act was concerned with allowing the enclosure of certain meadows in the parishes of Marden and the two Suttons because, as it states; 'after sickle and scythe all sorts of people turn in their cattle and within very short space eat up all the grass therof' with the result that 'the oxen and kine of the husbandmen are in danger to starve in summer and of necessity in many places must be sold away for want of [food]'.

Who these people with their animals were is not made clear but they obviously came from outside the three parishes. At a later date a vicar of Holmer complained of similar troubles with the grazing on his glebe lands and said that the cattle belonged to butchers and drovers. Perhaps these were being driven regularly down the lower Lugg valley. The 1606 Act mentions several Lammas meadows, in Marden and in the surrounding parishes, which were *not* to be enclosed, including Smeadal in Bodenham, Whitterday, Dole meadow, the Groves, Whistheys and the Wergins. It also states that they were not to 'inclose or alter the usage and course of the great Meadow in or near Sutton St Michael and Sutton St Nicholas called Lugg Meadow'. This meadow, probably the largest Lammas meadow to exist in the whole county, lay on the left bank of the Lugg and extended from Sutton down to Lugg Bridge Mill. It was finally enclosed in 1808.

Some enclosure awards relate to individual meadows on their own. These include Catley Rye Meadow (enclosed 1854), Volca Meadow (enclosed 1857) and Romney Meadow (enclosed 1862). These three were enclosed late after the tithe maps had been made.

The information given by tithe maps about Lammas meadows is mostly less specific than that given in enclosure awards but nevertheless provides many clues to the positions of former meadows and is of special value because the coverage of the county is almost complete.[22]

Where enclosure took place after the tithe map was made, or where it never took place at all, very detailed information about Lammas meadows is given. The tithe map for Volca Meadow shows not only all the strips but also indicates by tiny circles the dole stones or posts at the ends of every strip. The tithe maps that cover Upper and Lower Lugg Meadow and Hampton Meadow, which were never enclosed, still provide the best evidence for identification of strips in these meadows for legal transactions today.

Certain features of the tithe maps and their apportionments have proved to be particularly significant in the identification of Lammas meadows and these include:

(1) *Field names*. Some of the names that most obviously indicate a former Lammas

meadow are missing or rare in the county. There was, for example, only one named 'Lammas Meadow' but there were two examples of the variant, 'Midsummer Meadow', though neither were named on the tithe maps. The word 'Dole' was used as a field name fairly frequently in the county but often refered to arable fields; however, about fifteen 'Dole Meadows' have been found, the name being spelt variously. In contrast 'Lot Meadow' has not been found at all. The name 'Broad Meadow' has proved to be significant and can often be traced back to a definite Lammas meadow earlier on, but the name 'Great Meadow' had less significance.

The name 'Common Meadow' has been found misleading and often refers only to a bit of meadow that happened to be adjacent to commonland of the type derived from manorial waste held in common all the year round. However, when used with a suffix it may or may not indicate a Lammas meadow. For example 'Walney Common Meadow' certainly was a Lammas meadow but 'Staunton Common Meadow', recorded as such on a map of 1867 was not.[23] This is shown by the Staunton-on-Wye enclosure award of 1784 which was concerned with 'extinguishing the right of common' on 289 acres of waste ground called 'Staunton common' and 50 acres of enclosed land called 'Midleys'.[24] The commoners were said to claim rights of common on Staunton common at all times of year but on Midleys only from Midsummer day to the second of February. Clearly only Midleys was a Lammas meadow.

Some Lammas meadows took their names from the river by which they lay, notably the river Lugg, but although there were several 'Wye Meadows' none have been found to have been Lammas meadows.

(2) *The occasional unenclosed strip* in a meadow marked with dotted lines. Even after enclosure several former Lammas meadows retained a few strips owned by one person and surrounded by a meadow all owned by someone else. These strips were sometimes later forgotten by their owner, perhaps a charity or an absentee, and taken over quietly by the owners of the surrounding meadow.

(3) *Several adjacent meadows all having the same name*, indicating that they were formerly all part of one large meadow.

(4) The use of *the phrase 'in such and such a meadow'* to describe a piece of land.

(5) *Intricate, interlocking boundaries* where parishes meet and detached parts of parishes in areas of potential meadowland, the conjunction of the parishes of Adforton, Downton, Burrington, Leinthall Starkes and Wigmore being a case in point. Here in 1610 'doles' were frequently recorded in Dowl and Moore Meadows.[25]

6) *Numerous boundary stones* (marked BS) shown along a parish boundary on early, large-scale Ordnance Survey maps. Where a parish boundary passed through an unenclosed meadow the surveyors seem to have mistaken the numerous mere stones marking the ends of the strips for parish boundary stones. In places the strips certainly did end on a parish boundary, but the stones marking their ends were far closer together than parish boundary stones would have been. This mis-interpretation by the surveyors can be demonstrated on the Lugg Meadows (L 18) because many of the stones still stand, and it can be seen that the stones marked BS on the map are no different from the other mere stones nearby which are not on a

parish boundary and are not recorded on the map.

The meadows identified by the above methods from enclosure awards, tithe maps and other documentary evidence are shown in Figure 5. Each is given a reference number indicating the valley and position in which the meadow lay and these are shown in the table. Clearly the information is incomplete but nevertheless the meadows identified still show the same distribution pattern as in the two earlier periods. This is of course to be expected since most of the meadows marked are in fact the same meadows as those shown on the earlier maps.

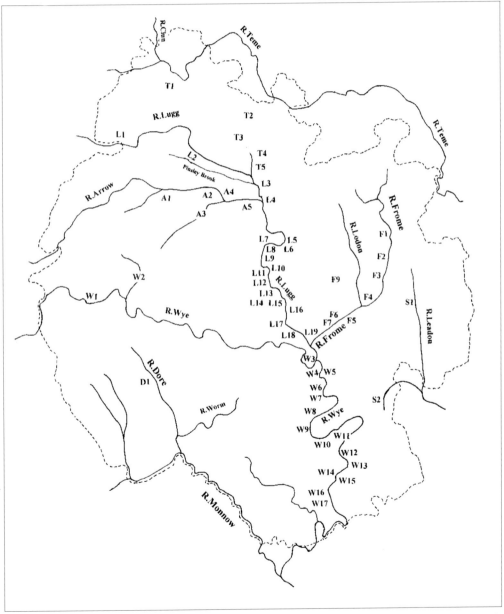

Figure 5. The distribution of Lammas meadows in Herefordshire, seventeenth to nineteenth centuries.

THE LOSS OF THE MEADOWS
LAMMAS MEADOWS IN HEREFORDSHIRE TODAY

The first move towards the loss of a Lammas meadow was probably the amalgamation of strips brought about by exchanges between neighbours. The Leintwardine Court rolls record many such exchanges of 'doles' of meadow and 'ridges' of arable land around 1620.[26] Doubtless many unrecorded exchanges took place as well. This amalgamation led to unofficial enclosure of the Lammas meadows in many parishes. In others enclosure was carried out rather later by Act of Parliament so that by the turn of the century all but three Lammas meadows in the county had gone. The survivors were Lugg Meadow (Upper and Lower L18), Hampton Meadow (L19) and Moor Meadow (W14). There had evidently been talk of enclosing Lugg Meadow in 1880, for a notice in the *Hereford Times* of that date, advertising strips for sale in these meadows, stated that 'after enclosure this land would be much more valuable'. But for reasons unknown this enclosure never took place and Lugg Meadow remained unenclosed. As a result under the Commons Registration Act of 1965 it became registered common land but because it was also a Lammas meadow the commoners could only register their rights for half the year.

In the country as a whole only fifteen or sixteen other Lammas meadows have survived and Lugg Meadow is the largest of them all.[27] Large parts of this meadow are now owned by the Herefordshire Nature Trust and Plantlife and are managed to preserve and enhance the rich meadow flora. Of the other two Herefordshire Lammas meadows, Hampton Meadow had come almost entirely into one ownership by 1994 with just two strips still belonging to the poor of Lugwardine being grazed all the year round. Because the continuous grazing was impoverishing the flora the meadow was bought by the Herefordshire Nature Trust and returned to the traditional management of a Lammas meadow. Moor Meadow, also in one ownership, was ploughed up during the war and reseeded afterwards and the flora has never recovered from this treatment.

And so the Lammas meadows, once a vital part of the economy of every parish, have almost disappeared from the county. However, of the three that remain two, making up 90% of the area, still lie in the lower Lugg valley fairly certainly just where the Domesday meadows lay, thus providing a very remarkable example of continuity of land use over a very long period of time – a fact that has important implications for the flora and fauna of the meadows and for their soil.

LANDSCAPE FEATURES OF LAMMAS MEADOWS

William Camden, antiquary, historian and traveller, writing of a Herefordshire valley in 1607 described it thus: 'The hills that compass it on both sides are clad in woods; under the woods lie corn fields either side and under these fields most gay and gallant meadows.'[28] These gay and gallant meadows were surely Lammas meadows when the buttercups were in flower and sheets of yellow stretched out for miles, as they still do today on the Lugg Meadows in May. However, although nearly all the meadows themselves have gone the landscape of which they formed a part can still be identified on the ground today.

Three landscape features characterised Lammas meadows: their position, their topography and their size.

(1) Position

The meadows lay in the flood-plain of a river or stream, often at a confluence, where they were flooded regularly in winter but were well-drained. They were usually bounded on the side away from the river by a slower moving watercourse called a *rhea* in many places in Herefordshire, the word being derived from *ea* meaning 'river'.[29] They did not necessarily take up the whole of the flood-plain which would also in the past have had ill-drained areas of marsh providing rough grazing or poor quality hay, such areas being identified by toponyms such as 'venn' or 'moor'.

(2) *Topography*

Their topography was very distinctive because they were absolutely flat, in sharp contrast with the rising or undulating land around. This flatness had arisen from long years of annual deposition of alluvium. The alluvium is particularly extensive in the lower Lugg, Frome and Arrow valleys and in the low-lying area stretching north from Leominster.[30] This latter area marks the former course of the river Teme, which at one time flowed south instead of east as now, was joined by the river Lugg as a tributary in what is now the Leominster area and, continuing south, carved out the wide valley now occupied by the river Lugg alone.[31] The extensive areas of alluvium deposited in this valley led, much later, to the number and size of the Lammas meadows established there.

Various writers have commented on the distinctive topography of Lammas meadows. Andrew Marvell, around 1650, vividly describes a Yorkshire Lammas meadow in the four different seasons of the year and compares the flatness of the meadow after the hay is cut and carted with a stretched artist's canvas.

> A levell'd space, as smooth and plain ,
> As Clothes for Lily stretched to stain
> The world when first created sure
> Was such a Table rase and pure.[32]

About the same time the local author, Silas Taylor , writing of Sutton and Marden said 'the meadow on both sides of the Lugg very much delighting the eye with its green prospect in summer being of a continued, even grasse platt in the winter of a water platt'.[33]

Rather later William Cobbett, writing of a Lammas meadow beside the River Ouse near Huntingdon in 1822, says 'here are no unevenness of any sort. Here are bowling-greens of hundreds of acres in extent with a river winding through them, full to the brink'.[34]

(3) *Size*

The meadows formed very large areas undivided by hedge or fence. This does not seem so unusual today when farmers have made so many 'prairie' fields by removal of hedges, but is nevertheless a very noticeable feature of the few surviving Lammas meadows.

By these three landscape features it is still possible to identify the positions and outlines of former Lammas meadows where these have escaped development.

Another once important feature of a Lammas meadow that sometimes survives is the lane along which the herds were driven to the meadow and by which the hay was carried out. Doll Lane formerly led to Dole Meadow, Volca and Smeadal lanes led to meadows of those names while Walney Lane still leads to the part of Lugg Meadow formerly known as Walney Meadow.

THE FUTURE

Old grassland is attracting a great deal of interest nationally at the present time mainly because so much of it has been lost in recent years – well over 95%. Flood-plain grassland, much of it former Lammas meadow, has suffered the most extensive losses of all partly due to development but mainly due to intensive, arable agriculture.

However, there is a new move aimed at respecting the importance of flood-plains and returning them to grassland cover where possible, so reducing flooding to nearby settlements and preventing further damage to the rivers and their wildlife through silting up, eutrophication and erosion.[35]   The success of such a move would be of particular importance for Herefordshire which has long lengths of three river Sites of Special Scientific Interest, the Wye, the Lugg and the Teme, within its bounds. The old Lammas meadows were established a very long time ago on the most fertile and valuable parts of the flood-plain and it would be very fitting if restoration were to start with these.

HEREFORDSHIRE LAMMAS MEADOWS
(Based mainly on eighteenth- and nineteenth-century evidence.)

Ref. No.	Meadow	Parishes
ARROW VALLEY MEADOWS		
A1	Long Meadow	Eardisland & Pembridge
A2	The Moors	Monkland
A3	The Fleets	Monkland
A4	Crowmore Meadow	Leominster
A5*	Passa Meadow	Leominster
A6 (L4)	Volca Meadow	Stoke Prior
(A7)	Broad Meadow (Tippets Brook)	Dilwyn
DORE VALLEY MEADOWS		
D1	Common Meadows	Peterchurch
FROME VALLEY MEADOWS		
F1	Romney Meadow	Bishops Frome, Bromyard & Stanford Bishop
F2	Long Froomy	Bishops & Castle Frome, Evesbatch & Much Cowarne
F3*	Stafforley	Castle Frome, Eggleton & Stretton Grandison
F4	Astney/Stretton Meadow	Ashperton & Stretton Grandison
F5	Stoke Great Meadow	Stoke Edith & Weston Beggard
F6	Dole Meadow	Bartestree, Dormington & Weston Beggard
F7	Froomy	Bartestree & Mordiford
F8 (L19)	Kymin Common Meadow (on R. Lodon)	Ocle Pychard, Westhide, Withington & Yarkhill
LUGG VALLEY MEADOWS		
L1	Doles Meadow	Byton, Coombe, Kinsham & Stapleton
L2	Great Common Meadow	Kingsland

L3	Lammas Meadow	Leominster
	Midsummer Meadow	Leominster
	Peps Meadow	Leominster
L4 (A6)	Volca Meadow	Stoke Prior
L5	Bowley Meadow	Bodenham
L6	Mitley & Smeadal	Bodenham
L7	Wichall Meadow	Bodenham
L8	Math Hom	Bodenham & Marden
L9	Whitterday Meadow	Marden
L10	Dole Meadow	Marden
L11	Wellington Meadow	Wellington
L12	Moreton Meadow	Marden & Moreton
L13	Wisthay	Marden
L14	Lyde Meadow	Lyde
L15	The Wirgins	Sutton
L16	Lugg Meadow (Sutton)	Holmer, Shelwick, Sutton & Lugwardine
L17	Midsummer Common	Holmer
L18	Lugg Meadow, Upper & Lower	Hampton Bishop, Tupsley, Holmer & Lugwardine
L19 (F8)	Hampton Meadow	Hampton Bishop

SEVERN VALLEY MEADOWS

| (S1) | Catley Rye (on R. Leadon) | Bosbury |
| (S2) | Rye Meadow (on Preston Brook) | Much Marcle |

TEME VALLEY & PROTO TEME (TP) MEADOWS

T1	Dowl & Moore Meadows	Burrington, Downton, Leinthall Starkes, Leintwardine & Wigmore
(TP2)	Shiel Meadow	Richards Castle
(TP3)	Long & Stake Meadows*	Brimfield & Burrington
(TP4)	Blackpole Meadow	Luston (& Eye?)
(TP5)	The Common Moors	Kimbolton & Luston

WYE VALLEY MEADOWS

W1	Great Meadow	Willersley & Winforton
W2	Midleys	Norton Canon & Staunton-on-Wye
W3	Tindings	Hampton Bishop
W4	Oxford & Fischers Meadows*	Holme Lacy
W5	Morney Meadows	Fownhope
W6	Crimes*	Holme Lacy
W7	Broad Meadow*	Holme Lacy
W8	Boat & Cary Meadows	Ballingham
W9	Common Meadow	Hoarwithy
W10	Common Meadow	Sellack
W11	Backney	Sellack
W12	Abbots Common Meadow	Brampton Abbots
W13	Broad Meadow	Ross-on-Wye
W14	Moor Meadow	Bridstow
W15	Broadholm	Ross-on-Wye
W16	Little Homme	Goodrich, Marstow & Trellech
W17	Ash Common Meadow	Goodrich & Marstow

* slight evidence only of Lammas meadow status

ACKNOWLEDGEMENTS

I am very grateful to the following people who have provided help and information: Pat Cross, Penelope Farquhar-Oliver, Joan Grundy, Geoff Gwatkin, Pauline Hitch, Beryl Lewis, Dr Alison McDonald, Jean O'Donnell, Liz Phillips, the late Elizabeth Taylor, Dr John Ross, Sue Hubbard and the staffs of the Herefordshire Record Office and of Hereford Cathedral Library.

REFERENCES

[1] R. Jefferson, 'Distribution, status and conservation of *Alopecurus pratensis-Sanguisorba officinalis* flood-plain meadow in England', *English Nature Research Reports*, 247 (1997).

[2] E. L. Jones, 'Agricultural conditions and changes in Herefordshire, 1660-1815', *TWNFC*, XX (1961).

[3] G. Lambrick and M. Robinson, 'The development of floodplain grassland in the upper Thames valley', *Archaeology and the flora of the British Isles* (1988) , 55-75.

[4] K. M. Kenyon, 'Excavations at Sutton Walls, Herefordshire, 1948-1951', *Archaeol. J.*, 110 (1953).

[5] F. & C. Thorn, *Domesday Book, Herefordshire* (1983); H. Darby & I. Terret, *Domesday geography of Middle England* (1954).

[6] A. W. McDonald, 'Changes in the flora of Port Meadow and Picksey Mead, Oxford', *Archaeology and the flora of the British Isles.* ed. M. Jones, Oxf. Univ. Committee for Archaeology Monograph 14 (1988), pp 76-85.

[7] H. L. Gray, *English Field Systems* (1915); F. L. Attenborough, *The laws of the earliest English kings* (1922).

[8] A. D. Brian, 'The allocation of strips in Lammas meadows by the casting of lots', *Landscape History*, 21 (1999), 43-58.

[9] HRO, B/64.   [10] HRO, B43/29.

[11] HRO, W76/55 & Jean O'Donnell, 'Stretton Grandison: settlement and landscape', *TWNFC* in press.

[12] op. cit. in note 8.   [13] HRO, AW28/13/23.   [14] HRO, C99/111/244.

[15] HRO, G38/1/28.   [16] HCL, G97/34/2A.   [17] HCL 4235.

[18] HCL 3556.   [19] HRO, Marden Enclosure, D5.

[20] D. Sylvester, *The rural landscape of the Welsh borderland*, (1969).

[21] HL, 1606 Enclosure Act, Pamphlet Book, vol. 34.

[22] *Herefordshire Field Name Survey*, Woolhope Club.

[23] HRO, C60/4.   [24] HRO, Q/R1/50.   [25] HRO, F76/I/48.

[26] HRO, F76/I/46.

[27] A. D. Brian, 'Lammas Meadows', *Landscape History*, 15, (1993) 57-69.

[28] W. Camden, *Britannia* (1610).

[29] E. Eckwall, *Oxford Dictionary of English Place-names* (1935).

[30] Soils of England and Wales, Sheet 3, *Soil Survey of England and Wales* (1983).

[31] A. Brandon, *Geology of the country between Hereford and Leominster*, HMSO (1989).

[32] Andrew Marvell, *On Appleton House*, c1650.

[33] Silas Taylor, *Valuation of estates in Co. of Hereford*, HRO, X8. ('platt' is a flat area.).

[34] W. Cobbett, *Rural Rides* (1822).

[35] English Nature. *Wildlife and fresh water - an agenda for sustainable management* (1997).

John Allen Jr. and his
Bibliotheca Herefordiensis

PAUL LATCHAM

In 1822 there was published in Hereford a serious and well-researched attempt to list and categorize the books, pamphlets and other materials relating to Herefordshire which until that time had appeared in print. It remains to this day the most detailed bibliography of the county for its period. It is a rare book and was deliberately made so by the restriction of the print run to just twenty-five copies, none of which was offered for sale; twenty-four copies were given away by the compiler and one copy he kept for himself.

Whilst histories of counties in the British Isles were being published as early as the sixteenth century, bibliographies of local history at county level only began to appear in the nineteenth century. Many English counties had no such bibliography until the twentieth century. It is, thus, a matter of some distinction that Herefordshire had a very competent county bibliography published as early as 1822. In fact, it may be the earliest publication of its kind in the British Isles. Such a claim needs the substantiation of detailed research, but it can be confidently asserted that Humphreys in his carefully researched and compiled *Handbook to County Bibliography* (1917) had encountered none earlier.

The British Isles had topographical bibliographers in the shape of Gough and Rawlinson in the eighteenth century. However, their work covering the kingdom or a whole nation, was not as detailed as individual county bibliography would later become. William Upcott published his *Bibliographical Account of the Principal Works relating to English Topography* in 1818, wonderfully detailed in its collations but, as its title implies, dealing with principal works only. The Herefordshire bibliography leaves out no printed material that the local historian might have needed to further his studies: pamphlets, broadsides, poll books, Acts of Parliament, sermons, miscellanies, fugitive poetry, maps, prints, portrait engravings, etc.

Sir Richard Colt Hoare of Stourhead, the historian of Wiltshire, published a catalogue of the topographical works relating to the United Kingdom in his library in 1815. Interestingly enough, the print-run was twenty-five copies, but catalogues of personal libraries necessarily leave out those books the owner does not possess. The county bibliography nearest in date to that of Herefordshire, and separately published, appears to be John Russell Smith's *Bibliotheca Cantiana* of 1837 for the county of Kent. Owen Manning and William Bray in their *History and Antiquities of the County of Surrey* (1804-14) included a county bibliography in volume 3 and in the appendices. I cannot say how comprehensive it is.

The compiler and printer of this elusive work entitled *Bibliotheca Herefordiensis; or a Descriptive Catalogue of Books, Pamphlets, Maps, Prints, &c. &c. relating to the County*

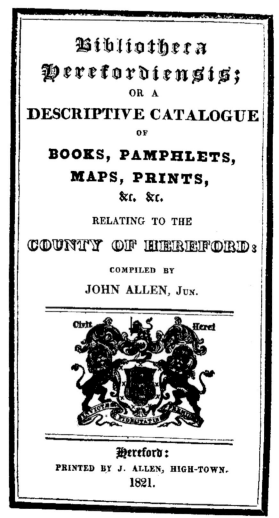

Plate 1. Titlepage of *Bibliotheca Herefordiensis.*

of Hereford was John Allen Jr., the son of a High Town bookseller and printer. For over forty years the father ran what was considered to be a very good bookshop, was made a freeman of the city, and retired in due course. Allen Jr. was associated with the business during his father's lifetime and had a passion for collecting materials towards the history of his native county, a passion which he pursued assiduously all his adult life.

John Allen Senior was born about 1753 and commenced business in Hereford in 1779.[1] His newspaper advertisement announcing the opening of his business states that he had come from London. A John Allen, son of John Allen of Greenwich, bookseller, was apprenticed to a Fetter Lane engraver in 1767.[2] Inspection of the IGI indexes reveals several John Allens born in London in the right time frame. John Allen was a common name and pinning down the relevant records without any corroborative data such as the mother's Christian name is difficult.

Allen made much of his London origins when advertising himself to his Herefordshire customers. He wished it to be known that the correspondence and connections with the London booksellers, which had been of singular service to him in assembling his stock, would also enable him to accommodate his customers with the newest publications from the capital, on the shortest notice, as well as to supply them with the most approved editions of the best authors, in elegant bindings, and at the most reasonable rates; an advantage not enjoyed by the generality of country booksellers.[3]

He made it clear that his business was to be further expanded as soon as possible by the addition of a circulating library of ambitious proportions. A little over six months after opening he was able to advertise a catalogue of its contents 'price 6d'.[4] The 'extensive and increasing' library comprised books on history, antiquities, voyages, travels, lives, memoirs, poetry, plays, novels, divinity, physic, surgery, anatomy, philosophy, mathematics, astronomy, trade, natural history, gardening, husbandry, &c. 'including the books which have been lately published in almost every branch of literature'.

In the days before any sort of free public library existed books could be borrowed from circulating libraries run by booksellers. For those who could not afford to buy many books the circulating libraries provided a means of keeping up their reading at a cost which was within their means. People could borrow books from Allen's circulating library at twelve shillings per year or four shillings per quarter. His premises were open from eight in the morning till eight at night for the choosing and exchange of books. Subscribers were allowed to take two books at a time and exchange them three times a week. Those living in the country were allowed to borrow extra books but they had to exchange them at least once a fortnight. According to Rees in his *Hereford Guide* Allen's circulating library was superior to those of most provincial towns.[5]

Allen advertised a new and enlarged catalogue of his circulating library in 1787 by which time its extent is described as 'upwards of two thousand volumes'.[6] One of Allen's catalogues survives in Hereford Library but it is undated.[7] At the time it was published the terms of subscription were twelve shillings per year or four shillings per quarter which is as advertised by Allen in 1780 and 1787. At a later date these figures were increased to sixteen shillings and five shillings as appears from a surviving label removed from one of the books.[8]

References to Allen speak of him as if he were a cut above the other

A

CATALOGUE

OF

ALLEN's extensive and increasing

CIRCULATING LIBRARY;

CONSISTING OF

A great Variety of the best Authors

ON

History, Antiquities, Voyages, Travels, Lives, Memoirs, Poetry, Plays, Novels, Divinity, Physic, Surgery, Anatomy, Philosophy, Mathematics, Astronomy, Trade, Natural History, Gardening, Husbandry, &c. including the Books which have been lately published in almost every Branch of Literature;

Which are lent to read at

Twelve Shillings per Year, or Four Shillings per Quarter.

By JOHN ALLEN, Bookseller, *Hereford.*

Where all new Books, on every useful and entertaining Subject, are purchased as soon as published, for the Use of the Subscribers.

The full Value given for any Library, or Parcel of Books.

[PRICE SIX-PENCE.]

Plate 2. Titlepage of John Allen Sr.'s circulating library catalogue. (HL)

booksellers in the county. In a letter to the *Gentleman's Magazine* in 1825 a correspondent mentions that he remembers Allen Sr., 'the principal bookseller in the county', 'nearly half a century ago'.[9] His business included the sale and purchase of secondhand books as was usual in the book trade. In 1786 he advertised a catalogue of books for sale which included the library of the late Canon Evans of Hereford and that of the Reverend Mr Baines of Upton.[10]

Most booksellers at this time were also printers but Allen applied himself for many years exclusively to his bookselling activities and his circulating library. There is no evidence for his having acquired a press before about 1810. In that year Allen printed and published a new edition of John Napleton's *Short and Plain Instruction for Young Persons before and after Confirmation*, and two sermons also by Napleton.[11] There are numerous items bearing his imprint in the second decade of the nineteenth century but Allen was not so prolific a printer as others. Probably it was by concentrating on the bookselling side of his business that he gained ascendancy in that field. His printing press was later described as 'well selected for a Job Office', implying that it was a basic and unpretentious piece of equipment.[12]

Allen Sr. traded at premises in High Town near the corner of Widemarsh Street. Early references to his address give his location as 'in the Market Place'. Later references are to No. 2 High Town. Thomas Theophilus Davies, another prominent bookseller and printer, traded next door.

In 1788 John Allen Sr. married Mary Thomas, daughter of Francis Thomas of the parish of All Saints.[13] Their first born, John Jr., was christened at St Peter's on 4th August of the following year. Another son, Francis, was born in 1790, a daughter Mary in 1792 and another daughter Elizabeth in 1794.[14]

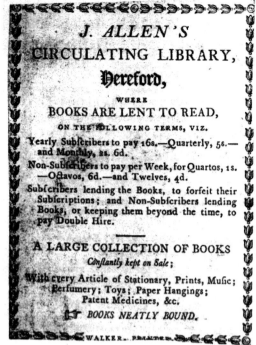

Plate 3. Circulating library label. (HL)

Allen Jr. exhibited something of a bibliographical bent at an early age. His *Waste Book for Things Concerning Antiquities* dated 1804 is in Hereford Library, as is a book of sketches of *Monuments in Hereford Cathedral* dated 1806. He corrected a plan of Hereford from Taylor's plan of the city for publication in the atlas for Britton & Brayley's *Beauties of England and Wales*, which appeared in 1806 when he was about 17. In 1807 he speaks of being shown at Enfield a rare book of Hereford interest by Richard Gough, one of the foremost antiquaries and topographers of his time, who travelled extensively and may well have known the Allen bookshop in Hereford and have met the younger Allen there. Young Allen was already showing signs of the commitment to bibliography as well as what would now be called local studies which were to be amongst the most important interests of his life.[15]

In 1808, the year which marked the commencement of the peninsular war, young Allen gained a commission as ensign in the local militia, the 1st Regiment of Herefordshire Volunteer Infantry, commanded by Lt. Col. John Matthews of Belmont, the successful physician with literary pretensions who had been MP for Herefordshire from 1803 to 1806. Two years later he was made up to full lieutenant and in 1811 found himself in the company commanded by Edwin Goode Wright, editor of the *Hereford Journal*.[16] By 1813 he was promoted to captain and given his own company. A pamphlet entitled, *Standing Orders of the Hereford Recruiting District*, Hereford, 1812 bears the imprint 'Printed by J. Allen, bookseller, printer, stationer, and bookbinder to the military districts of Hereford, Monmouth, and South Wales; where may be had all kinds of attestations and certificates'.[17]

Allen's career in the militia was confined to the period when England was under threat from France and his duty was close to home. It was left to his brother Francis to become a professional soldier. Francis was commissioned ensign in the 60th (or Royal American) regiment of foot in 1810 and promoted to lieutenant in 1811. He was placed on half-pay in 1814 doing duty with the militia and remained in that condition for many years.[18] He is also known as author of *The Ross Guide* (Hereford, 1827).

It is hard to tell just when John Allen began seriously to gather data with publication in mind. In 1819 it was stated that he was engaged in the composition of a history of his native county. A manuscript volume of extracts from various authors and copies of original papers relating to the city and county bearing his signature and dated 1818 was sold at the Stoke Edith Library sale at Sotheby's in June 1948. Allen certainly intended to publish a general work which he described as 'Antiquarian, Topographic and General Illustrations of the History of Herefordshire'. In a sense the gathering of data on all the printed sources, which was eventually to take form as his *Bibliotheca Herefordiensis*, was an exercise towards the history that he intended to write. His introduction to *Bibliotheca Herefordiensis* shows that he was equally familiar with the manuscript sources of county and family history, having documented every important collector of materials from the earliest times up to his own day and locating the materials wherever possible. It is also apparent that he spent time at the British Museum library consulting manuscripts some time before his becoming a resident in the capital made him an even more frequent visitor. His search for and recording of data of all kinds relating to his chosen study was indefatigable, but there is no evidence that he ever began to write the history that had been his declared ambition for so long.

In 1815 the first non-commercial library was founded in Hereford. Funded by subscription it was christened the Hereford Permanent Library and Allen Jr. was at the forefront of the body of people which brought it into being. The printed rules and regulations of the library for 1818 indicate the numbers allocated to the original subscribers.[19] Allen is number two preceded only by William Ravenhill, a fellow militia officer of Allen's and mayor in 1815. The Permanent Library was close to Allen's heart for the remainder of his life. He served on its committee for its first few years and probably had a prominent part in framing its rules. The Reverend John Duncumb, whose incomplete history of the county had by then been published, was honorary librarian. Edwin Goode Wright was a committee member and regularly printed the book list. The list of subscribers rings with the names of Arkwright, Bodenham, Baskerville, Garbett, Lingen, Pateshall, Symonds, Unett, Woodhouse, etc. but the mercantile classes with a smattering of the clergy and a handful of women formed the major part of the subscribers.

Allen Jr. was much involved in the parliamentary election of 1818 in the city of Hereford. The sitting members, T. P. Symonds and R. P. Scudamore, the former in the Duke of Norfolk's interest and the latter a kinsman of the duke's by marriage, were challenged for the first time in many years by a ministerial candidate, the Hon. John Somers Cocks.

The stage was set for a stiff contest and the pamphleteers had a field day. Allen Jr. was in the thick of it on the side of the sitting members. From his father's press issued a number of broadsides and pamphlets boosting Symonds and Scudamore and depreciating Cocks in none too delicate a fashion. The press of Watkins and Wright was much to the fore with similar material in Cocks's interest.[20] Allen himself was guyed in one of Watkins and Wright's pamphlets entitled *Selections from the Comedy of the Election, now performing, with applause, at the different Theatres in this City: consisting chiefly of Characteristic Soliloquies, Speeches, &c.*[21] The identities of the

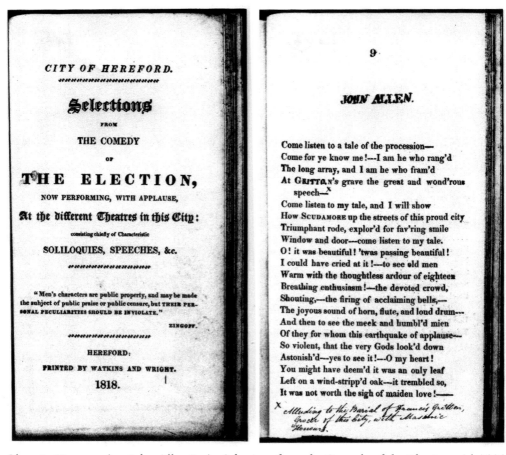

Plate 4. Verse guying John Allen Jr. in *Selections from the Comedy of the Election* with T. T. Davies's manuscript insertions. (HL)

persons supposed to have made the speeches or spoken the soliloquies, all in verse, are, of course, not given. Those in the swim would have had little difficulty in identifying them at the time. Fortunately the Davies copy at Hereford Library has the names supplied in manuscript. Allen is identified with the verse on page nine. The allusions are now clouded and to little purpose but serve to illustrate the high political profile Allen had assumed in the election of 1818. Allen stated that this pamphlet was written by John Pyndar Wright.[22]

It can be assumed that Allen Jr. was well known in Hereford by the time he was 30. Besides his association with the Permanent Library, his aggressive electioneering in 1818 and his career with the local militia he was also a freemason, becoming Right Worshipful Master of the Palladian Lodge, no. 196 in 1817.[23] Treasurer of the lodge was Thomas Bird, formerly the Duke of Norfolk's factor and clerk of the peace. Allen and Bird were further associated as two of the managers of the Hereford Savings Bank. Allen's stature as a local historian and putative compiler of a county history were well enough known for special mention to be made of them in a Hereford guide published in 1819, which acknowledged his help.

Allen's gathering of data for the compilation that would in due course appear as *Bibliotheca Herefordiensis* was, presumably, continuing throughout these years.

Another publication of his was to come from his father's press first, however: his translation from the original Latin of the charter of King William III to the city of Hereford, which he dedicated to 'the mayor, aldermen, common council, and citizens of the City of Hereford'. The titlepage bears no date of publication but the dedication is dated 16 August, 1820. The interest in the document lay in the fact that it is the last royal charter granted to the city and confirms the rights and privileges granted by previous sovereigns. Allen says,

> I procured a correct transcript of this last Charter, taken by the late B. Fallowes Esq., clerk of the Peace, and compared such translations as existed in mss. with the copy of the original Latin, and from a careful examination, word by word, wrote out a more complete translation than those I had seen; which I afterwards published, and dedicated to the Corporate Body and the Citizens. 300 copies printed.[24]

Allen was to suffer a double embarrassment, first as translator and second as printer, from the wrong date appearing in the title of this publication. As printed the title reads, *Translation of the Charter granted to the City of Hereford, by King William the Third, June 14, 1697*. The year should read 1696 and Allen says he did not notice the error until all the copies were printed.

Allen was a young man of considerable self confidence. His political awareness was highly developed and he had a taste for reform, which in 1821 manifested itself in his taking a leading part in inviting the 'aggressively independent radical' MP, Joseph Hume, to Hereford.

Hume's visit created great local interest. Not only was it fully reported in the *Hereford Journal* but Allen also published a pamphlet, with an introduction clearly written by himself, describing the whole proceedings.[25] He was chairman of the committee formed to discuss the idea of making a presentation to Hume of a hogshead of finest Herefordshire cider and a silver tankard. A public meeting of subscribers was then held with Allen as chairman. Allen was deputed to write to Hume extending an invitation to him to visit the county and attend a dinner in his honour at which the presentation would be made. Allen's letter and Hume's acceptance were published in *The Times*. Nearly 300 people sat down to dinner at the City Arms Hotel on 7 December 1821 amongst whom were many of the principal people of the county and its environs, bearing some of the longest established Herefordshire family names.

The dust had barely settled on the frenetic activity of Joseph Hume's visit when the annual general meeting of the Permanent Library loomed at the end of December. This was to be no routine affair. About forty-four of the 153 subscribers were present. Dr Samuel Hughes MD was elected president and the Reverend Mr Duncumb re-elected honorary librarian.[26] A motion was made to destroy Burdon's *Materials for Thinking*[27] and Hone's *Apocryphal New Testament*[28] on the grounds of their 'unmoral and irreligious tendency'. The newspaper report indicates that the motion was carried 'almost unanimously' and from a later account we learn that only John Allen and three others voted against. The two books were duly destroyed.

A further motion was put to the meeting to destroy Bayle's *Dictionary*, Hume's *Essays*, and Gibbon's *History*. If the first motion can perhaps be understood within the context of the theological strife of the time, the second motion is rather extravagant. Nevertheless, it was passed, but this time by a majority of only eight. Duncumb, 'the worthy librarian', moved that 'this sweeping sentence', in the words of the *Hereford Journal*, be 'postponed *sine die*', i.e. indefinitely.

Young Allen, then just over 30 years old, must have been recognized as a free thinker and a radical. His vote against burning Burdon's and Hone's books would alone have marked him out. Soon after this affair Allen was to take a step which it is difficult to believe he must not have regretted in the sequel. The matter touched upon the Permanent Library and left him facing a private prosecution for libel which became a *cause celebre*.

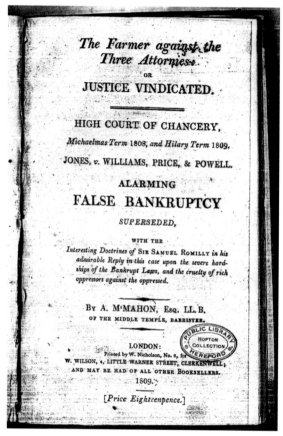

Plate 5. Titlepage of the pamphlet the depositing of which in the Permanent Library led to Allen's trial for libel. (HL)

The book burning incident at the Permanent Library occurred at the end of 1821 and it was 'soon after this took place' that Allen deposited a certain pamphlet in the library. The title of the pamphlet was *The Farmer against the three Attornies, or Justice Vindicated, etc.* by one A. M'Mahon, a London barrister. It had been published in London in 1809 and had been the subject of a libel judgment in 1810. By depositing the pamphlet in the Permanent Library where it was available to any subscriber Allen had, in effect, repeated the libel.

The case with which the pamphlet is concerned was heard in the High Court of Chancery in 1808 and 1809, fully twelve years previous to Allen's depositing the offending item in the library. The case had nothing whatever to do with Allen but had been brought by Richard Jones, a Herefordshire farmer, against one Robert Williams, a solicitor originally of Monmouth, and two others. The pamphlet paraphrases Sir Samuel Romilly as stating that '...Mr. Williams was on this occasion actuated by the most blind passion and prejudice against this poor man, and had actually undertaken by his wealth, importance and opulence, to utterly ruin him, which unhappily he has accomplished with a vengeance'.[29] When the pamphlet was published in London Williams filed an action for libel in which he was successful.

Allen states that the pamphlet 'was for some time openly sold by a poor fellow (connected with the injured party) on market days at Hereford, Monmouth, Gloster, &c &c, and who was subsequently indicted and imprisoned'.[30]

By the time Allen deposited the libellous pamphlet in the Permanent Library Robert Williams had moved from Monmouth to Hereford where he was living on 'Ailstone Hill'.[31] He would not have been best pleased to find that a matter which had caused him such tribulations more than twelve years previously, and had so damaged his reputation in the process, was now raising itself like a spectre before him once again;

the cause being a impulsive young man of 30 years of age. The wholehearted way Williams went about suing young Allen suggests that his reaction was immediate and decisive. He would have realised straight away that he could not lose the case in a legal sense since the libellous nature of the pamphlet had been established in court and was not at issue. Any 'publication' of the pamphlet, including making it available in a public library, was tantamount to a reiteration of the libel. There was no doubt Allen knew at the time he published the libel there had been a conviction for the same publication as far back as the year 1810.

The *Hereford Journal* trumpeted that this 'was an action which excited the most lively interest throughout this and the neighbouring counties'. The crowd which assembled with a view to gaining admittance to the assizes that day in early April of 1822 was 'immense' and the court was filled to capacity.[32] Mr Jervis, for the plaintiff, said Allen was well known, 'the son of a respectable bookseller and a very young man'. Jervis then proceeded to recall the recent events at the Permanent Library when at a meeting to consider 'whether books of an irreligious tendency should be suffered to continue on their shelves' a vote was taken to destroy certain 'deistical or atheistical' volumes. The only votes against being those of Allen and three others. Shortly after this Allen had 'thought fit to publish the libel in question'.

Mr Taunton, for Allen, accepted that some sort of damages would be awarded against his client but he warned that it would be 'incumbent on him to give evidence of what the circumstances of the case really were, and when the jury had adverted to the real circumstances, they would ask themselves what amount of damages the plaintiff had a right to demand at their hands'. He would not attempt to justify the entire contents of the pamphlet, 'but sufficient totally to annihilate any claim on the part of Mr. Williams to any thing beyond nominal damages'.

His lordship in summing up showed that he was quickly satisfied upon the fact of publication and of the libelous nature of the publication. The pamphlet was 'in itself of a scandalously libelous character' and the defendant, Allen, had certainly published the libel.

The jury took about half an hour to reach their verdict. When they returned it was to award Williams damages of £5, a derisory sum to compensate a man for defamation of his character. Allen notes that 'Baron Garrow is reported to have said, in allusion to the amount of the damages, that the sum (£5) was enough for the Defendant's "Freak", but too much for the Plaintiff's Character'.[33] Allen's pleasure and relief at the outcome would have been severely diluted by the realisation that he had to meet the plaintiff's costs. His own solicitors, James and Bodenham, gave their services free, charging only for their out of pocket expenses. Nevertheless, Allen faced a bill of over £400. Towards this amount he received £160 in voluntary contributions from well-wishers who 'well knowing Williams's character and vindictive disposition endeavoured to remunerate me in some degree for the loss I had sustained in the expences incurred on the trial at Hereford'.[34] Williams it seems had more enemies than one in Hereford. According to Allen he left the city in March 1823.

What Allen's father thought about his son's behaviour is not recorded. Almost certainly he would have considered that the placing of the pamphlet in the Permanent Library was a foolhardy thing to do, as indeed it was. It was the action of an impetuous young man and the resulting costs of it presumably fell upon the family. Allen Jr. was plainly outraged at Williams's behaviour. He considered that Jones 'was totally ruined by the iniquitous conduct of a man, whose station in society should, at least, have learnt him, that villainy, when once exposed, will never be forgotten by those who from public or private feeling take an interest in virtue or honesty'.[35] These are fine feelings but the method Allen chose of exposing Williams to further ignominy was a risky one and laid him open to financial consequences that he had not the substance to assimilate. One can only speculate as to how seriously the Allens' business was affected by the money paid out in this case or what effect it had upon the relationship between father and son. Certainly Allen Jr. was not to carry the business on. When Allen Sr. retired eight months later the shop and its contents were sold.

From the autumn of 1821, when he first began to organise Joseph Hume's visit to Hereford, to April 1822 when he faced the libel charge in court Allen had been fully occupied with matters, some pleasant, some not, which took up much of his time. In January his sister Elizabeth had died 'after a short but severe illness'. His *Bibliotheca Herefordiensis* was apparently intended for publication some time in 1821 for that is the date on the titlepage, which had evidently gone through his press during that year. The book, however, was not completed until 22 July 1822 as appears from the date in the colophon, the date on which the last sheets were printed.

The compilation of this book was the result of several years of effort. The printed introduction gives little idea of Allen's intention or purpose in publishing it. However, in a manuscript comment dated 1824 in his own copy he makes the following explanation:

> My object in printing this book was to afford to future writers on the history and antiquities of my native county a useful and compendious index to the printed and Ms. labours of their predecessors. To those who know anything of the trouble and expense of such pursuits and the little interest taken in general by those persons who having large or small estates in the county should be most interested in preserving records of their families and their possessions, – the want of pecuniary means to continue the collections, or patronage to publish, will be readily appreciated and felt.

Allen Sr., nearly 70 years old, announced his retirement and the disposal of his business to Thomas Bevan Watkins in January 1823. The nature of Allen's involvement with his father's business is not clear. Presumably he entered it after leaving school and learned the trade at his father's side. The character of bookselling should certainly have been congenial to him. References to the business as 'Allen & Son' are sparse but some have been noted in 1820. Allen Jr., who had no private means so far as is known, nor would it seem likely in the sequel, was left at his father's retirement without an income. Nowhere does he refer to these events other than matter-of-factly, but it is hard not to conclude that things had gone wrong between father and son.

Sometime in the year of his father's retirement Allen moved more or less permanently to London. That he had often gone there over the years is apparent from his many references to people he met there and his visits to the British Museum library. During 1822 he had been appointed one of the stewards of the Herefordshire Society in London, an organization he would have more to do with once he was fully resident in the capital. Nowhere does he state his reasons for leaving Hereford but the move coincided with his determination to give up his Herefordshire researches. In 1825 he wrote, 'intending to leave Hereford for the purpose of residing in London, I determined to give up, altogether, my favourite plan of publishing Antiquarian, Topographic, and General Illustrations of the History of Herefordshire...'.[36] He also disposed of his extensive collection of pamphlets. 'On my father's retiring from

Business, Jan'y 1823, I offered to H[ereford] P[ermanent] Library my collection of Herefordshire Tracts, &c. in 25 volumes of various sizes, at any valuation which they might affix, which offer being accepted with thanks the whole of this part of my collection is now deposited in the Library room and a printed index to their contents made.' Allen's pamphlets are still to be found in Hereford Library.

In 1824 Allen's address in London was 4 Furnival's Inn Court, a narrow lane off Holborn adjacent to Furnival's Inn, now demolished. He was a stroll away from the British Museum where he continued to go despite his intention of giving up his researches. At this time he wrote, 'My opportunities of collecting were great – my time – my own – my means at one period sufficient but circumstances change – times alter – and I surrender my Hobby to be ridden by those who are richer than the unfortunate J.A.' Despite his straitened circumstances, in the following year it appears he had not given up entirely. 'As several opportunities have presented themselves, from the nature of my pursuits, of continuing this book, I have from time to time, made such additions to my "Bibliotheca Herefordiensis" as may enable myself, or someone else into whose hands this volume may fall, to publish *a 2nd part* for the information of future collectors - to which I intend annexing *a digested index* to the contents of the Herefordian books, mss., &c. &c. in the British Museum, Bodleian, and other public libraries.'[37]

His antiquarian and literary interests continued to occupy his mind in London. In 1823 he contributed a description of a brass equestrian figure and candlestick belonging to Hereford cathedral to *The Portfolio*.[38] In 1824 a new and shortlived newspaper entitled the *Hereford Independent* appeared. Allen contributed a series of articles to this paper under the series title 'Collectanea Herefordiensia' dealing with matters relating to Herefordshire history. Twenty copies were printed 'in a separate form from the newspaper'. This was the last extensive writing Allen was to do. In March 1825 he contributed an item to the *Gentleman's Magazine* from his Furnival's Inn Court address on the tortuous bibliography of Coningsby's *Collections concerning the Manor of Marden* and other writings of the litigious earl. A list of titles of Herefordshire pamphlets 'extracted from my ms. additions to the Biblio: Heref:– a second part of which I have ample materials to publish' dated simply 1826 in Allen's hand may have been written out for the new edition of Rees's *Hereford Guide* (3rd ed. 1827).

At the election in Hereford in June 1826 Allen, 'resident in London' and described as 'Gent', voted for the Right Hon. John Somers, Viscount Eastnor (as Lord Cocks had become) and Edward Bolton Clive and not for Richard Blakemore. Lord Eastnor and E. B. Clive were elected. Allen Sr. is not listed as having voted.

The Herefordshire Society was formed in London 'in or about the reign of Charles I'. By Allen's time the records of the society prior to 1710 had been lost, but a sermon preached 'on the Anniversary Meeting of Herefordshire natives, June 24, 1658' was published and Allen reckoned the Herefordshire Society may have been the oldest county charitable society in the capital. Its purpose was the clothing and apprenticing in London of the children of poor natives of the county to give them a start in life by providing them with a trade. Allen calculated that from 1710 up to his time some 250 young persons had received the benefit of the society's charity.

By the 1820s when Allen first became associated with the society it had lost much of its vigour. There had always been a social element to the gatherings of the members. At one time they had met monthly, then quarterly, and by 1815 only annually for the general meeting. When Allen established himself in London he began to take an interest in the society. It needed someone to take a close look at it, decide what was needed to revitalise its activities and renew the interest of those Herefordians upon whom its existence depended.

Allen found that the existing rules of the society were not adequate to its circumstances and proceeded to draft new ones, which he as chairman presented at the general meeting on 3 May 1826 at the Albion Tavern, Aldersgate Street when they were unanimously agreed to. It was ordered that they be forthwith printed and delivered to every member.[39] The pamphlet that resulted consisted of rather more than just the new rules. Allen took the opportunity to include something of the history of the society, a list of stewards from 1743 to his time, as well as reprints of two Herefordshire songs written for the society by James Payne and J. M. Lacey. The committee's annual report was followed by the accounts and by a list of the seven apprentices still in indentures with the dates of their commencement and the names and trades of their masters.

In July 1826 John Allen had his 37th birthday. Two months earlier on 30 May he may have attended the anniversary dinner of the Herefordshire Society at the Albion Tavern. His multitude of hand-written additions, emendations and marginalia in his own copy of *Bibliotheca Herefordiensis*, which was always by him, come to an end around September with a note of the plan for the sale catalogue of the freehold estates of the late Thomas Evans in Herefordshire. The sale took place on 8 September 1826 and it is the latest dated item noted in Allen's hand. There is no evidence for any other activity until the beginning of the following year.

The auctioneer L. A. Lewis of 8 Wilderness Row, Goswell Street, published a catalogue of 'the Select Library of John Allen Esq' to be sold by him on Friday, 26 January 1827, at twelve o'clock at the Bank Coffee House, opposite the Bank of England.[40] The cream of the 264 lots was set out as follows:

Neale's Views of Gentlemen's Seats, 102 numbers; Neale's Parochial Churches, 2 vol.; Lodge's Illustrious Portraits, 23 parts; Sharpe's British Classics, 24 vols. LARGE PAPER, fine impressions; Canova's Works, 2 vols. morocco by C. Lewis; Dodsley's Old Plays, 10 vol LARGE PAPER; Pyne's Palaces, 3 vols. LARGE PAPER; Grose's Antiquities, 14 vols. half russia; Martin's Illus. ed. of Milton, LARGE PAPER; Beauties of Claude; Gems of Art; Rutter's Fonthill Abbey; Salt's Splendid Scenery of the East; Shakespeare's Plays, second ed.; Burnet's Own Time, 4 vols., IMPERIAL PAPER; Pantalogia, 12 vols.; Edinburgh Review, 43 vols.; Scott's Novels & Romances, 18 vols. calf extra; Lord Byron's Works, 16 vols; Walpole's Royal & Noble Authors; Dr. Syntax's various works, 8 vols.; Clarendon's Rebellion & Life, 9 vols. elegantly bound; Ireland's Hogarth, 3 vols.; Scott's Poetical Works, 8 vols.; Fontaine Contes et Nouvelles, 2 vols. red morocco; Shakespeare, 9 vol., morocco; Ritson's Metrical Romances; Bell's British Theatre, 34 vols., &c., &c.

The catalogue contains no Herefordshire material at all. If Allen had the intention at that stage to part with that portion of his library it was not to be in a London auction room. The sale made £247 12s 6d.

Lewis had sold the previous day what he had advertised as 'a portion of the Stock of a Dealer' which comprised 402 lots and realized £71 7s 6d.[41] The proceeds of this 25 January sale were added to the reckoning on the final page of Allen's 26 January catalogue, indicating a common vendor. Allen was the anonymous 'dealer'. Many of these books had not long been published, bearing dates as recent as 1825, 1826 and even 1827. This raises the question was Allen dealing in books in London and, if so, in what form? Was it his precarious financial position that led him to sell not only his 'stock' but also his own library? Or had he already begun that slide into mental illness which was to rob him of his sanity and any semblance of normal life?

The first sign of trouble is recorded in a scrappy little note on a misshapen piece of paper scrawled hastily and anxiously by Allen to his friend William Upcott, sub-librarian of The London Institution. The note is dated 21 March 1827 from Clerkenwell Prison and parts of it are illegible.[42]

> I have so often seen your kindness that I make no hesitation in requesting your kind interference in (????) me my release from this damned place. If you go Hatton Garden Police Office (????) you can Bail me and get me my Liberty.
>> Yours, &c.
>>> J. Allen Jr.

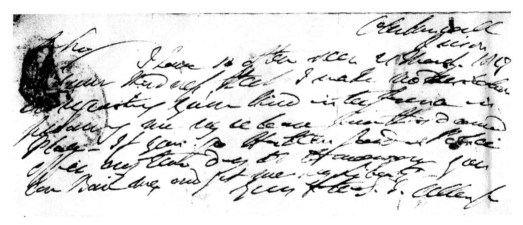

Plate 6. John Allen's scrawled note to William Upcott from Clerkenwell Prison. (HL)

Records of court or prison which would show why Allen was detained do not survive. Clerkenwell House of Detention was a long-established jail with an unpleasant reputation throughout its history. It was not a debtors prison, so it would seem unlikely that Allen was there for reasons of money, but it took in attempted suicides. The experience must have been horrible for him, as the desperation in his note to Upcott suggests. Had he made an attempt on his own life?

Upcott almost certainly got in touch with Allen's brother, Lieutenant Francis Allen. On 24 March just three days after Allen sent his note to Upcott a certificate of insanity was signed by Frederic Hunter, surgeon, of the parish of St Pancras, a necessary preliminary to Allen's admission to Bethlem Royal Hospital (Bedlam) where he was taken in as a lunatic on 12 April on the application of his brother.[43]

Francis Allen's petition for his brother's admission refers to John as of the parish of All Saints, Hereford, 'a lunatic, aged 37 years' who had been disordered in his senses about three months and was a proper object of charity. John Allen remained in hospital just short of eight months until 6 December when he was allowed out on one month's leave of absence. He was discharged 'well' on 3 January 1828.

Just under two months later his father died at Hereford aged 74. Old Allen had survived his wife by only a few weeks.[44]

Allen Jr.'s cure was not permanent. On 28 May he was admitted to Hereford

Asylum by the authority of his brother Francis 'having been removed from Bethlem Hospital'. This was to be his final incarceration. In the asylum return for the period to June 1829 compiled by John S. L. Pateshall, surgeon in charge, Allen is described as bookseller, age 39, single, and 'idiotic'.[45] Rees indicates that the asylum would hold twenty persons and 'in consequence of the inadequacy of the funds appropriated to this establishment, the expences of the patients are defrayed by those who procure their admission'. The conditions in the asylum under Pateshall can only be speculated upon. He was succeeded in 1834 by a Dr John Gilliland under whose regime a licence was refused by the county justices in 1838 owing to the bad conditions.

Allen remained an inmate of the asylum for little more than a year. Pateshall wrote to Thomas Bird, clerk of the peace and deputy custos rotulorum, on 18 August 1829 notifying him of Allen's death two days previously.[46] He was 40 years old. Bird himself, who shared Allen's passion for the collecting of Herefordiana and was

Plate 7. Allen's armorial bookplate engraved by Cross. His entitlement to the use of these arms is in some doubt. (HL)

to acquire much of the material from Allen's collection, died in 1836.

Allen's death was recorded in the *Hereford Journal* only in the most perfunctory way.[47] In fact, all later references to him disclaim any knowledge of his fate once he had moved to London; shame and disgrace were attached to the incidence of mental illness.

The *Dictionary of National Biography* devotes two paragraphs to Allen written by Henry Richard Tedder, which are not without inaccuracies. However, he is there described as a bookseller and antiquary, a label which no doubt Allen would have approved.

ACKNOWLEDGEMENTS I wish to record my gratitude to John Buchanan-Brown for generously providing me with references concerning the Allens gleaned during his as yet unpublished research on Hereford booksellers. My thanks also to Robin Hill and staff at Hereford Library and to Tim Pridgeon.

REFERENCES
[1] *Hereford Journal (HJ)*, 14 and 21 October 1779.
[2] D. F. McKenzie, ed., *Stationers' Company Apprentices, 1701-1800*, Oxford Bibliographical Society publications, new series 19, (1978).
[3] A good idea of Allen's stock in trade can be gleaned from his advertisements in *HJ*,14 October 1779 and 8 November 1787.

[4] *HJ*, 25 May 1780.   [5] [W. J. Rees], *The Hereford Guide* (Hereford, 1806), 65.

[6] *HJ*, 8 November 1787.   [7] HL, Pilley Collection.

[8] Pilley Collection. Allen's advertisement for another new catalogue in *HJ*, 21 February 1798 gives the rates as 16s a year, 5s a quarter or 2s 6d a month.

[9] *Gentleman's Magazine*, July 1825.   [10] *HJ*, 28 September 1786.

[11] John Napleton, *Two Sermons....preached at Hereford* (Hereford: John Allen, 1810). Napleton was a canon of Hereford Cathedral.

[12] When Allen's business was sold up to his competitor Watkins in 1823 the press was advertised for sale with this description. *HJ*, 29 January 1823.

[13] HRO, Hereford St Peter's parish registers, 1 April 1788.

[14] HRO, Hereford St Peter's parish registers: Francis, christened 9 October 1790; Mary, christened 6 November 1792; Elizabeth, christened 13 April 1794.

[15] Allen's own copy of his *Bibliotheca Herefordiensis* (*BH*) in HL contains many manuscript annotations and marginalia. These are mostly amendments and additions preparatory to a new edition which was never to be published, but also include some fragments of biographical information.

[16] PRO WO13/3500.

[17] Allen lists in his own hand the dates of his commissions at the end of this pamphlet in HL: Ensign Hereford Volunteers 26 May 1808; transfer to 1st Regiment of Herefordshire Local Militia 24 September 1808; lieutenant 14 March 1810; captain 14 May 1810. According to the militia returns in the PRO (WO13/3500) he was not made captain until 1812 or prior to 26 May 1813.

[18] 1811 Army List; List of the Officers of the Militia, 1820.

[19] HL, Herefordshire Pamphlets, vol.4.

[20] An interesting collection of these election 'squibs' can be found in the Pilley collection in HL, PC2271.

[21] HL, Davies collection, 'Collectanea Herefordensis', vol.1.   [22] *BH*, facing p.32.

[23] Allen's Masonic offices are listed by him in his lodge's rule book in HL, tracts vol.3. Pointed out to me by Dr John Eisel.

[24] Ms. note in Allen's own copy of *BH*.

[25] *The Proceedings in Herefordshire, connected with the visit of Joseph Hume, Esq., M.P...* (Hereford, 1822).

[26] *HJ*, 2 Jan. 1822.   [27] Published Newcastle, 1806.

[28] William Hone, *The Apocryphal New Testament, being all the Gospels, Epistles and other pieces now extant, attributed in the first four centuries to Jesus Christ, His apostles and their companions and not included in the New Testament by its compilers* (London, 1820).

[29] M'Mahon, 21.   [30] *BH*, facing 59.   [31] *BH*, 118.

[32] *HJ*, trial report, 3 April 1822. [33] *BH*, ms. note on 118.   [34] Ibid, opposite 118.

[35] Ibid, opposite 59.   [36] Ibid, opposite xii.   [37] Ibid, opposite xii.

[38] Sub-titled: *a Collection of Engravings from Antiquarian, Architectural, and Topographical Subjects, curious works of art, etc., etc., with descriptions*, vol.2, London, 1823 (by J. and H. S. Storer).

[39] *Rules and Regulations of the Herefordshire Society;...*(London, 1826).

[40] BL, S.-C.L. 1. (17.).

[41] This sale had been announced on the back of the catalogue of a sale held by Lewis 24 October 1825.

[42] The original is tipped-in before the half-title of Walter Pilley's copy of *BH* in HL.

[43] Information kindly supplied by the archivist and curator of The Bethlem Royal Hospital, Beckenham, Kent. In the midst of these tragic upheavals in Allen's life the *Hereford Journal* announced in its issue of 2 May 1827 that John Allen Jr. had 'lately' married a Miss Esther Lovell of Dudley at Dudley. The announcement defies explanation, for the John Allen who married Esther Lovell at Dudley was a life-long resident of that town and had nothing apparently to do with John Allen Jr. of Hereford.

[44] *HJ*, 5 March 1828. Hereford St Peter's parish registers: John Allen of Widemarsh Street buried 8 March 1828, aged 74. *HJ*, 2 January 1828. Mary Allen of Widemarsh Street buried 27 January 1828, aged 73.

[45] HRO, Q/AL/124.

[46] HRO, Q/AL/127. John Scudamore Lechmere Pateshall was mayor of Hereford in 1819.

[47] *HJ* of 26 August records the death of 'Mr. John Allen, age 40' but merely states 'in this city' without reference to the asylum. He was buried 20 August according to the registers of St Peter's.

The Green Lanes of Herefordshire

HEATHER HURLEY

The term 'green lanes' has no legal meaning, but they form an important network of minor routes.[1] Many are defined as rights of way or highways, and those that remain unclassified are in danger of being lost. Despite modern farming practices, Herefordshire retains a wealth of green lanes which vary in character depending on their location and former use. They are of carriageway width, usually unsurfaced, sometimes sunken, normally hedged, nearly always of historical importance, and also serving as wildlife habitats and features of the landscape.

CHARACTER AND DESCRIPTION

A typical green lane leads between stock-proof hedges consisting of holly, hazel, hawthorn, blackthorn, field maple and spindle, draped with bryony, bramble and dog rose. A solitary tree or row of oak, ash or yew has often been allowed to mature in the hedgerow. The age of the hedge may be determined by adding a century for each species found over a thirty metre stretch. A fine example of a green lane leads from the old school at Moreton which formed an ancient route to Orleton.[2] Its neatly cut hedges contain at least seven species over a short distance suggesting an age of six to seven hundred years. With this number of tree species along a green lane of historic interest, defined as a bridleway, its hedges are of sufficient importance to be protected under the Hedgerow Regulations of 1997.[3]

Throughout the seasons hedges change colour and character but always attract an abundance of plant life and a variety of insects, mammals, reptiles and birds seeking food and shelter. In Linton parish a dry-weather footpath leads from Bollitree to Fiddler's Cross above a former turnpike road.[4] A remaining sunken section is overgrown with creepers and fallen trees where badgers and other tunnelling mammals have made their homes. Circling above the old hedges are crows, rooks, pigeons and buzzards, while the keen eyed will also identify blue tits, sky larks, finches, robins, wrens and the rarer sparrow-hawk.

In some areas, weathered stone walls instead of hedges enclose the lanes. This is rarely found in Herefordshire, but at Welsh Newton a lane called the Market Path leads between the high stone walls of Newton Lodge and a dry stone wall clad in ivy. On the Great Doward, where stone was readily available from nearby quarries, walled lanes would be expected. Some lanes were discovered but their stone walls now lie in a tumbled state, attractively weathered with moss, ivy, fern and hart's-tongue.

Steep-sided banks are another feature of green lanes, termed as sunken lanes or hollow-ways. Their depth is usually attributed to the constant wear and tear of animals and men, combined with heavy rain washing away the loose soil and stone. It is noticeable that the deepest sections occur on hillsides where excess water flows at its fastest.[5] One to admire starts as Bridge Lane at Wellington and leads up through woods to Dinmore Manor. It possibly formed an earlier route leading to Ivington hillfort.

It is considered that some sunken lanes were made deeper and wider by the quarrying of stone. At Hope Mansell near the Gloucestershire boundary, an unsurfaced lane winds its way down from Deep Dean. Its rocky sides appear to have been quarried in the past to provide stone for building, road mending and for the lime kilns nearby. Along some of the more important lanes wayside quarries were constructed to provide passing places for wheeled traffic. This is apparent on the side of a green lane leading from Goodrich into Marstow. It is found on the left side of the lane before it levels and passes the site of Marstow's earlier church, where one or two leaning gravestones remain.

The study of maps, plans, deeds and documents reveals a fascinating distribution of lanes in Herefordshire with names that reflect their character, usage, place or destination. The popular 'Green Lane' is recorded in numerous parishes including Orcop, Little Birch, Ledbury, Whitchurch and Breinton. Green Lane at Sellack was closed in 1871 since it was considered 'unappropriate for public use'.[6] It survived as a hedged lane until the mid-1990s when its hedges were partly removed despite opposition.

Plate 1.
The Green Lane,
Orcop.

Names still in use include:

Well Lane and Llanfrother Lane – Hentland

Baynham's Lane – Much Marcle

Poltrough Lane – Little Dewchurch

Spoon Lane – Dorstone

Cutter's Lane, Holland Tuft Lane and Ferry Lane – Goodrich

Watery Lane – Dinedor

Hell's Ditch – Peterstow

Bodicott Lane – Bredwardine

Boat Lane – Walford

Red Lane – Brilley

Ochre Hill Lane – Wellington Heath

Cook Croft Lane at Leominster

Other named lanes, which have been partly surfaced, are Holywell Gutter Lane at Hampton Bishop, Holywell Lane at Dinedor, Ferry Lane at Fownhope, Pinford Lane at Linton, Bridge Lane at Wellington, Haymeadow Lane at Burghill, Brown's Lane at Dorstone and the Cleeve and Penyard lanes leading from Ross-on-Wye.

Unfortunately, for many former green lanes documentation is their only record, as all visible features have been destroyed or access has been lost. These are not easy to identify, but with historical research and field work they can be located. In the 1850s the Reverend John Webb described Colys Lane in Hentland as 'impassable and thrown in by 1820'.[7] This fact is confirmed by quarter sessions recording a highway leading from Pengethley to Aberhall which was 'stopped up' in 1825.[8] Now only a single hedge marks its former route and there is no public access.

Over the years many old names have been forgotten, while others have been recorded or remembered and now exist as rights of way. These include Puckeridge Lane leading from Ross-on-Wye to Deep Dean, Old Ford Road leading to a former river crossing at Ballingham, Gore Lane at Brampton Abbotts, Pudding Lane at Peterchurch and Crowmer Lane at Burghill.[9] At Linton and Whitchurch parish maps have been produced which feature names of paths, lanes and roads at Gorsley and on the Great Doward.[10] An interesting collection of names appears in a list of unclassified roads produced in 1936 by the Herefordshire County Council.[11]

DEFINITION AND USAGE

The name 'green lane' only describes the physical character of a lane, and the term 'white lane' refers to an uncoloured route on an Ordnance Survey map which in future will be identified as such. At present, neither has any legal meaning, but the lanes generally serve as rights of way or highways. In order to determine the status of these lanes it is necessary to inspect the definitive map which records all rights of way, and the county road map which notes unclassified roads.[12] Additional information is gained from the Ordnance Survey Pathfinder, Landranger, Leisure and the new Explorer series of maps.

A typical green lane leads from Hoarwithy to Carey along a ridge above the River Wye. It is unsurfaced, thickly hedged and used regularly by walkers and riders. This lane is not marked as a right of way on the definitive map, but is shown as an unclassified road on the county road map. A white lane to investigate climbs the northern slope of Garway Hill. It is obviously an ancient route and is still used by adventurous walkers who clamber up the steep and overgrown lane, which is not defined as a right of way or an unclassified road. This lack of definition is not conclusive proof that the public does not enjoy a right along its route.[13]

It is only since 1949 that rights of way have been legally defined.[14] The information supplied by parish councils varied considerably and errors were made which led to many green lanes being incorrectly defined or overlooked. Many previous cart tracks,

SOUTHERN DIVISION.
DISTRICT ROADS.—Area 1.

No.	Name of Road.	Point of commencement.	Termination.	Mileage.
1.	Ballingham	Hoarwithy P.O....	Ballingham Boundary	3 .2875
2.	Hoarwithy	Hoarwithy P.O....	Main 1, Poolmill	4 .075
3.	Ballingham Church	Ballingham School	Ballingham Court	.4375
4.	Tresseck	Hoarwithy	Central Div. Bdry.	.7125
5.	Laskett	Hoarwithy	Central Div. Bdry.	.6375
6.	Broadlands	Altbough Farm	Broadway Lands Bdry	.6375
7.	Altbough	Hoarwithy P.O....	Weaven Cottage	.975
8.	Paultro	Altbough Farm	Central Div. Bdry.	.3875
9.	Curatage	The Bibbletts	Altbough Farm	.3875
10.	Hentland	Red Rail	Harewood Cross	1 .525
11.	Hentland Church	Kynaston Lodge	Hentland Church	.575
12.	Treverran	Harewood Cross	Sandyway Cross	2 .375
13.	Fishpool Lane	Pencoyd Church	Gudgeons Cross	1 .250
14.	Marsh Lane	Windmill Hill	Treberran Farm	1 .6875
15.	Gillow Lane	Treberron Cross	Main 52, New Inn	2 .075
16.	Tretire	Tretire Bridge	Llanwarne Shop	3 .300
17.	Llanwarne	Main 54, Hill Gate	Broomy Close Lodge	.95
18.	Gibraltar	Lyston B'smith Shop	Llanwarne Shop	1 .000
19.	Netherton Lane	Pencoyd Court	Harewood Park Gate	2 .3625
20.	Pennygate	Pennygate Cross	Three Ashes	1 .2125
21.	Turkey Tump	Llanwarne Shop	Turkey Tump	.1875
22.	Ingston	Backney Shop	Ingston Farm	1 .975
23.	Picts Cross	Strangford Bridge	Picts Cross	1 .5000
24.	Strangford	Bridstow School	Strangford	2 .4625
25.	Ashe Lane	Poolmill Smithy	Wyeville	.5750
26.	Wells Brook	Peterstow Smithy	Poolmill	1 .2125
27.	Lovers Lane	Poolmill	Whitecross Farm	.1750
28.	Flann Lane	Peterstow	Flann Farm	.1000
29.	Monaston Lane	Dadnor Farm Turn	Grove Farm	.5375
30.	Sellack Common	Red Lion	Picts Cross	1 .1625
31.	Loughpool Lane	Grove Common	Loughpool Inn	.4125
32.	Carey	Rock Farm	Central Div. Bdry.	.4375
33.	Sellack Church	Sellack School	Sellack Church	.3875
34.	Sellack Marsh	Backney Bridge...	Baysham Court	.7250
35.	Belmont	Penault	Windsor Road	.3375
36.	Lynder	Perry Tump Cross	Greytree Bdry.	4 .5000
37.	Gurneys Oak	Gurneys Oak	Hoarwithy Bridge	4 .5000
38.	How Caple	How Caple Smithy	Armstone Turn	4 .9750
39.	Kings Caple	Ruxton Farm	Poulston Gate	1 .4875
40.	Clusters	The Clusters	Sellack Bridge	.9000
41.	Sellack Bridge	Sellack Bridge	Penault Corner	1 .125
42.	Maythorne	Falcon Farm	Brockhampton P.O.	1 .375
43.	Fawley Church	Fawley Cross	Fawley Church	.5250
44.	Fawley Court	Fawley Court	Wood Inn Corner	.2875
45.	Gatsford Lane	Brampton Abbotts	Gatsford Farm	.8250
46.	Brampton Church	Lynder Road	Townsend Farm	.5125
47.	Overton Lane	Lynder Road	Overton Pool	.1625
48.	Brampton Dingle	Grewtree	Lynder Road	.4500
49.	Totnor	Brockhampton Farm	How Caple Cross	1 .8500

DISTRICT ROADS—Area 2.

No.	Name of Road.	Point of commencement.	Termination.	Mileage.
50.	Wilton Lane	Bannut Tree	Wilton	.35
51.	Bannut Tree Lane	Bannut Tree	Bridstow School	.2375
52.	Bowers Lane	Weir End	Peterstow	.825
53.	Peterstow Common	Kyrle House	High Town Farm	.200
54.	Low Cop Lane	High Town	Wilsons Cross	1 .000
55.	Peterstow School	High Town	Peterstow Lr. Common	1 .275
56.	Benhall Lane	Wilton Cross	The Pound	.175
57.	Stowes	Pencraig	Mountcraig	.0625
58.	Glewstone	Glewstone P.O....	Red Lion Peterstow	2 .925
59.	Hollymount	Lower Weir End	Trorn Cross	1 .7125
60.	Glewstone Boat	Boat House	Chappel Cottage	.3000
61.	Hendra Lane	Biddleston	Wilsons Cross	1 .025
62.	Daffaluke Lane	Perks Cottage	Wilsons Cross	.725
63.	Blacknorle	Glewstone School	The Skates	.85
64.	Brelston	Stop Gates M.52	Old Mill	1 .900
65.	Marstow Lane	Marstow Church	Marstow Farm	.4875
66.	Nutshell	Cross Keys	Marstow Farm	.800
67.	Welsh Bicknor	Pencraig	Old Vicarage, Bicknor	2 .1750
68.	Coppet Hill	Pillar Box	Coppet Hill Corner	.275

Carried forward ... ... 82 .8125

7

Figure 1. List of unclassified roads, 1936. Herefordshire C.C.

carriageways and old roads were downgraded to footpath status, like the delightful green lane at Brockhampton leading from Plastre Tump to Brinkley Hill, which now forms part of the Wye Valley Walk.[15] On eighteenth-century maps this lane is shown to be a road.[16]

Other green lanes were given the higher status of bridleway, making them available for walking, riding and, since 1968, cycling.[17] Two bridleways at Walford, both leading down from Howle Hill are worth investigating on foot or horseback. Before the Hedgerow Regulations of 1997, many hedges were removed along bridleways sometimes leaving a single hedge or a row of trees as protection for wildlife.[18] From Weobley Church a bridleway leads to Dilwyn. It is mainly a headland path now, but was originally enclosed as recorded in 1817.[19] It leads into an unclassified road at Field's Place where the bridge was reported as being 'out of repair' in 1759.[20]

A green lane defined as a byway open to all traffic (BOAT) is used by walkers, riders and cyclists, with additional rights for horse-drawn and motorised vehicles. Byways are shown on the definitive map and on modern Ordnance Survey maps but sign-posting is rarely seen in Herefordshire. At Pipe and Lyde a sign directs the way along a partly surfaced byway leading from the main Hereford road to Lower Lyde. If green lanes were previously defined as 'roads used as public paths' (RUPPs) they are in the process of being re-classified as either byways, bridleways or footpaths under the Wildlife and Countryside Act of 1981.[21]

Another category of green lanes are unclassified roads, which are minor roads maintained as highways. The unsurfaced ones are the green lanes, which are mostly used by walkers and riders but are also open to cyclists and all other traffic. It is impossible to cycle or drive down from Middleton-on-the-Hill to Nurton Court in wet weather, or down the one leading from Llangrove to Welsh Newton, a wonderful lane leading to the Welsh border but its steep gradient, sharp bends and rocky surface are only negotiable by walkers or riders.

Plate 2. Unclassified road, Middleton-on-the-Hill.

ORIGINS AND HISTORY

Green lanes have evolved in a variety of forms, with their routes created long before the use of wheeled vehicles, when a direct line was preferable to a longer, less steep route.[22] Ridgeways were always considered to be the earliest routes, but many of these have been incorporated into our road system or remain as field paths. The ridgeway leading from Bullingham to Twyford is enclosed by hedges at its southern end below Aconbury hillfort, and although this stretch is not defined as a right of way or highway, it is in use and should be claimed as such.

In the past, sunken lanes were regarded as being of medieval origin, but there is growing evidence to suggest that they are much older. One such lane leads from Shenmore in the parish of Madley, where a sunken lane signed as a bridleway climbs up towards the hillfort in Timberline Wood. South of these wooded hills is the course of a Roman road known as Stane Street which led from the Roman town at Kenchester to Abbeydore.[23] Over Brampton Hill, this route follows a green lane into the Golden Valley. In spring 1998 there was confusion over access, but since then it is in the process of being claimed as a byway.[24]

Green lanes, which form parish boundaries, now have their hedges protected under the Hedgerow regulations of 1997. The age of these boundaries is difficult to determine as some probably existed long before the formation of parish boundaries.[25] Between Goodrich and Marstow an impressive parish boundary is worth viewing from the footpath leading from Newhouse Farm, an unusual house built in 1636 by Thomas Swift. He was the rector of Goodrich and the grandfather of Jonathan Swift.

With the spread of Christianity, pilgrim ways, corpseways and church paths were formed. The majority exist today as footpaths or highways, but some retain stretches of green lane. From All Saints church at Coddington, a linear path may be followed to Ledbury, closely resembling a route noted in 1817.[26] Sections of green lane remain near Coddington Church, through the bluebell wood over Raven Hill, across Wellington Heath and below the wooded Dog Hill, eventually reaching St Michael's church at Ledbury.

Plate 3. Footpath, Longtown.

Other green lanes reflect their former use. At Brobury Scar a sunken bridleway descends down the scenic sandstone cliff and terminates at the water's edge where a ferry crossed the river Wye to Moccas. Only the collapsed and overgrown ruins of a boathouse serve as a reminder of this crossing which was in use until the end of the nineteenth century.[27] On the outskirts of Leominster a well-defined lane, defined as a footpath leads into riverside meadows from Passa Lane, recorded as Passey Lane in 1799.[28] At Longtown short stretches of worn and weathered green lanes lead onto the slopes of the Black Mountains (Pl. 3).

Settlements which have developed on common land and waste have left a pattern of paths and lanes to investigate. From the Peterchurch road in the Golden Valley an unclassified road leads over a distance of 1.75 miles to Barrett's Boundary on Vowchurch Common.[29] From a height of 700ft wonderful views of the Golden Valley may be admired while exploring a delightful variety of green lanes linking isolated farms and cottages. Most lanes are defined as rights of way or highways, but one or two worthy of preservation need to be monitored.

With the introduction of wheeled traffic, packhorse trails were widened to carriageway width and important thoroughfares developed into roads. In order to improve and repair neglected networks of roads the turnpike system was adopted, spreading rapidly in Herefordshire from 1721.[30] New roads were constructed and alternative routes were used to ease the gradient for horse-drawn vehicles, while inconvenient narrow roads were abandoned. Puckeridge Lane, leading from Ross to Deep Dean, was discontinued as a turnpike road after the Ross Road Act of 1791 and officially 'stopped up' as a highway in 1820.[31] Now defined as a footpath, this lane provides a good example of an eighteenth-century road.

Another road that closed during the mid-nineteenth century was Didley Bridge Road in Kilpeck[32] (Pl. 4). Now a perfect example of a green lane leading from Gallows Knapp it proceeds past a semi-derelict cottage, over the Hereford-Abergavenny railway and across the course of an earlier tramway, which operated from 1829-53. Didley Bridge Road obviously formed part of a longer route, which

Plate 4. Footpath, Didley Bridge Road, Kilpeck.

COUNTY OF HEREFORD.

PARISHES OF
Kilpeck & Saint Devereux.

NOTICE IS HEREBY GIVEN,

That on the Third day of JANUARY next, application will be made to her Majesty's Justices of the Peace, assembled at Quarter Sessions, in and for the said County, for an **ORDER FOR STOPPING UP**, as useless and unnecessary, a certain **PUBLIC HIGHWAY**, situate partly in each of the said Parishes of KILPECK and SAINT DEVEREUX, commencing at a certain public Highway leading from Trelough and Kilpeck towards and into the Village of Kiverknoll and the City of Hereford, near to a place called Lath Bridge, in the said Parish of Kilpeck; and continuing from thence past a certain Cottage and Garden, occupied by Elizabeth Morgan, in the said Parish of Kilpeck; thence to the River Worm, the boundary between the said Parishes of Kilpeck and Saint Devereux; and from such boundary continuing through the said Parish of Saint Devereux, crossing the Abergavenny and Hereford Tram-road, and ending at a certain Cottage and Premises, in the occupation of John Built, at the Village of Didley, in the said Parish of Saint Devereux (excepting and reserving always to the Owners and Occupiers of the several Messuages, Lands, Tenements, and Hereditaments, adjoining and abutting on the said Highway so intended to be stopped up, a Road for Husbandry purposes, and also excepting and reserving a public Footpath along the same.) And that the Certificate of two Justices, having viewed the same, with a Plan of the said Highway, will be lodged with the Clerk of the Peace of the said County, at his Office, at the Shirehall, on the First day of December next.

Dated the Second day of November, One Thousand Eight Hundred and Fifty-two.

JAMES WILLIAMS, *Surveyors of the Parish*
JOSIAH RIDGWAY, *of Kilpeck.*
WALTER PROSSER, *Surveyors of the Parish*
JOHN BRISBANE, *of Saint Devereux.*

W. H. VALE, PRINTER, JOURNAL OFFICE, BROAD-STREET, HEREFORD.

Figure 2. Order for stopping up, 1852. Quarter sessions, HRO.

may be traced on an Ordnance Survey map, leading to Thruxton and Garway.

Droveways are adequately covered in various publications, but the actual routes remain undocumented and mainly undefined. It is estimated that every year 30,000 Welsh black cattle were driven through Herefordshire, using the byways in order to avoid paying a toll on the turnpike roads.[33] A green lane in Brilley parish was used by the drovers travelling from Newchurch in Radnorshire to the inn at Rhydspence. It is a continuation of Red Lane and features a typical wide droveway, which may be explored while following Offa's Dyke path.[34]

Industrial routes left a legacy of green lanes leading to mills, forges, quarries, limekilns and other sites. From the *Butcher's Arms* at Woolhope an unclassified road becomes a pleasant green lane winding its way to a quarry and limekiln on Bean Butts, where it continues as a footpath to Hooper's Oak. When lime was in demand for agriculture, building, tanning and medicinal purposes during the eighteenth century it was supplied from Woolhope at 12s a load and was ordered from Hereford or from the kiln itself.[35]

On some large Herefordshire estates avenues of trees were planted and laid out as rides, drives and walks for the gentry and their guests to enjoy. Although not strictly green lanes, those that have survived and are registered as rights of way ought to be included. From the *Harewood End Inn* a bridleway leads into Harewood Park, marked as Harewood Walk on an estate map of 1833 produced for Sir Hungerford Hoskyns.[36] At Monnington on Wye the Monnington Walk is a wide avenue of pines and yews probably planted during the seventeenth century by the Tomkyns family from Monnington Court.[37] It now forms a delightful stretch of the Wye Valley Walk between Byford and Brobury as admired by Kilvert in 1875.[38] From Stockton an obviously earlier route has been altered to form the Stockton Ride, which has recently been upgraded from a footpath to a bridleway (Pl. 5).

Plate 5. Bridleway, Stockton.

FUTURE PRESERVATION

Defining green lanes as footpaths or bridleways does not protect their physical character, although tougher hedgerow regulations under review in 1998 will help. Green lanes categorised as byways are in a stronger position. Landowners are not allowed to cultivate byways, so there is no advantage in grubbing up the hedgerows, which gives them a greater measure of protection.[39] Unclassified roads which remain unsurfaced still need to be monitored. One known as Bodicott Lane at Bredwardine is obstructed with barbed wire, and Hell's Ditch at Peterstow is unrecognisable as an unclassified road since a length of its hedges and banks were removed.[40] New legislation is required to protect the surviving green lanes, many of which serve as the only ancient monuments still in use thousands of years after their creation. This is a lengthy procedure and one that the local authorities did not recommend in 1997. Selected lanes of historical importance should be recorded on the Herefordshire Sites and Monuments Record, although the county archaeology service advises that lanes would be better protected through the planning process, hedgerow regulations, countryside stewardship or public rights of way.[41] The officer does welcome anything about green lanes if it is presented in a clear and concise way.

Perhaps the numerous green lanes of Herefordshire that are defined as footpaths and bridleways should be upgraded to byways. This reflects their former use, but also allows all traffic to use them. This is a controversial issue, which has led to the Department of the Environment producing practical guidelines.[42] It is from other sources that suggestions have been proposed for the preservation of green lanes defined as byways. An individual from Hereford and Worcester County Council appeals for an archaeological and historical status, while the Ramblers' Association seeks redefinition.[43] Meanwhile, the Countryside Commission is promoting 'greenways' as part of the government's sustainable transport policy.

The green lanes most at risk in Herefordshire are the unclaimed ones, which are shown as white lanes on Ordnance Survey Maps. In future they will be identified after liaising with local authorities.[44] Others need to be saved and added to the definitive map as byways. Any person can apply for a modification order as set out under the terms of the Wildlife and Countryside Act 1981, but the council must remain impartial before reaching a decision based on the facts presented.[45] If their application is successful and the green lane needs to retain its tranquil qualities, then a voluntary restriction agreement or traffic order may be necessary.[46] Another satisfactory method is the erection of a solid metal pole locked and placed 18in above the ground between the gateposts.[47]

The cycling fraternity describe white lanes as 'totally legal trails for cyclists, just waiting to be discovered and put on the Definitive Map'.[48] Riders are also pressing for the hundreds of miles of historic routes to be made legally available to equestrians. In the south of the county, the Ross-on-Wye and District Civic Society are campaigning to save unclaimed green lanes. With dedication and commitment they are compiling documentary and user evidence before applying for modification orders.

Finally, there is the question of green lanes in the future. At Walterstone, Perthe-Bach Lane is obstructed by overgrowth, but the dry weather path alongside is open and well signed. Holland Tuft Lane at Goodrich faces a struggle to survive as a bridleway, as the road it led to has been transformed into a dual carriageway where no horse or rider would be safe. If the bridleway at Peterchurch, called Pudding Lane, is not drained it will become out of use and the lane, which is now an unclassified road between Lewstone and Llangrove, is under threat if the gate at one end remains locked. These all face an uncertain future if their current situation is not resolved.

In 1998 the Countryside Commission's new proposals for 'Rights of Way in the 21st Century' was drafted. A number of their recommendations will need legislation and some will be controversial. Many points raised in this paper have been addressed. Perhaps the green lanes of tomorrow in Herefordshire will include disused railways, cycleways and the Countryside Commission's proposed 'greenways' which they propose as:

> a network of largely car-free off-road routes connecting people to facilities and open spaces in and around towns, cities and to the open countryside. For shared use by all people of all abilities on foot, bike or horseback, for commuting, play or leisure.[49]

APPENDIX

Examples of unclaimed lanes still in use but at risk of being lost:

Llanfrother Lane, Hentland   GRSO546289 to 543276

This ancient byway leading from Hoarwithy to Hentland probably pre-dates the sixth century, when St Dubricius founded his monastic college where Llanfrother Farm now stands. In 1633 Silas Taylor recorded some remaining foundations of this site in his history of Gavelkind. The lane has been in continual use and at its northern end forms the boundary between the parishes of Hentland and Harewood.

DOCUMENTATION: 1833 Harewood estate map, HRO AW22/1; 1835 Bryant's map; 1835 Knipe's map, 'parochial road'; 1842 Hentland tithe map; 1861 Llanfrother estate plan, 'Homestead road', HRO C15/3; 1870 Ross Highway Board minute book, 'Bridleway', HRO S36/M/9; 1895 Llanfrother deed, 'road', HRO C15; 1904 Ordnance Survey; 1910 Hentland Parish Council minute book, 'road', Hentland Parish Council; 1910 Finance Act plan and document, marked as public road, HRO AG9/14; 1926 Madeline Hopton, Notes of Hoarwithy, 'lane', HCL; 1935 Ordnance Survey; 1950 Hentland Parish schedule or information, 'cart road', Her.C.C; 1956 Ordnance Survey Sheet SO52; 1967 Ordnance Survey; 1988 Bartholomew Leisure Map of Hereford

Hell's Ditch, Peterstow   GRSO 554246 to 542235

An old road leading from Minnett Farm to Great Treaddow where hedges were removed in the 1980s, despite the green lane being defined as an unclassified road. The south-east end forms a parish boundary but is not claimed, although it is an obvious continuation of the road. It should be added to the definitive map as a byway together with the adjoining spur to Lower Hendre.

DOCUMENTATION: 1754 Taylor's map; 1819 Price's map; 1831 Ordnance Survey; 1835 Bryant's map; 1835 Knipe's map, 'parochial road'; 1839 Hentland and Peterstow tithe maps; 1867 Ross Highway Board minute book, 'road', HRO S36/M/9; 1896 Archenfield Magazine, 'road'; 1910 Finance Act map, marked as public road, HRO AG9/14 & 17; 1956 Ordnance Survey sheet SO52; 1985 Herefordshire County Road Map, UN71012 to Luke Brook, H&WCC; 1989 Ordnance Survey Pathfinder Sheet 1064; 1995 Peterstow News Issue 10 'to be given the status of a byway'.

The Green Lane, Orcop   GRSO481281 to 464281

A typical green lane, forming the boundary between Orcop and Much Dewchurch. The lane originally led to common land on Orcop Hill which was enclosed by an act of 1814. The lane was used by the landowner, and 'other persons', to reach an enclosure occupied by James Morgan in 1826. After this date the lane appears to have been extended to Lower Butts.

Although waterlogged in wet weather the lane is regularly used by walkers and riders. The eastern end at Lower Butts has become overgrown and obstructs the way, but definitive footpaths MD17 and OC16 give access onto the lane.

DOCUMENTATION: 1814 Inclosure Act, HRO; 1826 Inclosure award, HRO QS/RI/37; 1835 Knipe's map 'parochial road'; 1841 Much Dewchurch tithe map; 1843 Orcop tithe map; 1910 Finance Act plan, marked as 'Green Lane', HRO sheet 45; 1920 Mynde Park Estate sale particulars, HRO M5/23/77; 1956 Ordnance Survey sheet SO52; 1979 Ordnance Survey Landranger sheet 161; 1989 Definitive Map sheet SO42NE, H&WCC; 1992 Photograph of the Green Lane at Lower Butts, D. Coleman, *Orcop*.

REFERENCES

[1] J. Riddall & J. Trevelyan, *Rights of Way: A Guide to Law and Practice 2nd ed.* (1992), 32.

[2] I. Taylor, *Map of Hereford*, (1754).

[3] CPRE, Herefordshire District Hedgerow Regulations Update (1997).

[4] Ross Road Act, 1815.

[5] H. Hurley, *The Old Roads of South Herefordshire* (1992), 7-8.

[6] Quarter sessions, Trinity 1871, HRO Q/SRL/159.

[7] J. Webb, Pengethly and Scudamore Papers (*c*1850), HL.

[8] Quarter sessions, Epiphany 1825 HRO Q/SRL/113.

[9] Recorded as: Puckeridge Lane - Ross Road Act 1791; Old Ford Road - S.H Martin 'The Ballingham Charters' in *TWNFC*, XXXIV (1953), 71-73; Pudding Lane - Valuation Plan sheet XXXVII (1910); Gore and Crowmer Lane - A. Bryant, Map of Herefordshire (1835).

[10] The Footpaths of Whitchurch (1993); Map of Gorsley in the Parish of Linton (1993).

[11] Herefordshire County Council, Roads and Bridges Dept, List of Unclassified Roads (1936).

[12] H&WCC, Definitive Map 1989, County of Herefordshire Road Map (*c*1985).

[13] Countryside Commission, *Out in the Country* (1992), 26.

[14] National Parks and Access to the Countryside Act 1949.

[15] H. & J. Hurley, *The Wye Valley Walk* (1994), 43.   [16] op cit. note 2.

[17] Countryside Act 1968.   [18] Dept. of Environment, Hedgerow Regulations 1997.

[19] H. Price, *Map of Herefordshire* (1817).

[20] Quarter sessions, Epiphany 1759, HRO Q/SR/46-7.

[21] H&WCC Draft Milestones Statement 1996, 7.   [22] op. cit. in note 5.

[23] J. H Turner, *Herefordshire Countryside Treasures* (1981), 40.

[24] *Hereford Times*, 5 March 1998.   [25] Tom Greaves, *The Parish Boundary* (1987), 3-4.

[26] op cit. in note 19.   [27] op cit. in note 15, 71.

[28] Quarter sessions, Michaelmas 1799, HRO Q/SR/87.   [29] op cit. in note 11, 31.

[30] Ledbury Road Act 1721; Gloucester to Hereford Road Act 1726.

[31] Quarter sessions, Michaelmas 1820, HRO Q/SR/116.

[32] Quarter sessions, Epiphany, 1853, HRO Q/SR/139-41.

[33] S. & B. Webb, *Story of the King's Highway*, (1933), 68.

[34] J. B. Jones, *Offa's Dyke Path* (1976), 49.   [35] *Hereford Journal*, 30 April 1794.

[36] Maps of the Property of Sir H. Hoskyns (1833), HRO AW 22/1.

[37] *TWNFC*, VI (1870), 312-313.

[38] F. Kilvert, *Diary 1870-1879*, ed. W. Plomer (1977), 303.

[39] Herefordshire Council, Environmental Directorate, letter to author 1998.

[40] Ross-on-Wye Civic Society, Right of Way sub-committee, corres. with the society 1994-6.

[41] Hereford & Worcester County Archaeological Service, letter to author, 19 March 1998.

[42] Dept of the Environment, *Making the Best of Byways* (1997).

[43] Hereford and Worcester County Council, *Wayout* (Winter 1997/8), 5.

[44] Ordnance Survey, customer information (1997).   [45] op cit. in note 43, Summer 1997, 5.

[46] op cit. note 42.   [47] As seen by the author in Fife (1998).

[48] Countryside Commission, *Gearing Up* (1997), 8.

[49] Countryside Commission, Newspaper no. 87, Summer 1998, 4.

Roger of Hereford:
Astrology and the School of Hereford

ROGER FRENCH

INTRODUCTION

It is appropriate to mark the anniversary of the Woolhope Club with a record of Roger of Hereford, for he was in a sense a local product. He lived in the late twelfth century and held lands in Sufton, in the parish of Mordiford, where the shale breaks through the overlying Old Red Sandstone to form the northern edge of the Woolhope Dome. The family still live at Sufton Court; Roger was known in the medieval Latin of his time as *de Herefordia* and the family were 'de Hereford' until comparatively recently.[1]

The name is not unimportant for the topic of this chapter. This is because Roger was an astrologer. There were no pejorative connotations of the term among the laymen of the twelfth century; indeed astrology was seen as exciting and powerful, and Roger did his best to make it acceptable to the church. But it could not be had at home. Men who knew that Arabic culture contained desirable things concerned with the technical subjects of medicine, mathematics and astronomy (the theoretical basis of astrological practice) had to travel to places like Spain, where the Christians were slowly pushing Islam southwards and learning about its culture as they did so. We do not know if Roger travelled to Spain as a centre of translation (his writings were nevertheless very close to his Arabic sources) but he would have been known as *de Herefordia* only when away from home. His close friend, Alfred 'of Shareshill' only needed a toponymic for a surname when among strangers who asked him where he came from – in the first instance they were probably his countrymen in different towns; when he travelled and mixed with Spaniards and Jews who helped him translate some of Aristotle's works from the Arabic, he was known as 'the Englishman'.

Roger's historical importance is that he flourished just at the time when Aristotle's works on the natural world were becoming known again in Western Europe.[2] The importance of this for the intellectual and educational history of Europe was immense. It happened at the same time as the first European universities appeared, and the university arts course made Aristotle canonical down to the seventeenth century. To be educated, for the man who chose not to go on to be a doctor, a lawyer or a theologian, was to be Aristotelian. To be more precise, Roger flourished at a time when knowledge of the Aristotelian books on nature were known mostly only by medical men in Salerno, in southern Italy.[3] The universities were then simply schools of the arts, but they rapidly became *studia generalia*, schools teaching all the subjects, including the new Aristotle. Alfred, Roger's friend, spans the period in a way that Roger does not: Alfred translated from the Arabic a text on plants, apparently by Aristotle, and dedicated it to Roger. He addresses Roger generously as a learned man, but Roger's writings bear no evidence that he knew of the new Aristotle.[4] Alfred's translation became part of the curriculum in Oxford, and his treatise on the motion of the heart was statutory in the universities of thirteenth-century Italy. But the Aristotelianism of the university arts course promulgated a physical view of the cosmos, in which actual spheres carried the stars and planets round the central sphere of the earth. This was quite different from the purely mathematical model of the cosmos described by astronomers like Ptolemy, who explained the movements of the planets with the help of geometry rather than physical models.

Roger's importance, then, was that just before the creation of an 'official', or university, view of the heavens (based on physical spheres) he made available for the first time to Englishmen a mathematical and above all *predictive* science of astrology.[5] There had been a notable English interest in natural matters even before the Conquest and more recently before Roger's time the geographical concentration of this interest had been the west midlands. Walcher, Prior of Malvern, was the first Englishman to own an astrolabe. There was the scandal of the bishop of Hereford (and then of York) who died with a naughty astrological book under his pillow. There had been long-standing belief that the stars somehow governed one's life and that it was therefore important to know under what stars one had been born, but it was by Roger's use of Arabic material that English astrologers came to believe that precise predictions could be made.[6]

THE SCHOOL AT HEREFORD

Hereford was an important town for the Norman kings of England. Not only was it a major economic resource, but it was a border settlement, helping to hold the Marches against the Welsh. Borders are special places, where ruling ideologies have to be reinforced and where there is opportunity to discover about opposing ideologies in order to attempt to destroy them. It was a Norman-Muslim border, in Sicily, that was second only to the Christian-Muslim border at Toledo as a centre of translation where prelates and princes as well as scholars sought to understand aspects of Arabic culture. Medieval schools were efficient propagators of ideology. When in the first years of the thirteenth century (perhaps Roger was still alive) the fourth crusade was diverted against Byzantium, one of the first actions of the Western Church was, ironically enough, to set up a new school to re-educate the Greeks who had been, classically, the foundation of Western Latin learning. When, a little later, there was heresy around Toulouse the school there was hastily upgraded to be a *studium generale* to teach Aristotelian doctrines useful against the heretics.[7] Resources may well have been put in to the school at Hereford, where the proximity of a different culture was well known.[8] The resistance of the Welsh to Norman claims of sovereignty came to a head in the fierce revolt towards the end of the thirteenth century.

Like most schools that at Hereford was an outgrowth of the cathedral. Cathedrals since Carolingian times had had the duty to educate the clergy for purposes of liturgy and administration, and the man with the responsibility for the school was the chancellor, acting for the bishop. With the growth of urbanisation in the eleventh and twelfth centuries the clergy of towns found that they were practising a more practical and pastoral care than had been needed in the reflective and cloistered life of the monasteries. Instead of contemplating the levels of meaning of the sacred page the urban clerical teachers taught more practical subjects like the seven liberal arts.

Logic above all was valued for its merit in communication and persuasion, and a famous teacher of logic could attract pupils from across Europe. This was 'heroic' teaching, and the fame of a heroic teacher was such that pupils would be attracted to him rather than to the school. But at some point in the late twelfth century, the masters of the big schools decided they could do better for themselves by collaborating rather than competing as heroic teachers. They formed a *consortium*, essentially a medieval guild of teaching masters, deciding on a curriculum and sharing out the work. This formal organisation of the schools came at the same time as the translation and use of the physical works of Aristotle. These were adopted with enthusiasm in Oxford by teachers like John Blund and, in the earlier thirteenth century, Adam of Buckfield; and Alfred of Shareshill's commentaries of some of the physical works formed part of slightly later formal commentaries. In Paris, in contrast, the physical works of Aristotle were banned in 1210 and again in 1215 and did not become part of the curriculum until the middle of the century, when the church had given thought to how the works of Aristotle, who did not mention a Creator, could be taught in Christian schools.[9]

The school at Hereford fits into this context.[10] It was the school of the cathedral. There is some evidence that Roger was a canon of the cathedral, and there is abundant evidence that bishops of Hereford were patrons of the new learning. We know about the school mostly from a poem written by another canon, Simon du Fresne, who hoped to attract to the school the famous scholar Gerald of Wales, Giraldus Cambrensis.[11] The school he describes – in rather fulsome terms – taught the whole range of subjects we should expect in a *studium* that had not yet adopted the physical works of Aristotle as part of the curriculum. Simon mentions the *trivium*, a group of three subjects, grammar, rhetoric and logic, that made up the early parts of the arts course and which later, when the universities turned their attention more to philosophy, were pejoratively labelled *trivial*, indicating their introductory nature. The later part of the arts course was the *quadrivium*, a group of four quantitative subjects that, as Simon says, with the *trivium* comprised the seven liberal arts. The quadrivial subjects were firstly arithmetic (Simon says that the *ars numerosa* discusses solid, plane and cubic numbers) and secondly music, the art of proportions.

The third quadrivial subject was geometry and the fourth astronomy. It is in these that we feel the presence of Roger in the school at Hereford. Simon spends no more than a couplet on each of the other seven arts but devotes a much greater space to the subjects we would expect Roger as an astrologer to be concerned with. What was important for Simon in the practice of geometry was not so much diagrams on flat surfaces as the use of the astrolabe in surveying, for example in determining the height of towers. The astrolabe was primarily an instrument for taking celestial observations and was central to the astrology practised by Roger, who assumes his readers will be familiar with the parts and use of the device. Simon also gives a couplet to this astrolabe-based 'geometry' and another to astronomy, the art in which the motions of the sun and moon are studied and in which eclipses are predicted (he says).[12] The motion of the moon and the occurrence of eclipses was again central to astrology, more so in fact than to astronomy. But it is when Simon comes to the person of the astrologer – the *astrologus* – that we see Roger most directly. Eight lines of the poem are devoted to this teacher and his topic, four times as much as to others. Simon does not mention Roger by name, for he was after all describing the offices or establishment of the school, but there can be little doubt about Roger's pre-eminence at the school; he was almost an heroic teacher.

Simon's poem tells us more about the school in Hereford. Two lines are given over to the teaching of the 'new' and 'old' law, where the new seems to have been the recently re-discovered Roman or Civil Law which had been of so much interest earlier in the twelfth century in Bologna. It was primarily the law of the Emperor Justinian and so of great interest to the medieval Holy Roman Emperor, who claimed the old imperial powers and jurisdiction in Italy. It is not clear from Simon's words whether Canon Law was included, but it is notable that both kinds of law came to be higher faculties in the developing universities, and the presence of law in Hereford indicates the extent to which the school was complete. Of the two other higher faculties, theology and medicine, we know from other sources (of rather later date) that there were theologians in Hereford and we can perhaps take for granted that as a cathedral school it was not failing in its duties to educate its clergy in the queen of the sciences.[13] It has been suggested that medicine was also taught in Hereford. Finally, Simon mentions, in another couplet, the subject *fisis*. This was *physis*, or 'nature'. Sometimes in medieval sources the term means 'medicine', for the doctor presented himself as an expert on the natural world (the term gave rise to 'physician'). But Simon's terminology suggests natural philosophy, of a pre-Aristotelian kind: how the world is composed of elements and matter. It was within this topic in a school that the components of Aristotle's natural philosophy would have been assembled as they became known to the learned world.

There seems to have been no ideological clash between astrology and church doctrine in Hereford. Simon, a canon of the cathedral, clearly thought that predicting the future was among the attractions of the school. Having spent as much as ten lines on the art of the astronomer and astrologer, he goes on at once to the *geomanticus*, the geomancer who may not have been Roger, who seems not to have written on the topic. But it was an art closely related to astrology. It was the technique of making predictions from patterns made on a diagram by throwing down some earth. Like astrology, this art was derived from the new translations from the Arabic, and Gerard of Cremona said that geomancy was derived from the truth of astrology. It took its technical terms from astrology and had the same 'houses', judgments and signs. It was based on the motions of the celestial bodies, like astrology. Like astrology, with the aid of calculations it made predictions about events on earth that were important to the geomancer's client. Geomancy was often seen as a branch of astrology that had the attraction of not needing tables of planetary motion nor observation of the skies. It was important enough for Simon to spend six lines on the topic, second only to the eight he spent on astrology. Clearly the predictive arts and the theory (astronomy) necessary for their practice were important to Simon and were a major feature of the school at Hereford.[14]

HEREFORD AND OXFORD

Simon did not succeed in attracting Gerald of Wales to Hereford. Perhaps Gerald did not approve of astrology, which Simon had recommended so energetically and possibly a little naively. Certainly Gerald did not like the new translations of the Aristotelian physical works, fearing that they would lead to heresy. Gerald was one of a number of men connected with each other, with the developing *studium* in Oxford and with Hereford. Gerald read his *Topographia Hibernia* to the assembled scholars of Oxford in 1190, the year in which the bishop of Hereford, William de Vere gave him a Hereford prebend.[15] We have seen that Alfred of Shareshill addressed his translation of the pseudo-Aristotelian work on plants to Roger; he also dedicated his tract on the motion of the heart to Alexander Neckham. The first work was used in teaching natural philosophy in Oxford and the second became statutory in Paris. Neckham taught in both Oxford and Paris, and records that sometimes the new Aristotle was read rather secretly, no doubt as a result of the church's ambivalent attitude towards it.[16] One of the biggest names in the history of medieval natural philosophy, Robert Grosseteste, was in the service of the bishop of Hereford in the 1190s and may well have been, therefore, in Hereford when Roger was there. It has been claimed that Grosseteste was a Master of Oxford, and it is clear from Gerald of Wales that Grosseteste was a Master of some *studium* before 1198.[17] The evidence that Roger was a graduate of Oxford is more tenuous.[18] Grosseteste may well have returned to Oxford when bishop de Vere died in 1199.

The circle of men that related Hereford to Oxford had links with the English west midlands. As late as Roger's time the influence of the Celtic church was considerable. At Deerhurst, near Tewkesbury, there had been considerable interplay between the Celtic and Saxon traditions (the remarkable Saxon church at Deerhurst is well known). A major point at issue was the church calendar, the topic of the computists. The story of Walcher of Malvern with his astrolabe, knowledge of which soon spread to other western towns, is matched by the Worcester chronicles that record an eclipse, the whole of the story of the Hereford school, and the connections with Oxford.

PATRONAGE

The group of men in the Hereford–Oxford circle may have been held together partly through patronage. As it was a cathedral school, we have to assume that the astrology taught at Hereford had not attracted the censure of the church, and in some sense it patronised those of its canons who taught astrology and the men to whom it gave prebends. It may be that the bishops of Hereford, well known for their philosophical interests, were particularly accommodating. But there was the potential for a considerable clash of ideologies. The principal feature of Roger's astrology was that it was *predictive*, offering rules for foretelling future events with the promise of mathematical precision. But to churchman elsewhere this seemed to detract from the freedom of the human will, and from the nature of God, to whose omnipotence alone the future was known. Daniel of Morley, meeting the great translator Gerard of Cremona in Toledo in the previous century, had been fascinated and horrified at the promise of Arabic predictive astrology, for these reasons. When Daniel had an embarrassing interview on the way home with the bishop of Norwich, he remembered that Gerard had explained that the predictions of astrology were concerned with the *tendencies* of sublunar matter to move in ways determined by the motion of the celestial bodies, and that these tendencies could be averted by human action.[19]

Outside the *studia*, astrology was important in princely courts, where the outcome of military, political and dynastic endeavours was of direct concern. The English and French monarchs vigorously defended the schools of Oxford and Paris, a form of patronage that ensured a supply of educated masters for administrative and political tasks. While the church was ambivalent to the new Aristotle and to astrology, the king could patronise the new learning to advantage at court. This was the world where Roger's texts were important. He cast a horoscope for Eleanor of Aquitaine, wife of Henry II. Henry had been taught some astrology when young by Adelard of Bath and seems to have retained an interest in the subject. He appointed Roger a Royal Justice as part of a new scheme of appointing learned men rather than local magnates as justices. A colleague of Roger's in this position was Walter Map, another learned man and a correspondent of Gerald of Wales. Walter was also a protégé of Gilbert Foliot, bishop of Hereford, and so (perhaps like Roger too) benefited from both sources of patronage. Indeed, whatever the views of the church on astrology, it needed technical expertise to determine the date of Easter, the sort of expertise developed by Roger in his *Compotus*. This sort of material had been of interest in Hereford since at least the time of Robert of Losinga, who had been made bishop of Hereford in 1079, partly as a result of his attention to the new learning. He too was known as an astronomer and his computistic works are extant, as are those on the motion of the moon, a topic equally important in ecclesiastic as in astrological calculations.

ROGER'S ASTROLOGY

Mathematically predictive astrology depended on accurate knowledge of the motions of the heavenly bodies. It was believed in Roger's time that the earth was a fixed sphere around which revolved the stars, which were always in the same position relative to each other, and were consequently called 'fixed'. This simple picture was enormously complicated by the two facts that the whole fixed 'map' of stars varied in time in its position to any fixed point observable on earth (generally the horizon); and that the planets, while generally sharing this characteristic motion, also varied in the speed of rotation, sometimes even going backwards in relation to the fixed stars. The whole practice of predictive astrology, based on the motions of the planets rather that that of the constellations, depended on being able to find their position accurately. This depended in turn on calculated tables of planetary appearance, and these tables differed according to the latitude of the place from which the observations were made. For these purposes Hereford was in the distant north, for Arabic and Greek treatises had been based on observations to the south. Roger based his tables on those of Toledo, where the translations from the Arabic had been made.

The rules of the astrological art as set out by Roger are very complex.[20] It is best to approach them from a practical rather than theoretical direction. The astrologer served his customer by answering questions important in his life.[21] Would he have sons? Would he recover the stolen gold? Was this a good time to begin a voyage? The technique was first to make a note of the time when the question was asked. This supplied, via the planetary tables, the position of the celestial bodies. One of these, often the moon, was then identified with the 'querent', the man who had asked the question. If it was not appropriate to choose the moon, the astrologer sought the 'Lord of the Ascendant', a planet identified by means of the sign that was rising at that moment. The matter in hand – the querent's question – also had a 'Lord', determined by its astrological affinities. The outcome of the querent's question was then answered from a knowledge of the course of the two 'Lords' through the features of the heavens.

These features were complex. The whole of the great sphere of the heavens revolved around the earth once in 24 hours. The great broad circle in which the sun, moon and other planets moved was divided into the twelve signs of the zodiac, 'signs' because, as Roger knew, the constellations that had given rise to the names of Aries, Taurus and so on had shifted their relative positions since ancient times and no longer marked the divisions of the zodiac. But there was also a frame of reference based on fixed points on the immobile earth, so that all the revolving celestial bodies passed through these 'houses' every day, but at different positions according to the seasons, just as the sun was higher in the summer than the winter. Arabic astrologers differed somewhat in their method of constructing the houses (domification) and Roger adopted a comparatively simple method.

Moreover, each planet had its favoured location in these houses, one for the day and another for the night. In its favoured position it exerted its influence most strongly on the earth, and each planet had its characteristic powers. Mars was baleful, hot and warlike, Venus soft, moist and beautiful, Jupiter (the Greek Zeus) masterful and just. The mathematics of the situation was largely a question of 'aspects' of the planets, that is, the geometrical angles presented by their relative positions. Planets at opposite sides of the sky were 'in opposition' at 180 degrees apart, a position where their influences were largely mutually negated. Planets in conjunction, that is, within a few degrees of each other generally acted in concert with each other. The position of 45 degrees was 'square' and of 30 degrees was 'trine', and astrological lore was very much concerned with the good and bad implications of such geometry. A planet 'in retrograde', that is, moving backwards across the 'map' of fixed stars, did not portend well for the querent.

The signs had special relationships with parts of the body, so that Aries for example as the first of the signs, was concerned with the head, and Taurus, the second, with the throat. The other signs followed, finishing with Pisces, the last of them, governing the feet. Moreover, the planets too had special relationships with the body, relationships that changed systematically as the planets moved through the signs, that is, the seasons that made up a full year. Thus, for example, Saturn in Aries controlled the chest while in Aries, but in Taurus had moved to the belly. By Sagittarius it had reached the feet, and in the next sign, Capricorn, it started again at the head. Jupiter, the next planet, started lower in the body – the belly – when in Aries, and worked down the body, beginning the cycle again at the head in Sagittarius, one sign before Saturn began again. The starting points were shared out among the planets so that each of them in turn (in the order Saturn, Jupiter, Mars, Sun, Venus, Mercury and Moon) began at a subsequently lower place on the body and followed the others in a cycle.

These relationships enabled the astrologer to say something about diseases and their outcomes, and many an ill person consulted astrologers, especially at Roger's time, when the medical men had not yet given their subject an Aristotelian rationality. Like the medical man, the astrologer had to convince his client that he knew what he was about, indeed, that he had an unrivalled knowledge of cosmic causality and could fit the client's problems into that and so explain them. Medical men were quite explicit about the advantages of dazzling their patients with their science, and much of the technical detail of both medicine and astrology could be used as consulting-room patter.

The astrologer's clients also fell into categories determined by the planets, and Roger gives the details of the characteristics of a Saturnine or Martial man, taken from the qualities of the planets: the Martial man was warlike and angry. Planetary patronage of this sort added greatly to what the astrologer could say about and to his clients. In a similar way different countries on earth, different human institutions, from families and monarchies to prisons, inheritance, power and even death, were categorised in groups, largely on the basis of the 'houses' of the heavens. These were the divisions of the sky fixed in relation to the earth, so that all revolving heavenly bodies passed through them. At the most direct level all celestial bodies passed through the houses every 24 hours, and the astrologer could observe and calculate the positions, particularly the risings and settings, down to a second of time. This was the basic motion of the celestial bodies. More elaborate 'motions' were the yearly motion by which the bodies moved higher and lower in the sky, and the more elaborate motions of the planets (literally 'wanderers') as they moved across the map of fixed stars. What we loosely call a horoscope was for Roger and the astrologers a 'nativity' – a plan of the houses and the position of the planets at the precise moment of birth. This was the celestial environment of the client, through which moved the celestial body chosen to represent him.

CONCLUSION

The rules set out by Roger for making astrological judgments were reconstructed from newly-recovered Arabic sources (it is just possible that he knew of these sources, or had help in translating them, from the Jewish community in Hereford). The rules were long lived, ultimately Greek in origin, and they survived in popular culture in a surprisingly conservative way at least down to William Lilly in the seventeenth century. The chief characteristic of this astrology was that it allowed prediction of particulars with a great show of theoretical apparatus and mathematical precision. None of this was known in England, as far as we can tell, before Roger, who accordingly has an important place in the circle of Englishmen who are becoming increasingly well known among historians for their adaptation of the new arts and sciences being sought from Arabic sources.

REFERENCES
[1] See John Duncomb, *Collections towards the History and Antiquities of the County of Hereford*, vol. 1 (1804), vol 2 part 1 (1812) vol 3, W. H. Cook (1882), 68. By tradition Walter of Hereford, sheriff of Hereford in 1155 and Robert de Hereford, fined in 1158 for homicide, are members of Roger's family. Major Robert Hereford recalls the family once had court rolls of the twelfth century. (Personal communication.)
[2] There has been some interest in Roger and the west midlands of England since Haskins: C. H. Haskins, 'The reception of Arabic Science in England', *The English Historical Review*, XXX (1915) 56-69; 65. See also J. C. Russell, 'Hereford and Arabic science in England about 1175-1200', *Isis*, XVIII (1932) 14-25. Fundamental for recent work is the unpublished M. Phil. dissertation (1991) in History and Philosophy of Science, University of Cambridge, by N. Whyte: '*Roger of Hereford's* Liber de astronomice iudicandi: *A Twelfth-Century Astrologer's Manual*'. Important also are Jennifer Moreton, 'Before Grosseteste: Roger of Hereford and calendar reform in eleventh- and twelfth-century England', *Isis*, XVIII (1995) 562-586 and (on the importance of the Hereford region) C. Burnett, 'Mathematics and astronomy in Hereford and its region in the twelfth century', in *Hereford: Medieval Art, Architecture and Archaeology*, The British Archaeological Association, Conference Transactions, XV, ed. David Whitehead, Leeds, 1995, 50-59. See also Roger French, 'Foretelling the future. Arabic astrology and English medicine in the late twelfth century', *Isis*, LXXXVII, (1996) 453-480.
[3] On Salerno see D. Jacquart, 'Aristotelian thought in Salerno' in P. Dronke, ed., *A History of Twelfth-Century Western Philosophy*, (1988), pp. 407-428.
[4] Alfred calls him *dilectissimi mi Rogere*: See the critical edn. of the text by H. J. Drossaart Lulofs and E. L. J. Poortman, *Nicholas Damascenus De Plantis. Five Translations*, (1989), p.516.
[5] On the utility of the study of the heavens, see C. Burnett, 'Adelard, Ergaphalau and the science of the stars', in C. Burnett, ed., *Adelard of Bath. An English Scientist and Arabist of the early Twelfth Century*, (1987).
[6] Roger's claim to originality was that he was the first to bring together into a working

system the scattered fragments of astrology for the benefit of its practitioners. Cambridge, University Library mss I.11, f.40r: *Quoniam regulas artis astronomice iudicandi non nisi per diversas opera dispersas invenimus utili astrologorum desiderio satisfacere cupientes eisque ubi necesse fuerit explanacionem sive supplemencionem apponentes in unum breviter colligemus.*

[7] See Roger French and Andrew Cunningham, *Before Science. The Invention of the Friars' Natural Philosophy* (1996).

[8] Hereford was sometimes referred to as if it were in Wales, and Pits says that Roger was born *apud Herefordium in confinibus Cambriae.* See *Ioannis Pitsei Angli S. Theologiae Doctoris...Relationum Historicarum in Rebus Anglicis tomus primus* (1618), 964.

[9] Many of the documents relating to heresy, the masters' consortium and the bowdlerizing of Aristotle can be found in *Chartularium Universitatis Parisiensis,* ed. H. Denifle, O.P.(1889) vol. 1.

[10] This never became a university, but rivalled a number of English provincial schools, like that at Northampton, which were the kind of material from which Oxford, and a little later Cambridge, were founded.

[11] The relevant portion of the poem is given by R. W. Hunt, 'English learning in the late twelfth century', in R. W. Southern, *ed. Essays in Medieval History,* (1969), 106-128.

[12] Roger refers to the eclipse of 1178 that was visible in Hereford. Roger's work was composed, the scribe, or Roger himself, wrote, *a magistro Rogero super annos Domini ad mediam noctem Herefordiae anno ab incarnatione Domini m⁰c⁰lxx⁰viii⁰ post eclipsim quae contingit Herefordiae eodem anno.* Quoted by Thomas Wright, *Biographica Britannica Literaria* (1846), 218.

[13] Simon's name appears on a charter together with that of another Simon, whose surname was probably Melun and who is described as a theologian. See Russell, 'Hereford and Arabic science'.

[14] On geomancy see T. Charmasson, *Recherches sur une Technique Divinatoire: la Géomancy dans l'Occident Médiéval* (1980), 9, and Burnett, 'Mathematics'.

[15] On de Vere see Julia Barrow, 'A twelfth century bishop and literary patron: William de Vere', *Viator,* XVIII (1987) 175-189; 179.

[16] He taught in Oxford in the last decade of the twelfth century. Hunt 'English learning', p.107.

[17] On Grosseteste see J. McEvoy, *The Philosophy of Robert Grosseteste* (1982); and R. W. Southern, *Robert Grosseteste. The Growth of an English Mind in Medieval Europe* (1986).

[18] It has been suggested that Alfred's address to Roger is of a kind that would be made to master. See Southern (Grosseteste) p.91. Fuller asserts that Roger was in Cambridge in about 1170: see Thomas Fuller, *The History of the University of Cambridge from the Conquest to the year 1635,* ed. M. Prickett, (1834). Pits, *op. cit.* in note 8, claimed that Roger was a product of Oxford. Roger himself, in a *Compotus* written in 1167, said that he spent many years in the schools (*regimen scholarum*): see C. H. Haskins, 'The reception of Arabic Science in England', *The English Historical Review,* XXX (1915) 56-69; 65.

[19] See Roger French, 'Astrology in medical practice' in Luis Garcia-Ballester, Roger French, Jon Arrizabalaga and Andrew Cunningham, eds, *Practical Medicine from Salerno to the Black Death* (1994), 30-59

[20] Although Roger was an important figure too in the school of Hereford, his writings have no features of the classroom. He expected his readers to be familiar with the astrolabe and with the methods of dividing the heavens. He is didactic at the comparatively advanced level of 'domification', the different methods of finding the astrological 'houses'.

[21] The astrologer strove to make judgments and the astrology practised by Roger was therefore 'judicial' astrology. This is reflected in the titles of his two most important works, the *Liber de Tribus generalibus Judiciis Astronomie* and the *De iudiciis astronomie.* Neither has been published; I have used the following MSS.: Cambridge, CUL I.1.1., CUL Gg vi 3, Oxford, Bodleian, Selden supra 76 and Digby 149.

Parish Boundaries in Greytree Hundred

ROSAMUND E. SKELTON

INTRODUCTION

The object of this study is to look at the physical nature and location of parish boundaries shown on the tithe maps to find what evidence they yield for the history and inter-relationships of the parishes. Such boundaries can show the presence and form of cultivation at the period of their establishment.

GREYTREE HUNDRED

Greytree Hundred was selected because it was accessible. The hundred is a subdivision of the shire in theory composed of approximately 100 hides, and provided the basis for tax collection, local courts of justice and the pursuit of criminals.[1] The later medieval hundred of Greytree was formed from two Domesday hundreds, Greytree in the north and Bromsash in the south with a few additions and subtractions of parishes.

   The hundreds provided the basis for civil administration and taxation for 800 years. Their boundaries began to be altered after 1563 when responsibility for administering the poor law was given to parishes. In the Middle Ages some parishes were split between different hundreds; however, in the 1801 census the whole of the parish appeared in the same hundred.[2] As this study is concerned with information on the early boundaries it is proposed to study the hundred of Greytree with the townships recorded in the medieval tax lists.[3]

DEANERY AND PARISH

The parish is the basic unit of the ecclesiastical administration, grouped into deaneries as administrative units within the diocese. The boundaries have been recorded in documents from early times, often in Anglo-Saxon charters because of the obligation to pay tithes to support the parish church. Unfortunately, few such charters survive in Herefordshire so this study is based on the boundaries as recorded on the nineteenth-century tithe maps. Hereford diocese is thought to represent the extent of the early kingdom of the Magonsaete before it was absorbed into Mercia.[4] The parishes represent one of the earliest physically identifiable territorial units. However within the parishes were local communities represented in Domesday[5] terminology by the 'vill' and later equated with the township or tithing.[6] In this hundred many of the parishes contain more than one vill or township. The hundred is based on a group of townships so that some parishes lie partly in one hundred and partly in another. Foy is an example where the church is in the hundred of Wormelow while the township of Eaton Tregoes, separated from the church by the River Wye, is in Greytree hundred.

THE PHYSICAL NATURE OF PARISH BOUNDARIES

One of the reasons for carrying out this study is that modern farming methods increasingly threaten the physical survival of parish boundaries. Apart from the direct destruction by bulldozing hedgerows and banks and ploughing over them, there are more subtle changes such as piping small streams and rivulets, realigning winding streams in straight ditches, as has happened along the N.W. boundaries of Mordiford and Dormington. The plan (Fig. 1) shows which boundaries are along natural and which are along man-made features (Pl. 1). Physical features can be any of the following; rivers, streams, ridges, watersheds, while the man-made features are roads, tracks, footpaths, and field boundaries. Undefined boundaries are separately identified as there is no indication of their original state. Physical features such as streams and ridges form clearly recognisable boundaries in an area which was otherwise waste or woodland and are likely to be early. Next in age would be prehistoric tracks and Roman roads, followed by tracks of unknown date. The use of field boundaries indicates a very late definition of a boundary, after the land was in agricultural use. This could arise from (a) the splitting up of an earlier unit between other parishes e.g. Brockhampton, Buckenhill and Woolhope (see later) or (b) the detachment of individual manors from a township, where a powerful lord could unite detached manors into one parish, e.g. Woolhope and Putley (see later). This probably occurred at an early period in the development of parishes.

Plate 1. Boundary along a watershed - a large willow on the left marks the site of a spring from which the parish and county boundary between Aston Ingham on the left and Longhope, Gloucestershire, on the right snakes up the hillside along a hedge full of holly which separates the streams flowing north to the Ell Brook from the streams flowing south to the Longhope Brook. Three of the trees along the hedge are very ancient pollarded oaks.

Some boundaries are an intermixture of natural and man-made features, and some natural features can be shown on the ground to have been 'improved' by the digging of a deeper ditch and creation of a hedge-bank on one side. Elsewhere the absence of a natural feature is met by creating a hedge, bank and ditch to link two streams used as boundaries. Both these examples occur on the Upton Bishop and Much Marcle boundary at grid references SO674.269 and SO668.272 respectively (Pl. 2).

Plate 2. Man-made boundary - ditch and bank marking the boundary between Much Marcle on the left and Linton on the right, it links two lengths of boundary along streams.

The scale of the plan showing Greytree hundred (Fig. 1) only allows a distinction to be made between natural and man-made features as these show the most significant difference in terms of age of definition. Comments will only be made on the most significant interpretations arising from the nature of the boundaries while considering the inter-relationships between groups of parishes. Due to lack of time it has not been possible to study all the relevant documentary sources, but the study has raised a number of queries which further documentary study might elucidate.

INTER-RELATIONSHIPS OF GROUPS OF PARISHES
MORDIFORD AND DORMINGTON
The boundaries of both these parishes converge on the Pentaloe Wells near Seager Hill on the Woolhope boundary while their N.W. boundaries lie on the rivers Lugg and Frome (Pl. 3). The adjacent parishes of Stoke Edith and Tarrington in an adjoining hundred also fan out in the same way from the Pentaloe Wells. Each parish therefore had a proportionate amount of the wooded hills and riverside meadows. It appears likely that these four parishes are subdivisions of an earlier territorial unit at the junction of the Frome and Lugg valleys.

FIG. 1
PARISH BOUNDARIES IN GREYTREE HUNDRED
as shown on 19th century Tithe Maps

LEGEND

⌒	Natural Boundaries
- - -	Former line of river
· · · ·	Man-made Boundaries
....	Undefined Boundaries
○●○●	Documentary Evidence for Boundary
·—·	Hundred and Township Boundary only
✳	Iron Age Hillfort
+	Site of Church or Chapel
FOY	Parish Name
Hom	Chapel Name
⊢——→	Detached portion of a parish

Mordiford church is located in the extreme S.W. corner of the parish about 2km and 3km respectively from Priors Frome and Checkley, the main settlements. Priors Frome is mentioned in 1086[7] and in all the subsequent tax lists, while Mordiford is not mentioned until 1148 and is said to be 'in the Henry de Ferrers' manor of Frome

Plate 3. The Pentaloe Wells are just to the left of the white tree guard just below the track on the right of the photograph. This is the meeting point of five parishes, Woolhope in the foreground, the conifer wood on the left is in Mordiford, the adjacent field and wood beside a track is in Dormington, while the field on the right is split between Stoke Edith and Tarrington.

in 1086'.[8] This manor was held by Alfgeat from Bishop Aethelstan before 1066 and the survival of a Norman doorway and a central tower in the church indicates an early church of some status.[9] Since the majority of the population of the parish was located in Priors Frome and Checkley the reason for the church being on the edge of the parish requires some explanation. Geographically it is on the main access roads to both Woolhope and Fownhope and could equally serve these areas as well as Mordiford parish, so it may have been an early minster church serving the whole area.

FOWNHOPE, FAWLEY AND STRANGFORD

By 1086 Fownhope also had a church with two priests, half a hide of land and a central tower, indicators that it too may have been a minster church.[10] In the Middle Ages Fawley and Strangford were chapelries of Fownhope. Fawley with Fownhope was in Greytree hundred but Strangford in 1086 was recorded as being in Sulcet (Sellack) hundred and later in Wormelow hundred. It was only in 1835 that it was shown on Bryant's map as being in Greytree hundred along with the rest of Fownhope parish to which it belonged.

The origins of the close relationship between Fownhope, Fawley and Strangford may date back to before 1086. In the Domesday survey Fawley is not mentioned by name, but Fownhope and Strangford were both held by Thorkel White.[11] In an early gospel book of Hereford Cathedral is an interesting record from the reign of Canute of a gift by Enneawne a lady at Feligley (Fawley) of all her lands to her kinswoman Leoflaed, wife of Thurkill the White, 'and never anything at all to my own son'.[12]

This arose from a complaint made by her son Edwine about a share of lands at Wellington and 'Cyrdeslea'. It should be noted that by 1086 Thorkell also held five hides at Wellington.[13] If the Fawley mentioned in this record is the one lying in the parish of Fownhope this would explain its relationship with Fownhope parish, and the possession of both Fownhope and Strangford by Thorkell the White seems to confirm it.

The boundaries around Fownhope village are nearly all along streams, but the boundaries of Fawley and Strangford are almost entirely either along field boundaries or are undefined, except where they both abut the river Wye (Pl. 4). Fawley has a natural boundary along a valley with Brockhampton but the boundary with How Caple is now wholly undefined. This may suggest that in the past How Caple and Fawley were part of the same larger unit. A closer look at the tithe map shows that by 1840 Fawley manor held fields that extended into How Caple. Without further documentary evidence there is no way of telling whether this acquisition occurred after or before enclosure from common open fields. On the How Caple side of the boundary two of the adjoining parts of fields are called 'In Upper Yew Tree Field' and 'In Yew Tree Field', while on the other side of the undefined parish boundary one field is called 'Thirty Acres' and the other is not given a name. This suggests that Yew Tree Field might be the name of a common field extending across the boundary.

Plate 4. Natural boundary - Pentaloe Brook in the foreground with a tributary in the centre separating Woolhope parish on the left from Fownhope on the right. Behind the camera position is Mordiford parish.

WOOLHOPE, BROCKHAMPTON AND PUTLEY

Woolhope and its medieval chapelry of Brockhampton contain the Iron Age hillfort of Capler Camp and stretch from land abutting the river Wye on the W. right across a concentric series of ridges and valleys to the broad lowlands of the Leadon vale on the E. It is not a physically coherent unit although it includes all the varied types of terrain in the locality. Woolhope, Brockhampton and Putley are considered together because their boundaries are interdigitated, and in the case of Putley and Woolhope detached parts of each lie within the other. This means that these parish boundaries, mainly along man-made features, were decided upon after the area was under open-field cultivation or in separate intermingled ownerships. In the case of Woolhope and Brockhampton it is very clear that people living within Woolhope parish were culti-vating unenclosed strips in the open field of Walboro in Brockhampton in 1834.[14] Therefore, when it was decided to make the old medieval chapel of Brockhampton into a parish church, the boundary zigzagged through the open-field strips. In 1086 Brockhampton manor had five English and three Welsh hides.[15] It has been suggested that Buckenhill (township)[16] represents the Welsh hides, but when Brockhampton was separated from Woolhope parish, Buckenhill was included in Woolhope. The breaking up of the earlier unit of Brockhampton and Buckenhill may be why the open field of Walboro is split between the two parishes.

There is also evidence of an ancient chapel site at Buckenhill described as 'the shrine of the Holy Trinity at Hope Wolwith commonly called St Dubricius' by Bishop Mayhew in 1514.[17] There is field-name evidence of a boundary just S. of Wessington and N. of Buckenhill. The names are 'Meerfield' and 'Meer Green'.[18] This may indicate an ancient boundary between Buckenhill and Woolhope since St Dubricius is a Celtic dedication and may predate the Anglian conquest of this area.[19] However, the precise location of this boundary is not clear.

Putley, on the other hand, seems to have larger blocks of land possibly representing whole holdings which have been taken out of Woolhope and given to Putley parish. The church contains Norman work and is listed as a church in 1291.[20] It appears to be taken out of Woolhope because three landholdings of Woolhope called The Brainge, Aylhill and Hatsford lie on the far side of Putley adjacent to Pixley, Aylton and Much Marcle parishes respectively. Putley has four small, detached fields in Woolhope on the tithe map of 1838, presumably at one time part of holdings where the homestead was in the main part of Putley parish. From this it seems likely that either these small parcels were assarted from the original woodland cover before Putley was separated from Woolhope, or these lands may have been allocated to specific holdings as their proportion of woodland waste at the time it was being enclosed, possibly after the creation of Putley as a parish. Another interesting point is that Woolhope had three townships of its own, Buckenhill, Woolhope and Putley which suggests that the Putley parish may represent only part of the original settlement of Putley. Alternatively it may be that some of the lands in the original parish of Putley were given to the dean and chapter of Hereford, which owned the manor of Woolhope, and were then annexed to that parish at an early period. Putley has within its bounds and close to the church, evidence of the remains of a Roman villa found in the last century indicating early settlement here.[21] The boundary with Tarrington is mostly along natural features except where it is undefined as it crosses part of Devereux Park, which is a late creation and may have eliminated an earlier boundary. The boundaries of Putley and Woolhope with Pixley, Aylton and Much Marcle are however mainly man-made, using roads and field boundaries and indicating their late establishment.

MUCH MARCLE AND YATTON

Much Marcle itself was a post-conquest addition to Greytree hundred. Only about a third of the eastern boundary of the parish is along the top of Ridge Hill, the limestone ridge forming the western flank of the valley of the Leadon and its tributaries. At the northern end Woolhope parish overflows the ridge and extends down to Putley on the valley floor, while to the south the boundary with the chapelry and township of Yatton is along a road. Marcle means 'Boundary wood' and the boundary is thought to be that between the Hwicce and the Magonsaete, two early Anglian sub-kingdoms.[22] This lay along the eastern side of the parish, half along streams and low ridges linked intermittently by field boundaries. It seems very poorly defined as the topography is generally only gently undulating and the streams small and insignificant. When the wood itself was present no doubt this created a more effective barrier as it was on heavy and wet clay soil. Woods still survive along this boundary; Hall Wood, Stone Redding, and Queens Wood confirm the difficult nature of the soil when, even with modern methods of cultivation, these woods have been left alone. A detached portion of Much Marcle lies in Queens Wood on the other side of Kempley parish and the man-made boundaries suggest that Kempley at one time may have formed part of Much Marcle. Kempley has more surviving woods, which may have been part of the original *Marc leah* such as Allums Grove and Haind Park Wood. Within Much Marcle parish were at least three medieval townships, Yatton, Kynaston and Bickerton, of which the first two had chapels.

Plate 5. Road forming boundary between Yatton on the left and Much Marcle on the right. The species-rich hedge on the right contains a lot of spindle as seen in the foreground.

The boundary with Yatton is almost entirely along one road and a track. The hedge on the E. side of the road, although very decayed still has many surviving spindle bushes, a shrub not often found in roadside hedges (Pl. 5). This road leads up to Oldbury Camp, an Iron Age hillfort, and may be a prehistoric route. The W. boundary of Yatton lies along the top of the ridge overlooking the Wye valley. Some of the ridge is followed by a trackway and some by a modern road, as this 'ridgeway' provides dramatic views E. and W. it could be prehistoric in origin. In 1086 Yatton had one hide which before 1066 was 'thane' land but subsequently had become 'reeve' land, a drop in status.[23] At about 1000 AD the building of a church could assist in conferring 'thane' status on a ceorl, thereby encouraging the building of churches.[24] The specific mention of this status suggests this might be the reason for the 'thane land' status of Yatton, as most churches were associated with manors of five or more hides. The chapel was rebuilt in the twelfth century and displays a tympanum in the style of the Herefordshire school of sculptors.

SOLLERS HOPE
Sollers Hope includes most of the valley of the brook, which rises near Westnors End Farm and flows down through the middle of Sollers Hope as far as Falcon Farm, making a compact geographical unit. The E. boundary along the Marcle ridge and abutting Oldbury Camp seems most likely to be an ancient and well established boundary, while the location on not very well defined or continuous natural features of the other boundaries suggests that Sollers Hope may originally have been part of Woolhope (Pl. 6). The boundary with How Caple is formed by straight field boundaries enclosing a ridge of land dropping down to the brook, its straightness suggests an artificial and late boundary.

Plate 6. The curving hedge in the foreground is the boundary between Yatton in the right foreground and Sollers Hope in the left middle distance. The ridge on the skyline separates Sollers Hope from Much Marcle beyond the ridge. The thin scatter of trees on the skyline marks the position of Oldbury Iron Age hillfort.

HOW CAPLE AND EATON TREGOES
How Caple has an entirely natural boundary with Brockhampton to the N., but the E. boundary with Sollers Hope, Yatton and Eaton Tregoes (Foy parish) is only natural along the ridge with Yatton; the other boundaries are all man-made features. The physical location of the boundary with Eaton Tregoes implies that How Caple may originally have been part of a larger unit including them both. Eaton Tregoes has a

long finger extending north interposed between How Caple and Yatton. In fact Eaton Tregoes occupies the ridge along the boundary with Yatton, leaving the boundary of How Caple some metres lower down the hillside along a trackway (Pl. 7). There could be two reasons for Eaton to retain this piece of land, either as a lookout point over the surrounding countryside, particularly to the E and W., or to maintain access and control of the road leading eastward to Oldbury and Ledbury. The highest land on the Foy side of the river is only 64m while the highest point within Foy Parish on this finger of land is 165m with a good view of the surrounding landscape. This strategic point may have been retained by the more important estate at a time when security depended on awareness of people's movements.

Plate 7. The oak in the centre is the first of a line of trees on the right of an old track which marks the boundary between How Caple on the left and Foy on the right. The wooded ridge on the skyline marks the boundary between Foy and Yatton.

Eaton Tregoes was the site of a medieval castle and this may be the continuation of an earlier tradition. In 1086 it was only taxed at 2½ hides but the area was much bigger than the 5-hide manor of How Caple.[25] The E. boundary of Eaton Tregoes with Upton Bishop is entirely along the old road from Ross to Ledbury via Old Gore, which suggests that the road was a well established early route-way. There is an interesting record of a ditch substantial enough to be thought to be Offa's Dyke to the west of this road on Park Farm land.[26] Since this was also the E. boundary of Foy, a parish where the church township was part of Wormelow hundred in Archenfield, this dyke just might have been a defensive or territorial boundary dating back to the period before the Angles penetrated as far as the river.

UPTON BISHOP AND BRAMPTON ABBOTTS
A gently sloping ridge separates Upton Bishop and Brampton Abbotts, but there is a

detached part of Upton Bishop at Overton surrounded on two sides and interdigitated by Brampton Abbotts, with Eaton Tregoes on the third side. A pollarded Gospel oak marks the boundary on the interdigitation (Pl. 8). In the S.E. Brampton Abbotts has an almost detached portion reaching down to the Rudhall Brook. There is evidence of iron-working in the form of dark soil containing slag 250m S.W. of the detached portion of Brampton Abbotts.[27] Possibly iron-working was the reason Brampton Abbotts retained this small area by the Rudhall Brook, or it may have provided access to a mill site.

Overton, the detached part of Upton Bishop, is a roughly triangular shape with the E. point on top of the highest hill here, at 102m, the track forming the N. boundary with Eaton Tregoes runs E. to W. over this hilltop. There are some sloping banks around this high point which may indicate the presence of a ploughed-out Iron Age

Plate 8. Pollarded Gospel oak between Brampton Abbotts behind and Upton Bishop in front of the tree. Identified in 1806 description of the boundary.

hillfort. Isaac Taylor on his map of 1786 shows a 'camp' to the W. of Hill of Eaton. There is no physical evidence at that location for a hillfort, while this site to the E. of Hill of Eaton shows some possible physical evidence. The man-made nature of the boundaries between these three parishes seem to confirm an early link between them. The other significant survival is a Roman tombstone embedded in the walls of Upton Bishop church showing the antiquity of settlement here.

ROSS AND WALFORD

The Iron Age camp on Chase Hill lies right on the boundary between the two parishes, which follows the S. rampart of the camp and descends the W. face of Chase Hill along a footpath. At the foot of the hill the tithe map shows a straight field boundary going W. past Ashfield School site, and then following the path down to the bridge and the ford over the river. This straight boundary is the north side of the Cleeve tithing, one of the few tithings identified on the tithe maps as a physical entity. In 1086 Cleeve with its berewick of Wilton on the other side of the river, was a 14½-hide manor, twice the size of Ross manor with only 7 hides.[28] At some time in the intervening centuries Cleeve tithing became part of Ross Parish. The close link between the tithing boundary and the access to the south entrance to the hillfort suggests that this may be the remains of an Iron Age boundary. Unfortunately it is now difficult to locate as it is mostly behind modern developments. The parish boundary S. and W. of the *Vine Tree* pub zig-zags along field boundaries, while the site of the old Hom Green chapel lies within a quarter of a mile of the Walford parish boundary. The churchyard cross still stands in the wood marking its site. In the *Valor Ecclesiasticus* 'Home' contributed £4 to Ross church so the area served by the chapel must have been within Ross parish. Therefore Ross had three dependent chapels in the Middle Ages: Brampton Abbotts, Weston-under Penyard and Hom. The first two later became independent churches but Hom, like its near neighbour Cleeve, faded away.

The W. boundary of Ross is the river Wye, except for a length opposite the town where all the river frontage back to the Rope Walk and an old field boundary line west of Dock Pitch and north of the road leading to Wilton Bridge and the ford just downstream, was part of Bridstow parish. This is puzzling, but Bridstow church has an early dedication to St Bridget which suggests that it was probably established before Ross church. Also, much of Wilton manor in Bridstow parish was held by Earl Harold before 1066,[29] and may have been a royal manor before that. In the Anglo-Saxon period kings were responsible for bridges and fords and this piece of land would ensure that the crossing point remained in the hands of the king after the manor of Ross was given to the bishop. Control of a crossing point was a strategic matter in the defence of the kingdom when it was in border territory, as this was in the early Anglian period. The other possibility is that one of the mills of Bridstow was located on the cut made from the Rudhall Brook along the Rope Walk down to the location of the *Hope and Anchor* inn. Such a water supply would be easier to control than a mill on the river itself with the constant fluctuations of water level. Either or both of these explanations could account for the retention of this land by the royal manor in Bridstow parish.

The W. and S. boundaries of Walford are both along natural features but the E. boundary with Hope Mansell is entirely along man-made features.

HOPE MANSELL

This is a small parish occupying the whole of a small enclosed valley on the edge of the Forest of Dean, at one time lying within the forest. There is one detached portion, which is a section across the Castle Brook valley, separated from the rest of the parish by part of Weston-under-Penyard containing Bill Mills. The detached portion of Hope Mansell includes fields with the names Lower and Upper Weavington which may indicate a farm or hamlet here.[30] Bill Mills appears to have been an early iron-working site which may account for its retention within Weston-under-Penyard.[31] The boundary of the main part of Hope Mansell with Weston is along a stream and similarly the E. boundary with Gloucestershire and the Forest of Dean is mainly along a stream, using paths in the S.E. corner. Along the S. boundary a ridge is followed by a path, now lying immediately adjacent to a deep active quarry. Hope Mansell has boundaries along man-made features with both Walford and Weston-under-Penyard but, as it is Weston which separates the detached part of Hope Mansell from the rest of the parish, it seems more likely that Hope Mansell may originally have formed part of a territory which included Weston-under-Penyard.

LEA, ASTON INGHAM, LINTON, AND WESTON-UNDER-PENYARD

This is an interesting group in which three large parishes of 2,300 to 3,000 acres surround one of only 700 acres. Lea, the smallest, has few natural boundaries and was divided in two by 1086, 1 hide being owned by St Peter's Abbey in Gloucester, which caused it to be treated as part of Gloucestershire.[32] The shape of the parish is rather like a starfish with bits protruding into all the surrounding parishes and the boundaries are largely man-made. It appears to be a focal point of the three parishes. Aston means the 'East-ton' and Weston the 'West-ton' and these are only E. and W. of either Lea or Linton. Linton was a royal manor prior to 1066 and so was probably the more important place with Aston and Weston as its subsidiaries.[33] This suggestion is supported by the man-made boundary between Weston and Linton. Aston however has 50% natural boundaries with Linton, which may indicate a much earlier separation before cultivation or occupation was extensive.

The name Lea is supposedly derived from *leah* meaning either 'wood' or 'clearing' (in a wood), although the earliest spellings are *Lecce* 1086, *Leche* 1160-70 and *Lacu* 1201.[34] According to A. H. Smith, *lece* OE, *leche* ME, and *lacu* OE all mean 'stream'.[35] Coplestone-Crow suggests that *Lacu* is erroneous, but it is the medieval name applied to the forest bailiwick which in 1282 had Lea as its administrative centre.[36]

The old centre of the village is located at the confluence of three small tributaries in the valley bottom, along the line of the old road from Gloucester to Ross, which crosses the valley at this point. This would be an appropriate location for a place with the name of 'stream'. In the centre of the parish was the hide owned by St Peter's Abbey at Gloucester in 1086 and within that hide is the parish church. After the dissolution of the monasteries this chapel was annexed to Linton church. None of this really explains why Lea is such a small parish compared with the adjacent parishes. However, it may have been the administrative centre of the forest bailiwick of *Lacu* or Lea, which was desmesne wood of the king in 1282 when 'Nicholas of Lea had custody of it'.[37] This might be the explanation.

The E. boundary of Aston and Linton was in early times the boundary between the Hwicce and the Magonsaete and could be expected to be a readily identifiable natural boundary. Although fairly equal in area Weston, Linton and Aston are not equal in hidage. In 1086 Weston had four and Linton had five hides while Aston had only two hides but there is a remark about Aston having '8 other men'.[38] These 'other men' may have occupied another two or three hides between them but paid no tax, possibly because they owed duties in relation to forest management.[39]

Weston has man-made boundaries not only with Linton but also with Ross. Since Weston was a chapelry of Ross throughout the Middle Ages, this is to be expected. However, the historical ownership of the major manors in these linked parishes indicates the presence of an early royal estate which, in the pre-conquest period, had already been split up but still left evidence in the the Domesday survey. Ross manor, with additional lands in Walford, was given to the bishop by the king well before 1066. Cleeve and Wilton had remained in royal hands just prior to 1066, while Linton was still held by the king in 1086. Only Aston Ingham and Hope Mansell did not have any hint of previous royal ownership, but Aston as noted above, appears to have been an early subsidiary of Linton while Hope Mansell demonstrated a similar link with Weston-under-Penyard. All these parishes could therefore have been part of one large royal holding which had gradually been split up in the Anglian period. The Normans reorganised it again, segregating it into smaller separate units and detaching them from royal ownership.

SMALL DEVIATIONS IN BOUNDARIES
WESTON-UNDER-PENYARD AND ROSS

The boundary in the S.W. through the medieval Penyard Park has been wooded for centuries. Here there seems to have been a change of boundary between the seventeenth century and the 1834 tithe map. The eighteenth-century documentary description clearly indicates that the boundary followed a pathway, up to the Gospel oak. This path is still there, but the boundary is shown following a route up a very steep hillside, where there is absolutely no evidence of there ever having been a path, and along a field boundary to the Gospel oak.[40]

FOWNHOPE AND HOLME LACY

The W. boundary of Fownhope follows the river Wye except for one field on the banks of the river called 'Bye field Meadow', which is excluded and belongs to Holme Lacy parish on the other side of the river.[41] A study of 'byefield' names shows that this field was given to Craswall Priory 'that they may cause the pond of their mill of Hamme (Holme Lacy) to be affixed to my land of Hope (Fownhope)' by Roger de Chandoys in the thirteenth century.[42] This gift resulted in the land also being transferred to the parish of the estate to which it belonged. There is a similar field belonging to Bolstone parish further down river on the Fownhope side, which may also represent the location of a weir for a mill.

CONCLUSIONS

The split between natural and man-made parish boundaries does seem to identify groupings of parishes which can be explained by earlier linkages. In some of the cases there is additional evidence for the linkages, but in others the explanation must for the time being be proposed and await further evidence to confirm or disprove them. The following are suggested groups together with possible explanations.

(1) The convergence of the boundaries of Mordiford, Dormington, Stoke Edith and Tarrington demonstrate the break up of an earlier unit. This could be a multiple estate of four vills as found in Wales. What seems certain is that this early grouping pre-dates the formation of the *parochia* around the minster church of Stoke Edith,[43] as this excludes Mordiford and Dormington and includes several other parishes. In fact the form and location of Mordiford church seems to indicate that this may itself have been an early minster church, possibly serving Dormington, Lugwardine and Woolhope all of which contained substantial manors owned by the Hereford college of canons in 1086. Fownhope may or may not have formed part of this early *parochia*; its proximity to the church would make it a logical addition. However, by 1086 it already had a church and two priests with half a hide, which together with the presence of a central crossing tower suggests an important church of similar status in its own right. It is possible that this was a later development than the Mordiford church, but the lack of early records makes it difficult to prove.

(2) Woolhope with its chapelries of Brockhampton and St Dubricius in Buckenhill township, and the townships of Woolhope and Putley suggests the presence of a multiple estate of the Welsh type previously mentioned. In addition in 1086 it had two clerks holding 1 hide and 1 virgate[44] which could be diagnostic of a minster church.[45] Sollers Hope may have formed part of the *parochia* of such a minster church, as it had a link with the priory of Hereford in 1291; but there is no obvious link in the *Valor Ecclesiasticus*.

(3) Much Marcle is another church with a central crossing tower, half a hide owned by the church of Lyre,[46] which also owned the church itself.[47] This again suggests it may have been a minster church. Within its own parish were two chapels, one at Yatton and another in the township of Kynaston, which was swept away by 'The Wonder' land slip. The man-made boundary with Kempley and the fact that there is a detached portion of Much Marcle on the far side of Kempley suggests that Kempley also may have been part of the *parochia* of this minster church.

(4) Upton Bishop, Eaton Tregoes and Brampton Abbotts and possibly How Caple show evidence of links. Brampton in 1546 still paid a pension of two shillings to the vicar of Upton Bishop, which may well indicate that Upton Bishop was a minster church with Brampton within its *parochia* before Brampton became a chapelry of Ross church.[48] The other links between these parishes may relate to Iron Age times rather than the Anglian or medieval periods.

(5) The links between Linton and its neighbouring parishes of Weston, Aston, Lea and possibly Hope Mansell may be those of a multiple estate, as there is no evidence to suggest that Linton was a minster church. These links were superceded when Weston became a chapelry of Ross.

(6) These early groupings seem to suggest that the links between Ross and the two largest of its medieval chapels were formed relatively late, perhaps after the acquisition of the manor of Ross by the bishop.

REFERENCES

[1] A hide is an Anglo-Saxon measure of land sufficient to support one family.

[2] *Abstract of the Answers and Returns to the Population Act 41* GEO. III (1800),129.

[3] These are the *Nomina Villarum* 1316, the Lay Subsidy 1334 and the Poll Tax of 1377.

[4] J. Hillaby, 'The Origins of the Diocese of Hereford', *TWNFC* XLII (1976).

[5] *The Domesday Survey of Herefordshire 1086*, eds. F. & C. Thorn (1983), (hereafter cited as D.B.)

[6] Both these names appear in Greytree hundred, Cleeve tithing as a territorial division on the Ross tithe map, and Dormington as a township in the 1801 census.

[7] D.B. fols. 2, 58; 13, 1; 26, 1.

[8] B. Coplestone-Crow, *Herefordshire Place-Names* (1989),148.

[9] D.B.fo.13, 1.   [10] D.B.fo.29, 2.   [11] D.B.fos.29, 2; 29, 20.

[12] J.W. Leigh, 'Some Archives and Seals of Hereford Cathedral', *TWNFC* (1901), 109-10.

[13] D.B.fo.29, 11.   [14] Woolhope tithe map, 1845 [15] D.B.fo.2,15

[16] Op cit. in note 8, 214.   [17] *Register of Bishop Mayhew*, 285.

[18] Op cit. in note 14.   [19] E. Taylor, *Kings Caple in Archenfield* (1997), 10.

[20] *Pope Nicholas' Taxation 1291* (Record Commissioners, 1802).

[21] E. C. Davies, *Herefordshire Countryside Treasures* (1981),62.

[22] Op cit. in note 8, 142.   [23] D.B. fo.1, 75.

[24] J. Blair, *Early Medieval Surrey* (1991), 109.   [25] D.B. fo.19, 7.

[26] H. C. Moore, 'Offa's Dyke and Rowe Ditch', *TWNFC* (1901),146.

[27] Personal observation.   [28] D.B. fos.2, 24; 1. 8.   [29] Ibid.

[30] Hope Mansell tithe map, 1840   [31] Personal communication from H. Hurley.

[32] D.B.fo.5, 2.   [33] D.B.fo.1, 1.   [34] Op cit. in note 8, 119.

[35] A. H. Smith, *The Place-name Elements* Part II, (1970), 8,10. (OE = Old English, ME = Middle English).

[36] C. Hart, *The Regard of the Forest of Dene in 1282* (1987), 39.

[37] Ibid.   [38] D.B. fo.21, 3.

[39] Op cit. in note 17, 27. 'Walter of Aston Ingham (a forester of fee) had custody of it[the bailiwick of Blakeney]'.

[40] Documents in Ross parish chest.   [41] Holme Lacy tithe map, 1840.

[42] E. Taylor, 'An Investigation of the Byefield, Bylet, Cinder, Forge and Furnace, Cae Tref and Cover Names for the County of Herefordshire', *TWNFC*, XLVIII (1996).

[43] J. W. King, 'Two Herefordshire Minsters', *TWNFC*, XLVIII(1995).

[44] D.B. fo.2,13.

[45] Op. cit. in note 24, 92. 'The work of the last twenty years makes it possible to accept Domesday terminology with more confidence as evidence for former minsters.' '...any description [of a church] more elaborate than the ubiquitous *ibi ecclesia*...seems generally a mark of superior status.'

[46] D.B. fo.4,1.   [47] Op. cit. in note 20   [48] Op. cit. in note 46

Caradoc Court

RON SHOESMITH & RICHARD MORRISS

It was during the fourth field meeting of 1928 that the Woolhope Club paid their first visit to Caradoc Court. This followed an arduous day visiting the church and the Black Swan at Much Dewchurch, the hall and chapel at Harewood Park, and Hentland and Sellack churches. They were entertained by the owner of Caradoc, Colonel Heywood, who then showed them around the house. They saw and photographed some sixteenth-century fresco work on the sloping ceilings of an attic room.[1] In July 1952 some seventy members made another, unscheduled visit in two coaches and a number of private cars, but Mrs Heywood rose to the occasion and entertained them hospitably.[2] The building was gutted by a fire in 1986 and was surveyed and analysed by members of the City of Hereford Archaeology Unit in 1989.[3]

INTRODUCTION

Caradoc Court is in the western part of Sellack parish some four miles N.W. of Ross-on-Wye. It sits on an outcrop of sandstone rock above the river Wye. The earliest parts were built in the late sixteenth century and alterations and additions were made principally in the early seventeenth and mid-nineteen centuries.

The building was gutted by a fire in 1986 and was abandoned for several years. Eventually Finchfield Ltd., who intended to convert it into residential units, bought it. Finchfield commissioned the then City of Hereford Archaeology Unit (now Archaeological Investigations Ltd.) to carry out an analytical survey of the building. The project included the provision of fully measured elevations of all the timber-framed elements to accompany a complete report on the history and development of the complex. As a preliminary to this work unit staff supervised the clearance from the building of the large amount of debris resulting from the fire. All burnt and charred timbers were tagged and removed to an open area in the grounds where they were laid out in a facsimile 'plan' of the building to aid future identification. After the building was scaffolded the remains of the external timber frames were drawn *in situ*. The internal frames, where they still existed, were also drawn. All the loose and burnt timbers that had survived the fire, were then examined and the evidence thus obtained was used to reconstruct sections of the main frame drawings. Finally all the available evidence was used to produce a phased constructional history of the building.

Finchfield Ltd. eventually went into liquidation and the ruins were sold. Some parts have since been reconstructed and building work continues.

OUTLINE HISTORY

The early history of Caradoc is lost in legend. It is the reputed home of the British

Plate 1. Caradoc Court from Robinson's *Mansions and Manors of Herefordshire*, 1873

chief Caradoc Vraich-Vras, or Strong Arm, a knight of King Arthur's round table and hero of the *Ballad of the Boy and the Mantle*.[4] According to Matthews, there are traces of a British camp near to Caradoc, but the precise locality is uncertain and it has been suggested that he was referring to the Iron Age hill fort at Gaer-Cop in Hentland[5]. However, the late nineteenth-century directories are mainly quite confident that 'Caradoc…occupies the site of a castle reputed to have belonged to "Caradoc Vreich Vra," prince of the country between Severn and Wye…'[6]

Sellack is not mentioned in the Domesday Book, but in the twelfth-century *Book of Llandaff*, there is a ninth-century entry for *Lann Suluc*, meaning Suluc's Church.[7] *Suluc* is a hypocoristic form of Tysilio, to whom the present church is dedicated.[8]

The earliest documentary reference to Caradoc occurs in 1291 when Roger de Somery died, seized of the manor of Caircradoke in Irchenfield. In 1308 Robert de la Mere held Carycraddock, a sub-manor of Tretire. The messuage on the site was worth 12d per annum, as was the garden; a dovecote was worth 6d and there were 160 acres of ploughland together with pasture and woods. There were nine freeholders.

By 1443 Caradoc belonged to John Abrahale and remained in his family, although tenanted, until 1569 when it was sold to the Mynors family. In 1596 it was again sold, this time to Rowland Scudamore of Churcham in Gloucestershire. He was a brother of Sir John Scudamore of Holme Lacy, one of the most important families in the county. Rowland Scudamore, who added the Baysham estate to increase his landholdings in the area in 1619, is credited with the building or re-building of Caradoc Court.[9] He died in 1630-1 but Caradoc continued to be owned by the Scudamores.

In a memorandum dated 14 March 1639 the 'olde house & kitchinge garden att Cradocke' was leased for six years by Viscount Scudamore to Richard Phelps 'of Rolston'. The same lease allowed the tenant of the 'new howse' to 'brue in the sayde olde hous att such time and times and so often as hee shal have occasion so to doe'.

In addition, whenever Scudamore wished to come back to Caradoc, Phelps and his family had to move to Baysham. The implication of an old and new house might be that Caradoc Court was divided into two large dwellings at this time.

Members of the Scudamore family continued to reside at Caradoc from time to time, including James who died in 1688. His grandson John, who died at Caradoc in 1714, aged 27, left a widow, Elizabeth, who remained in the house, although the estate passed to John's elder brother, James, 3rd viscount Scudamore. He died, aged 31, in 1716 and the estate then passed to his wife's family, the Lord Digby's. Elizabeth eventually re-married William Dew of Sellack and, after her death in 1760, the Dew family continued to lease Caradoc from the Digbys until 1864.

The estate had to pay £21 17s in the 1776 land tax; this made it the second largest estate in the two large parishes of Sellack and Foy, but by 1809 the Baysham portion was in separate ownership. At this time Caradoc belonged to the Hon. Reverend Robert Digby, a younger son of the family, who lived at Rigswood in the same parish, but by 1840 it had reverted to Lord Digby.

In 1864 Elisha Caddick bought Caradoc and radically rebuilt the house and re-modelled the gardens and the grounds. In 1910, Edward Whitehouse Caddick sold it to Colonel George Basil Heywood and the remaining Caddicks then moved to Sidonia, Sellack. In 1914 the house was still tenanted, by Montague MacClean, but by 1919 the Heywood family was in full residence. Colonel Heywood died in 1944, his widow in 1960, and both were buried within the estate on the summit of Fair Hill, overlooking the River Wye. Caradoc Court then passed to Mrs Katie Gaze, the Heywoods' youngest daughter, and her husband, Tony Gaze, a national hunt trainer. Mrs Gaze died in 1976, and in 1978 the estate was sold to another racehorse trainer, John Edwards. In 1984 it was again sold, this time to John Onslow-Edwards, but he did not live in the house. It was in 1986, when the estate was about to change hands, that the whole building was gutted by fire (Pl. 2).

Plate 2. The eastern wing looking south in June 1989.

THE PHASES OF CONSTRUCTION (Fig. 1)

It is not possible within the confines of this article to describe in detail the fourteen timber frames that were identified within the building and which made up a large proportion of the seventeenth-century house. These frames were partly drawn *in situ* and partly reconstructed from the burnt and charred timbers. The following phases of construction are based on an analysis of these drawings and on the overall survey of the building.

PHASE ONE

In its primary phase Caradoc Court was a large and sophisticated timber-framed building constructed in the latest architectural style of the day. It was unlikely to have been designed by a Herefordshire architect and its structural carpentry is also far removed from the usual vernacular styles of this area.

The original house consisted of a long, two-and-a-half-storied main range, from which two cross-gabled wings of the same height projected forwards to create a 'half-H' plan with a central open courtyard facing south. There would have been an entrance porch on the central part of the south frame, which would have answered the two-and-a-half-storied, cross-gabled oriel that projected from the northern face of the building. The overall design would then have been the typical E plan of the second half of the sixteenth century.

However, the focal point of Caradoc was its ground floor, cross-axial hall – a very early example of such a plan in England. Such halls did not become common in English houses until well into the seventeenth century. Until this time the hall, although of gradually diminishing importance in the room hierarchy of a large house, continued to reflect its medieval ancestry and was open to the roof. The important rooms of the house were attached to the 'high' or dais end of the hall, with the service wing opposite at the 'low' end and separated from the hall by the screens passage.

In the cross-axial hall the room is turned through a right angle – thus at Caradoc the 'high' end is represented by the projecting northern oriel. Sufficient evidence remained to show that the south wall of the hall was originally close-studded, indicating that it was an external wall facing onto the courtyard. The position of the traditional screens passage at this end of the hall was simply reflected by the two opposing doorways – one leading from the hall into the residential rooms to the west and the other leading to the service wing on the east. There is no trace of any wall or partition separating this 'screens passage' from the rest of the hall and, indeed, it would appear unlikely that any such wall was ever contemplated.

The west wing contained the main residential quarters of the owner. On the ground floor, a grand stairwell separated the parlour from the dining room. The main bedchambers were on the floor above with another principal chamber over the hall. One or both of the phase 2 chimney stacks in the west wall may well have replaced earlier ones in similar positions.

The service wing would have contained the kitchen and usual offices on the ground floor, with lesser chambers above. A passageway led from the southern end of the hall, through the service wing, to a single-storied, close-studded side porch, probably primary, which survived all the alterations until the fire of 1986. Cellars ran underneath the east wing and the hall. There would have been a second stairwell in this range although not as grand as the one in the west wing.

Structurally, this timber-framed building had many traditional features, but also some highly unusual ones. The close-studded external walls with mid-rails for each

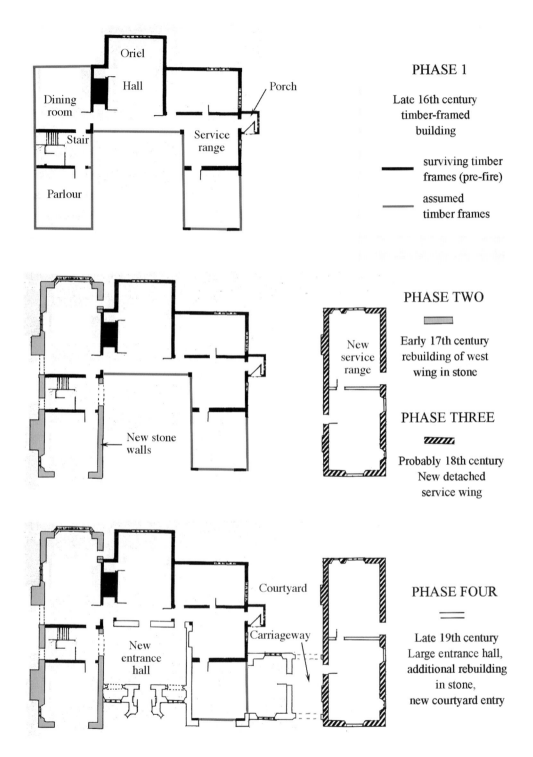

Figure 1. The four main phases of development of Caradoc Court

floor are typical of the western school of carpentry, and of a well-built house of the period. The timber framework was erected on a continuous high stone plinth, which also formed the upper walls of the cellars; the remainder of the depth of the cellars being carved out of the bedrock of the site.

The main rooms had very large windows throughout the north elevation and the oriel, a feature probably matched in the southern gable of the west wing and in some of the side walls, though not, apparently, in the south gable of the east services wing. The size of these windows is typical of the fashionable architecture of the time – thus Hardwicke Hall was well described as being 'more window than wall'. The original windows did not last – the surviving windows in the timber framing were all found to be replacements, although probably in a similar style to the originals with ovolo mouldings.

The unusual features of this late sixteenth-century building are mainly associated with the design of the basic framing and roof, the method of fixing the internal partitions, and the way the oriel was connected to the main north frame. Although the main northern range was divided by roof trusses into seven bays, the framework was separated into just three wide bays with two principal posts for the bays on each side of the axial hall. The two end bays were each sub-divided into two by a truss, and the central bay was similarly separated into three. Apart from the two gables, each of the tie-beam trusses was tenoned into the side of the wall plate with a pegged, horizontal tongue-and-tooth tenon, instead of resting on top of the post or the wall plate. The first-floor cross-beams beneath each truss were similarly tenoned into the first-floor wall plate, apart from those joining the principal posts, which had plain, vertical tenons. The spine beams, running between the cross-beams, also had tongue-and-tooth tenons. (Because there are many missing elements it has been assumed that the two wings were designed in an identical fashion).

This type of design had all the makings of a potential problem from the start. Not only did the trusses not sit on top of and thus rely on the strength of the principal posts, but also the integrity of the building relied on the maintenance of compression on the tenoned joints. If there were a failure in any part of the building, then the stress on the joints would have increased. Thus, if there was any tendency for the side frames to splay outwards, this would have meant that the structural stability of the building would rely on the strength of the tenons holding the girding and tie beams. If the splay worsened, the building would then have had to rely entirely on the pegs holding the tenons in place.

The projecting oriel that formed the northern end of the hall appears to be a primary feature. Its close-studding and large windows would have matched the overall symmetry and it was clearly designed as the central feature of the north, or riverside elevation. The first floor girding beams of the side frames have cavetto and ovolo mouldings, which were copied in the late nineteenth-century replacement bressumers of its jettied end gable. For maximum structural stability the side frames should have been tenoned into principal posts on the main north frame, but this was not the case. Instead, the oriel was designed to be narrower than the wide central bay of the north range. Intermediate posts were then incorporated into the design of the north frame. These posts were given additional rigidity at first floor level by the insertion of an extra rail. Having gone to this trouble, it would have been logical to tenon the side frames of the oriel into these intermediate posts, but instead the whole structure was designed as a separate edifice, which was, effectively, free-standing. The southern posts of each side frame were only fixed to the intermediate posts by free-tenons. One possible reason for this odd method of construction could have been to reduce the possibility of the weight of the oriel pulling the north frame over slightly, thus adversely affecting the compression of the unusual jointing of the cross-beams and trusses.

All the internal partitions throughout this sixteenth-century building were apparently of square panels, being three panels high on each floor. None of the partitions appear to have been properly tenoned into the main frame timbers, with the exception of the frames flanking the stairwells. There was no evidence of mortices in the soffits of any of the other beams to show how the partition frame was held in place and, similarly, there were no suitable mortices in the surviving posts. The partition frame forming the east wall of the hall is the only one that survived virtually intact at least at ground floor level. It was structurally independent of the rest of the building, and not tenoned into any part of the main frame.

The existing L-shaped cellar, underneath the hall and the original east wing, is probably primary. Original square-headed cellar-lights survive in the north wall, and blocked lights exist in the east wall and in the original south wall beneath the present hall. The existing stair access is secondary, possibly connected with the rebuilding of the main east stairwell during phase 4. It is unlikely that the cellar ever continued underneath the west wing.

There is some evidence to indicate how the interior of the sixteenth-century building was originally decorated. It is clear that all of the major rooms were fully wainscoted, though all the surviving wainscoting is of late nineteenth-century date. The lack of ornate chamfers on most of the beams, together with the lower runs of sockets and cut-backs indicate that the main ceilings would have been ornately plastered and the beams hidden. However, beams were left exposed in some of the rooms in the service wing, where they were plain chamfered.

The fireplace and stack standing on the west side of the hall appear to be primary, though clearly altered. The ground floor fireplace originally had a large, chamfered, timber lintel. The chamfer was carried on down the stone jambs with a half-pyramid stop near the floor. This lintel was partially removed and part of the stack rebuilt in brick at a later date. A second lintel, now visible in the masonry above the first one, was probably related to an ornate over-mantle. Parts of the original first floor fireplace also survive although partially blocked behind a later insertion, probably of nineteenth century date.

PHASE TWO

The timber-framed external walls of the west bay of the main northern range and the whole of the west wing were totally removed and rebuilt in the local red sandstone, although the floors, roof trusses, cross-beams and stair-well partitions were all retained. This new, ashlar-faced, two-and-a-half-storey stone wing was also extended to the north so that the new gable was in line with the original oriel projection of the cross hall. Internally the basic room pattern was retained, but new cross-beams, morticed into the surviving original frame beams to take the floor joists of the extension, lengthened the northern room on each floor.

The new masonry work included two chimney stacks in the west wall – the northern one was incorporated into the rebuilt gable-end of the northern range and the southern stack was of similar design. At first floor level, in the thickness of masonry on the north side of the south stack there is a small recess with a timberlintelled head, probably a closet or garderobe. One or both of these stacks may have been built during phase 1 and then incorporated into the phase 2 works.

The new north gable included a two-storied canted bay window of eight lights, with a high transom, demonstrating the importance of these chambers. It is possible that there was a similar canted bay on the new south gable, but there is no surviving evidence. The windows in the new wing had square drip moulds. The north rooms on the ground and first floor levels each originally had, in their west walls, three-light transomed windows on each side of the chimney stack, whilst a larger four-light window, probably of full wall height, lit the stairwell. The southern rooms each had a small two-light transomed window in the west wall south of the stack. These rooms and the stair well also had larger windows in the east wall overlooking the front courtyard. In addition, there were small windows in each of the attic gables and smaller windows in the cross-gables.

The ovolo moulding of the windows, the square drip moulds, the style of the canted bay, and the projecting stone string course articulating the ground and first floors, all seem to point to a date no later than the 1620s.

Assuming that the phase 1 building was put up in the late-sixteenth century it should not by then have needed replacing – unless it had suffered a structural failure or, possibly, a destructive fire. As the main roof timbers, cross-beams and staircase frames appear to have survived, a fire would seem unlikely, and a structural failure is more probable, especially considering the unusual carpentry used in the original building. There is always the alternative, of course, that the then owner had a simple preference for stone rather than the old fashioned timber-framing.

PHASE THREE

This broad phase incorporates all the changes made during the two centuries or more up to the mid-nineteenth century. Few of these changes can be accurately dated.

The most significant addition during this phase was a new two-and-a-half storey rubble-built range erected to the east of the main house and parallel to the existing east wing. This range was clearly re-fenestrated during phase 4-5 and then gutted and totally rebuilt internally during phase 6, thus leaving few traces of the original work and little dating evidence. The central truss was originally of timber but it was rebuilt in brick and, beneath a thick layer of later plaster, one of the door or window jambs leading into the phase 5 easternmost range is of chamfered stone. In its present state it is not even clear how long this range was when it was built, although it was obviously designed to fit in with the overall symmetry of the south façade of the whole building complex. When it was built it was not connected to the main range and was probably used as a secondary service wing.

On the 1870s drawing in Robinson's *Mansions and Manors of Herefordshire* there is, in the approximate position of the north end of this wing, a single storey building with one doorway and apparently no roof.[10] The building may well have been in the process of reconstruction at this time (Pl. 1).

It was during this period that the southern timber-framed gable of the original east wing of the main house was rendered, laths being nailed onto the close-studding to provide a key for the render. This was before the addition of the rubble-stone front; the scars left by the laths being visible on the inside of the stone wall after the fire.

Several of the fireplaces in the main house have bolecton-moulded surrounds and appear to be of early eighteenth century date, perhaps indicating some internal re-modelling at this time. The high garden wall running both west and east of the house

Plate 3. Caradoc Court in 1872.

predates the phase 4 rebuilding work and could also be of early eighteenth-century date, perhaps even earlier.

PHASE FOUR

It was during the latter part of the nineteenth century that the house was radically reconstructed and took on the general form that was present before the fire. The main change was the construction of a large ceremonial entrance hall with a large entrance porch in the original courtyard area between the two wings. This involved the construction of a new cross-wall, the blocking of the eastern windows in the phase 2 west wing, and the rebuilding in rubble stone and brick of the west wall of the east wing. The south wall of the original hall was rebuilt in rubble stone and the short return from the front gable to the new south wall of the hall was ashlared. The new hall was two stories high with an attic above lit by a gabled dormer.

A new range of ashlared stone was added to link the original east wing with the phase 3 service wing. A carriageway with a neo-Tudor four-centred head pierced this and led to a new courtyard at the rear of the buildings. Access from the main house to the first floor of this range was complicated. From the first half-landing of the eastern stairwell a flight of stairs was enclosed by a timber framework built into the south-western corner of the new rear courtyard and supported by a large bracket from the old timber-framed wall. There was a small cupola containing a bell on top of it. This flight led into the new range at first floor level.

There was considerable internal re-modelling at this time, although much of the evidence has disappeared in the fire. It appears that both of the main staircases were substantially rebuilt, although some of the original timber-work was probably re-used. Externally, all the gables (which were originally plain) were remodelled with shaped 'Flemish' gables and stone balustrades were placed between them on the south wall of the new hall and the west wall of the west wing. A large semi-circular bay window, two stories high, replaced the existing window in the south gable of the west wing. A canted bay was added to the first floor of the corresponding gable of the east wing. Curiously, the ground floor had no such window and instead two pillars supported the new upper window. All the windows in the new eastern ranges were copied in the style of those of phase 2. New chimney stacks were inserted in the service wings and most of the chimney tops were rebuilt in stone. The most prominent new feature was a huge octagonal timber-framed view tower perched on top of the roof over the new entrance hall.

Apart from the oriel extension of the original cross-hall, most of the surviving external timber-frames were radically reconstructed and re-fenestrated. The eastern part of the original north frame lost virtually all of its primary infill timber work, only the main beams being left in place. The new inserted timbers, although superficially similar to the old, were little more than match boarding and were unrelated to the original mortices in the main frame. The new windows, though copying the general style of the old, were much smaller. In addition, increased attic space was created by the construction of a pair of dormer gables on this façade.

Most of the exposed section of the east frame was also repaired with match boarding and its windows were changed. Only the courtyard porch appears to have been unaltered. It was either during this phase, or possibly at an earlier date, that the southern part of the east wall of the original east range was rebuilt in stone and brick.

PHASE FIVE

Further alterations took place towards the end of the nineteenth century, but all in the same style as the phase 4 work. These included a shallow single-storey extension between the stacks on the west elevation and a new addition to the service end of the house, running from the north-eastern section of the phase 3 wing. A wall was built across the northern boundary of the phase 4 courtyard, which was then covered with a glazed conservatory roof. The entrance carriageway to the courtyard was blocked up at the same time (Fig. 2).

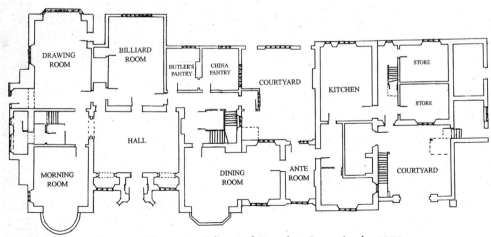

Figure 2. The ground floor of Caradoc Court in the 1970s.

PHASE SIX

In the early twentieth century a few minor changes took place. Electric light was installed throughout the mansion before 1910, by which time it had three bathrooms. Some time before 1929 the view tower was removed and the lower section of the southern wall of the original east wing was removed and the upper sections supported on steel joists. Shortly afterwards a canted bay was added to the ground floor of the southern gable of this wing, beneath the existing phase 4 oriel window. The phase 3 service wing was redesigned to create a large south-facing dining room, which included the adjoining ante-room, and the ground floor fireplace was moved to the north wall. Central heating was installed and steel girders supported a series of water tanks in the attics. Much of this later work was left precariously hanging in space after the fire.

A PRE-FIRE DESCRIPTION

The clearance of the debris after the fire and the careful laying-out and drawing of the burnt and charred timbers from the various frames provided the information for the detailed historical analysis of the building. But what was the building like before the fire when it was still in use as a large twentieth-century house? Fortunately there are sufficient descriptions and photographs to provide a reasonably complete picture of this Herefordshire mansion.[11]

THE GROUND FLOOR

The single-storey stone entrance porch is essentially neo-Tudor, but incorporated a variety of other styles. It led into the late nineteenth-century grand entrance hall (Pl. 4). The flat pine ceiling with carved decoration was 6.7m high and the floor was covered with fine encaustic tiles made by Godwins of Hereford. The roof beams were supported on short wall posts, resting on corbels, with carved pendants hanging from the brackets. The architectural features of this new hall were a typical mixture of medieval and Renaissance. The first floor gallery, which linked the west and east wings, was given an Italianate arcade looking down into the new hall. This had moulded heads to the openings, which were flanked by free-standing pillars of Grinshill stone and incongruously fitted with wooden neo-Jacobean balustrades. Large four-centre headed open doorways, also flanked with Grinshill stone pillars led from the hall into the window alcoves on either side of the porch, and a similar doorway led through into the west stairwell. Three symmetrically placed doorways led through the north wall of the new hall, the central one into the old hall, whilst those on either side gave access into the west and east wings. Each opening was deep-set into the wall with panelled reveals, moulded jambs and square cornices – copies of a typical design of *c*1700. The walls were plain plastered, with seventeenth-century style panelling covering the lower sections.

The western wing contained the main staircase, still timber-framed and continuing up to the second floor, with a small cloakroom behind it in part of the large western bay window. Through the south wall of the staircase a doorway led into the morning room with its large semi-circular bay window. It had an oak-panelled dado, a carved oak and marble fireplace, and a late nineteenth-century moulded plaster ceiling. The drawing room, which was to the north of the staircase, had a door in part of the large western bay that led out onto the western terrace and a shallow bay window on the north. It had an open fireplace with a timber surround on the eastern wall and a moulded plaster ceiling.

Plate 4. The entrance hall in 1978.   *Photo: Foster & Skeffington*

The original axial hall, to the north of the entrance hall, was above part of the cellars. It was in use as a dining room in 1910, but was used as a billiard room until the 1970s. By 1983 the billiard table had been moved into the northern room of the west range and the old hall had become the drawing room. The half-timbered walls were covered in mid-seventeenth-century moulded panelling and there was a seven-light window in the north wall. The fireplace in the west wall had a bolecton-moulded surround of about 1700 and the moulded plaster ceiling was of nineteenth-century date.

The dining room, which was to the east of the entrance hall, was originally two rooms. The western half was part of the service range of the phase 1 building and had stopped and chamfered ceiling beams. The eastern half was part of the new link block. The separating wall, which had originally contained the chimney stack, was removed in the early twentieth century when a new marble fireplace was installed in the central part of the north wall. The room was lit with a modern bay window and a three-light window in the south wall and by another three-light window on the court-yard side. There was an ante room on the east leading into the service wing. The wall to the west of the fireplace, which separated the dining room from the central stairwell, was timber-framed.

There was a stone staircase leading down to the cellars that ran underneath the billiard room and part of the original east range. This central staircase suffered several complex changes in order to provide access into the eastern part of the building and was eventually abandoned in favour of a first floor passageway from the entrance hall balcony.

To the north of the central staircase position was a passageway that led from the hall and billiard room into the courtyard where there was a timber-framed porch lined with seventeenth-century panelling. On the north side of the passageway were two small rooms – the butler's pantry and china pantry (used as breakfast room and kitchen in 1983). Both were timber-framed and above the cellars.

The courtyard separated the main building from the servants quarters to the east. It was originally approached from the south through the ante-room area by a passageway. The western side was timber-framed and included the porch and the first-floor timber-framed corner projection for the servants' staircase. The courtyard had a tiled floor and an iron-framed conservatory roof. The rubble-built eastern range, which contained the main kitchen, servants' hall, rear stairwell, and various storage areas, suffered least damage during the fire.

THE FIRST FLOOR

The main staircase in the centre of the western range was reconstructed in the nineteenth century. It provided access to the south bedroom above the morning room. This room was lined with seventeenth-century moulded oak panelling. To the north of the staircase was a short passage leading to the north-western bedroom and a bathroom. The passage also led to the front hall balcony from which there was a doorway leading into the bedroom above the billiard room. This timber-framed room had a seven-light window in the north wall and a fireplace with a stone surround. It also had a connecting doorway with the north-western bedroom and a second doorway leading to a bathroom and WC above the butler's pantry. The remainder of the eastern range of the original building contained two more bedrooms and the passageway that had replaced the central staircase. There was one bedroom over the ante room and several more in the service range to the east.

SECOND FLOOR

The second floor was essentially within the roof spaces and was in two parts – the main building and the eastern service wing. There was no connection between the two at this level.

Only the western staircase approached the second floor in the main building. The central staircase may at one time have provided a secondary access, but of this there was no trace. The stairwell led to a long west-east passageway on the northern side of the central gully. In the western wing, both the southern and the central attic bed-rooms contained early seventeenth-century fireplaces with square-chamfered heads and continuous jambs onto shaped stops. The north-western attic bedroom retained

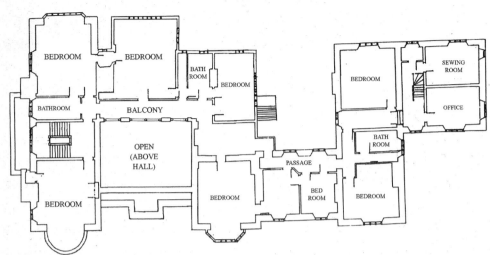

Figure 3. The first floor of Caradoc Court in the 1970s

a considerable amount of early seventeenth-century wall painting on stucco, set between the main timbers of the roof. On the sloping west and east walls the lower part consisted of two bands of conventional foliage and a few birds, arranged in scroll patterns, and painted in black line tinted with red and blue colour. The same decoration continued on the south partition wall. Above the upper purlins were two friezes of landscape in panels, separated by a truss, with trees and outlines of buildings.

Plate 5. The wall paintings in the attic.   *Photo: Foster & Skeffington*

There was a series of small box/bedrooms on the northern side of the passageway and in the original eastern range. Above the entrance hall were two rooms. The western one, without any illumination, was apparently the chamber underneath the large cupola shown on late nineteenth- and early twentieth-century photographs.

In 1978 the second floor of the service range had been converted into a self-contained flat.

CONCLUSION

It is rare to be provided with both the opportunity and the finance to carry out a survey and analysis of a building of such interest as Caradoc Court. Although the basic design of the building was appreciated, the details of its construction, the unusual carpentry, the gradual replacement in stone, could only be hypothetical. The fire, tragic though it was, opened up the building and allowed the long-hidden details of its complex constructional history to be studied and analysed. The many drawings and photographs made by the City of Hereford Archaeology Unit during the survey, which are far too complex and lengthy to be included in this article, will be deposited in the Herefordshire Record Office.

REFERENCES
[1] 'Fourth Field Meeting, Tuesday, August 28th, 1928,' *TWNFC*, XXVI, (1926), lxix-lxxv.
[2] 'Third Field Meeting, Saturday, 12th July, 1952,' *TWNFC*, XXXIV, (1952), ix-x.
[3] 'Caradoc Court – Preliminary Report July 1989,' Hereford Archaeology Series 56 (internal publication).
[4] J. W. Hales & F. J. Furnivall (eds), *Bishop Percy's Folio Manuscript: Ballads and Romances*, (3 vols, 1868) ii, 304-11; C. J. Robinson, *A History of the Mansions and Manors of Hereford-shire*, 1872, 248.
[5] Matthew in J. Duncumb, *Collections towards the History of Herefordshire*, vi, Upper Division, pt. 2, 130.
[6] eg Kelly, *Directory of Herefordshire*, 1891, 150.
[7] W. Davies, *The Llandaff Charters*, 1979, 230b.
[8] B. Coplestone-Crow, *Herefordshire Place-Names*, 1989, 179.
[9] C. J. Robinson, *A History of the Mansions and Manors of Herefordshire*, 1872, 248.
[10] Ibid. note 9.
[11] The following sale catalogues were consulted: John D. Wood & Co., London, (1910); W. H. Cooke & Arkwright, Hereford, (1978); Russell, Baldwin & Bright and Knight, Frank & Rutley, Hereford, (1983); Coles Knapp Residential, Ross, (post fire). Further details were taken from the Royal Commission index card for Caradoc (1929).

Ullingswick: A Study of Open Fields and Settlement Patterns

JOAN E. GRUNDY

The present day countryside of Herefordshire, with its neatly hedged fields, orchards and hopyards, overlies an earlier landscape characterised by wide tracts of unfenced arable land. Under the open field system, the arable land of each settlement had a regular layout and was cultivated, in common, by all the farmers of the settlement. There is a broadly accepted recognition of two main types of rural settlement with contrasting geographical distributions: (a) nucleated villages, which are most numerous in a broad expanse of Midland England and (b) hamlets and scattered homesteads, which are more typical of western regions including Herefordshire.[1]

The open field system is usually associated with nucleated villages, which are scarce in eastern Herefordshire, yet here open fields were formerly much in evidence. The relationship between settlements and open fields was recognised as long ago as 1915, when H. L. Gray, in his classic *English field systems*, chose to compare Herefordshire, a county of hamlet settlement with irregular field systems, with Oxfordshire where nucleated villages and a more orderly arrangement of two-field or three-field systems were most common.

Gray drew attention to the parish of Ullingswick, which he considered to be one of the more convincing examples of a three-field system in Herefordshire, and which survived in a recognisable form well into the nineteenth century.[2] Additional maps have since come to light which enable us to examine the parish in greater detail. Parish and estate plans with schedules of landholding, occupation and land use, combined with printed maps, enable detailed examination of the agrarian landscape of the parish as it was in the late eighteenth and early nineteenth centuries. A systematic study has not been made of earlier sources, but reference will be made to certain earlier documents which are fundamental to understanding the later period. The focus of the study is the open arable fields, their structure and form, and the evidence they provide for the changing landscape of Ullingswick.

The features of an open field system are:[3]

(1) the cropping land of a settlement is divided into two or three *fields* of roughly equal size;
(2) within these fields the land is subdivided into *open* or unfenced *strips* or *parcels*, grouped into interlocking bundles or *furlongs*;
(3) the land of each holding is distributed equally between the fields, in strips intermingled with those of other holdings;

(4)There is communal regulation of all aspects of husbandry. (This feature relates to function rather than form, and will not be considered here.)

Ullingswick lies in the eastern part of Herefordshire, where Dorothy Sylvester identified the anomaly that, despite dispersed settlement and an almost complete absence of villages, there was wide distribution of open fields. She considered it a challenging puzzle that open fields in the county were most numerous where nucleated villages were fewest.[4] Although today Ullingswick appears amorphous, the parish can be shown to have been highly structured, organised on ecclesiastical, seigneurial and agrarian lines, all forming overlapping and interlinking layers.

THE ANCIENT PARISH OF ULLINGSWICK
The study is based on the ancient parish of 1,245 statute acres (504 hectares). This was smaller than the present parish, but included a detached portion about 8 miles (13km) S.W. in Lugg Meadow. The area and boundaries shown on the tithe map and schedule (sealed 1842) have been taken as the standard; the tithe schedule acreage was accepted by the registrar general in the printed census returns of 1851.[5]
    Bryant's map published in 1835 shows the boundaries of the ancient parish, together with the roads and tracks and the main areas of settlement (Fig. 1).[6] The parish is recognisably similar to that of the present day, showing two main clusters of dwellings about 1 mile (1.6km) apart. These are: (a) Lower Town, where the church is situated. Three farmsteads and the Old Rectory are the only other buildings. Lower Town has been identified as a shrunken medieval settlement with earthworks S of the church.[7] (b) Upper Town, which is sited along and around a low ridge overlooking former marsh land.
    In addition to these two main groups, Bryant indicates widely scattered homesteads in other locations, at Cornets, Crosen, Criftage and elsewhere, which are distant from the main settlements. Bryant differentiates by dotted and solid lines where the roads cross open and enclosed land. His map indicates that large areas of the parish were as yet unenclosed.

THE ANCIENT PARISH IN 1783
(1) Lordship
Fig. 2 shows the distribution of leasehold and copyhold land held under the dean and chapter of Gloucester in 1783. It covers 840 acres, which is 69% of the total parish, or just over two-thirds of the tithe map acreage.[8] A document of 1186 records that two parts of the entire land of 'Ullyngwyk' remained the abbot of Gloucester's, and the third part remained Walter Giffard's.[9] This seems remarkable persistence of land-holding, but Christopher Taylor has drawn attention to the long-standing continuity of tenurial estates in the hands of perpetual institutions such as the church.[10] This must be significant, because certain portions of land are also divided in the propor-tions two-thirds and one-third (Fig. 2).[11] (See below, Lugg Meadow; and p.292).
(2) Layout
The dean and chapter land does not lie in a large self-contained estate, but is scattered throughout the parish in 702 relatively small plots, intermingled with land in other ownership.
    It cannot be assumed that the *layout* of 1783 is any indication of that of the late twelfth century, but, whenever it was surveyed, it seems clear that the layout in Fig. 2 is unlikely to have been devised from choice. Being neither rigidly planned nor

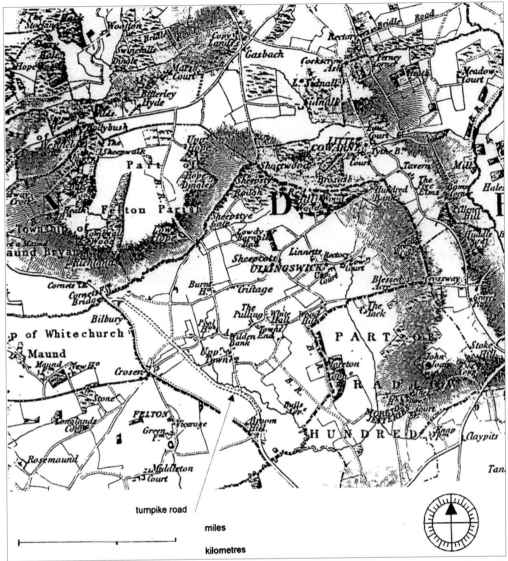

tumpike road

miles

kilometres

Figure 1. The ancient parish of Ullingswick. (Detached portion not shown). From A. Bryant's map of Herefordshire, surveyed 1822, 1833 and 1834, pub. 31 October 1835. Scale of original 1.5in to 1 statute mile.

completely random, it must have had some relationship to another underlying pattern or patterns (not necessarily earlier). The layout need not be ancient, indeed, it may be the latest of a series of reorganisations, and it may not have covered the whole parish at the same time. But the perpetuation of pre-existing shares was clearly a vitally important part of any reallocation of land.

(3) Detached portion

On the Coningsby map of the manor of Marden, surveyed c1720, a large section of Lugg Meadow is annotated: 'The first vesture of this part of the Meadow belongs to the several Townships of Thinchill, Livers Ockhill, Morton, Holmer, Preston,

Figure 2. Ullingswick lands of the dean and chapter of Gloucester. From 'Map of the Several Leasehold & Copyhold Estates in the Manor of Ullingswick and County of Hereford. Held under the Dean and Chapter of Gloucester. Survey'd by T. Harris 1783'.

Ullinswick, and Felton.'[12] This means that the named places were entitled only to the first cut of the meadow, and this is confirmed by a terrier of 1790.[13]

Around 1785, the area of the detached part of the parish was about 13.7 acres.[14] Of this, 10.5 acres was divided in the proportions two-thirds and one-third and was also changeable land, i.e. the occupiers of this common meadow 'yearly interchanged' their allotments.[15]

The area was affected by the Marden enclosure, signed in 1818, and the Ullingswick tithe map of 1839 shows just over 10.5 acres in a layout of rectangular parcels.

SUMMARY The parish is the unit of land area studied, but there is unconformity between the parish boundaries and those of the two estate plans on which FIG. 3 is based. Both plans include land adjoining the parish to the N: 73 acres at Sidnall in Pencombe parish and 99 acres at Shortwood and Brocks[ash] Coppice in Little Cowarne parish (all named in Fig. 1). This may mean that, at the time of the agreement between Walter Giffard and the dean and chapter of Gloucester, the parish boundaries were ill-defined, or that there was in existence another, larger, territorial unit.

THE TOWNSHIPS

The term township refers to the two agricultural territories of Lower Town and Upper Town.[16]

Lower Town occupies the more favourable site from a farming point of view. The land faces S., and is sheltered from the N. and E. by the escarpment of Hundred Bank and from the W. by Wood Hill. A small stream flows around the edge of the settlement.

Upper Town has a more open, rolling landscape with long, bare ridges exposed to all winds except the N., yet providing localised shelter for livestock. Streams run only around the base of the ridge, so running water is less accessible than in Lower Town.

TABLE 1

AREAS OF ARABLE LAND IN OPEN FIELDS, *c*1785

Holding	Site	Tenure c = copyhold f = freehold l = leasehold	Acres of open arable in:	
			Lower Town	Upper Town
Linnett	L	c	4.6	0.0
Lower Court	L	l	75.5	3.9
Sheepcot	L	l	53.3	0.0
Upper Court	L	f	60.0	0.0
Brooking	L	l	5.0	28.2
Criftage	U	c	0.0	0.3
Pool House	U	c	5.8	17.9
Pulling	U	c	3.4	63.3
Steps	U	c	0.0	48.5
Stonehouse	U	c	0.0	21.6
Good, Geo.	U	c	0.0	13.3
Love, Ann	U	c	0.0	34.6
Mason, John	U	c	0.0	10.8
TOTALS			207.7	242.3
Lower Town (L)			198.4	32.1
Upper Town (U)			9.3	210.2

Holdings 5 hectares (2 acres) and over. 1.0 hectare = 2.471 acres.
Sources: Dean's map 1783; Book of Reference to Dean's map; Estate map 1788; Ullingswick enclosure map and award 1856. [17]

Each township is a separate economic unit, with its own open fields, as indicated by the following:

- the enclosure of 1856 deals only with Upper Town and the three fields, Bebury, Broomhill and Wood. Therefore, any other open fields must belong to Lower Town. Separating the townships by open fields gives the conjectural division shown in Fig. 3 and allocates to them approximately equal acreages.
- the farm homesteads are sited within each loosely clustered settlement, with the exception of Criftage and Brooking. The latter lies close to Sheepstye Gate (see Fig. 1). Although a few farms have a small acreage of arable land in another township, the open arable land of each holding is normally confined to the township in which the homestead lies (Table 1).

There are differences between the two townships.
- Tenure. All dean and chapter holdings in Upper Town are copyhold, while in Lower Town most are leasehold. In the period under review, copyholds were for three lives and leases for twenty-one years.
- Layout. Upper Town has three large compact open fields; Lower Town has eight fields of irregular size and shape (Fig. 3).
- Parcels in the open fields are generally larger and more rectangular in Upper Town.
- Open field land covers a higher proportion of the farmed land of Upper Town: 53% as opposed to 44% in Lower Town (Table 5).
These factors may account for differences in the timing of change in the two townships.

Two further distinctions are:
- the glebe land, the arable portion of which lies in the open fields, is confined to Lower Town.
- in Lower Town are certain lands divided in the proportions two-thirds and one-third, as is the changeable land in Lugg Meadow. One of these is Red Hill, a steep escarpment on the N. boundary of the parish (hatched in FIG. 2). Another tiny plot, Church Green, lies in Redway Field. The shared use of Lugg Meadow suggests that these two areas were also shared, perhaps as common pasture.

SUMMARY At community level, there were two agricultural territories within the parish in the late eighteenth century. These were separate economic units with different features and different patterns of evolution.

THE OPEN FIELDS
The cropping land of the townships lay mainly in the open arable fields.

UPPER TOWN
This township conforms more closely to Gray's classic arrangement of three open fields. Gray considered that, as in Upper Town, open-field arable should predominate over closes as a characteristic feature of the 'Midland' system (Table 6). The land of the individual holdings lies in intermingled strips within each field. In addition, the Dean's, tithe and enclosure maps, with their accompanying schedules, provide reliable and detailed information about the size, shape, layout and occupation of the fields.

(1) 1783. Since the Dean's map excludes part of the township, tithe survey

evidence combined with enclosure must be used to reconstruct the layout of the open fields in their entirety. The total area of the three open fields at enclosure in 1856 was 258.75 acres.[19] This agrees closely with the 1842 total in Table 2. Copyholds in the open fields amounted to 63% of the total area, approximating to the two-thirds share of the dean and chapter in 1186.

Figure 3. The open field landscape of Ullingswick, *c*1785. Figure 3 is based on two late eighteenth-century estate plans: 1. The Dean's map. 2. *A MAP of an Estate in the Parish of Ullingwick* [sic] *in the County of Hereford; the property of* [BLANK]. *Survey'd by Tho. Buckle 1788.*[18] The two plans can be combined jigsaw-fashion, and together cover 990 acres which is 81% of the tithe map area of 1,217 acres, excluding roads and waste; and 91% of the *farmed* area (see Glossary) at the time of the tithe survey. Despite the incomplete coverage of the two plans, the only holding of significant size to be omitted is Wilden, 87 acres in 1842.

TABLE 2   OPEN FIELDS IN UPPER TOWN

Field name	1783		1842	
	acres	no. of parcels	acres	no. of parcels
Bebury	81.5	100	93.2	142
Broomhill	70.5	117	62.3	118
Wood	90.3	135	101.7	106
Total	242.3	352	257.2	366
Mean parcel size	0.69		0.70	

Source: 1783: as Table 1. 1842: tithe map and schedule; enclosure map and award.[20]

The jagged edges of all three open fields suggest that piecemeal enclosures were nibbling them away before formal enclosure took place. Several adjoining closes have intermingled strips within them (Fig. 2). It may be speculated that the three fields were originally equal in area and more extensive, perhaps each of 90 to 100 acres.[21] The fields abut the very edges of the parish, leaving neither wastes nor commons. However, the ample enclosed land allowed each farmer to control grazing arrangements in his own way.

The open field layout of 1783 may represent reallocation or relocation of the township's arable land, as there is evidence of a possible earlier field system. *Longlands* and *Old Acre* field names are found very close to the settlement, and virtually all of the enclosed land of Upper Town is intermingled between copyholders and freeholders in the same way as that of the open fields. There are also several enclosures, particularly to the N. of the settlement, in which intermingled strips are held by the occupiers of the township's holdings (Fig. 2). These are demonstrated clearly in FIG. 2 and may be the fossilised furlongs of an earlier open field.

(2) Enclosure. Between c1785 and 1842, some areas in Bebury and Broomhill Fields were enclosed and the new holding of Broomhill was created. The newly built Leominster to Ledbury turnpike road (Fig. 1) was probably the catalyst for this, slicing across strips, creating awkward corners and impeding access. Plans for the road were drawn up in 1824,[22] and in 1826 it was noted that the commissioners of the new road through the parish were to pay each proprietor for the damage to, and loss of, land.[23]

Final enclosure of the three open fields of Upper Town took place in 1856.[24] After this date there were no open fields in the parish.

LOWER TOWN

(1) c1785. As the open arable land in Lower Town was enclosed before 1842, evidence is restricted to the Dean's map and a series of estate plans. Certain small freeholds are therefore not represented.

Lower Town has eight open fields of irregular size and shape (Fig. 3 and Table 3). As in Upper Town, the land lies in intermingled parcels, but these are generally larger and more rectangular than the long, narrow strips in Upper Town (Fig. 2). Again, field patterns outside the open fields indicate that these were once more extensive. The multiplicity of fields and greater irregularity of size and shape support Gray's comments on Herefordshire, that irregular fields were indicative of progress towards enclosure.[25]

Despite the apparent complexity of eight fields of widely differing area, earlier documents suggest that they comprised a three-field system. The glebe terrier of 1589 describes Callow Hill as being in Broxash Field. This is confirmed by the 1614 terrier, which also lists Little Field under Lowdy, and combines Marsh Field and Little Marsh.[26] A seventeenth-century terrier includes Great and Little Marsh and Redway in Church Field, and confirms Little Field as part of Lowdy Field.[27]

Such combination of fields may indicate extensions of the originals – for instance Lowdy and Little Fields. In the case of Church Field, however, it is possible that Marsh Field may have been a substitute for early-enclosed areas in Church Field. Perhaps also the western tip of Wood Field (in Upper Town) had originally been part of Church Field.

In Lower Town, it appears that the three fields may have also been about 90 acres

TABLE 3
OPEN FIELDS IN LOWER TOWN, c1785

Field name	as eight fields:		as three fields:		
	acres	no. of parcels		acres	no. of parcels
Broxash	51.2	33	Broxash & Callow	66.2	46
Callow	15.0	13			
Church	34.7	32			
Great Marsh	22.9	21	Church, Marsh	63.7	60
Little Marsh	4.4	4	& Redway		
Redway	1.7	3			
Lowdy	73.0	69	Lowdy & Little	78.4	76
Little	5.4	7			
Total	208.3	182		208.3	182
Mean parcel size	1.1			1.1	

Source: as Table 1.

when first laid out. However, it seems likely that the layout of c1785 represents a major reorganisation. The parcels are larger than those in Upper Town, their shapes more regular, and there are fewer holdings (Table 1). There is evidence from the sixteenth century and later of complete reorganisation of field patterns. Certain very regular divisions of arable land into three fields, with orderly allocation of land between holdings 'make it clear that schemes to rationalise field systems were being put into practice'.[28] In some east Yorkshire townships during the sixteenth and seventeenth centuries, exchange of lands gave each tenant fewer but larger parcels, known as 'flatts', perhaps in contrast to 'ridges'.[29] Broxash, Church, Marsh and Lowdy Fields could all be interpreted as examples of such a procedure.

(2) Enclosure. Between c1785 and 1832, the open arable fields became enclosed and the land allocated to separate holdings. This took place as a series of piecemeal enclosures of varying size, affecting different parts of the fields, amidst a background of constant trafficking in land, changes of leaseholders, and reallocation of parcels between holdings. The open fields of Lower Town had been obliterated by the time of the tithe map of 1839.

SUMMARY It has been shown that a layout of three open arable fields was present in each township. The fields represent the economic wealth of the community; its working assets.

The fields of Upper Town have the more archaic layout – large and compact, with long, narrow strips. Yet there are clues that these may replace earlier open fields of similar layout, sited closer to the settlement.

In Lower Town, the more rectangular parcels indicate amalgamation or reallocation of land between holdings, and the large number of irregular fields may indicate progress towards more flexible rotations or a wider choice of crops.

HOLDINGS

The land was worked by the occupiers of the farm holdings.[30] At the time of the tithe survey in 1842, there were eighty-seven occupiers of land in Ullingswick, forty having less than 1 acre. In order to focus on those who might be described as farmers, analysis has been restricted to holdings of 5 acres (2 ha) and over. The land occupied by these holdings is the farmed land of the parish. There is evidence of considerable flexibility of land holding – farms subdivide and amalgamate, enlarge and contract, appear in and disappear from the records. Including the glebe, twenty-seven separate holdings can be identified between 1783 and 1870, but no more than nineteen appear in any one of the three main sources.

TABLE 4
FARMED LAND IN THE PARISH

	c1785	1842	1870
No. of holdings	13	19	19
Total farmed land: acres:	940.7	1037.4	1043.7
In Upper Town	410.7	523.5	517.0
In Lower Town	530.0	513.9	526.7
Total open field land (acres)	450.0	237.8	0

Source: *c*1785 and 1842: as TABLE 2; 1870: Tithe re-apportionment.[31]

The relationships between townships, fields and holdings *c*1785 are shown in Table 5. Although the farmed land of each township was approximately equal in area (Table 4), there is a difference in the number and size of the holdings sharing each set of open fields. In Lower Town *c*1785 there were three holdings of over 100 acres, and these totalled 82% of the farmed land. In Upper Town there was only one holding of this size (Table 5). This suggests that, even within an open field system, Lower Town had made more progress towards amalgamating smaller holdings, thereby creating larger farms.

Gray noted that a Herefordshire parish 'usually consisted of several hamlets, each with its group of fields in which seldom so many as ten tenants had holdings of any size'. In Oxfordshire, there were normally more than ten, sometimes as many as thirty. He thought that departures from a regular system could be more easily made among fewer tenants, easing moves towards irregular systems and towards enclosure.[32]

The land of several holdings is fairly evenly distributed by area between three open fields (Table 5). In Lower Town, Upper Court is a clear example. In Upper Town, there are Steps, Stonehouse, Geo. Good, Ann Love and John Mason. Tithe survey data show that Wilden (with 14, 14 and 15 acres in each of the fields), and possibly Gobbott (4, 3, 5), may be added to the list.

There is little evidence of the sequential allocation of strips to holdings within each furlong. However, some areas of each township show systematic recurrence of freehold strips (Fig. 2), and the strict adherence to the allocation of proportionate shares has already been noted.

The holding of Upper Court (both house and lands are in Lower Town) is of particular interest. It is freehold, but also holds one-third of the changeable land in Lugg Meadow and one-third of Red Hill (the other two-thirds of Red Hill were held by leaseholders). In 1700, 'the Upper Mann[o]r or Court in Ullenswicke' held the perpetual advowson of the rectory of Ullingswick.[33]

TABLE 5
TOWNSHIPS, FIELDS AND HOLDINGS, c1785 (acres)

| Holding | Open Fields in | | | | | | Total Holding | Land in Open Field (%) |
| | Upper Town | | | Lower Town | | | | |
	Bebury	Broom-hill	Wood	Broxash & Callow	Church Marsh & Redway	Lowdy & Little		
Upper Town								
Criftage	0.3						17.2	2
Pool House	8.1	3.9	6.0			5.8	41.1	58
Pulling	16.0	18.1	29.2		1.7	1.7	135.1	49
Steps	16.6	17.2	14.6				77.4	63
Stonehouse	7.6	7.4	6.6				35.5	61
Good, Geo.	5.0	5.0	3.3				23.7	56
Love, Ann	10.8	10.6	13.1				56.2	62
Mason, John	3.3	3.2	4.4				24.5	44
Lower Town								
Linnet				1.9	0.8	2.0	19.9	23
Lower Court			3.9	35.9	21.8	17.8	196.0	41
Upper Court				19.3	21.0	19.6	131.6	46
Brooking	13.8	5.2	9.3		1.0	4.1	76.2	44
Sheepcot				9.2	16.8	27.3	106.4	50
Total acreage farmed by:								
Upper Town	67.7	65.4	77.1	0.0	1.7	7.5	410.7	53
Lower Town	13.8	5.2	13.2	66.2	61.4	70.9	530.0	44
Total Open Field	81.5	70.5	90.3	66.2	63.1	78.4	940.7	48

Note: the total acreage of Church, Marsh and Redway Field differs from that shown in Table 3 because 0.6 acres in this field is not part of a 'holding'. Source: as Table 1.

These shreds of evidence point towards the tentative identification of Upper Court with the site of the principal estate of 1186: '...the third part remained Walter Giffard's, with the advowson and the chief house and the orchard'.[34]

The house is situated adjacent to the churchyard; Roberts considers that magnate farmstead and church relationships were important in the twelfth century[35], whilst Morris shows association between manorial sites and Anglo-Saxon churches in Essex, gives medieval examples from the Welsh Marches, and suggests the possibility that churches adjoined the houses of local power-owners.[36]

The regular layout and larger parcels of freehold and leasehold land in Lower Town, suggesting relatively recent reorganisation, has already been noted. Alone among holdings in Lower Town, Upper Court has equal areas of land in each open field. In addition, mean parcel size is half of the size of other parcels, confirming the very precise allocation of open-field land between freeholders and leaseholders.

TABLE 6
PARCEL SIZE IN OPEN FIELDS, LOWER TOWN, c1785

	Mean parcel size (acres)	
	Upper Court land	Land of other occupiers
Broxash	1.0	2.1
Callow	0.7	1.6
Church	0.7	1.5
Great Marsh	0.9	2.0
Lowdy	0.7	1.3

Source: Dean's map 1783, Estate map 1788; both as Table 1.

For total area and other details c1785, see Table 5.

SUMMARY The right to farm land in the open fields was probably restricted to home-steads within the township, and perhaps originally within the settlement cluster. There is a high probability that the cropping land of each holding was allocated equally between the three open arable fields by area.

The above features provide very strong evidence for each township having an open field system of classic form, as set out by Gray.

DISCUSSION
Beneath the apparent formlessness of Ullingswick at the dawn of the twenty-first century lies a highly organised landscape and agrarian system, operating at several different levels.

The open field system
The functional basis was the township, a community with rights over sufficient land for its support. The parish was functionally unrelated to this agricultural territory, but had its own layer of complexity. Division by lordship into two-thirds and one-third proportions affected every field and furlong, open or enclosed, regardless of township. However, this did not preclude reallocation of layout, provided that the proportions were retained in the new arrangement.

The arable land of each township was laid out as three open fields, and the land in these fields was shared by all farmers of the township, whether freeholders or tenants of the dean and chapter. The relatively standardised layout of the two field systems therefore conceals complex patterns of landholding and tenure.

Settlement and open fields

Ullingswick townships (assuming them to be half the parish) are 622 acres, but evidence shows that small size did not preclude them from the open field system. The average size of an English lowland township is 2,320 acres; in Herefordshire it is 1,811 acres.[37]

Perhaps what is now seen as dispersed settlement simply means smaller townships, and therefore *settlement clusters* which are closer together. Population loss and removal of homesteads (which occurred in Ullingswick) would fracture these small nucleations into fragmentary survivals. Once enclosure had obscured and made obsolete the earlier structures, the individuality of the settlements was lost, particularly when they were too small to become civil parishes.

CONCLUSIONS

Late eighteenth-century and later sources can be valuable in interpreting the patterns and forms of earlier landscapes, but do not allow dating of the various stages. However, they provide numerous pointers to the direction of future enquiry, using earlier sources.

Della Hooke notes that 'in the West Midland region we are only just at the stage of identifying early township communities and the nature and extent of their field systems can only be guessed at'.[38] Detailed examination of Ullingswick parish over a relatively short time-span has contributed to understanding field systems and settlement patterns in the Welsh Marches.

ACKNOWLEDGEMENTS

The assistance of the following is gratefully acknowledged: Staff of Gloucestershire Record Office; Mrs M. J. Hallam, Graffham, Sussex; Staff of the Reference Library and Local Collection, Hereford Library; Staff of Herefordshire Record Office; Mr W. D. Turton, Leominster.

GLOSSARY

Township: a community comprising a settlement and its agricultural territory.

Holding: 5 acres (2 hectares) and over, occupied by the same person, with homestead site in the parish. Land in the occupation of persons resident outside the parish is therefore excluded.

Farmed land: total area occupied by the holdings defined above.

Open field: unenclosed field, with land in intermingled strips, but not necessarily communally regulated. Sale particulars in the eighteenth and nineteenth centuries often refer to 'common fields' in the sense of 'unenclosed'. Here, the term 'open' means 'unenclosed'; 'common' is confined to situations where there is evidence of common agriculture.

REFERENCES

[1] B. K. Roberts, *The making of the English village* (1987), Fig. 1.1.

[2] H. L. Gray, *English field systems* (1959), 143.

[3] Ibid, based on Gray's 'Midland' system', 39-47.

[4] D. Sylvester, *The rural landscape of the Welsh Borderland: a study in historical geography* (1969), 32, 371.

[5] *Census, Printed Returns*, 1851.   [6] HRO 6/24/4, a copy of HRO T70/27.

[7] S. C. Stanford, 'The deserted medieval village of Hampton Wafer, Herefordshire', *TWNFC*, XXXIX (1969), 71-92.

[8] Compared with the Tithe map, the Dean's map over-estimated the area by 6 to 8 per cent. This would make the true total about 790 acres, 65% of the parish. Gloucestershire Record Office (GRO) bundle D936 E227.

[9] J. H. Parry (ed.), *Register of Lewis de Charlton, Bishop of Hereford, AD 1361-1369* (1913), p35; another copy in: W. H. Hart (ed), *Historia et cartularium Monasterii Sancti Petri Gloucestriae* (1863), II, 156.

[10] C. Taylor, *Village and farmstead: a history of rural settlement in England* (1983), 104.

[11] GRO D1740 P3. The map includes 73 acres in Pencombe parish.

[12] HRO J94/1. A possible link between the named places may lie in Sheppard's speculation of a territorial unit based on the hill fort of Sutton Walls, overlooking Lugg Meadow. June A. Sheppard, *The origins and evolution of field and settlement patterns in the Herefordshire manor of Marden* (1979), fig. 9 (Dept. of Geography, Queen Mary College, University of London, Occasional Papers No 15.)

[13] GRO Bundle D636 E224: *A Particular of an Estate situate at Ullingswick...1790.*

[14] Totals from the two sources of MAP 3 differ.

[15] HRO G37/II/265 of 1700. However, GRO Bundle D636 E224: sale particulars, 1783 gives 'every other year', as does the document named in note 13.

[16] B. K. Roberts, *Rural settlement in Britain* (1977), 77, has township - economic area of a cluster settlement. *Hamlet* suggests settlement rather than tract of land, yet Sylvester uses the term for 'small agricultural communities'. op cit. in note 4, 199. Ullingswick townships do not become separate nineteenth-century civil parishes with delineated boundaries.

[17] *Book of Reference to Dean's Map, n.d. c1800*: GRO D1740 E4. (From internal evidence, the Book may be dated between 1789 and 1800.) Estate Map 1788: see p.6 and note 18. Ullingswick Enclosure Map and Award, 1856: HRO Q/R1/54.

[18] Collection of Mr W. D. Turton, Leominster. The map includes 99 acres in Little Cowarne parish.

[19] But op. cit. in note 2, 140: 290.5 acres; W. E. Tate, 'A hand list of English enclosure acts and awards. Part 15. - Herefordshire' *TWNFC*, (1941), 193: 260 acres; W. E. Tate and M. E. Turner *Domesday of English enclosure acts and awards* (1978), 135: 248 acres awarded.

[20] Tithe map and award : HRO HD429/L146; enclosure map and award: as note 17.

[21] Noted by Gray, op cit in note 2, 143.   [22] HRO Q/RWt/21 and Q/RWt/23.

[23] GRO Bundle D936 E230.

[24] op. cit. in note 17. The award lists five 'old enclosures', all under half an acre.

[25] op. cit. in note 2, 153.   [26] 1589: HRO HD2/1/71; 1614: HD2/1/73.

[27] GRO bundle D936 E218.

[28] A. R. H. Baker and R. A. Butlin (eds) *Studies of field systems in the British Isles* (1973), 647 (Cambridge).

[29] J. A. Sheppard , 'Field systems of Yorkshire', Baker & Butlin, loc. cit., 155.

[30] Defined in Glossary above.   [31] HRO HD 721.   [32] op. cit. in note 2, 153, 407.

[33] HRO G37/II/265.   [34] op. cit. in note 9.   [35] op. cit. in note 1, 152-5.

[36] R. Morris, *Churches in the landscape* (1989), 248-9, 270-4. See also J. Blair, *Early medieval Surrey: landholding, church and settlement before 1300* (1991), esp. 134-5. (Stroud, Glos.)

[37] op cit. in note 1, 168; note 16, 181.

[38] D. Hooke, 'Village development in the West Midlands', in D. Hooke (ed), *Medieval villages: a review of current work* (1985). Oxford University Committee for Archaeology, Monograph no. 5.

LIST OF SUBSCRIBERS

THE NAMES OF THE SUBSCRIBERS TO *A HEREFORDSHIRE MISCELLANY* IN THE YEAR 2000 AT THE BEGINNING OF A NEW MILLENNIUM

1   Not for Sale
2   Not for Sale
3   Not for Sale
4   Not for Sale
5   The Right Reverend Lord Bishop of Hereford and Mrs Oliver
6   The British Library (copyright)
7   The Bodleian Library (copyright)
8   Cambridge University Library (copyright)
9   National Library of Scotland (copyright)
10 Library of Trinity College Dublin (copyright)
11 National Library of Wales (copyright)
12 Basil Butcher
13 David Postle
14 Peter & Alison Young, Bosbury
15
16 Tim Pridgeon
17 The London Library
18 Dr J. H. Bowman, London
19 Mrs R. H. Locker, Lichfield
20 M. Phillips, Sutton Coldfield
21 Eric Lewis, Scarborough
22 Christopher Over, Dinedor
23 Christopher Over
24 J. W. & M. Tonkin, Wigmore
25 Woolhope Naturalists' Field Club
26 Woolhope Naturalists' Field Club
27 Woolhope Naturalists' Field Club
28 Frank Bennett, Tupsley
29 Frank Bennett
30 Herefordshire Record Office
31 Donald Moore, Aberystwyth
32 H. R. Lloyd, Hereford
33 Mr A. J. & Dr A. K. Malpas, Kimbolton
34 Ronald W. Perry, Wellington

35 John A. Farr, Sutton St Nicholas
36 Marches Archaeology, Lyonshall
37 Collette Kendall, Gladestry
38 Jamie Mason
39 Derryan Paul, Aberystwyth
40 Marjorie Jones
41 Helen Davies
42 Kerstin Paul
43 Colin Paul
44 J. G. Nendick, Hereford
45 Archaeological Investigations Ltd.
46 Jon Hurley, Hoarwithy
47 Heather Hurley, Hoarwithy
48 Sandra Carole Fletcher
49 Hereford Sixth Form College
50 Hereford Sixth Form College
51 Dr Richard Parker, Ross-on-Wye
52 Donald J. H. Baker, Droitwich
53 Linda Hansen, Zürich
54 Dr A. Heijn, Pudleston
55 Dr A. Heijn
56 Dr A. Heijn
57 Lawrence Banks, Kington
58 Professor John A. Blair
59 Dr David Boddington, Bromyard
60 R. J. Bray, Tarrington
61 R. J. Bray
62 John Dent, Withington
63 John Dunabin, Warrington
64 Edward Bulmer, Pembridge
65 Edward Bulmer
66 Edward Bulmer
67 Edward Bulmer
68 Jean Sharples, Eardisley
69 Mrs O. L. Champion, Callow
70 Mrs O. L. Champion
71 Peter Newman, Kington
72 Peter Newman
73 Peter Newman
74 Peter Newman
75 Mary Hawtin, Ledbury
76 Mary Hawtin
77 John Taylor, Essex
78 Sir Thomas Dunne

79   George Charnock, Newton St Margarets
80   The Hon. Lady Morrison
81   Graham Sprackling, Ewyas Harold
82   R. W. Clarke, Bodenham
83   Hereford Cathedral Library
84   Hereford Cathedral Library
85   B. R. Edwards, Dulas
86   David & Bridget Halpern, Hereford
87   Doris Charlton, Eardisley. I.M. D.W.C.
88   Pam Cochrane, Tupsley
89   Pam Cochrane
90   Thelma P. Evans, Hereford
91   Trevor Nash
92   D. J. Collins, Pembridge
93   J. Harnden, Tupsley
94   Mr & Mrs J. W. King, Ledbury
95   Valerie Goodbury, West Malvern
96   C. F. Huntley, Linton
97   C. F. Huntley
98   Martin Colman, Ledbury
99   Elizabeth Colman
100 Mr & Mrs G. Shetliffe, Cross Keys
101 Bill Jackson, Breinton
102 Sir John Cotterell
103 Allan Wyatt, Edvin Loach
104 Allan Wyatt
105 Mr & Mrs Ron Drew, Carlisle
106 Kevin Mason, Fownhope
107 William Chinn, Walford
108 Nicholas & Victoria Keeble, Glasbury
109 Mary I. Jones, Bosbury
110 Reverend D. J. Enoch, King's Caple
111 Brian Thomas, Garway
112 Joan Fleming-Yates, Garway
113 Mark Lawley, Ludlow
114 Helen J. Simpson, Eardisland
115 I. & E. Evans, Tupsley
116 Peter Garner, West Malvern
117 Alan Lloyd, Ledbury
118 David Gorvett, Leominster
119 Janet Lawrence, Lyde
120 Peter & Anna Wolley, Leintwardine

121　Jane Rose
122　Muriel E. Hall, Hereford
123　Muriel E. Hall
124　Muriel E. Hall
125　E. A. Morgan, Dorstone
126　Clive Richards, Ullingswick
127　Colin J. Manning, Hereford
128　Peter & Jackie Morgan
129　Richard Mather
130　John M. White
131　Jeremy Wilding, Hereford
132　Helen E. Breen
133　R. Olivia Morris
134　Sophie V. Morris
135　Dr A. J. Warsap, St Margarets
136　Eddie Hatton, Hereford
137　R. W. W. Pantall, Staunton-on-Wye
138　John Meredith, Garway Hill
139　H. T. Pierson, Fownhope
140　Don & Shan Preddy, Lyonshall
141　Margaret & Ernie Kay, Malvern
142　Norman C. Reeves, Leominster
143　Sam Wilson
144　Edward Wilson
145　Mrs U. I. Pyke, Hereford
146　Mrs U. I. Pyke
147　Charles Renton, Hereford
148　Alan & Janet Parry, Coddington
149　Dominic Williams
150　Adam Williams
151　Mary McGhee, Hartpury
152　Anonymous
153　Elizabeth Patrick, Fordbridge
154　A. Welch, Hereford
155　Julian Mitchell, Llansoy
156　Peter M. Scott, Colwall
157　Bromyard & District Local History Society
158　Jennifer Weale
159　Ian McCulloch
160　James & Judith Hereford, Sufton
161　Philip Anderson, How Caple
162　A. Egerton Parker, Hereford
163　B. B. Sutton
164　D. M. Annett, Beauchamp Newland

165　A. MacC. Armstrong, Colwall
166　A. MacC. Armstrong
167　A. MacC. Armstrong
168　Alfred & Nina Dowson, Birtley
169　Mr & Mrs E. H. Ward, Much Marcle
170　Charles & Jean Hopkinson, Little Cowarne
171　Harry & Gillian Bridges, Colwall
172　W. D. Emrys Evans, Whitbourne
173　Rosemary Athay, Much Dewchurch
174　Rosemary Athay
175　Rosemary Athay
176　Pamela C. Roper, Hereford
177　Dr P. R. & Mrs M. L. Morris, West Malvern
178　David Davenport, Mansel Lacy
179　David Davenport
180　David Davenport
181　Peter Quilliam, Hereford
182　Dr G. E. Aylmer, Ledbury
183　Kathleen & Barry Freeman, Eardisland
184　Kathleen & Barry Freeman
185　Phillippe Gill
186　Ian Sanderson, Leeds
187　R. Bradshaw, Brilley
188　Dr Paul Olver, Canon Pyon
189　John Arnett, Little Cowarne
190　Brenda & Edward Mears, Belmont
191　S. Brinded, Kent
192　Dr & Mrs Michael Haggie, Shucknall
193　A. A. Rees, Ross-on-Wye
194　Reverend Ronald Smith, Ledbury
195　Christine Hamer
196　Miss J. R. Davies, Hereford
197　Sheila R. Butt, Hereford
198　Elizabeth Layton Jones, Hereford
199　P. J. Jones, Hereford
200　Nigel S. Carter, Ewyas Harold
201　Captain C. P. Hazlehurst, Llandinabo
202　Sheila & Arthur Davis, Kimbolton
203　Mrs E. J. Ingram, Kings Thorn
204　Mrs B. M. Winser, Hereford
205　Mrs B. M. Winser

206　Mrs P. Cartwright, Hereford
207　Mrs P. Cartwright
208　Mrs V. Caton, Hampton Bishop
209　Mrs V. Caton
210　Mr & Mrs M. C. Lupton, Holmer
211　Robert D. McDuff, Much Birch
212　Bryan & Elizabeth Betts, Canon Pyon
213　Bryan & Elizabeth Betts
214　Miss P. D. Hitch, Sutton St Nicholas
215　Rosalind Lowe, Goodrich
216　Miss M. E. B. Leonard, Hereford
217　Miss M. E. B. Leonard
218　Mr & Mrs C. B. Nixon, Ledbury
219　Linton & District History Society
220　John Tuchfeld, Hereford
221　Dr J. G. M. (Ian) Mortimer, Yarpole
222　John Edwin Lewis, Hereford
223　Dr M. L. Moncrieff, Eye
224　Derek Shorthouse, Highnam
225　Susan Wood, Eardisley
226　Susan Wood
227　David N. Williams, Monmouth
228　John Grove, Llanbadoc, Usk
229　Geoffrey Newman, Hereford
230　Dr D. E. St. J. Burrowes, Wellington Heath
231　Paul R. Hadley
232　Robert Blackith, Dublin
233　H. J. Dance, Yarpole
234　Daphne Rutter
235　Mrs. B. A. Newton, Hereford
236　R. Erle Sparry, Trowbridge
237　Sir Colin Shepherd
238　Mr & Mrs P. J. T. Barbary, Hereford
239　Prebendary Andrew Talbot-Ponsonby
240　John Buchanan-Brown, Hereford
241　Derek A. Price, Woolhope
242　Derek A. Price
243　T. F. Bradstock, Ashperton
244　F. A. Leeds, Wellington Heath

245 Glyn Morgan
246 Mrs A. P. Poppleston, Hereford
247 Longtown Historical Society
248 Dr Richard J. Collins, Bodenham
249 Dr Richard J. Collins
250 Dr Richard J. Collins
251 John Butler, Bewdley
252 Tom Wall, Lydbury North
253 John Osborn
254 John Bray
255 Bruce Coplestone-Crow, King's Norton
256 C. F. Tomaszewski, Tintern
257 Mary & Rosemary Mumford, Swainshill
258 Dr D. J. L. Smith
259 Celia Beckham
260 Michael Neal, Presteigne
261 Edward Harley, Brampton Bryan
262 Edward Harley
263 Edward Harley
264 J. G. Calderbank, Ross-on-Wye
265 Mary Pullan, Abbeydore
266 Carolyn M. Eaton, Garway
267 David Williams, Solihull
268 Roger Hall Jones, Malvern
269 Sidney Roberts, Colwall
270 Mr & Mrs A. W. James, Poston
271 K. F. Coles, Almeley
272 Mr & Mrs E. A. Hadley, Hereford
273 A. G. Brown, Bristol
274 F. E. Skinner, Cradley
275 F. E. Skinner
276 Neil Barnes, St Margarets
277 Sara Stringer, Tupsley
278 Roland Owen-George, Garway
279 Garry Stokes, Sutton St Nicholas
280 Susan Edwards
281 Sir Roy Strong, FSA
282 J. S. Hopton, Buckinghamshire
283 Mr & Mrs S. Guest, Pencombe
284 John Ward, CBE
285 N. Peabody, Madley
286 D. H. Pennington, Linton Hill
287 Gwen Watkins, Hereford

288 Gwen Watkins
289 Dr D. Joan Marsden, Hereford
290 Jim Budd, Brilley
291 C. Hafner, Hay-on-Wye
292 Miss E. R. Gale, Hereford
293 Jeremy Soulsby, Hereford
294 Clive & Rosemary South
295 Elizabeth Lees-Smith, Hereford
296 Margaret L. S. Guy, Hereford
297 Ivor B. Lesser, Abbeydore
298 Anne M. Thompson, Birmingham
299 Anne M. Thompson
300 Jerome Betts, Torquay
301 Tony & Angela Colmer
302 Jennifer Newnham
303 L. J. Gibson, Walsall
304 L. J. Gibson
305 Patricia M. Barrett
306 G. Rees, Leominster
307 Mr & Mrs J. Hyde-Smith, Llanwarne
308 Mrs. F. M. Probyn, Welsh Newton
309 Dr Joan Lane, Leamington Spa
310 Mrs R. Walton, Upper Colwall
311 Paul & Susan King, Eardisley
312 Richard Bartholomew, Malvern
313 Marjorie Hallam
314 Joan Balding, Leominster
315 W. B. Dickinson, Lugwardine
316 W. B. Dickinson
317 Dr David Slater, Sheffield
318 Geoff & Sue Warren, Bodenham
319 Patrick & Margaret Ellis, Hereford
320 C. E. D. Jackson, London
321 C. E. D. Jackson
322 Evelyn Evans
323 Beverley James Whitehouse, Hereford
324 Elizabeth M. Thomas, Leysters
325 Christopher Lyons, Hereford
326 Michael H. Statham, Richmond, Surrey
327 D. C. Layton, Hereford
328 Patrick Lowry, Tupsley
329 Ena Bissell, Abergavenny

330 Mr & Mrs J. E. Dunn, Hereford
331 Charles R. Hereford, Texas
332 Ray & Valerie Hands, Leominster
333 Dr & Mrs. F. W. Pexton, Burghill
334 R. G. Deane, Newton St Margarets
335 Mrs M. M. Rendall, Hereford
336 Mrs L. Harbottle
337 F. E. Okell, Ross-on-Wye
338 Graham Hodgetts, Orleton
339 Tim Hodgetts
340 Dr M. E. Speight, Craven Arms
341 Susan Thomas, Michaelchurch Escley
342 Dr Brian Trueman, Powick
343 Charles Watkins, Ledbury
344 Charles Watkins
345 Mrs R. M. Dunnico, Essex
346 C. R. Mayos, Darlington
347 V. G. Rye, Dorstone
348 Howard F. J. Painter, Tenbury Wells
349 Mr & Mrs T. Teale
350 Shirley Hurlbatt, Ballingham
351 Mr & Mrs Michael Jolley, Ledbury
352 W. S. Phillips, Hereford
353 Mr & Mrs C. R. Riches, Hereford
354 Reverend Felix Watkins
355 Dilys M. Spurrell, Somerset
356 Major B. A. May, Staunton-on-Arrow
357 Joan Nash, Ludlow
358 Philip J. Nicholas, Port Talbot
359 Dr Geoffrey Vevers, Berkshire
360 J. W. Eggar, Hereford
361 Kenneth & Irene Hutchinson, Leicester
362 David Greenhalf, BSc.
363 R. C. Perry, Bromyard
364 Bryan A. Garland, Hereford
365 Mr & Mrs A. B. Mills, Newcastle-upon-Tyne
366 Stephen John Merrick, Bristol
367 Mrs E. Russell, Almeley
368 S. C. Stanford, Leinthall Starkes
369 M. M. Storey, Leominster

370 Wendy Angove, Caerphilly
371 Myrtle Middleton, Hereford
372 A. W. Gunn, Woolhope
373 Paul Morgan, Oxford
374 William Mountney, Germany
375 Dr L. K. Harding, Edgbaston
376 Dr L. K. Harding
377 Dr L. K. Harding
378 Dr Vivien Helme, Lugwardine
379 M. Barbara Wallis, Cambridge
380 J. C. Sockett, Hereford
381 R. A. Sockett, Hereford
382 D. M. Hopson, Monmouth
383 B. & K. Showler, Hay-on-Wye
384 C. & K. Brook
385 The Venerable Len Moss, Ledbury
386 Mrs John Comyn, Turnastone
387 L. W. Powell, Birmingham
388 H. T. Randolph, Abingdon
389 H. T. Randolph
390 Dr J. H. Ross, Hereford
391 Dr J. H. Ross
392 L. J. A. Phipps, Moccas
393 L. J. A. Phipps
394 Doreen Matthews, Llangwm, Usk
395 Paul L. Hunt, Cradley
396 S. B. Kings, Northampton
397 Mr & Mrs L. E. Washer, Hereford
398 Judith Ericksen, Bishops Stortford
399 Norah Lloyd
400 Sarah Hinton
401 Mrs A. F. Peacock, Clehonger
402 Shirley Preece, Ross-on-Wye
403 Frances Rosamond Searson, Derbyshire
404 G. C. Griffith, Peterchurch
405 John V. Addis-Smith, Bedford
406 John V. Addis-Smith
407 Michael J. E. Gater, Northampton
408 Reverend G. D. Restall, Hereford
409 Josephine Bromley, Stansbatch

410 Josephine Bromley
411 Lady Wakeman, Shrewsbury
412 Michael Jones, South Shields
413 Clarence Attfield, Hereford
414 P. Cotton, Much Marcle
415 K. W. Prosser, Leighton Buzzard
416 Dr & Mrs D. M. Spencer, Eardisley
417 The Lady Cross, Leintwardine
418 Derek Jackson, Exeter
419 George Phillip Lancett, Presteigne
420 J. Owen, Caerphilly
421 Darryll Seabourne, Bognor Regis
422 K.T. & A. J. Dolling, Weobley
423 Betty Philpott, Kingsthorne
424 Mrs B. A. Hussey, Kent
425 Alan A. Powell, MA, Gwent
426 Mrs S. Jones, St Austell
427 C. A. Virginia Morgan, Walford
428 Mr & Mrs R. E. J. Watkins, Bush Bank
429 A. N. Davis, Eardisley
430 Esmond & Caroline Gale
431 Andrew Sweetman, Moreton on Lugg
432 John Sweetman
433 Mrs R. J. Thorn, Stamford, Lincs.
434 K. C. G. Lucas
435 Edward Clive, Whitfield
436 Albert D. Matthews, Plymouth
437 K. Margaret Brunwin, Chalfont St Giles
438 Christopher J. James, Droitwich
439 Reverend Dr C. J. Armstrong, Pontrilas
440 Marjorie Trimmer, Bembridge, IOW
441 Rachel Jenkins, London
442 Rachel Jenkins
443 Brian & Chris McEvoy
444 Miss Estelle Davies, Hereford
445 Miss Estelle Davies
446 G. R. R. Treasure, Kington
447 Rosa M. Binstead Lee, Berks.

448 Rosa M. Binstead Lee
449 Ronald A. Buckland, Abertillery
450 Eric Turton, Luston
451 John Hawkins, Dymock
452 Mrs C. C. Harley, Brampton Bryan
453 Paul Selfe, Monkland
454 Diana Kelly, Ullingswick
455 Mrs P. A. Price, Bromsgrove
456 J. F. Brazier, Ross-on-Wye
457 A. J. Weston, Hereford
458 Chris Gunson
459 Michael Pollitt, Wigmore
460 Terry Watts, Holme Lacy
461 Wilhelmine Blower, Newchurch
462 Douglas Story, Bromyard
463 A. M. Begg
464 Michael Webb, Anglesey
465 Michael Webb
466 Mary Dolphin, Ludlow
467 Isobel Gough, Maidenhead
468 Mrs F. L. J. Williams, Aymestrey
469 Mrs P. Williams, Skenfrith
470 J. H. Coates, Onibury
471 Mrs R. Harvey, Bredwardine
472 Ian Skyrm, Tenbury Wells
473 Ian Skyrm
474 Geoffrey Crofts, Leominster
475 Geoffrey Crofts
476 Geoffrey Crofts
477 Dr Yolande Heslop-Harrison, Leominster
478 Joy & Thomas Roderick, Hereford
479 Mrs K. R. Stokes, Tupsley
480 Mrs K. R. Stokes
481 D. Taplin, Marden
482 Madeleine Townson, Hampton Bishop
483 R. F. Birchenough
484 Sheila Rowlands, Aberystwyth
485 John David Caldicott
486 J. C. U. James
487 Christopher Mitchell, London
488 Mrs K. V. A. Thompson
489 Simon Allen, Hereford
490 David & Margaret Rose, Hereford
491 David & Margaret Rose, Hereford
492 Dr Elizabeth O'Donnell

493 Catherine Treadaway
494 Dr Elizabeth Lockwood
495 Jane Mary Jenkins (née Longman), Hereford
496 Pip Clark, Bodenham
497 Mrs R. J. Nash, Little Dewchurch
498 Robert Chappell, Hereford
499 Robert Chappell
500 Leslie Morris Kedward
501 Dr Keith Ray, County Archaeologist
502 Herefordshire Archaeology (Herefordshire Council)
503 Ludlow Museum
504 Ann Waite, Ludlow
505 Herefordshire Family History Society
506 Worcestershire Archaeological Service
507 Barbara Tyler, Shrewsbury
508 Peter Reed, Lucton
509 Stanley Baugh, Carmarthenshire
510 Stanley Baugh
511 Orta Books, Bristol
512 B. C. Redwood, Weobley
513 John Vickers, Wellington
514 Richard C. Lett, Leominster
515 Mary Lewis, Shrewsbury
516 Mrs J. M. Bentley-Taylor, Ivington
517 Brian A. Holborow, Lyonshall
518 Miss N. de Baskerville, MA Hons., Powys
519 B. J. Barnett, Torquay
520 Doreen Davis, Leominster
521 Doreen Davis
522 Rhydwyn H. Lewis, Lugwardine
523 K. Palmer, Llangua
524 J. A. Hudson, Leominster
525 W. Grant Kidd, Renfrewshire
526 Karen Tracie Freeman, Kent
527 Jean Tucker, Pembridge
528 Shirley Telfer, Hereford
529 David L. Plowman, Hereford
530 Joan Morris, Kenchester
531 Joan Morris
532 Brian Willder, Stretton Grandison
533 Lady Lorraine Earlshall

534 Dr Geoffrey Franglen, Hereford
535 Marion Percy, Colwall Green
536 Joyce James-Lewis, Hereford
537 Joyce James-Lewis
538 Graham Hurst, Weston-under-Penyard
539 Mrs M. Fieth, Tarrington
540 Richard Hancock, Knapton
541 John R. Collins, Hereford
542 William Ernest Preece, Staffordshire
543 Patrick Lee, Checkley
544 B. & H. Beach, Staunton-on-Wye
545 B. & H. Beach
546 Dr J. H. Ross, Hereford
547 A. S. T. Body, Wellington
548 John Vickerman, Salisbury
549 Margaret Smith, Caversham
550 Janet Moult, Hereford
551 Brian S. Smith, Vowchurch Common
552 Gillian Bulmer
553 Gillian Bulmer
554 Geoffrey Evans, Cardiff
555 Robert Dolling, East Dulwich
556 A. R. Knott, Bishopstone
557 Mrs E. M. Mitchell, Clehonger
558 Susan Bond, Colwall
559 Philip Weaver, Ledbury
560 Herefordshire Libraries and Information Service
561 HLIS
562 HLIS
563 HLIS
564 HLIS
565 HLIS
566 HLIS
567 HLIS
568 HLIS
569 HLIS
570 Peter O. McDougall, Durham
571 John Holland, Burghill
572 Lieutenant Colonel T. B. d'E. Powell
573 A. E. Brown, Leicestershire
574 Mike Williams, Norton Wood
575 Keith Mason, Hereford
576 Donald Mash, Minehead
577 P. A. Phillips, Ledbury
578 Mrs P. A. Farquhar-Oliver, Little Marcle

579 Hereford Cathedral School Library
580 Chris Spencer
581 Paul Thornley
582 Peter Tomlinson, Bodenham
583 Joan Milligan, Tupsley
584 Maurice R. Morgan
585 Brian Draper, MBE, Martley
586 Ray Whiley, Llanwarne
587 Ray Whiley
588 David & Jennifer Higham, Broadmoor Common
589 Dr Charles F. Donovan, Burghill
590 Robin Charles Donovan
591 David Watkins, Hereford
592 S. V. Jones, Tenbury Wells
593 Anthea Brian, Bodenham
594 Anthea Brian
595 The Reverend S. Barnaby Bell, Clungunford
596 Hazel Wagner, Ruckhall Common
597 Dr & Mrs H. Connor, Hereford
598 P. J. Holliday, Leominster
599 E. L. Crooks, Holmer
600 Veronica Thackeray, Hopton Castle
601 Mrs M. Powell, Longtown
602 Mrs B. Lydiard, Leominster
603 Sybil Parry, Hereford
604 Julie M. Jones, Clifford
605 Alan & Joan Tucker, Stroud
606 Alan & Joan Tucker
607 Alan & Joan Tucker
608 Miss M. A. E. Whittal, Hereford
609 Mr & Mrs B. Curr, Clodock
610 Mr & Mrs B. Curr
611 B. W. Lawrance, Kingstone
612 John Norton, MBE, FGS, FRES, FMA, ARICS
613 Mrs W. J. Bailey, Ross-on-Wye
614 Sydney Trenchard-Morgan, Fownhope
615 Roger Jones
616 Basil Jones
617 Edmund Jones
618 Mrs W. V. Morgan-Brewer, Hereford
619 Reverend Prebendary G. F. Holley, Renfrewshire
620 David C. Brooks
621 J. R. W. Paige, Hereford

622 Reverend Michael Cluett
623 Mrs E. M. Lloyd, Colwall
624 John Freeman Bonnor, Upminster
625 Henry Moore, Shucknall
626 Charles Moore
627 Emma St John
628 Julian Moore
629 Toby Moore
630 Alice Moore
631 David G. Bissell, Stratford upon Avon
632 Ernest Briggs, Lyde
633 Michael Barker, Archenfield (Hay)
634 Lynne Ardrey, Bosbury
635 Catherine Rees
636 Janet Parry, Hereford
637 Mrs J. Herbert, Bromyard
638 L. G. Williams, Breinton Common
639 J. M. Jones
640 Dr G. E. Atkin, Hereford
641 Marilyn Price, Powys
642 R. B. Haig, Much Dewchurch
643 Kenneth Bowe, Staffordshire
644 Marjorie & Brian Roby, Felton
645 James Mattock, Putson
646 Mike Horwood
647 Peter & Margaret Skelton, Fownhope
648 Dr W. Powell, Dunstable
649 L. B. Pilgrim, Bridstow
650 Liz Phillips, Hereford
651 Winston Baldock, Newent
652 Gillian R. Rampling, Wilton
653 Mr & Mrs Colin Dickerson, Fownhope
654 Eileen Gosling, Dorset
655 G. E. Wickens, OBE, East Sussex
656 B. Jones, Fownhope
657 John F. Nunn, Cirencester
658 Patrick Cannings, Hereford
659 Mr & Mrs V. Gammage, Hereford
660 Mr & Mrs Peter W. F. Jones, Hereford
661 Mr & Mrs D. O. Williams, Clehonger
662 Peter F. Pitt, Hampshire
663 M. K. Rist, Colwall
664 Austin & Daphne Crathorn, Hereford

665 Colin Storey, Hereford
666 James Hervey-Bathurst, Eastnor
667 Judy Nicholas, Hereford
668 David Elvins, Bucks.
669 Julie Meech, Lower Broadheath
670 Mrs B. Millington, Shropshire
671 Mrs D. M. Nicholson, Upper Sapey
672 Mrs D. M. Nicholson
673 Laurence Le Quesne, Shrewsbury
674 C. Fuller, Powys
675 S. G. V. Milligan, Fownhope
676 Howell & Beryl Haines, Hereford
677 Anne Burnett, Hereford
678 Miss A. J. Witts, Hampton Bishop
679 Jane S. Lissimore, Ross-on-Wye
680 J. H. Robinson, Swainshill
681 Pete Barley, Walford
682 Lachlan Sturrock, Walford
683 A. J. Norman, Pembridge
684 The Hon. Mrs Morris-Jones, Eardisley
685 The Hon. Mrs Morris-Jones
686 Mark O'Brien, Kenilworth
687 Roger & Brenda Tingley, Hereford
688 Miss C. M. M. Roberts, Hereford
689 Graham Powell, Ledbury
690 Chris Ridler
691 Sandra Apps, Uphampton
692 Mr & Mrs A. C. Barraclough, Moccas
693 Mrs R. C. Evans, Cambridge
694 Dr D. McGlashon, Burghill
695 Mrs M. C. Aspland, Malvern
696 Dr Jonathan Sleath, Kingstone
697 Reverend Ralph E. Fennell, Burghill
698 David Machin, Bath
699 Allan Shaw Wright
700 Alan Stone, Bredwardine
701 Clive Young, Ewyas Harold
702 Michael J. Reynolds, Powys
703 A. W. Morris, Bartestree
704 Michael Bolt, Hereford
705 Margaret & Glyn Morris, Dewsall

706 Margaret & Glyn Morris
707 Roderick Dew, Eastbourne
708 Mrs Phyl King
709 Mr & Mrs W. J. Wells, Leominster
710 Mr & Mrs W. J. Wells
711 H. C. Wooler, Fownhope
712 Dr & Mrs J. A. F. Evans, Hereford
713 Dr & Mrs J. A. F. Evans
714 Dr & Mrs J. A. F. Evans
715 Dr & Mrs J. A. F. Evans
716 Colonel A. R. Anslow, Kempsey
717 Roland Burr, Leominster
718 Katelyn Olivia Jones
719 Angela Helen Jones
720 Rose & Leslie Wiles, Kimbolton
721 Biddy Fosdike
722 Mrs C. McNaughton, Kingsland
723 Mr & Mrs J. F. Allan, Whitbourne
724 Mr & Mrs R. W. Middlemiss, Powys
725 Duncan James, Combe
726 Tom Nellist, Eau Withington
727 Dr Dan & Mrs Jacky Thomas, Hereford
728 Gary and Susan Thomas
729 A. E. Gray, Malvern
730 Miriam Irvine, Devon
731 Phyllis Gordon Williams, Hereford
732 Weobley & District Local History Society
733 Leonard Chase, Stretford Bridge
734 Mrs Leonard Chase
735 Sylvia Rumney, Ledbury
736 Mrs K. Rogers, Bartestree
737 Mrs K. Rogers
738 Jane Wise, Breinton
739 Janet Epps, Ledbury
740 Janet Epps
741 Mr & Mrs J. Fisk, Bishopstone
742 Mr & Mrs J. Fisk
743 John Olney, Bringsty Common
744 John Olney
745 Mary Watkins, Hereford
746 Aneurin Thomas, Hereford
747 Mr & Mrs. G. D. Wilkinson, Risbury
748 Mr & Mrs. G. D. Wilkinson

749 Peter M. Jones, Tredegar
750 Marches Archaeology, Lyonshall
751 Michael J. Antcliff, Cambridge
752 P. C. C. Brookes, Weston-under-Penyard
753 Brian Cummins, Wellington
754 Brian Cummins
755 Richard Wille, Hereford
756 Siân Cook
757 Mrs P. Rowberry, Bodenham
758 Reverend & Mrs P. J. Nash, Hereford
759 Sybil P. James, Birmingham
760 Jean Carter, Llanveynoe
761 Judith Wilson, Hereford
762 Miss M. Lewis, Somerset
763 Anne Milne, Edinburgh
764 Richard J. W. Evans
765 Ken & Veronica Harris, Sollers Hope
766 David & Pauline Deakin
767 Ralph Ralph, Credenhill
768 Graham Hornsby, Hereford
769 Sir Richard & Lady Mynors
770 Peter Mynors
771 Peter Whittle
772 Elizabeth Russell
773 Harold L. Brade, Stretton Sugwas
774 Harold L. Brade
775 Nigel Eckley
776 Derek Roberts
777 R. N. Williams, Weobley
778 Alan M. Meredith, Ross-on-Wye
779 Alan M. Meredith
780 Alan M. Meredith
781 Dr D. M. Parker, Wirral
782 Miss J. R. Jonson, King's Caple
783 Mrs A. M. Eagling, Norton Canon
784 Mrs A. M. Eagling
785 Mrs A. M. Eagling
786 W. S. & E. Pollitt, Holmer
787 Christina Margaret Mills
788 Michael & Jennie Francis, Marden
789 Bryan Markham, Kingsland
790 Bryan Markham
791 Donald Slade, South Croydon

792 Rev. Prebendary C. M. Oldroyd, Tupsley
793 D. M. W. Bishop, Tillington
794 D. M. W. Bishop
795 Dr W. H. J. Baker, Lugwardine
796 R. W. Binnersley, Hereford
797 Judith Cadigan, Pennsylvania, USA
798 J. A. Cooper
799 Molly Wright, Derbyshire
800 Dr Anne E. Caunt, Kington
801 Sarah Cadwallader, Kington
802 Sue & Roger Norman, Ivington Green
803 Roger W. Stokes, Canon Pyon
804 Nan Raper, Kings Thorn
805 Nan Raper
806 Vicki & Paul Murray, Callow
807 Harriet Murray
808 Ms S. E. Macintyre
809 John S. Turner, Lower Bullingham
810 R. L. Wheeler, Monkland
811 R. A. Jones
812 Mr & Mrs Mark Lloyd, Tillington
813 Mary J. Wood, Much Birch
814 A. W. Wood
815 E. J. McCormick, Ross-on-Wye
816 Dilla Greening, Ledbury
817 A. C. Brown, Tillington
818 C. R. Craven, Staffordshire
819 Dr J. L. T. Birley, Longtown
820 R. J. E. Justham, Newent
821 Edward Blackwell
822 Adrian & Alison Cook, Orleton
823 R. D. Birch, Lichfield
824 R. D. Birch
825 P. G. Calderbank, Hereford
826 Glyn & Pamela Roberts, Shrewsbury
827 Glyn & Pamela Roberts
828 Glyn & Pamela Roberts
829 David J. Baldwin, Much Birch
830 Dr J. B. Wood
831 Anonymous
832 Anonymous
833 Anonymous
834 Anonymous
835 Anonymous
836 E. W. Taylor, Orcop
837 Anonymous

838 Anonymous
839 Avian M. Gray, Wellington
840 Michael Fieldsend, Wigmore
841 Peter Wollen
842 Catherine Percival
843 Jonathan Sant, Bodenham
844 Diana Grimwood, West Sussex
845 John E. Barnett, Weston Beggard
846 Malcolm Allport, Mordiford
847 Stanley Simons, MBE
848 Dr A. Knight, Risbury
849 Dr Geoffrey Vevers, Berkshire
850 Alma Crump, Delaware, USA
851 Alma Crump
852 Timothy Allen, Kidderminster
853 Timothy Allen
854 Mrs E. M. Wilson, Dorstone
855 John B. Westcott, Risca
856 Sophia Wetherell
857 Virginia Wetherell
858 D. R. & L. B. Thomas, Madley
859 D. R. & L. B. Thomas
860 Roy Palmer, Dymock
861 R. Preece, Hereford
862 Mrs C. A. M. Garrett, Callow
863 R. Michael Garrett
864 Rosalie Lilwall, Pembroke
865 A. J. Reeve, Kimbolton
866 Gillian Murray, Hereford
867 Brian Weekes, Hereford
868 Margaret West, Pembridge
869 Mrs. H. V. Croxton, Clunbury
870 J. R. Hosking, London
871 Valery MacDonald, Kingsland
872 Richard J. Barnett, Surrey
873 Richard J. Barnett
874 Maureen L. Newport, Worthing
875 David Terry, Bromsgrove
876 Mrs P. Edden, Westhope Hill
877 Mrs P. Edden
878 Frank Robert Green, Hay-on-Wye
879 R. I. Hall, Checkley
880 Dr R. W. Mills
881 Frances L. Mills

882 Michael Young, Rugby
883 A. L. Yoxall, Charlton
    Kings
884 Daphne Trumper, Surrey
885 The Reverend Richard H.
    Smith, Leominster
886 Robert Marsland,
    Hallwood Green
887 R. J. E. Barker
888 Mrs P. Lancaster,
    Hereford
889 Mrs P. Lancaster
890 Pamela Hurle, Storridge
891 M. D. Thompson, Much
    Birch
892 Robert Powell, Blockley
893 Brenda Tubbs, St Albans
894 L. K. Hayward, Hereford
895 John B. L. Faulkner,
    Ruckhall
896 Tom Goddard, Hay-on-
    Wye
897 Jennifer Hughes, Hereford
898 Philip W. Baldwin,
    Moreton Eye
899
900 Ian Brown
901 Ian Brown
902 Ian Brown
903 Ian Brown
904 Ian Brown
905 Sinclair Johnston, London
906 Sinclair Johnston
907 Sinclair Johnston

THE CONTRIBUTORS
908 Anthea Brian
909 John Eisel
910 Roger French
911 Joan Grundy
912 Beryl Harding
913 Heather Hurley
914 Alan Morris
915 Richard Morriss
916 Jean O'Donnell
917 Derryan Paul
918 Ruth Richardson
919 Graham Roberts
920 John Ross
921 Ron Shoesmith
922 Rosamund Skelton
923 Brian Smith
924 Peter Thomson
925 Jim Tonkin
926 Muriel Tonkin
927 David Whitehead

Index

Page references in *italics* refer to illustrations.
Named buildings and streets, where indexed at all, are entered under the place where they are situated. Names of individual species of birds, plants, etc., are not indexed.